T. ALEXANDER ALEINIKOFF

Semblances of Sovereignty

The Constitution, the State, and American Citizenship

HARVARD UNIVERSITY PRESS
Cambridge, Massachusetts, and London, England
2002

Printed in the United States of America

Library of Congress Cataloging-in-Publication Data

Aleinikoff, Thomas Alexander, 1952–
Semblances of sovereignty : the constitution, the state, and American citizenship / T. Alexander Aleinikoff.
p. cm.
Includes bibliographical references and index.
ISBN 0-674-00745-X
1. Constitutional law—United States. 2. National state. 3. Sovereignty. I. Title.

KF4552 .A43 2002
342.73'02—dc21 2001051519

In memory of Elizabeth Wise Aleinikoff,
with whose respect for the diversity of life
I have attempted to fill these pages

Preface

> This world, our world at the end of the century, our world at the end of the millennium, is blind to itself, unable to take in the horror of the mutilations it suffers or the marvels of the plentitudes it conceals, filled with colors we are not allowed to see and with voices we are not allowed to hear. In the midst of this era of mandatory globalization . . . these colors and voices keep alive powerful evidence that the best of the world lies in the quantity of worlds the world contains.
>
> Eduardo Galeano, acceptance speech for the 1999 Lannan Prize for Cultural Freedom

This book began more than a decade ago when I pulled together materials for a seminar at the University of Michigan Law School on pluralism, citizenship, and sovereignty. In ways that I had not previously appreciated, late-nineteenth-century constitutional decisions declared in similar terms virtually unreviewable congressional power to regulate Indian tribes, the territories, and immigration. I set out to try to discover why, and—more important—why the "plenary power" cases continued to be good law.

At the same time, I wondered why constitutional scholarship and casebooks had generally neglected these important cases. First-year constitutional law students are routinely told that the federal government is one of delegated powers, and yet power to regulate immigration is nowhere mentioned in the Constitution. Nor is a general power to regulate the internal affairs of Indian tribes. Students are taught about a structure of dual sovereignty, with no mention of the sovereignty of Indian tribes or the status of Puerto Rico, Guam, or the District of Columbia. The progressive recognition of individual rights is usually featured as a central part of the constitutional story told about the twentieth century. Yet these areas of federal regulation appeared to have remained largely immune from general constitutional developments. Remarkably, few of these issues had received serious attention from constitutional theorists, and most constitutional law teachers were unfamiliar with the foundational cases. Constitutional scholarship, it seemed, began in the middle—ignoring first-order questions about the establishment and meaning of sovereignty and the bestowal of membership.

This book is an attempt to open up these kinds of questions for serious scrutiny. I address a selected set of issues, well aware that many others need attention (such as the status of the District of Columbia, extraterritorial application of U.S. law, and the impact of international organizations and norms on U.S. sovereignty). I hope that my arguments on specific issues are persuasive (or at least interesting); but perhaps more important, I hope to spark interest in "sovereignty studies"—a field of inquiry that will only grow more important in the years ahead as national states are pressured from above and below.

I want to acknowledge the wonderful assistance I have received from colleagues and institutions. The University of Michigan Law School and the Institute for the Humanities at the University of Michigan lent crucial support at the beginning of the project. Dean Judith Areen and the Georgetown University Law Center have provided me with an ideal environment in which to finish the work. I am grateful to faculties and conference attendees at Fordham Law School, New York Law School, the University of Toronto, and the University of North Carolina School of Law for valuable comments on portions of the book. I have benefited greatly from conversations with, and comments from, Hope Babcock, Linda Bosniak, Sarah Cleveland, Rachel Cohen, David Cole, Jim Fleming, Willie Forbath, Phil Frickey, Gary Gerstle, Tom Green, David Hollinger, Vicki Jackson, Will Kymlicka, Larry Kramer, Arnold Leibowitz, Sandy Levinson, David Martin, Mari Matsuda, Hiroshi Motomura, Nina Pillard, Robert Post, Sue Deller Ross, Mike Seidman, Rogers Smith, Gerald Torres, Mark Tushnet, Lorraine Weinrib, Robin West, and Wendy Williams. Two reviewers for the Harvard University Press posed tough—and appreciated—questions.

Special thanks are owed to Gerry Neuman, whose line-by-line critique of the manuscript was enormously helpful, and to David Scobey, who helped me think through just about every significant issue in the book.

Research assistants Allison Baker, Stephen Ballas, Brian Lambert, William Rahm, Paul Supple, Jon Michael Thompson, and Daniel Wadley have saved me from egregious errors, and Mike Thompson also served as indexer. Fran Mulligan, Anna Selden, and John Showalter provided invaluable technical support in preparation of the manuscript.

Portions of the book have appeared previously. Chapter 4 is a revised version of "Puerto Rico and the Constitution: Conundrums and Prospects," 11 *Const. Comm.* 15 (1994). Chapter 7 borrows from "Citizens, Aliens, Membership, and the Constitution," 7 *Const. Comm.* 9 (1990), and Cornelia T. L. Pillard and T. Alexander Aleinikoff, "Skeptical Scrutiny of Plenary Power: Judicial and Executive Branch Decision Making in *Miller v. Albright*," 1998 *Sup. Ct. Rev.* 1 (© 1998 by The University of Chicago. All rights reserved).

Contents

SEMBLANCES OF SOVEREIGNTY

CHAPTER 1

Introduction

On July 4, 1992, a procession of Tall Ships graced New York Harbor, gliding past the Statue of Liberty, saluting the skyscrapers of Wall Street, and pleasing holiday crowds in Manhattan and Brooklyn and a national television audience as well. In language more understandable to newspaper readers of another age, the *New York Times* declared the procession at sea

> a sight to behold: barks and barkentines, brigs, full-rigged ships and schooners from yesteryear, sailors lining rails and yardarms like rows of magpies, steepled shrouds straining at mastheads, gaff-rigged spankers and jibs set, rakish bowsprits and dolphin-strikers churning froths of wind and wave, a ballet whose beauty seemed all the greater in the leaden fog.[1]

In a world "crowded with noisy artifice," the Tall Ships offered "something quietly authentic."[2] The Tall Ships will perhaps become an enduring American symbol, having visited New York several times in recent years. Originally brought to the 1964 World's Fair, they returned for the bicentennial celebration of 1976 and the Statue of Liberty centennial ten years later.

A flotilla of largely foreign-built sailing ships is not an obvious choice for commemorating a declaration of independence from a European empire. The 1992 appearance was more curious still, as it was billed as being in celebration of the five-hundredth anniversary of Columbus's first landing in the Caribbean—an event rather distant in time, geography, and meaning from the nation's independence 284 years later. (Why was the quincentennial celebration not scheduled for the October Columbus Day holiday?) On July 4, 1992, rather than providing self-congratulatory speeches on the beginnings and ultimate triumph of American democracy (not an inappropriate theme on the first Independence Day since the fall of eastern European communism), New York celebrated its Old World origins. On the brink of a new century, the nation looked back.

The newspaper account attempted an explanation: the Tall Ships "evoked a sense of America's immigrant experience, of commerce and the dangers of life at sea, of skills and ideas in a new land."[3] Surely there is something to this narrative of rugged individualism and capitalism. But the celebration also seemed to represent a collapsing of time, a placing of formative events in an equally distant past. Columbus's discovery occurs alongside the colonization of the eastern seaboard, the Revolutionary War, and the great migrations of the nineteenth and twentieth centuries. There is no prioritizing here, as both Jamestown and Ellis Island are evoked. The Tall Ships in New York Harbor are thus able to construct an inclusive past, which is, at least on the surface, remarkably free of ideological content. The silence of sail, on this account, is no accidental trope.

It has become common for scholars to recognize that silence frequently connotes domination more than consensus, erasure as much as inclusion.[4] As New York mayor David Dinkins noted in his speech at the Governor's Island reviewing stand, the sea trade brought slaves as well as explorers and immigrants. So, too, the Tall Ships did not tell the stories of American Indians massacred and enslaved by the Europeans or Mexicans who became Americans upon the annexation of their homeland. Accounts of the "welcome" accorded Asian migrants at San Francisco's Angel Island are overshadowed by the mythologizing of New York's Ellis Island.[5]

The Tall Ships celebration was one manifestation of the story that the United States tells about its origins, its people, and its authority and legitimacy—in short, its "stateness." A state will invariably have a "creation myth" identifying its founding and founders (more often reflecting a country's current self-conception than reporting historical truth).[6] The 1992 version grasps the dominant account of the preceding threescore years. "We" are a nation of immigrants, and though the ancestors of some of us "missed the Mayflower," they "came over on the first boat they could find."[7]

But it was not always so. The somewhat confusing current national narrative—the *E Pluribus Unum* melting pot imagery coexisting with affirmations of cultural pluralism—contrasts sharply with the less tolerant, more exclusionary American self-image that arose as the nation confronted challenges at home and abroad around the turn of the twentieth century. Imperialist adventures, Indian policies, and race-based immigration restrictions were justified on narrow conceptions of "how wide the circle of we."[8] These federal policies raised fundamental questions for constitutional law regarding the source, scope, and nature of American national sovereignty. Did the Constitution authorize the ruling of distant territories not thought fit for statehood? Did Congress possess power to exclude and remove "friendly" aliens? What was the source of federal authority to regulate Indian tribes? What constitutional rights could each of the regulated groups assert against the predatory actions of the United States government? To a remarkable degree, the Court's answers to these questions more than a century ago continue to dominate constitutional understandings of sovereignty and membership. Thus, while our national narrative has undergone significant change, our constitutional law has remained largely locked in nineteenth-century conceptions of statehood.

Modern constitutional law has considered questions of sovereignty primarily in cases involving the distribution of powers between the federal government and the states. The invocations of state sovereignty are more than mere makeweights: since the early 1990s a majority of the Court has been firmly committed to protecting state governments from overregulation by federal authorities.[9] The Court has offered various accounts of exactly what should be protected and why,[10] but the concept of "sovereignty" helps level the federal-state playing field. States are not mere interest groups vying for federal dollars or private associations entitled to constitutional protection against governmental regulation. Rather, the Constitution affirms "an indestructible Union, composed of indestructible states."[11] It is their sovereignty that distinguishes states from other organizations and endows them with special constitutional status.

For most constitutional casebooks and scholarship, issues of state-federal relations exhaust the interesting questions to be asked about sovereignty.[12] This conception of the field suppresses the recognition of other governmental structures in the United States that have plausible claims to some form of sovereignty: Indian tribes, U.S. territories (Puerto Rico, Guam, the Virgin Islands), the District of Columbia. It also avoids deep and important questions about the scope and power of the American state—such as the source of the immigration power, voting rights for residents of the District of Columbia and the Commonwealth of Puerto Rico, and extraterritorial application of U.S. law and the status of international law in U.S. courts. These issues, it should be apparent, have potentially significant implications for theories of liberal democracy.

In a rather unconscious manner, most U.S. constitutional law scholarship "assumes the state."[13] Analysis about limits on the exercise of national power begins with an already constituted state exercising authority over an already constituted body of citizens. Exactly who We the People are and by what right the United States exerts sovereignty over a beautiful and bountiful land are questions rarely examined.

In the pages that follow, I take up some of these generally unexplored questions about sovereignty and the Constitution. I intend this study to be representative of a nascent field of inquiry I will label "sovereignty studies." By "sovereignty" I mean the supreme legal authority in a national state.[14] I use the term "national state" to mean a political organization exercising sovereignty over a bounded territory.[15] A national state may find its ability to exercise its sovereignty limited by practical considerations (such as the military aggression of other states, transborder pollution, or civil war), and national states may cede aspects of their sovereignty by way of treaty or other international agreement. But to say that sovereignty is not absolute as a matter of fact is not to deny its existence as a matter of political theory. The sovereignty of a national state has both an external and an internal scope, identifying an entity that both acts in the foreign sphere and rules over the domestic affairs of that portion of the world's territory acknowledged by other national states as the state's own.[16]

As Rogers Brubaker has noted, states are membership organizations.[17] Liberal democratic states exercise power in the name of, and on behalf of, state members (usually designated "citizens"). This is so not because the state has entered into an agreement with its members—as if it were an insurance or telephone company that signs up customers based on a promise to serve them well. Rather, the state's power is understood to derive from its members. The idea of popular sovereignty is that a contract has been formed among the members to establish a state and to delegate to it powers to act on their behalf.

It is important to see from the start that although the citizenry may be the location of sovereignty, citizenship defines neither the category of the governed nor that of the governors. States exercise power over nonmembers—immigrants—located within state boundaries (and sometimes over nonmembers beyond territorial borders). And the category of those who either exercise state power or elect those who do has never been coterminous with citizenship. Throughout the nineteenth century, white male immigrants were entitled to vote in a number of states,[18] even as women and African-American citizens were not. Today, residents of Puerto Rico and of the District of Columbia are not represented by voting members in Congress, and millions of citizens who have been convicted of felonies are disenfranchised.

This book examines the relationship of sovereignty and membership in constitutional law. My central thesis is that a constitutional law for the twenty-first century needs understandings of sovereignty and membership that are supple and flexible, open to new arrangements that complement the evolving nature of the modern state. Yet our constitutional law, at least as declared by the Supreme Court, is moving in the opposite direction, adopting wooden conceptions of sovereignty and membership as citizenship and statehood are brought into close —almost congruent—association. The Court has drawn or affirmed hard lines between citizens and immigrants, a narrowing of the sovereignty of Indian tribes, and a second-class constitutional status for the territories.

In telling this story, I begin with the late-nineteenth-century Supreme Court decisions involving federal power over immigration, Indian tribes, and newly acquired territories.[19] In each instance the Justices concluded that Congress possessed "plenary power" to regulate in these areas; the Court would apply virtually no constitutional limitations on congressional authority. Despite tectonic shifts in our constitutional law, these cases remain largely untouched and continue to dominate their areas of law. Indeed, their longevity is now cited against assertions that they ought to be reconsidered. They are viewed by the Court as part of the fabric of American constitutional law.

Chapter 2 locates the foundational cases in their time. I argue that behind these cases lay a vision of the United States as a *nation-state:* a *state* endowed with the power to control its territory and take its place as an equal among other foreign states and a *nation* that defined itself in ethno-racial terms as Anglo-Saxon. According to the received wisdom of the day, tribal Indians, Filipinos, and immigrants from China and southern and eastern Europe were plainly not prepared to participate in the governing structures or institutions of American society. Federal policy called for either assimilation or exclusion of the groups, based on assumptions about whether the particular group was ultimately able to be "civilized."

In Chapter 3 I aim to sustain the claim that in the twentieth century the United States moved from a *nation-state* to a *citizen-state*[20]: from a society whose primary story of belonging shifts from an ethnic and racial account to one based on the legal equality of citizens. By the mid-twentieth century, acceptance of cultural pluralism became the norm, the repeal of the exclusion of Asian immigration began, and the federal government took sustained and serious action again racial inequality. The Supreme Court, during Earl Warren's tenure as Chief Justice, was an active participant in the drive for equality, striking down discriminatory state laws and validating congressional legislation and executive regulations. I argue that at the core of the Warren Court's work was a concept of *full and equal citizenship.* The Warren Court ordered wholesale restructuring of electoral processes in the pursuit of political equality. Its muscular use of the equal protection clause sought to make real the Fourteenth Amendment's condemnation of second-class citizenship based on race, and the Court took strong measures to protect United States citizenship—described as "a most precious right"—by virtually denying Congress the power to remove it.

For the Warren Court, citizenship was an expansive and inclusionary project, removing barriers to equal participation and equal treatment. The message was ultimately assimilatory. But the focus on citizenship was also exclusionary; the Court did virtually nothing to advance the constitutional rights of immigrants. That task fell to the Burger Court, which in a surprising decision announced that aliens constituted a "discrete and insular minority" for whom special judicial protection was warranted. The Burger Court, also more attuned to issues of local governance, was in some respects more supportive than the Warren Court of Indian self-determination—again a topic that the

Warren Court largely ignored. Citizenship figures little in the work of the Burger Court; its important constitutional decisions emphasize the rights of *persons* and the powers of state and local governments.

Citizenship returns as a theme under the Rehnquist Court. As the Warren Court had recognized, citizenship could be a powerful unifying concept. In the hands of the Rehnquist Court, it becomes a vehicle for resisting multiculturalism and the "special rights" sought by groups organized around identity. Thus, the Court has mobilized citizenship in cases limiting the sovereignty of Indian tribes and sustaining harsh government policies against immigrants.

While the concept and content of citizenship change, the plenary power doctrines regarding congressional power over immigration, the territories, and the tribes stand as monuments to an earlier time. The continuing vitality of the plenary power cases and current readings of citizenship are linked. They are two sides of the national state: the plenary power doctrines endow Congress with unfettered authority to deal with "others" by crafting policies of assimilation, partial inclusion, or exclusion as deemed necessary. Citizenship provides the measure of full membership in the state—the *demos* on whose behalf the state acts.

I urge the abandonment of the plenary power cases and argue for more flexible understandings of membership that would legitimate new arrangements intended to promote self-determination and equality. The later chapters take up these themes in specific contexts. Chapter 4 considers congressional power to regulate territories of the United States. The rules established by the *Insular Cases*—early-twentieth-century decisions of the Court regarding federal power over territories acquired after the Spanish-American War—remain largely intact. Congress has the power to establish governments for the territories as it deems fit, and constitutional restrictions on federal power are not fully applicable. Paying particular attention to Puerto Rico, I examine a number of conundrums implicit in the Court's doctrine. In considering the continuing debate over the status of Puerto Rico, I am skeptical of the federal government's constitutional argument that casts doubt on a more robust form of "commonwealth." Looking fresh at the status debate can put in play new understandings of sovereignty that provide space for subnational governance without undermining the national state.

The Constitution was written against a backdrop of preexisting, sovereign Indian nations. Several hundred years of contact with Europeans, however, brought devastation on the tribes. Throughout the eighteenth and nineteenth centuries, their lands were taken as the tribes were forced west. By the late nineteenth century, reservations set aside for the tribes were opened to white settlement, and further land was lost. The New Deal brought a new day to Indian self-governance, but Indian policy veered again in a different direction with the so-called termination policies of the 1950s. In its latest phase—tracing from the administration of Richard Nixon—the federal government has announced its dedication to tribal self-determination. Federal policies, from child adoption laws to casino gambling, recognize broad notions of tribal sovereignty.

As I describe in detail in Chapter 5, the Court—throughout all the changes in federal policy—has affirmed congressional "plenary power" to structure federal, state, and tribal political relationships. At the same time, it has increasingly restricted inherent tribal sovereignty. Thus, while the tribes possess significant power over tribal members, they have little authority over nonmembers on reservations. This is a peculiar notion of sovereignty, one more akin to the power of private associations to write rules for members than nationhood. I suggest that the current Court's crabbed view of tribal sovereignty is based on concern about the exclusion of nonmembers from reservation governance, a racialized conception of the tribes, and the implications of its focus on citizenship.

In Chapter 6 I examine constitutional claims that would support a fuller conception of tribal sovereignty. I argue for a new relationship between the federal government and the tribes based on binding agreements rather than exercises of plenary power. For this arrangement to provide a firm foundation, the Court must abandon the century-old doctrine that permits Congress to abrogate treaties despite provisions in the treaty that require tribal consent to such changes.

In both the territorial and tribal cases, plenary power has stood for federal *unilateralism:* the authority of the national government to impose governing structures and substantive legal norms as it deems appropriate. Frequently the federal rules have pursued what the national government believed was in the best interests of the tribe or territory. But those judgments have just as frequently been based on assumptions of racial and cultural inferiority. The central theme of these chapters, then, is that these political arrangements need to be established on a *bilateral* basis, able to take into account cultural and normative commitments of the subnational polities. Futhermore, to provide a secure space for self-governance, negotiated agreements must be binding on future federal authorities.

A second major theme in the chapters on the territories and the tribes is the Court's conception of citizenship. The Court's implicit model of indivisible national sovereignty is complemented by a strong notion of national citizenship. Citizenship defines national state membership, and the idea of equal citizenship argues against subnational political arrangements that appear to provide "special rights" to certain classes of citizens (particularly when those classes are perceived to be defined by race). Thus, citizenship functions to undermine some conceptions of tribal sovereignty and to affirm the legitimacy of policies that favor citizens over aliens.

In Chapter 7 I look at the difference that citizenship makes, examining the basis for the Court's recognition of Congress's plenary power to regulate immigration and to draw lines based on alienage in the distribution of benefits and opportunities. I make two broad arguments: first, that the plenary power doctrine is based on the Court's institutional concern that it not interfere with the political branches, not on an interpretive theory that different constitutional norms apply to immigration regulations; and second, that federal power to discriminate against aliens is based on an implicit model of citizenship-as-membership. I argue that the reasons for judicial deference are unpersuasive and that the Court ought to subject immigration laws to the usual constitutional norms applied to other exercises of federal power. (A 2001 decision of the Supreme Court points in this direction.) I further propose a broader model of membership—one that includes settled immigrants. I borrow the term "denizenship" to describe the broader class. Under this conception, citizenship identifies those who "belong to" and, ideally, are committed to America; it does not, however, supply a basis for discriminating against settled immigrants. I conclude the chapter by responding to the objection that my "decentered" version of citizenship strips citizenship of significance.

By focusing on both sovereignty and membership, I do not propose to dismiss or "deconstruct" either concept. Rather, I attempt to chart a course between a postnational account that declares the end of the national state and a nationalism that seeks to preserve a certain cultural or ethnic definition of the national state. The national form has never been, and is not now, static. But as the national state increasingly becomes a site for transnational public and private interactions,[21] as understandings of indigenous rights and imperial wrongs become stronger, as America grows more diverse (but no less powerful), then notions of sovereignty and membership must adapt. By this I do not mean a transcending of older categories as much as a transforming—figuring citizenship as commitment, not privilege, and viewing sovereignty as empowerment, not domination.

CHAPTER 2

The Sovereignty Cases and the Pursuit of an American Nation-State

A national state confronts issues of sovereignty when it determines its borders, its members, and its powers. In the eighteenth and nineteenth centuries, U.S. constitutional law faced a host of sovereignty-based questions: the constitutionality of the Louisiana Purchase, congressional authority to prohibit slavery in the territories, theories of union and secession, federal and state power to regulate commerce, the citizenship of free blacks, the status of Indian tribes. By the late nineteenth century, the nation's attention turned to empire. The Union had been preserved and the West had been won. Huge waves of immigrants brought the world to America just as the United States sought a larger role on the world stage.

This chapter begins with an exploration of turn-of-the-twentieth-century constitutional doctrine on questions of statehood and sovereignty. In brief, I argue that cases considering federal authority over immigrants, Indian tribes, and territories reached essentially the same result: that Congress had plenary power to construct the American state and its membership largely immune from judicial review.[1] Congress, in exercising its power, adopted a range of policies aimed variously at excluding, dominating, and assimilating "non-American" "races." Behind the policies lay a conception of the United States as a white, Anglo-Saxon nation-state—an ideal never fully attained and finally rejected by the second quarter of the twentieth century. Not surprisingly, the Supreme Court found itself deeply embroiled in the political and cultural battles of the day, and the decisions in the sovereignty cases both reflected and helped formulate representations of American statehood.[2]

In the middle decades of the twentieth century, America's self-conception changed dramatically. Drastic reductions in immigration, combined with the largely successful incorporation of earlier immigrants, permitted the emergence of a public philosophy of "cultural pluralism" that celebrated the many roots of the American family tree. European immigrants and their descendants became "white"[3]—their national origins now describing their cuisine and culture, not their race. This "whitening" of second-generation European immigrants, however, contrasted sharply with treatment afforded other groups. Jim Crow and the exclusion of Asian immigrants lasted until after World War II. Mexican immigrants were sought after as low-paid agricultural workers, not as potential members of the American polity.

Throughout this period, the foundational plenary power cases were not questioned. And Congress used its authority in important, and sometimes beneficent, ways: the Philippines were readied for independence, citizenship was granted to Puerto Ricans and Native Americans, and Indian policy under the New Deal took a significant turn toward recognizing tribal sovereignty.[4] But no doubt was cast on Congress's power to deal with these matters as it saw fit.

Sovereignty at the Turn of the Century

In the late nineteenth and early twentieth centuries, the Supreme Court constructed an account of state sovereignty that it applied to a number of salient legal (and political) issues. Relying on well-established principles of the law of nations, the Court understood the United States to be endowed with the powers normally associated with statehood: (1) authority to control one's borders and the entry of aliens; (2) authority to acquire new territory by conquest, treaty, or purchase; (3) exclusive jurisdiction over the territory of the United States, implying (4) limited—or perhaps no—jurisdiction in the territory of foreign states; and (5) power (if not an obligation) to protect U.S. citizens overseas. In short, the Court ensured that the ship of state was outfitted with the requisite constitutional authority to assume its role as a world power.

The Court's decision in *Chae Chan Ping v. United States*[5] (usually referred to as the *Chinese Exclusion Case*) provides an example. At issue were the exclusion laws of the 1880s, the first significant federal immigration legislation enacted since adoption of the Constitution.[6] Chae Chan Ping had entered the United States in 1875 and left for a visit home to China twelve years later. Before departing, he obtained from the federal government a certificate authorizing his reentry. While he was outside the United States, Congress enacted the Chinese Exclusion Act of 1888, which, in contravention of a prior treaty with China, prohibited the entry of Chinese laborers—including those in possession of duly issued certificates for reentry.[7] When Chae Chan Ping attempted to return to his home in the United States, he was stopped at the border and prohibited from entering under the terms of the Exclusion Act.

In an opinion for a unanimous Court, Justice Field wrote that the power of the government of the United States to "exclude aliens from its territory is a proposition which we do not think open to controversy."[8] His analysis began:

> Jurisdiction over its own territory to that extent is an incident of every independent nation. It is a part of its independence. If it could not exclude aliens it would be to that extent subject to the control of another power . . .
>
> . . . [I]n their relation to foreign countries and their subjects or citizens[,] [the United States] are one nation, invested with powers which belong to independent nations, the exercise of which can be invoked for the maintenance of its absolute independence and security throughout its entire territory.[9]

Preserving the state's independence and protecting it from foreign aggression, according to Field, was "the highest duty of every nation, and to attain these ends nearly all other considerations are to be subordinated."[10] Foreign encroachment could come from many sources, from either aggressive acts of foreign states or the cumulative acts of individual aliens; the latter Field referred to as "vast hordes . . . crowding in upon us."[11] There is a double sense of danger here, which Field's analysis conflates. Unchecked immigration threatened both the territorial security of the American state (the invading army analogy) and its racial and cultural composition. Sovereignty meant more than control of borders. It also implied power to construct an "American people" through the adoption of membership rules.

Field's conception of the state as a sovereign exercising jurisdiction over territory—and recognized as such by other states of the world—was not novel. It was rooted in an international law paradigm that had dominated American jurisprudence at least from the time of John Marshall,[12] and it was reflected in other important decisions of the Court in the late nineteenth century that involved extraterritorial application of law. A model that conceived of the world as a collection of separate and equal states implied limits on the power of one state to adopt laws that applied to the territory of another (the "territorial principle"). Certainly the United States would resist attempts by foreign states to impose its law on American domestic affairs, and norms of reciprocity (or self-protection) argued for equally limiting the scope of U.S. legislation. Thus, Justice Holmes, in the influential 1909 *American Banana* decision, labeled as "rather startling" the proposition that conduct outside the jurisdiction of the United States could be governed by an act of Congress.[13] Similar reasoning supported the "Act of State" doctrine, announced by the Supreme Court in 1897: "Every sovereign State is bound to respect the independence of every other sovereign State, and the courts of one country will not sit in judgment on the acts of the government of another done within its own territory."[14]

In a world in which people cross national borders, strict adherence to the territoriality principle would be unworkable and not conducive to friendly relations among sovereigns. For example, under traditional international law norms, sovereigns had the power to regulate the conduct of their citizens no matter where their citizens were located in the world. Any assertion of such power beyond the state's borders necessarily implicated the territorial jurisdiction of the foreign state in which the citizen of the regulating state found himself. So despite Holmes's strong language in *American Banana,* the rule against extraterritorial application of law was not a constitutional command; it was rather an interpretive presumption—in modern parlance, a "clear statement" rule: "[I]n case of doubt" the Court would construe a statute "as intended to be confined in its operation and effect to the territorial limits over which the lawmaker has general and legitimate power."[15]

Territoriality also produced conundrums for choice of law cases. If

Smith (a citizen of country A) injured Rodriguez (a citizen of country B) in country A and Rodriguez sued Smith in country B, what law should the courts of country B apply? Not to apply the law of country A would arguably deny sovereign A full authority to prescribe rules for its territory, but to apply automatically the law of country A would be to derogate from the sovereignty of country B to prescribe law for its courts. The solution at the turn of the century, usually identified with the writings of Harvard professor Joseph Beale, was to understand the wrongful conduct as creating a cause of action that the injured party carried with him—even across state borders. Thus, the court in country B was bound to apply the law of country A because not to do so would be to deny the "vested rights" of Rodriguez, which vested in him at the time and place of his injury at the hands of Smith.

Holmes, again, wrote the leading opinion of the day: "The theory of the foreign suit is that although the act complained of was subject to no law having force in the forum, it gave rise to an obligation . . . which, like other obligations, follows the person, and may be enforced wherever the person may be found."[16] The solution was a neat one for the territorial model because it allowed the law of the country where the conduct occurred to control without asking the country in which suit was brought to yield its sovereignty. It was the vested right of the individual, not the superior sovereignty of the country where the act occurred, that required the forum country to apply the foreign law.[17] (Even here there was a catch. A court in the forum country had no duty to permit the suit to go forward if its law did not recognize a cause of action similar to that established under foreign law.)

There is a similar story to tell about the recognition of foreign judgments. The leading case on "comity," *Hilton v. Guyot,*[18] decided in 1895, again drew its premises from a territorial model. The idea of equal and independent sovereigns suggested that states generally respect judgments duly rendered in the courts of another state. But the model was not fully satisfactory. In *Hilton,* for an American court to find the French court's judgment against American litigants conclusive would be to abdicate the sovereignty of the United States; yet to permit the U.S. court to try the action anew would be to deny the principle of territoriality that the United States hopes foreign courts would apply to its courts' judgments. The accommodating solution was that foreign judgments should be entitled to presumptive but not conclusive authority. In *Hilton,* the Court ultimately held that the presumption was overridden because French law did not treat foreign judgments as conclusive in its courts.[19] The notion of "reciprocity" helpfully supplemented strict territoriality, in effect requiring a contract between sovereigns under which each agreed to recognize the judgments of the other in the pursuit of international peace and convenience.

In a bundle of cases around the turn of the century, then, the Supreme Court constructed a fairly powerful model of the sovereign state exercising sole authority over its territory and its people. To be sure, conflicts arose, and a model of strict territoriality provided no necessary resolutions. But answers and doctrines were crafted that sought accommodation within the model.[20] It is thus apparent that Field's invocation of "sovereignty" in the *Chinese Exclusion Case* was but one aspect of a larger model regarding the source and extent of the regulatory power of the American state. Though Field might have derived congressional authority from powers expressly delegated by the Constitution,[21] his appeal to prevailing international law understandings was hardly controversial and sparked no dissent among his brethren.

The reliance on notions of statehood and sovereignty put a spin on the analysis that had significant implications. First, the linking of immigration controls to both national security and the conduct of foreign affairs argued against a judicial role in restricting congressional exercise of the immigration power.[22] Field put it rather strongly: "The government, possessing the powers which are to be exercised for protection and security, is clothed with authority to determine the occasion on which the powers shall be called forth; and its determination, so far as the subjects affected are concerned, are [sic] necessarily conclusive upon all its departments and officers."[23] Here is born the *plenary power doctrine,*[24] a phrase encompassing two ideas that add up to a virtually unlimited congressional power to decide admissions policies for the United States: (1) Congress received (either by way of the Constitution or as an attribute of national statehood) all the power that a sovereign state may have to regulate the entry of aliens,[25] and (2) the courts would not subject congressional choices to any limitations on federal power located elsewhere in the Constitution (such as the First Amendment or the prohibition against retroactive legislation).

Second, conceiving of the immigration power as an aspect of international relations had implications for the remedies that aliens harmed by the law could pursue. Under the international law doctrine of the day, an individual's claim could not be brought directly against a foreign state; rather, it became the property of the citizen's state to "espouse" in whatever way its diplomatic personnel thought fit (and the citizen was bound by the recovery, if any, that the sovereign was able to obtain). Accordingly, any injury suffered by the excluded alien became a matter of international negotiation, not private right: "If the government of the country of which the foreigners excluded are subjects is dissatisfied with this action it can make complaint to the executive head of our government, or resort to any other measure which, in its judgment, its interests or dignity may demand; and there lies its only remedy."[26] Although China complained bitterly about the exclusion laws, the U.S. Congress held fast (not repealing them until 1943!). Chae Chan Ping was refused entry into the United States despite his possession of a federally issued certificate guaranteeing him a right to return to his lawful residence of twelve years after a short visit to his Chinese home.

The power to control borders may reasonably be inferred from the idea of a sovereign state, but the second half of the plenary power doctrine—limited judicial review—is not a necessary implication.[27] If the national government is a creature of the Constitution, then there is no obvious reason why the limits established in the fundamental law would not restrain the exercise of all powers delegated to the national government.[28] But this was plainly not the Court's view in the immigration cases (and, as we shall see, in the other sovereignty cases).

One way to understand the Court's results is to return to the concept of a national state as land plus people. The "normal" setting of a constitutional case is the operation of a challenged governmental action on state members (citizens) in state territory; in such circumstances, constitutional restrictions on governmental power should be fully operative. Deviating from the "norm" by having the regulation either fall on less than full members or apply beyond U.S. borders opens up the possibility of the relaxation of constitutional limits. A simple two-by-two model (citizen/alien/inside United States/outside United States) can go a long way in explaining the late nineteenth century sovereignty cases.

Chae Chan Ping is in the least favored position, being both (nominally) outside the country and a less than full member. He can object to neither the substance of the congressional decision nor, as later cases establish, the procedures established for determining admissibility.[29] Attaining entry improves an alien's constitutional status, permitting the Court to apply due process norms to deportation proceedings.[30] But, as the Court made clear in *Fong Yue Ting v. United States,* Congress retains unfettered power to establish the substantive grounds on which aliens may be sent home.[31] In contrast, citizens are understood to benefit from full constitutional protections while inside the United States; outside U.S. territory, however, the constitutional rights of U.S. citizens stand on less sure footing.[32]

Complications for the Sovereignty Model: Indians and the New Territories

So far so good. A simple territory-plus-membership model explains much of what is going on in the sovereignty cases, fitting nicely with prevailing understandings of "sovereign statehood." But the real world invariably complicates neat categories like sovereignty, membership, and territory. In the late nineteenth century, the status of Indian tribes and the new Caribbean and Pacific possessions raised difficult questions for the territorial model. What was the constitutional status of residents of the new possessions and Indians born in the United States? Did the Constitution "follow the flag"? In both the Indian and the possessions cases, the indigenous peoples were neither aliens nor nonresidents, yet despite their birth and residence on U.S. soil, the Supreme Court was not prepared to include them within the circle of full membership. Rather, the Court recognized in Congress the power to resolve these troubling membership questions largely free from judicial constraint. The legal doctrines, which will be briefly described here and examined in greater detail in subsequent chapters, follow the lines of the alien cases.

The Status of Indian Tribes

By what right did European settlers assert sovereignty over the indigenous people and territory of the New World? John Marshall's early-nineteenth-century "solution" for American constitutional law ratified in law what had been true in fact for several hundred years: that white claims to the land of the United States were superior to those of the Indians.[33] But Marshall never found a fully satisfactory theoretical construct for describing the relation of Indian sovereignty to U.S. sovereignty. His term "domestic dependent nations"[34] has dominated the field of Indian law ever since, although emphasis has shifted back and forth between the "dependent" and the "nation."[35] To this day, Supreme Court opinions refer to the status of Indian tribes as "anomalous."[36]

For much of the nineteenth century, Congress regulated affairs with Indian tribes by way of treaties. The obvious underlying idea was that tribes, though not foreign states, were "distinct, independent, political communities."[37] The Constitution supported such a characterization by excluding "Indians not taxed" in counting the population for apportionment purposes.[38] Conceptualizing regulation of Indians as akin to relations with foreign nations supported, as it did in the alien cases, assertions of plenary federal power.[39]

In 1871, Congress enacted legislation ending the treaty system,[40] thereby rendering regulation of Indian tribes a matter of the normal statutory process. The statute provided the House of Representatives (excluded from the treaty process) a more significant role in crafting federal Indian policy.[41] But there was a broader story as well. Subdued by federal military power, removed from their homelands and largely confined to reservations on federal land, the tribes looked less and less like (even quasi-) sovereign nations capable of entering into treaties with the United States.[42]

Significantly, the new shift in conceptualization of tribal relations was not seen as undercutting congressional "plenary power" over Indian affairs. Instead, it merely provided a different justification for federal power. Citing an earlier Marshall opinion (but with an important change in emphasis), the Supreme Court in 1886 characterized Indians as "wards of the nation" and "communities dependent on the United States."[43] Thus federal power "over these remnants of a race once powerful, now weak and diminished in numbers, is necessary to their protection, as well as to the safety of those among whom they dwell."[44]

That the Court's understanding of "plenary power" over the Indians was of a piece with its analysis in the alien cases is made clear in the 1903 case of *Lone Wolf v. Hitchcock.*[45] At issue in *Lone Wolf* was a federal statute ratifying an 1892 agreement that had purported to transfer more than 2 million acres of Indian land to the federal government for the purpose of opening the land to white settlers. Members of the affected tribes had sued, claiming that the transfer had been fraudulently obtained and had violated the terms of an 1867 treaty that prohibited cession of any jointly held reservation land unless agreed to by three-quarters of all adult male Indians occupying the land.

In language echoing the *Chinese Exclusion Case,* the Court held that Congress had plenary power to regulate Indian tribes, preexisting treaty rights to the contrary notwithstanding:

> Plenary authority over the tribal relations of the Indians has been exercised by Congress from the beginning, and the power has always been deemed a political one, not subject to be controlled by the judicial department of the government. Until the year 1871 the policy was pursued of dealing with the Indian tribes by means of treaties, and, of course, a moral obligation rested upon Congress to act in good faith in performing the stipulations entered into on its behalf. But, as with treaties made with foreign nations, *Chinese Exclusion Case,* 130 U.S. 581, 600, . . . the legislative power might pass laws in conflict with treaties made with the Indians.[46]

As in the alien cases, plenary authority here had the dual sense of being both complete and unreviewable. The actions complained of "were solely within the domain of the legislative authority and its action is conclusive" upon the judiciary.[47] "If injury was occasioned, which we do not wish to be understood as implying, by the use made by Congress of its power, relief must be sought by an appeal to that body for redress and not to the courts."[48]

The Indian cases complicate the two-by-two matrix of territory and membership sketched earlier. Born and residing on U.S. soil, Indians seem to fit into the "full membership" category. But in *Elk v. Wilkins,* decided in 1884, the Supreme Court held that the Fourteenth Amendment did not confer citizenship on Indians born under the jurisdiction of a tribe—even those who had separated from their tribe and taken up residence "among white citizens."[49] Such Indians were not deemed to be subject to the jurisdiction of the United States.[50] Inclusion was a political question to be decided not by the Court but "by the nation whose wards they are and whose citizens they seek to become."[51] Indeed, acquisition of citizenship under later federal statutes was not deemed to remove "wardship" or undercut the "plenary authority" of Congress to regulate Indian affairs.[52]

The Territories and the Insular Cases

There was no doubt in the first decade of the twentieth century that Congress possessed inherent power to acquire territory and plenary authority to craft (nonrepresentative) institutions for the territories' governance.[53] The tougher issue was what constitutional limits applied to congressional regulation of the territories. In nineteenth-century cases involving the western territories, the Court regularly concluded that the Constitution constrained the federal and territorial governments.[54] The question posed by acquisition of the Philippines, Puerto Rico, and other lands was whether these norms for the continent applied to far-flung islands.

The Supreme Court came to grip with these issues in a series of cases usually referred to as the *Insular Cases*.[55] In *Downes v. Bidwell*, a major case examining congressional power over the possessions acquired after the Spanish-American War, the Court splintered, mirroring the powerful political debates of the day; Justice Brown announced the "conclusion and the judgment of the court" in an opinion that no other Justice joined.[56] Within a few years, however, the majority of the Court had fixed on a doctrinal solution, one that purported to maintain the rule from the earlier territory cases but granted Congress flexibility toward the new possessions. Adopting Justice White's suggestion in his *Downes* concurrence, the Court focused on "the relation of the particular territory to the United States."[57] For those territories that, by treaty or statute, had been "incorporated" into the United States, the Constitution applied in full.[58] Thus, a provision of the Alaska Code providing for criminal trials with six jurors was unconstitutional under the Sixth Amendment, since the Alaskan Territory was deemed to have been "incorporated" by way of the U.S. treaty with Russia and subsequent congressional legislation.[59] Residents of the Philippines and Puerto Rico, however, were not entitled to the same amendment's guarantee of a jury trial because Congress manifested no intent to "incorporate" those territories into the United States.[60]

Unincorporated territories were not wholly bereft of constitutional protection. Congress, "in legislating for the Territories[,] would be subject to those fundamental limitations in favor of personal rights which are formulated in the Constitution and its amendments."[61] The question for decision in cases involving "unincorporated" territories, then, was whether the constitutional right alleged to have been violated was "fundamental."[62]

Despite the doctrine's reliance on the "occult"[63] and difficult-to-apply concept of "incorporation," its purpose and effect were apparent. In a time when the nation itself was uncertain about the future status of the former Spanish possessions and quite sure that most of the indigenous inhabitants should not be granted citizenship immediately, the Court opted for constitutional rules that gave Congress a rather free hand in fashioning arrangements for the new territories and their people. Complete and direct application of the Constitution, it was thought, could severely hamper congressional policy options and perhaps undermine empire building altogether. For example, the Court concluded that the right to jury trials did not extend to the Philippines on the following reasoning:

> [To hold that the Constitution applied in full to the territories would mean that if] the United States, impelled by its duty or advantage, shall acquire territory peopled by savages, and of which it may dispose or not hold for ultimate admission to Statehood, . . . [then it] must establish there the trial by jury. To state such a proposition demonstrates the impossibility of carrying it into practice.[64]

Not only could Congress decide the rules that applied in "unincorporated" territories, but also the question of incorporation itself would turn on congressional intent and action.

As in the *Chinese Exclusion Case,* the Court believed that the power to acquire and rule territory was an inherent aspect of statehood in the nineteenth-century world, enabling the United States to "move with strength and dignity and effect among the other nations of the earth to such purpose as it may undertake or to such destiny as it may be called."[65] But it is clear that the Court was thinking here of more than theoretical equality in a world of national states; it was thinking rather of the ability and authority of the United States to be an imperial power of a stature equal to that of the European states. "A false step at this time," wrote Justice Brown with refreshing candor in *Downes,* "might be fatal to the development of what Chief Justice Marshall called the American Empire."[66]

In short, in the *Insular Cases*—as in the Indian cases—the logic of territoriality ran into the impossibility of full membership for "savage peoples." The Court found a middle position that neither sacrificed the Constitution nor unduly hindered American empire building.[67] The possessions could be "subject to the jurisdiction of the United States, [but] not *of* the United States."[68]

Sovereignty and the "Uncivilized"

Formally, then, a conception of national sovereignty could be translated into doctrine that more or less satisfactorily resolved the constitutional issues of the day. But the results of the turn-of-the-century cases were clearly not the product of the exercise of logic or the abstract manipulation of categories or models. Other solutions, after all, were conceivable. Location of the immigration power in mystical notions of sovereignty[69] added strength to the Court's claims of national security and unreviewability. But the power to admit aliens could well have been derived in less dramatic fashion from Congress's delegated power to regulate commerce or provide a uniform rule of naturalization.[70] Dissenting justices in the *Insular Cases* provided plausible legal theories for application of the Constitution to the territories. A judiciary willing and ready to enforce the government's promises made to Indian tribes would have been true to deep American conceptions regarding the sanctity of property rights. Remarkably, the plenary power cases arise in a constitutional era usually remembered for its judicial activism on behalf of private rights—typified by the Supreme Court's decision in *Lochner v. New York,* which invalidated a maximum-hours law for bakers.[71] Can *Lochner* and the sovereignty cases coexist?

An answer begins to come into focus when we recognize that the reasoning of the sovereignty cases reflected late-nineteenth-century views on the superiority, and therefore legitimate supremacy, of Anglo-American culture and institutions. Put simply, "uncivilized" peoples were unfit for self-governance or for full membership in the American polity. Congressional power to exclude inassimilable aliens from the territory of the United States appeared self-evident; and for resident aliens, Indians, and other "less civilized" groups already located on U.S. soil, congressional plenary power was justified, perhaps even morally required, as a way to raise up the lower orders by "Americanizing" them.[72] In the sovereignty cases, the Supreme Court announced that it would not restrict congressional prerogatives as the nation decided how, and to what extent, it would "take up the White Man's burden."[73] The plenary power cases, then, parallel the Court's willingness to tolerate protective legislation for women in the age of *Lochner*.[74]

In the late nineteenth century, American notions of "civilization" were largely a function of race, which was understood to be both biologically fixed and closely linked with nationality, culture, and national character.[75] As John Higham has explained, "Nationalism was naturalized; and 'race' in every sense came to imply a biological determinism."[76] In this schema, superiority was assigned not simply to "whites" but rather to the Anglo-Saxon (or Teutonic) branch of the Caucasian race.[77]

The cult of Anglo-Saxonism at the turn of the century replayed familiar older themes in the national repertoire. Before the Civil War, Indian policy, slavery, and the war with Mexico had been defended on grounds of the superiority of the Anglo-Saxons and Anglo-Saxonism.[78] The march to the west coast of the United States was seen as part of the inevitable movement of liberty and democracy that had followed the sun since the beginning of civilization—from the mountains of the Caucasus to the forests of Germany to the British Isles and then across the Atlantic. Anglo-Saxonism, it was assumed, would continue its spread and domination of the world, subduing and ultimately assimilating or supplanting the less capable races. As Reginald Horsman has argued, by the 1850s, American Anglo-Saxons understood themselves as a "separate, innately superior people who were destined to bring good government, commercial prosperity, and Christianity to the American continents and to the world."[79] Earlier Enlightenment ideas of the common humanity and educability of other groups had been replaced by a racial arrogance that condemned "most of the world's peoples . . . to permanent inferiority or even to extinction."[80]

By the late nineteenth century, Anglo-Saxonism had force in both foreign and domestic policy spheres. U.S. expansionism was fueled not only by economic and military considerations but also by racial and cultural ideology.[81] "American expansion," Nell Irvin Painter concludes, "was not interpreted simply as the spread of the American polity . . . It was emphatically and explicitly the expansion of the Anglo-Saxon."[82] To many, the American people—understood in turn-of-the-century terms as primarily Anglo-Saxons—were agents in a teleological process. U.S. imperialism was good for the world because it continued the ineluctable spread of free and democratic institutions. Josiah Strong, an influential Congregational minister of the day, put it this way in his enormously successful book *Our Country:* "Is there room for reasonable doubt that this race . . . is destined to dispossess many weaker races, assimilate others, and mold the remainder, until, in a very true and important sense, it has Anglo-Saxonized mankind?"[83]

The rhetorical project hit the ground in the Philippines. Dewey's victory over the hapless Spanish fleet at Manila in 1898 presented the expansionists with an instant overseas empire. The question then became whether the United States should grant the archipelago independence or continue to hold the islands in furtherance of U.S. imperialist designs. Some of the proponents of empire imagined a long-term arrangement with substantial American settlements overseas (as had occurred in Hawaii from mid-century on). Others thought that a continued American presence was advisable at least until the pagan inhabitants could be schooled in the arts of self-government. But no domestic group, imperialist or anti-imperialist, thought the Filipinos were ready for U.S. membership. Indeed, the antiexpansionist constitutional argument that "the Constitution follows the flag" was pressed more in order to prevent empire building (since the inapplicability of the Constitution to the "savages" of the Philippines seemed apparent) than to ensure that all residents on U.S. soil would be guaranteed basic civil rights. President McKinley's account of his decision in 1898 to maintain dominion over the Philippines provides a candid statement of the American view that prevailed. He reported that, after kneeling in prayer for several nights seeking divine guidance on what course of action to take in the Philippines, an answer came: the archipelago could neither be returned to Spain ("that would be cowardly and dishonorable") nor handed over to France or Germany ("our commercial rivals in the Orient").[84] Nor could the United States "leave them to themselves—they were unfit for self-government—and they would soon have anarchy and misrule over there worse than Spain's was."[85] So "there was nothing left for us to do but take them all, and to educate the Filipinos, and uplift and civilize and Christianize them, and by God's grace do the very best we could by them, as our fellow-men for whom Christ also died."[86]

Domestically, the preservation of Anglo-Saxonism was sorely challenged by the mass migrations of the late nineteenth century. In the 1850s, the influx of Irish immigrants had helped to spark the "Know-Nothing" movement that captured more than one hundred seats in Congress and six governorships on an anti-alien, anti-Catholic platform. The second great wave of immigration, from 1880 to 1920, brought more than 20 million aliens to the United States. The arrival of the "heathen" Chinese[87] was stopped by the exclusion laws of the 1880s, but southern and eastern European immigration rose to unprecedented levels in the first decade of the twentieth century.[88] By 1910, almost 15 percent of the population was foreign-born.[89] The United States could hardly fulfill its destiny of world domination if it was permitted to rot from within. As Robert Wiebe notes, "Mixing contempt with fear, [U.S.] natives pictured the newcomers as dispirited breeders of poverty, crime, and political corruption, and simultaneously as peculiarly powerful subversives whose foreign ideologies were undermining American society."[90]

The superpatriotism of the day cultivated worship of Constitution and flag.[91] But it was not only the American state as political entity that was at risk; the arriving masses of foreigners also threatened the American nation-state conceived of as an Anglo-Saxon polity. To construct the nationness of the United States, American nationalism needed to tell a story of the nation's roots that emphasized Anglo-Saxon ancestry and the Anglo-Saxon dedication to democratic self-rule. It is thus not surprising that the late nineteenth century witnessed the birth of the Society of Mayflower Descendants, the Sons and Daughters of the American Revolution, the National Society of Colonial Dames,[92] and what Werner Sollors has termed myths of "Plymouth origins."[93] According to Sollors, prior to the Civil War, Plymouth Rock played only a minor role in the American public memory, sharing space with the Virginia colonies in the origin myths.[94] But by the end of the century, Plymouth had attained prominence, largely in response to the new immigration: "The more heterogeneous the country was perceived to be, the more Plymouth origins came to be stressed as a mark of distinction."[95] In a characteristically felicitous formulation, Mark Twain noted that the Pilgrims "took good care of themselves, but they abolished everybody else's ancestors."[96]

To retain Anglo-Saxon domination of American institutions, the massive migration of un-American groups had to be stanched, and those who had already gained entry had to be effectively "Americanized."[97] The upshot was the enactment of laws excluding and deporting aliens for their political beliefs, the restrictive Immigration Act of 1917,[98] the Palmer Raids of 1919, and ultimately the national origins quota system of the 1920s.[99]

American Indians presented another domestic challenge for Anglo-Saxonism. Throughout the nineteenth century, Euro-Americans constructed conflicting images of the Indians. That they were "uncivilized" went without saying, but characterizations varied from the brave and honorable "noble savage" (who was able to be lifted up with proper religious and secular education) to the "wild savage" (who was unable to be civilized, and thus an appropriate candidate for removal and extermination).[100] Completion of the military project in the second half of the nineteenth century gave greater scope to the missionary project. Thus, the reservation policy put in place after the Civil War could be defended as establishing locations where Native Americans could be taught "the arts and industry" of European civilized life.[101]

By the 1880s, "friends of the Indians" had become skeptical of the reservation system. Rather than inculcating civilization, it appeared that "[t]he reservation line [was] a wall which fence[d] out law, civil institutions, and social order, and admit[ted] only despotism, greed, and lawlessness."[102] The major piece of reform legislation, the General Allotment Act of 1887,[103] took a different approach to the "civilizing" of the natives. Self-sufficiency and independence, it was argued, could be attained by helping the Indians become farmers, who could then acquire the Puritan virtues of hard work, thrift, and individualism—in short, by replacing the communally based reservation system with privately held parcels of arable land. (Not incidentally, the breakup of reservations would also open up huge tracts of land to white settlement and ownership.)[104] "[T]ake [the savage] by the hand," declared Senator Henry L. Dawes, sponsor of the Allotment Act, "and set him upon his feet, and teach him to stand alone first, then to walk, then to dig, then to plant, then to hoe, then to gather, and then to *keep*."[105] Under the Allotment Act, the president was authorized to distribute reservation land "advantageous for agriculture and grazing purposes" to individual Indian families.[106] The secretary of the interior would hold such allotments in trust for twenty-five years, at which time title would vest in the allottees.[107] Indians receiving allotments were granted U.S. citizenship, as were Indians who had taken up residence apart from any tribe and had "adopted the habits of civilized life."[108]

The allotment policy has properly been declared a disaster for the Indians, costing them almost two-thirds of the 138 million acres of land they inhabited in 1887. But at the time, the Allotment Act displayed, in part, the more optimistic side of white American views on the "civilizability" of native peoples. Unlike Chinese laborers, Indians could not be "sent home" to a place outside the United States. Instead they should be "dispersed or diffused throughout our population," wrote former Supreme Court Justice William Strong in 1885.[109] "[T]hey should not maintain their own language and habits, but be brought into contact with the better portion of our communities scattered throughout the land, where they might be brought under good influences, and ultimately be Americanized."[110] In this way, Indian policy provides an early example of the Americanization programs established for immigrants in the first decades of the twentieth century. In time, the idealism of the reformers would fade, and the assimilationist project would be declared a failure. In the harsh glare of turn-of-the-century racism, Indians appeared "naturally" able to enter American life only at the lower rungs.[111] But whether Indians were deemed assimilable or inherently inferior, the benchmark against which they were measured was Christian "civilized" society.

The Sovereignty Cases and the Idea of Civilization

It is against this background that we can begin to make fuller sense of the sovereignty cases. At issue for the Court was not just the working out of a set of nineteenth-century international law norms, but rather the greasing of the wheels of an American machine that would project Anglo-Saxon civilization overseas and affirm it at home. This conclusion requires no between-the-lines reading of the cases or psychobiographies of the Justices. The opinions themselves display a clear—and, to the modern eye, rather remarkable—account of the assumed superiority of Anglo-Saxon culture, usually described in terms of "civilization." According to the Court, destiny had forced a "civilized" American polity to confront "savage" Indians and "inassimilable" Chinese at home and "alien races" in the territories abroad, all of whom required suppression or domestication for their own good and for the progress of the United States.[112]

Thus, in sustaining the Chinese exclusion laws of the 1880s, the Court held that Congress had the power to prohibit immigration if it "considers the presence of foreigners of a different race in this country, who will not assimilate with us, to be dangerous to its peace and security."[113] Even the dissents in *Fong Yue Ting* (the case upholding the power of Congress to expel resident Chinese laborers) are laced with phrases such as "the obnoxious Chinese" and "this distasteful class."[114]

Similar characterizations of the peoples of the new territories bestrew the pages of the *Insular Cases.* The doctrinal innovation of the cases was the distinction between incorporated and unincorporated territories. But that question was deemed to turn on congressional intent, as manifested in treaties and legislation, and there was no doubt that the congressional judgment was based largely on the race and perceived level of civilization of the inhabitants of the newly acquired territories. Areas populated by "barbarians" not thought fit for full U.S. membership were found not to have been incorporated into the United States, and those persons living in such territories were therefore not entitled to full constitutional protection.[115] Limited application of the Constitution was justified in terms of the impracticability of the extension of rights and the cultural differences separating the superior and inferior races:

> If those possessions are inhabited by alien races, differing from us in religion, customs, laws, methods of taxation and modes of thought, the administration of government and justice, according to Anglo-Saxon principles, may for a time be impossible; and the question at once arises whether large concessions ought not to be made for a time, that, ultimately, our own theories may be carried out, and the blessings of a free government under the Constitution extended to them. We decline to hold that there is anything in the Constitution to forbid such action.[116]

Indian tribes, who could neither be excluded like the Chinese nor granted independence like the Filipinos, could perhaps be civilized. From the Court's late-nineteenth-century perspective, they were "in a state of pupilage, advancing from the condition of a savage tribe to that of a people who, through the discipline of labor and by education, it was hoped might become a self-supporting and self-governed society."[117]

The "savageness" of the tribes not only supported plenary federal authority but also argued against the application of "civilized" standards and procedures to tribal governmental operations. The case of *Ex parte Crow Dog* provides a vivid example. In 1883 Crow Dog killed Spotted Tail, a Sioux chief popular with federal authorities. Pursuant to Sioux custom, Crow Dog's relatives approached Spotted Tail's family and offered compensation acceptable to the aggrieved family. That Crow Dog could go free with neither a trial nor sentence so outraged public opinion that federal authorities arrested him and tried him for murder. He was convicted by a federal jury and sentenced to death. Upon appeal, the Supreme Court read federal statutes as not authorizing federal criminal jurisdiction in such a case. It therefore overturned the conviction and sentence. Crucial to its interpretation of federal law were the cultural differences between tribal and U.S. systems. To find federal jurisdiction under existing laws, the Court stated, would be to extend federal law "over aliens and strangers; over the members of a community separated by race, by tradition, by the instincts of a free though savage life, from the authority and power which seeks to impose upon them the restraints of an external and unknown code."[118] A federal criminal proceeding

> tries them, not by their peers, nor by the customs of their people, nor the law of their land, but by superiors of a different race, according to the law of a social state of which they have an imperfect conception, and which is opposed to the traditions of their history, to the habits of their lives, to the strongest prejudices of their savage nature; one which measures the red man's revenge by the maxims of the white man's morality.[119]

The country apparently was not ready for such cultural relativism. Concluding that Sioux customs demonstrated the low value that savages placed on human life, Congress responded by enacting the Major Crimes Act two years later.[120] The statute granted federal courts jurisdiction in criminal cases involving designated serious offenses committed by an Indian on federal territory or on an Indian reservation. The

Supreme Court upheld the exercise of federal power in the landmark case of *United States v. Kagama* in 1886.[121]

The "uncivilized" nature of foreign cultures also had an impact on the rights of Americans overseas. In the important case of *In re Ross,*[122] the Court upheld the constitutionality of criminal trials conducted by U.S. consular courts. Ross, a crew member on an American ship anchored in Yokohama Harbor, stabbed and killed the ship's second mate. A treaty with Japan yielded jurisdiction in such cases to the American authorities, and Ross was subsequently tried and convicted of murder before a consular court. Ross's appeal, which claimed violation of his constitutional rights to a grand jury and a petit jury in criminal proceedings, was rejected by the Supreme Court. Tracing the history of such tribunals back to the Middle Ages, Justice Field's opinion for a unanimous Court noted that consular proceedings benefited U.S. citizens by withdrawing jurisdiction from the "often arbitrary and oppressive" courts of non-Christian countries.[123] "It is true," Field conceded, "that the occasion for consular tribunals in Japan may hereafter be less than at present, as every year that country progresses in civilization and in the assimilation of its system of judicial procedure to that of Christian countries."[124] Nonetheless, the system of consular courts "is of the highest importance, and their establishment in other than Christian countries, where our people may desire to go in pursuit of commerce, will often be essential for the protection of their persons and property."[125]

Throughout this period, then, the Supreme Court ratified federal policies aimed at furthering and preserving Anglo-Saxon domination of "inferior" races. In the *Chinese Exclusion Case* and *Fong Yue Ting,* in the *Insular Cases,* in *Kagama* and *Lone Wolf,* and in *In re Ross,* the Court affirmed the "plenary power" of the federal government to create, in effect, an American nation-state in which Christian institutions and benevolence would suppress, reform, or replace uncivilized peoples not deemed capable of proper self-government or participation in the American polity.[126] The Court was resolute in its unwillingness to interfere with Congress's sovereign power to build an empire and regulate the peopling of America.[127]

It should be emphasized that leaving such matters to Congress did not invariably result in the adoption of subordinating and racist policies. Under federal treaties, Indians were able to attain citizenship as early as 1861,[128] and in 1924 a federal statute extended citizenship to all Indians born in the United States.[129] Puerto Ricans were made citizens in 1917.[130] Furthermore, congressional civil rights legislation was written to protect aliens as well as African-Americans.[131] Of course, such protections, like the early Indian treaties, frequently amounted to little more than words on paper. In this period few African-Americans or American Indians exercised the right to vote guaranteed by citizenship, and most discriminatory state legislation survived until the middle of the twentieth century.

It was an odd mix of orthodoxies, perhaps peculiarly American, that believed enough in the fundamental dignity of all men[132] to extend basic civil (and, for blacks and Indians, political) rights irrespective of race and at the same time permit the blatant abridgment of such rights because of the equally firm conviction of the inherent inferiority of nonwhite races. If the system held together, it was because a deep social prejudice—left untouched by the Court and Congress—policed the borders of racial caste.[133] That is, civil and political rights could be guaranteed because they ultimately posed no threat to the social hierarchy. Wrote one "friend of the Indian" in 1886:

> We are descended from a common father; God made us "of one blood;" nor have we any right, except that derived from power, to withhold from them [i.e., the Indians] any privileges or immunities which we grant to the more civilized people. In all this I do not *recommend* the intermingling of the races; but I do not fear it. Long as the African has lived side by side with the Caucasian on these shores, it is very seldom, even now, that a marriage takes place between a negro and a white. It may safely be left to the tastes and prejudices of individuals to avert the nightmare of a confusion of races or the degradation of the Caucasian by either Indian or African infusion.[134]

Ten years later the Supreme Court would place its imprimatur on the great oxymoron of "separate and equal" with similar certainty that the Constitution did not promise social equality, nor would Anglo-Saxon America tolerate it.[135]

Toward Cultural Pluralism—for Whites

In 1915 Woodrow Wilson told newly naturalized citizens that "[a] man who thinks of himself as belonging to a particular national group in America has not yet become an American."[136] But other voices spoke of nonwhites and immigrants contributing a healthy diversity to the nation. The idea of America as a mosaic was at war with both the metaphor of the melting pot and Anglo-Saxon superiority.

A deep essentialism ran through much of this counterdiscourse. In 1897 W. E. B. DuBois had praised black culture and character, seeking its preservation in a time of virulent racism. Black people, he wrote, had a duty to "conserve our physical powers, our intellectual endowments, our spiritual ideals" and to strive "by race organization, by race solidarity, by race unity to the realization of that broader humanity which freely recognizes differences in men, but sternly deprecates inequality in their opportunities of development."[137] Horace Kallen, in a widely cited two-part essay in *The Nation,* challenged the idea of the melting pot, arguing that America was in the process of becoming "a great republic consisting of a federation or commonwealth of nationalities."[138] In that republic, different nationalities would "cooperat[e] voluntarily and autonomously in the enterprise of self-realization through perfection of men according to their kind."[139]

Perhaps the most interesting—and far-sighted—intervention in this debate came from Randolph Bourne, a journalist and social critic, who saw immigrants as providing the fresh blood needed to reinvigorate a declining Anglo-Saxon race. His supple reading of the social text—today we might label it "postmodern"—saw a "transnational America" in which immigrant groups neither melted nor maintained preexisting characteristics; rather, they took on a kind of dual nationality, being citizens of both the Old World and the New. Bourne's "cosmopolitan vision" figured America as "a novel international nation" and "a weaving back and forth, with the other lands, of many threads of all sizes and colors." He criticized "Americanization" movements that sought to "thwart this weaving, or to dye the fabric any one color, or disentangle the threads of the strand." Progress toward a "cosmopolitan America" would "liberate and harmonize the creative power of all these peoples and give them [a] new spiritual citizenship."[140]

The call for a "transnational America" was drowned out by the drumbeat of war and demands of 100 percent Americanism. The nation witnessed its worst race riots,[141] the heyday of the Ku Klux Klan, and the Palmer Raids.[142] According to John Higham, the "historic confidence" in the process of assimilation weakened. And with "the passing of faith in the melting pot there perished the ideal of American nationality as an unfinished, steadily improving, cosmopolitan blend."[143] Demands for immigration restriction came front and center and eventually resulted in enactment of the national origins quota system in the 1920s. Under the new statute, sending countries were assigned quotas based on their share of the foreign-born population in the United States according to the 1890 census—a date safely before the dramatic increase in immigration from eastern and southern Europe. The point of the new immigration system was direct: if assimilation of new "stocks" could not be guaranteed, then the nation would return to earlier, more assimilable flows.[144]

And yet within a decade or two, the idea of hyphenated Americans—as we understand it today—was ascendant for white European immigrants and their descendants. Restrictions on immigration had produced fewer first-generation immigrants and more second- and third-generation Americans. The "old country" served more as a nostalgic memory than as a set of ongoing connections. These social developments coincided with, and were supported by, the rise of the modern social sciences. Academics dramatically undermined Anglo-Saxonism by demonstrating the fallacies of race essentialism and Nordic superiority;[145] and they argued for the "relativity of cultural habits."[146] At the same time, they theorized the assimilation of immigrants as a natural and inevitable process."[147] In this era, Native American culture was rediscovered and newly valorized.[148] America had, in effect, been made safe for Kallen's "cultural pluralism"[149]—not as a federation of nations, but as a nation united by a civic and political culture that tolerated (at times celebrated) cultural diversity. In Lawrence Fuchs's terms, America had come to believe that "the hyphen unites."[150]

The rosy narrative of ethnic assimilation was, however, limited by race, geography, and politics. The exclusion of Asian immigrants was not relaxed until World War II, and then only partially. (Full equality was not achieved for another two decades.) In the post–World War II years, communism was deemed the major threat to social peace, and the immigration system was mobilized to prevent the entry of this pathogenic alien ideology. The McCarran-Walter Act of 1952, enacted over President Truman's veto,[151] set its sights on "undigestible blocks" of immigrants—defined in ideological terms. Thus, new grounds for exclusion and deportation were added to the immigration code to keep the nation safe from those who "advocate the economic, international and governmental doctrines of world communism or the establishment in the United States of a totalitarian dictatorship."[152] Although overall levels of immigration were not reduced, the McCarran-Walter Act maintained the national origins quota system.[153] The thinking was that assimilation would proceed apace, and pluralism could be tolerated, provided the right kinds of immigrants were granted entry.[154]

Race remained the great dividing line. The scientific prediction of assimilation did not apply to racial minorities. According to Robert Park, "The Negro, during his three hundred years in this country, has not been assimilated. This is not because he has preserved in America a foreign culture and an alien tradition." Blacks, unlike recent immigrants, were American citizens. Yet the African-American was regarded as "in some sense a stranger, a representative of an alien race."[155] In the immediate post–World War II era, social segregation remained the rule. Racial intermarriage was extremely low; indeed, in the mid-1960s a dozen states still had antimiscegenation laws on the books. Gunnar Myrdal's *An American Dilemma,* published in 1944, demonstrated in painful detail the gap between American ideals of equality and the treatment of blacks. Nonwhite immigrant groups faced similar isolation and nonassimilation.[156]

Indians were somewhere between immigrants and African-Americans, viewed as assimilable but nonassimilated. The New Deal's Indian Reorganization Act (IRA)[157] had sought to transform the guardian-ward relationship between the federal government and the tribes. The act ended the allotment policy and provided for Indian self-government over reservations. By the end of World War II, however, critics claimed that living conditions on the reservations had not materially improved and that what was needed was an explicit policy of assimilation. The so-called termination policies of the 1950s sought to end the special relationship between Indians and the federal government by eliminating the reservation system and subjecting Indians to general state authority.[158] As stated in the concurrent resolution declaring termination as official federal policy, Congress's goal was to make Indians "subject to the same laws and entitled to the same privileges and responsibilities as are applicable to other citizens of the United States."[159] Pursuant to the policy, more than one hundred tribes and bands were terminated (representing about 3 percent of all federally recognized Indians); with their lands offered for sale, the Indians' tribal sovereignty came to an end. Other termination policies included the transfer of educational programs from the tribes and the federal government to the states and the transfer of federal health programs from the Bureau of Indian Affairs (BIA) to the federal Department of Health, Education, and Welfare.[160] Most significant was the enactment in 1953 of Public Law 280, which extended—without tribal consent—state criminal and civil jurisdiction over reservations in California, Minnesota, Nebraska, Oregon, and Wisconsin. The statute authorized all other states to assume similar authorities over reservations within their borders, again without the need for tribal consent.[161]

Plenary Power in the Mid-Twentieth Century

Whatever the change in public rhetoric or social science regarding the ultimate assimilability of various groups, the Supreme Court continued to affirm Congress's plenary power over immigration, Indians, and the territories in the broadest possible terms. In immigration cases laced with cold war language, the Court upheld summary exclusion procedures with the chilling words that "[w]hatever the procedure authorized by Congress is, it is due process as far as an alien denied entry is concerned."[162] The Court sustained the retroactive application of deportation grounds, fully embracing the plenary power cases of the late nineteenth century.[163] And, applying an anemic First Amendment standard, it permitted the deportation of persons under a 1940 statute based solely on their past membership in the Communist Party.[164] Justice Jackson, writing for the Court, made clear the linkage between immigration and national security; the former attorney general stated that the Court would not declare that "congressional alarm about a coalition of Communist power without and Communist conspiracy within the United States is either a fantasy or a pretense[.]"[165]

The Indian cases likewise reflect continued allegiance to the plenary power doctrine. Despite New Deal policies aimed at reinvigorating tribal self-determination, the Court never doubted that Congress retained full and complete control over tribes and reservations. Felix Cohen's *Handbook of Federal Indian Law*, prepared during his tenure at the Department of the Interior, provided the leading summary of the doctrine at mid-century. Examining the sources and scope of federal authority, Cohen described a broad congressional power to regulate Indian affairs—including the power to manage and dispose of tribal lands, supersede tribal membership decisions, alter tribal property distribution rules, control tribal funds, and prohibit the sale of liquor on or near reservations.[166] A sympathetic observer, Cohen attempted to rein in plenary power talk.[167] "Plenary power," he wrote, "does not mean absolute power, and the exercise of the power must be founded upon some reasonable basis."[168] But throughout this period, as Cohen's survey makes clear, the Court simply deferred to congressional policy choices; it played no role in supervising federal regulation of the tribes.[169]

The territories cases of the day display similar results. Despite changes in the political relationship of the territories to the United States, the Court continued to confirm Congress's plenary power. Thus in a 1937 case involving a federal tax on the processing of coconut oil in the Philippines, the Justices took note of the passage of the Philippine Independence Act and the adoption of a constitution for the Commonwealth of the Philippine Islands (formal independence occurred in 1948). These developments, however, did not alter Congress's power over its dependency. According to the Court, Congress "is not subject to the same restrictions which are imposed in respect of laws for the United States considered as a political body of states in union."[170]

Congress plainly relied on such representations. After a lengthy process, federal legislation affirmed the establishment of commonwealth status for Puerto Rico in 1952.[171] President Truman, in his letter transmitting Puerto Rico's constitution to Congress, stated that the new relationship vested "full authority and responsibility for local government" in "the people of Puerto Rico."[172] Nonetheless, the House report recommending approval of the constitution stated that congressional approval "will not change Puerto Rico's fundamental political, social, and economic relationship to the United States."[173]

By the mid-twentieth century, then, the Supreme Court had cast no doubt on Congress's power to structure immigration, Indian, and territories law as it saw fit. The Court was just warming to the task of tackling head-on the great contradiction in U.S. citizenship—race discrimination—and it was decades away from recognizing conditions that imposed second-class citizenship on women. Enter the Warren Court.

CHAPTER 3

The Citizen-State: From the Warren Court to the Rehnquist Court

First-time readers of *Brown v. Board of Education* might well be surprised that the case is neither a paean to constitutional color blindness (Chief Justice Warren's opinion does not cite Harlan's dissent in *Plessy v. Ferguson*) nor a wholesale condemnation of state-imposed segregation. The case is about education and, more broadly, citizenship. It concludes that segregated schools harm the academic performance of black children, a harm that is egregious because of the "importance of education to our democratic society." Education, says the Court, is "the very foundation of good citizenship."[1]

Citizenship was not a major focus of the Court in pre–Warren Court days.[2] Birthright citizenship for African-Americans and Mexican-Americans was not seen as a challenge to deep structures of legal discrimination and social segregation. Citizenship was understood as a status connoting state membership—a right to a passport, diplomatic protection, and (for men) the duty to serve in the armed forces. It guaranteed neither the right to vote nor entitlement to social welfare programs. Citizenship had been extended to Puerto Ricans and Indians in the early part of the century with no idea that it entailed a fundamental shift in their rights or their relationship to the federal government.[3] President Franklin Delano Roosevelt would, by 1944, come to talk of a second Bill of Rights that would establish rights to "a useful and remunerative job," "a decent home," "adequate medical care," "a good education," and "adequate protection from the economic fears of old age, sickness, accident, and unemployment."[4] But the rhetoric of the New Deal is primarily not one of the rights of citizens.[5]

But *Brown* signals a major shift. Segregation in public schools is condemned for producing second-class citizenship for African-Americans both because it imposed a stigma on them (as persons not fit to go to school with whites) and because it did not adequately prepare them to be effective citizens.[6] In this formulation three concepts—citizenship, equality, and rights—are linked, and each concept is central in the constitutional workhorse for the Warren Court, the first section of the Fourteenth Amendment. It provides the following:

> All persons born or naturalized in the United States, and subject to the jurisdiction thereof, are citizens of the United States and of the State wherein they reside. No State shall make or enforce any law which shall abridge the privileges or immunities of citizens of the United States; nor shall any state deprive any person of life, liberty, or property, without due process of law; nor deny to any person within its jurisdiction the equal protection of the laws.[7]

The affirmation of birthright citizenship rejected Chief Justice Taney's holding in the *Dred Scott*[8] case that *free-born blacks* in the United States were not American citizens (no one supposed that slaves were citizens). The remainder of the section sought to ensure that the new citizens—those born free and those born slaves and now free—would not suffer a second-class citizenship. Race discrimination was objectionable when it denied persons fundamental rights guaranteed to members of the polity; indeed, the denial of equal treatment branded one as a less-than-full member.[9]

Kenneth Karst has identified "equal citizenship" as a key theme of the Warren Court.[10] There is much to this account.[11] Many of the important equality decisions involved rights closely identified with national citizenship, such as effective participation in the electoral process,[12] the "right to travel,"[13] and access to courts;[14] and the race cases sought to remove barriers to full and effective participation in society. Equal citizenship was a measure of the success of that project.[15] An emphasis on the equality strand, however, understates the Court's protection of substantive citizen rights as well as the super-strong protection afforded the status of citizenship. A better rendering might be the Court's regard for "full citizenship," a notion that encompasses both substantive and equality norms.

The Substantive Rights Agenda of the Warren Court

The Warren Court's work on behalf of citizenship started early. Chief Justice Warren signaled in a 1958 dissent his disagreement with prevailing doctrine that had granted Congress broad power to take away U.S. citizenship.[16] A decade later, a majority of the Court joined in striking down a statutory provision that provided for loss of citizenship for voting in a foreign election. In a series of cases, the Court erected extraordinary limits on Congress's power to denationalize U.S. citizens: naturalized citizens could not be treated differently from native-born;[17] denationalization following conviction by court-martial for desertion in time of war constituted cruel and unusual punishment;[18] and, most significantly, citizenship could not be lost unless the citizen possessed an intent to give it up.[19] By settling on this last rule, the Court effectively substituted for Congress's denationalization power an individual's right to expatriate.

Invoking florid language—describing U.S. citizenship as "a most precious right"[20] and "the right to have rights"[21]—the cases turned on both international and domestic considerations. World War II and its aftermath had demonstrated with clarity the vulnerability of "stateless" persons,[22] and membership in the leading state of the "free world" was surely a valuable commodity. Also of concern was the possibility that current majorities of Congress might seek to denationalize political opponents.[23]

The denationalization cases, combined with the Fourteenth Amendment's broad *jus soli* principle (that birth on U.S. soil confers citizenship), meant that all persons born in the United States would be secure in their citizenship from cradle to grave unless they voluntarily relinquished it. At the same time, the Warren Court increased the value of citizenship in terms of the rights it guaranteed the possessor. This happened in two ways. First, the Court expanded the substantive reach of rights. Decisions on criminal procedure,[24] due process in civil cases,[25] voting cases,[26] speech,[27] and privacy[28] recognized new rights or extended prior protections.[29] (This "rights revolution" was paralleled in the political sphere with a broad new array of "Great Society" social programs.)

Second, the Warren Court expanded enforcement of the Bill of Rights against the states. This might have been accomplished easily and at once through the Fourteenth Amendment's guarantee that "[n]o State shall make or enforce any law which shall abridge the privileges or immunities of citizens of the United States." But the Supreme Court's 1873 decision in the *Slaughter-House Cases*[30] had rendered the clause a virtual nullity (from which it is just beginning to recover).[31] In important prewar cases, the Court had held that the free speech and free exercise provisions of the First Amendment applied to the states as an aspect of the "scheme of ordered liberty" protected by the Fourteenth Amendment's due process clause.[32] The process of case-by-case "incorporation" of the Bill of Rights picked up steam under Earl Warren's Chief Justiceship, and in short order all but a few of the amendments' protections were deemed applicable to the states.[33]

The Court likewise extended constitutional protections to U.S. citizens overseas. In *Reid v. Covert,*[34] the Court considered the constitutionality of military trials of civilian spouses accused of murdering their husbands who were members of the armed forces in England and Japan. Four Justices representing the core of the Warren Court (Warren, Brennan, Black, and Douglas) held that "[w]hen the Government reaches out to punish a citizen who is abroad, the shield which the Bill of Rights and other parts of the Constitution provide to protect his life and liberty should not be stripped away just because he happens to be in another land."[35] Justices Frankfurter and Harlan concurred in the result, using more of a balancing test that stressed that the case involved a capital offense in time of peace.

The decision in *Reid* reversed a decision reached by the Court in the same case the previous year.[36] The shift was made possible by Justice Brennan's ascension to the Court and Justice Harlan's change of heart. The prior decision had relied heavily on the nineteenth-century decisions in *In re Ross* (involving trials conducted overseas by consular officials)[37] and the *Insular Cases.* The new majority relegated *Ross* to the past—a result that squared with recent congressional action terminating the practice of consular trials.[38] The *Insular Cases,* however, proved harder to deal with; this was significant because Puerto Rico, Guam, and other possessions remained territories of the United States. Justice Black's resolution is instructive. He was unwilling either to jettison the cases or to expand their holding that only certain "fundamental rights" applied abroad and in unincorporated territories.[39] For Black and his three brethren, the *Insular Cases* could be distinguished on the ground that "they involved the power of Congress to provide rules and regulations to govern temporarily territories with wholly dissimilar traditions and institutions whereas here the basis for governmental power is American citizenship."[40] Though open to quibble (after all, the residents of Puerto Rico were also citizens of the United States), the reasoning is an important window on the Warren Court's overall approach. Citizenship is a powerful concept and a broad sword, but it applies in only limited fashion in subnational polities (territories and tribes) that traditionally have operated under different rules. Ultimately, as will be discussed later in this chapter, the Bill of Rights would be brought to the territories and the tribes as an exercise of Congress's plenary power.

Race, Equal Protection, and Citizenship

The Warren Court's substantive rights agenda was complemented by a powerful equality agenda committed to ending the second-class citizenship of black Americans.[41] The victory over Nazism and the battle with communism gave great impetus to the domestic fight against racial discrimination. If modern social science had weakened academic claims supporting biological notions of race, the war against National Socialism put extreme pressure on any continuing attempt to justify racist governmental policies. Not only had Hitler's racism been the cause of unimaginable destruction, but also African-American, Native American, and Hispanic U.S. soldiers had fought to end it. What could this nation say to soldiers of color who, after risking their lives for democracy, were returning to a Jim Crow South and a largely segregated North and West?[42]

Ending second-class citizenship had several facets. It surely meant getting rid of race-based laws and practices that denied blacks political rights and mandated segregation in schools, on buses and trains, and in public facilities. Legal segregation imposed on blacks the crushing cumulative burden of unequal and inadequate facilities as well as the stigma of being deemed unfit to associate with whites.[43] At its broadest, equal citizenship might imply entitlement to the basic means necessary for political and social participation: education, employment, relief from poverty.[44]

During the Reconstruction period following the Civil War, the program of a "radical Congress" had been resisted by the Court. During the Second Reconstruction, the federal branches worked together to advance the nondiscrimination agenda. Congress enacted laws protecting civil rights in employment contracts[45] and housing.[46] It adopted dramatic protections of the right to vote, obliging most jurisdictions in the South to seek approval of the Department of Justice before altering voting rules and practices.[47] In the social sphere, Congress prohibited discrimination in public restaurants and accommodations,[48] denied federal funds to institutions and programs that discriminated on the basis of race, and directed the executive branch to promulgate regulations for school desegregation.[49]

The Court played a crucial role in the Second Reconstruction, crafting constitutional doctrine to uphold new statutes prohibiting discrimination[50] and adopting novel interpretations that breathed new life into statutes enacted after the Civil War.[51] It also directly enforced the Fourteenth Amendment on its own. Beyond the school cases, it invalidated other state segregation laws (including antimiscegenation laws),[52] set aside racially gerrymandered voting districts,[53] and condemned race discrimination in the selection of grand juries.[54] In important cases it brought private conduct within the purview of the equal protection clause by finding "state action" entangled with the conduct of the private discriminator.[55] It also used a variety of routes to invalidate the criminal convictions of the freedom riders and persons involved in desegregation efforts.[56]

Social Citizenship

The elements of citizenship discussed so far involve what may be viewed as negative rights and requirements for formal equality. There can be a more substantive side to citizenship as well, what T. H. Marshall in a well-known essay labeled "social citizenship."[57] By this Marshall meant "the whole range from the right to a modicum of economic welfare and security to the right to share to the full in the social heritage and to live the life of a civilised being according to the standards prevailing in the society."[58]

Social citizenship—like civil and political citizenship—can be conceived of in both equality and rights terms. In antidiscrimination law, attaining social citizenship demanded the demise of racial segregation. Gunnar Myrdal's monumental 1944 study of racial inequality, *An American Dilemma*—cited in *Brown*—pulled no punches in its lengthy discussion of the nature of social inequality based on race, stating that "what we are studying is in reality the survivals in modern American society of the slavery institution."[59] Blacks were seen as unfit to associate or swim with whites, to drink from the same water fountain or ride in the same railroad car as whites, or to go to school with or marry whites. Whatever the purported neutrality of segregation, it was patently clear that "social segregation and discrimination is a system of deprivations forced upon the Negro group by the white group . . . The rules are understood to be for the protection of whites and directed against Negroes."[60] The social inequality was mutually supportive of economic and political inequality: "There is a fundamental flaw in that distinction between what is purely social and all the rest of discrimination against Negroes. *Social discrimination is powerful as a means of keeping the Negroes down in all other respects.*"[61] The majority opinion in *Plessy v. Ferguson* had declared that "[i]f one race be inferior to the other socially, the Constitution of the United States cannot put them upon the same plane."[62] There may be some sad truth to this remark, if one takes it to be about personal prejudice. In using the equal protection clause to dismantle Jim Crow, however, the Warren Court showed that the Constitution could go a long way toward securing equal social citizenship.[63]

During the Warren Court era, Congress pursued another version of social citizenship focused more on the positive rights side of T. H. Marshall's concept. The New Frontier and Great Society programs of the 1960s greatly expanded social programs that provided entitlements to the fulfillment of basic needs such as food, housing, income support, medical care, and legal assistance.[64]

Ultimately, the substantive and equality versions of social citizenship were linked. President Johnson, in a 1965 speech at Howard University, stated that it was "not enough just to open the gates of opportunity. All our citizens must have the ability to walk through those gates."[65] This was a "more profound stage of the battle for civil rights," one seeking "not just equality as a right and a theory but equality as a fact and equality as a result."[66] As William Forbath has shown, civil rights leaders understood that "without social citizenship for all Americans, many black Americans would remain part of a subordinate caste."[67] Thus, Martin Luther King, Jr., in 1964 proposed a Bill of

Rights for the Disadvantaged that called for programs to improve education and housing and provide jobs at a living wage.[68]

In its most heady moments, the Warren Court appeared willing to proceed on a parallel path, taking aim at unequal social conditions that contributed to political and economic exclusion or subordination.[69] Perhaps education or welfare would be declared a "fundamental interest" whose unequal distribution would be subject to "strict scrutiny" under the equal protection clause.[70] But the substantive equality movement had pretty much run its course by the time Richard Nixon was elected president, and whatever initiative the Court might have taken on this front died with the appointment of Warren Burger as Chief Justice in 1969.

Exclusion and the Citizenship Project: Immigrants, Indians, and Territorial Residents

Alexander Bickel would warn a few years after the passing of the Warren Court that its reverence for U.S. citizenship undermined a constitutional tradition (and a Fourteenth Amendment) dedicated to the protection of the rights of *persons* not *citizens*. Indeed, Bickel found echoes of—of all cases—*Dred Scott* in the Warren Court cases that linked rights to citizenship.[71] Perhaps it is unfair to criticize the Warren Court for an approach to constitutional law that did so much but could not do everything. But the respects in which the Court's citizenship project seems, today, to have been inadequate are noteworthy. The Warren Court paid virtually no attention to the rights of immigrants residing in the United States—perhaps the predictable result of a piercing focus on the rights of citizens. And apparently unwilling to take on the *Insular Cases,* the Court never followed through on the suggestion of *Reid v. Covert* that the Constitution applies in full whenever and wherever the government acts against U.S. citizens.[72] Finally, the Court did not come to grips with the conflict between sovereignty claims by subnational groups and the rights of U.S. citizens.

In all these areas—immigration regulation, territorial governance, and federal Indian policy—the Warren Court accepted the plenary power cases of the late nineteenth century. Although various Justices expressed misgivings from time to time about the scope and implications of the cases, no plenary power case was overturned during the Warren Court era.[73]

The Immigration Cases

The immigration cases of the early 1950s were in tune with the xenophobic and anticommunist policies of the McCarran-Walter Act of 1952. In language one might think too harsh to be sustainable, the Court had declared aliens seeking entry into the United States rightless.[74] Henry Hart's celebrated "Exercise in Dialectic" published in the *Harvard Law Review* in 1953 took on these cases, powerfully arguing that they were inconsistent with the idea of a rule of law. Noting that the Justices on the Court "are only the custodians of the law and not the owners of it," Hart ended with the declaration that an "appeal to principle is still open."[75]

The Warren Court did not heed that call. The logic of *Reid v. Covert* might well have carried over to the alien cases. In *Reid,* the four-Justice plurality opinion had stated: "The United States is entirely a creature of the Constitution. Its power and authority have no other source. It can only act in accordance with all the limitations imposed by the Constitution."[76] But the Court never embraced the idea that the Constitution applied to government action irrespective of the status or location of the persons asserting rights.

In an early Warren Court case, *Galvan v. Press,* the Court upheld the retroactive application of a provision in the 1950 Subversive Activity Control Act mandating the deportation of any alien who had been a member of the Communist Party. Justice Frankfurter's opinion for the Court stated: "[T]hat the formulation of [immigration policies] is entrusted exclusively to Congress has become about as firmly imbedded in the legislative and judicial tissues of our body politic as any aspect of our government. And whatever might have been said at an earlier date for applying the *ex post facto* Clause, it has been the unbroken rule of this Court that it has no application to deportation."[77]

In 1967, with the Warren Court in high gear, a majority upheld the government's interpretation of the immigration statute as barring the entry of homosexuals.[78] The immigrant had asserted that the statutory provision under which he had been excluded—it appears incredible today: persons "afflicted with [a] psychopathic personality"—was unconstitutional on "void for vagueness" grounds. The Court rejected the claim, stating that "[t]he constitutional requirement of fair warning has no applicability to standards . . . for admission of aliens to the United States." It followed with a reaffirmation of Congress's plenary power doctrine nailed down by a cite to the *Chinese Exclusion Case*.[79]

Earlier Courts had held that aliens could assert equal protection claims under the Fourteenth Amendment. Those cases had condemned discrimination based on national origin or, in effect, race,[80] and they were embraced by the Warren Court.[81] But the Warren Court —despite its strong use of the equal protection clause elsewhere— took no steps to strike down state laws that discriminated on the basis of alienage. Neither did it signal that it was prepared to cast constitutional doubt on discriminatory federal immigration laws, such as the national origins quota system.

Why the Court's equality work did not extend to aliens is unclear. The 1950s were a period of relatively low immigration to the United States.[82] Nevertheless, it is not as if immigration was nowhere on the legal and policy radar screen: the McCarran-Walter Act was a major piece of legislation, passed over the vociferous veto of President Truman.[83] Cases involving lengthy detention of aliens at the U.S. border had reached the Court in the early fifties, and their dénouements several years later were featured in the national press.[84] Legislation enacted after the Soviet invasion of Hungary in 1956 brought thousands of refugees to the United States. In the Southwest, the 1950s saw mass deportation efforts launched against Mexicans, unfelicitously dubbed "Operation Wetback," as well as the continuation of the Bracero Program under which hundreds of thousands of Mexican temporary farm workers entered the United States. These statutes and policies bristled with human rights issues that might have ripened into important litigation invoking the Warren Court's rights and equality paradigm.

The Court's reluctance to undercut the plenary power cases, I believe, is a consequence of its focus on citizenship. For those in the inner circle, the Court was willing to do a lot of work both in expanding rights and in ensuring that all citizens were treated equally. As I will discuss, however, an emphasis on citizenship has inevitable exclusionary implications for noncitizens.[85]

Liberal scholars who have sought to provide theoretical foundations for the work of the Warren Court have generally neglected the Court's poor record on immigration issues—even as they have attempted to show how the general themes of the Court could be mobilized to extend protection to aliens. John Hart Ely argues that aliens, as traditional victims of prejudice, constitute a discrete and insular minority for whom heightened judicial protection is justified because they are unlikely to receive fair representation in the political system.[86] Charles Black, well attuned to the Warren Court's citizenship theme, would protect aliens from state discrimination on grounds that state regulation is preempted by the federal immigration power—although he is silent as to the plenary power cases.[87] Kenneth Karst attempts to bring aliens within his "equal citizenship" perspective, obviously a difficult position to sustain on the face of it.[88] The variety and ingenuity of the arguments make clear the awkward fit of aliens within the Warren Court jurisprudence.

Congress proved less reticent than the Court, repealing the national origins quota system in 1965. Presidents Truman and Kennedy had announced their opposition to the race-based system of distributing immigrant visas, and Lyndon Johnson's signing statement—read at Liberty Island—characterized the repealed act as "un-American in the highest sense, because it has been untrue to the faith that brought thousands to these shores even before we were a country."[89] The 1965 act should be seen as of a piece with Congress's other civil rights statutes of the day.[90] So too the Great Society programs adopted in the 1960s generally included permanent resident aliens. The Warren Court, permitting Congress to sort out the equality issues, appears—as a constitutional matter—to have been content with the process of American assimilation that would lead to naturalization and entry into the inner circle of membership.[91]

The Tribes and the Territories

A citizenship model may necessarily exclude nonmembers, but what is more surprising is how the Warren Court fell short in two areas involving U.S. citizens: the Indian tribes and the territories.

Members of tribes and persons born in U.S. territories are not understood to come within the Fourteenth Amendment's birthright citizenship rules. The 1884 case of *Elk v. Wilkins*[92] decided the issue for children born within tribes in Indian country. Indians born on reservations were virtually stateless, even if they subsequently took up residence off the reservation. The noncitizenship of children born in the unincorporated territories has always been assumed,[93] but the issue has never reached the Supreme Court.[94] In the late eighteenth century and early decades of the twentieth century, territorial residents were "nationals" but not citizens of the United States—owing allegiance to the United States but not entitled to political rights.[95] The fact that persons born on reservations or in unincorporated territories were not deemed to be "in the United States" and "subject to the jurisdiction thereof" for the purpose of establishing birthright citizenship under the first sentence of the Fourteenth Amendment is evidence of just how anomalous their situation was.

Indians and territorial residents ultimately acquired citizenship by way of federal legislation. Various laws had offered citizenship to members of certain tribes during the allotment era.[96] In 1924 Congress adopted general legislation conferring citizenship on all Indians born within the territorial limits of the United States.[97] Puerto Ricans received citizenship under the Jones Act in 1917, as part of the ongoing and contentious status debate. Proponents of statehood generally approved of the federal legislation; *independentistas* were likely to be more skeptical, seeing citizenship as establishing a closer relationship between the island and the mainland and thereby undermining their political goals. The United States took little notice of the change. From the perspective of the federal government, the grant of citizenship neither altered political arrangements nor undermined congressional plenary power.[98] The Supreme Court agreed. Five years after the Jones Act, the Court held that the grant of citizenship had not changed the status of Puerto Rico as an unincorporated territory; accordingly, only "fundamental" constitutional rights applied there.[99] (The other major territory, the Philippines, had early on been slated for independence, so residents of the archipelago were never granted U.S. citizenship.)[100]

This might well have become fertile ground for the Warren Court's citizenship project, but it turned out not to be. Perhaps preoccupied with the race question and the expansion of rights against the states, the Court decided no cases of importance involving the territories. In *Reid v. Covert,* four Justices had stated that "neither [the *Insular Cases*] nor their reasoning should be given any further expansion,"[101] but the

Court as a whole made no move to cut back on the earlier cases. Cases "incorporating" the Bill of Rights in the territories would be the work of a later Court.

Exactly what forward motion on behalf of the tribes could mean from the perspective of citizenship is difficult to say. It might have meant overturning the 1896 ruling in *Talton v. Mayes*[102] (decided the same year as *Plessy*) that the Bill of Rights did not apply to actions of the tribal governments. This move would have paralleled the Court's ongoing incorporation of the Bill of Rights against the states. But it presented real problems in the tribal context. Unlike in the fight against race discrimination—where the extension of rights to individuals went hand-in-hand with advancement of the goal of antisubordination—the goal of tribal autonomy put the rights and antisubordination agendas in potential conflict: a focus on individual rights might well call into question acts of tribal self-governance, thereby supplying an argument for limiting tribal autonomy. One can move toward resolving this tension by settling on a constitutional value of self-determination, but the metric of citizenship provided no easy way out for a Court concerned about historically oppressed groups.

Instructive is the Court's decision in *Williams v. Lee,*[103] holding that a state court had no jurisdiction in a case brought by a non-Indian merchant (Lee) against Indians to whom he had sold goods on credit. Lee operated a general store on the reservation where the transaction had occurred. The Court's decision has been hailed as a "watershed" opinion and "a leading example of the special rules that the Court has recognized during the modern era in order to protect tribal government in Indian country."[104] But *Williams* appears to have been more about Congress's plenary power than about inherent sovereignty. The Court repeatedly noted that no federal statute expressly granted the state court jurisdiction over such cases, and the opinion ends by recognizing Congress's power to oust tribal court jurisdiction.[105] Furthermore, under Public Law 280, Arizona could have assumed all civil jurisdiction over the tribes (without tribal consent) by following procedures established by the statute, but it had declined to do so.

More important, the case discloses the tension between the citizenship and tribal sovereignty agendas.[106] Because the Bill of Rights did not apply to the tribal court, subjecting the merchant to tribal jurisdiction might seem to cut against the Warren Court's efforts to expand rights accruing to citizens (compare *Reid v. Covert*). But this concern is nowhere stated in the Court's opinion—in contrast to Burger and Rehnquist Court decisions, where the concern receives explicit mention. Instead, the Court comes down on the side of sovereignty, holding that "[t]here can be no doubt that to allow the exercise of state jurisdiction here would undermine the authority of the tribal courts over Reservation affairs and hence would infringe on the right of the Indians to govern themselves."[107] The point here is not that the Court reached the wrong decision in *Williams;* rather, *Williams* demonstrates the limitations of the citizenship approach.

The Warren Court era coincided with the national policy of termination. Those seeking to justify the termination policies did so in terms of helping the Indians take steps toward full membership in the American polity, which would end the guardian-ward relationship with the federal government that had left Indians second-class citizens.[108] Perhaps in tune with this goal, the Court may have believed that Indians would become full citizens when they cast aside their dependent status and took their place among other citizens of the United States and the states in which they resided. The Court would stand ready, at that point, to protect their rights, as it protected the rights of all persons within the innermost membership ring.[109] As the Court noted in *Williams,* referring to the termination policies:

> Congress has followed a policy calculated eventually to make all Indians full-fledged participants in American society. This policy contemplates criminal and civil jurisdiction over Indians by any State ready to assume the burdens that go with it as soon as the educational and economic status of the Indians permits the change without disadvantage to them.[110]

The Warren Court registered no dissent from this view.[111]

In sum, the Court's dramatic work on behalf of U.S. citizenship ran aground in the territories and Indian sovereignty cases. In *Reid v. Covert,* the plurality opinion distinguished the *Insular Cases* as involving congressional power "to govern temporarily territories with wholly dissimilar traditions and institutions."[112] No doubt the Court had a similar view of the tribal governments. Thus, the Court simply put these situations to the side, outside the purview of the citizenship project—despite the fact that both Indians and territorial residents were citizens of the United States.[113] The complexities raised by these polities in the

American system of sovereignty bear witness to Alexander Bickel's remark that citizenship is "a simple idea for a simple government."[114]

The Warren Court's modesty in these areas did not leave residents of the territories and reservations without rights. Congress, exercising its plenary power, ensured equal citizenship by statute on U.S. soil. Thus, the 1917 Organic Act for Puerto Rico applied most of the Bill of Rights to the colonial legislature,[115] and the statute initiating the commonwealth process in 1952 required that any constitution drafted by Puerto Rico include a bill of rights.[116] (The 1952 constitution did so.)[117] In Guam, the 1968 Guam Elective Governor Act extended most constitutional protections to the island.[118]

In the same year, Congress enacted the Indian Civil Rights Act (ICRA) to overcome the Court's decision in *Talton v. Mayes,* which had held that the Bill of Rights did not apply to tribal governments. Under ICRA, most of the Constitution's protections of individual rights were made applicable to the tribes.[119] (The statute was added as a title to the 1968 Civil Rights Act, which passed in the aftermath of the assassination of Martin Luther King, Jr.) ICRA was adopted without the formal consent of the tribes to which it would apply, although some effort was made to take into account the special nature of the tribes.[120] For example, the law did not include the First Amendment's protection against established religion, which would have created significant problems for theocratic Pueblo tribes.[121] Senator Sam Ervin, author of the legislation, justified ICRA as providing to Indians protection against tribal actions that would be unconstitutional if undertaken by federal, state, or local government.[122]

These legislative developments perhaps offer another reason for the Warren Court's willingness to abide the plenary power cases. A beneficent federal government could be trusted to provide for the progressive legal assimilation of anomalous categories of citizens. It is not clear whether the Court was attuned to the unfortunate echoes of the *Insular Cases* here, or whether it fully appreciated the risk that another Congress might use its plenary power to deny rather than extend rights.

Citizenship and Assimilation

The Warren Court's protection of citizenship was a bringing in, not a coming together. The Court attacked social and political exclusion by allowing outsiders to share equally what the insiders had had for so long. To be successful, outsiders had to learn how to look and dress the part. The movement required little of the insiders, other than a commitment to pretend that the newcomers were really no different from them.[123] To use the odd phraseology of the 1866 Civil Rights Act, the idea was that the previously marginalized were now entitled to the same rights "as [are] enjoyed by white citizens."[124] This is hardly a surprising construction: in a society where racism had so degraded blacks, making whiteness the measure of equality could provide significant gains to nonwhites.

There was thus a theme of assimilation at the core of both the civil rights strategy of the day and policies for Indians and immigrants.[125] In the 1950s and 1960s it was a widely held view that members of these groups could be brought into the American mainstream. As noted, congressional "termination" policies expressly pursued this goal for Indians. For immigrants, the assimilation process was regarded as natural and largely inevitable, even if not expressly supported through government programs. Assimilation was aided by a dramatic decline in immigration throughout the century, as the national origins quota system, the Great Depression, and the Second World War brought immigration levels to historic lows. From 1900 to 1920, about 14.5 million immigrants entered the United States. From 1930 to 1950, the rate of immigration had declined by nearly 90 percent (to 1.5 million immigrants). In 1920, almost 15 percent of the U.S. population was foreign-born; by 1950, that number had dropped to just over 5 percent. White ethnics as a group continued to melt, as second- and third-generation Americans took the place of turn-of-the-century immigrants. The declining significance of alienage led public scholars to see race and religion, not ethnicity, as the key social variables in American society.[126]

By the late 1960s, however, American sociologists were less sanguine about the inevitability of assimilation. In an influential 1964 book Milton Gordon saw "structural assimilation," which he defined as entry of an out-group into primary relationships with the host society, as the core measure of the full integration of groups. (Structural assimilation was thus more than the adoption of host society cultural behaviors, a process Gordon labeled "acculturation.") If structural assimilation could occur, it would inevitably produce marital assimilation, "identificational" assimilation, and a reduction in prejudice and discrimination. Looking at the United States of his day, Gordon found no structural assimilation of blacks, Jews, or Puerto Ricans in the United States, and he argued that structural assimilation of immigrant groups that enter the United States in large numbers "is both impossible of attainment in most cases and undesirable as a goal toward which pressure on the immigrant might conceivably be exercised."[127]

The 1960s recognition of the resilience of ethnicity is also evident in a comparison of the first and second editions of Nathan Glazer and Daniel Patrick Moynihan's classic study of New York, *Beyond the Melting Pot.* The 1963 edition, based on data gathered in the 1950s, reached the conclusion that religion and race were becoming the salient characteristics of group identification while the "national aspect of ethnicity declines."[128] Seven years later the authors conceded the weakening of religious identity and the resurgence of ethnic identities.[129]

The theoretical work was surely influenced by what was happening in the streets, from urban riots to strong assertions of black nationalism and race-consciousness by militant groups who saw "integration" as a demand that oppressed groups assimilate to the culture of their oppressors.[130] Stokely Carmichael and Charles Hamilton's manifesto *Black Power* assailed integration as "a subterfuge for the maintenance of white supremacy," a strategy by which "black people must give up their identity, deny their heritage."[131] Assimilation meant conformity with Anglo-Saxon norms and institutions, a position that sustained racism.[132] No hyphen united "black" and "American": "I'm not an American," Malcolm X declared in 1964. "I'm one of the 22 million black people who are the victims of Americanism."[133]

But if all this meant that assimilation was not inevitable, it may have made it that much more necessary. In the search for a unifying concept, citizenship appeared ideal: it could promise equal rights while rejecting the relevance of race or ethnicity. Charles Black, writing in 1969, argued that citizenship embodied "a sound and healthy rhetoric" that could be used to provide "the beginning of an answer to the growing separatism of the Black Power movement"; it could "sum up in a word the thing we ought to be offering in place of that withdrawal to which many Negroes—in my view, naturally but regrettably—feel themselves driven."[134]

Equal citizenship, as a legal project, could be achieved through laws and courts. It was thus, Black argued, preferable to "another concept—that of brotherhood—which played so prominent a part a few years ago in the utterances of opponents of racism."[135] For Black, "brotherhood"

> suggested that the public demand was that some men had a duty to feel toward and to treat other men as brothers. This, I submit, is an overreaching, a basic defect in theory, a radically wrong symbolism . . . Brotherly love may stand somewhere in the shadow of time, waiting. There is not very much the law can do about that. But fellow-citizenship is for now, for the day before yesterday.[136]

Thus rendered, citizenship was a common bond around which the nation could rally in a time when things seemed to be spinning out of control. Its idealism could be realized through the pragmatics of law; it did not require change in human hearts.

In sum, the Warren Court took great strides forward in extending the protection of the Bill of Rights to citizens wherever located,[137] and it was aided in this endeavor by Congress's imposition of rights-based limits on tribal and territorial governments. The promise of "full citizenship" was an end to class legislation and a prohibition on discrimination that excluded citizens, usually on a group basis, from the political and civil rights that mark full membership in a society.[138] Perhaps even social inequalities were within the purview of a progressive constitutional law.

Citizenship was not just a status that guaranteed equality; it was a place where equality could exist. It was an inner circle, and all those within it shared the same rights. Furthermore, there could be no smaller circles, nothing "fuller" than full membership. Consistent with the Constitution's prohibition of titles of nobility,[139] there could be no platinum citizenship. Citizenship levels up and it levels down; it is a sword for equal rights and a shield against assertions of special rights and the politics of division.

As idealized, citizenship had no race, no official ethnicity or established religion. The notion of an Anglo-Saxon state was long gone. What the New Deal began, the civil rights movement and the Warren Court completed: the construction of a new sense of America—not as a *nation-state* but as a *citizen-state,* united not by national origin but by the common sharing of a status that guaranteed equal rights to participate in government, equal rights to social benefits, and equal rights held against the government.[140]

The Burger Court: Toward Race Consciousness

For the Warren Court, the vision of equal citizenship in the race cases (and the civil rights legislation of the 1960s) was a world of "equal opportunity" in which race played no role in the distribution of rights or the imposition of harms.[141] It was, in short, a vision of color blindness.[142] A regime of color blindness was the death knell of Jim Crow, without the need to explain why separate could never be equal in schools, swimming pools, railroad cars, or cemeteries. Color blindness was also an answer to the growing race consciousness urged by Black Power advocates and the potential divisiveness it entailed. Color blindness was not, however, color-neutral. To be accepted, blacks, immigrants, and Indians had to join the existing mainstream; they had, in effect, to become "white."

By the 1970s, the attack on color blindness was no longer the province of militant groups. It was becoming increasingly clear that, given the cumulative harms of several centuries of racism, formal equality in employment, housing, and voting would not and could not produce substantive equality for African-Americans. As Justice Blackmun would write in his opinion in the *Bakke* case, "In order to get beyond racism, we must first take account of race."[143]

The Burger Court's response was complicated, and to some extent, unexpected.[144] The Court sustained race-conscious policies crafted on behalf of disadvantaged minority groups. It extended the protection of "higher scrutiny" to laws that discriminated on the basis of alienage and gender.[145] The Court affirmed the sovereignty of tribes over their members, although it limited tribal authority over non-Indians living on reservations. The Burger Court also extended the Warren Court's rights, recognizing the application of the Bill of Rights to territorial governments.[146]

The Burger Court did not adopt or advance the Warren Court's emphasis on citizenship. The Justices also made clear that the Warren Court's interest in protecting "fundamental interests" under the equal protection clause would not be pursued.[147] If there was an underlying theme to the Court's decisions in these areas, it might best be understood as respecting the authority of groups and institutions to operate under norms, traditions, and even cultures that they have evolved over time and that serve important group or institutional interests. From this perspective, the imposition of norms from outside the group—for example, in the name of an overarching theme such as citizenship—threatened the integrity of the group and potentially upset its ability to attain its functional goals. This approach is apparent in the Court's resurrection of federalism limits on exercises of congressional power that were seen as interfering with "traditional" or "core" state functions.[148] One also sees it at work in Burger Court decisions that deferred to school,[149] military,[150] and prison authorities,[151] and that rejected constitutional claims that would have intruded into "Western civilization concepts of the family as a unit with broad parental authority over minor children."[152]

An approach that takes seriously group traditions and functions implicitly tolerates a social, and even political, pluralism. Thus the Burger Court made strong statements on behalf of the "inherent sovereignty" of Indian tribes.[153] But the approach is also consistent with restricting the scope of group authority to group members. The Court's 1972 decision in *Wisconsin v. Yoder* is emblematic. Chief Justice Burger's opinion for the Court sustained the right of the Amish under the First Amendment's free exercise of religion clause to remove their children from public high school. In *Brown,* the Warren Court had noted that "[c]ompulsory school attendance laws" demonstrated recognition of "the importance of education to our democratic society," and that education was "the very foundation of good citizenship."[154] But in *Yoder* the Burger Court concluded that the state interest in "prepar[ing] citizens to participate effectively and intelligently in our open political system" was not significantly impinged upon by permitting the Amish to keep their children out of public high school. Not only had the Amish shown themselves to be "a highly successful social unit within our society, even if apart from the conventional 'mainstream,'" but also the group's qualities of "reliability, self-reliance, and dedication to work" would equip members for life outside the group should they choose to leave.[155]

Yoder represents a regard for community life that may at times trump assertions of individual rights. (Interestingly, Justice Douglas dissented from the Court's opinion primarily on the ground that the policy of the Amish unduly burdened the ability of a child to choose a lifestyle in the future.)[156] The tension between group claims and individual rights was apparent in discussions of the constitutionality of race-conscious government programs. In the 1970s, strong arguments were advanced for group-based approaches to equal protection,[157] and some members of the Court held that race-conscious programs adopted on behalf of minority groups should be judged by a more lenient standard of review than laws that discriminated against such groups.[158] The Burger Court, to the surprise of many, proved open to race-based remedial programs. Justices appointed pursuant to Richard Nixon's "southern strategy" upheld wide-ranging school desegregation decrees that explicitly assigned students based on race[159] (although the Court was not prepared to enlist the suburbs in the desegregation of urban schools,[160] a decision that was consistent with the Court's protection of local governments against an overreaching federal government). In *Bakke,* a splintered Court signaled support for some versions of affirmative action under a variety of justifications,[161] and in *Fullilove v. Klutznick,* the Court sustained federal legislation (enacted during the Carter presidency) that established minority business set-asides for projects funded under the 1977 Public Works Employment Act.[162]

Whereas an emphasis on citizenship made the Indian cases problematic for the Warren Court, the Burger Court had an easier time affirming tribal sovereignty. Significantly, however, it largely limited tribal governance to persons within the tribe's sphere of authority—defined in terms of membership rather than geography. Three cases decided in 1978 typify the approach. In *United States v. Wheeler,* the Court, without dissent, permitted a federal prosecution of a Navaho for statutory rape following a tribal court conviction for disorderly conduct and contributing to the delinquency of a minor. The defendant had asserted that the subsequent prosecution violated the constitutional prohibition against double jeopardy because the tribes were, like territorial governments, arms of the federal government exercising delegated power. The Court rejected the claim, holding that "the power to punish offenses against tribal law committed by Tribe members" was part of "the Navajos' primeval sovereignty" and that Congress had neither explicitly nor implicitly removed that power. *Wheeler* is, admittedly, a bit of an odd case and may be more in tune with Burger Court views on criminal justice than on Indian sovereignty. Moreover, under the version of the federal Major Crimes Act then on the books, the tribe was not permitted to impose punishments in excess of six months' imprisonment or a $500 fine—even against its own members. Thus, to conclude that tribe prosecution barred subsequent federal prosecution would have permitted major crimes to go unpunished as felonies.[163] Nonetheless, *Wheeler* includes particularly strong language about the inherent power of tribes to punish offenses by members and goes out of its way to note that federal preemption of tribal jurisdiction would "detract substantially from tribal self-government, just as federal preemption of state criminal jurisdiction would trench upon important state interests."[164]

When tribes sought to exert jurisdiction over nonmembers, the Burger Court adopted a restricted view of Indian sovereignty. The cardinal case is *Oliphant v. Suquamish Indian Tribe.*[165] In *Oliphant,* the Court held that tribal courts did not have inherent jurisdiction to try non-Indians who commit crimes on the reservation.[166] (*Oliphant* will be discussed in detail in Chapter 5.)

A third case, *Santa Clara Pueblo v. Martinez,*[167] presented the Court with a conundrum. At issue was a tribal ordinance that recognized the membership of children of male members who married outside the tribe, but denied membership to children born to female members who married outside the tribe. Julia Martinez, a tribe member, had married a nonmember, with whom she had a daughter, Audrey. Although Audrey Martinez had been raised on the reservation and continued to live there as an adult, the membership rules meant that she could not vote in tribal elections, hold office, remain on the reservation in the event of her mother's death, or inherit her mother's home or interest in communal lands. Both mother and daughter sued, alleging violation of the equality guarantees of the 1968 Indian Civil Rights Act.

The case presented exquisite issues of self-determination and gender justice.[168] Membership rules lie near the heart of sovereignty, yet the explicit discrimination of the tribal ordinance would not withstand the usual scrutiny applied to sex-based laws. Furthermore, the insider-outsider (*Wheeler-Oliphant*) distinction could not supply an answer when it was the definition of insider and outsider that was at issue. Unable to solve the puzzle on the substantive level, the Court reached a procedural solution. It held that ICRA did not authorize a civil suit in federal court against the tribe alleging violations of the statute's protections.[169] Thus, Martinez would have to press her daughter's claim in the tribal court. The resolution both affirmed tribal sovereignty over membership rules and left Martinez a forum for raising the sex discrimination claim.[170]

Respect for group self-determination might be seen as consistent with state policies that excluded aliens from social programs. But here the Burger Court moved considerably beyond the Warren Court's equality agenda. In the 1971 decision in *Graham v. Richardson,* Justice Blackmun declared that aliens were "a prime example of a 'discrete and insular' minority" and that state laws that classified on the basis of alienage merited strict judicial scrutiny.[171] Even more startling was the Court's decision in *Plyler v. Doe*[172] invalidating a Texas statute that permitted local school districts to exclude undocumented immigrant children. The case has been widely criticized for its clumsy and unpersuasive manipulation of equal protection doctrine.[173] But the heart of the case lies elsewhere.[174] Crucial to the majority was the recognition of the strong likelihood that the undocumented children would stay in the United States, growing to be a part of American society:

> [T]he record is clear that many of the undocumented children disabled by this classification will remain in this country indefinitely, and that some will become lawful residents or citizens of the United States. It is difficult to understand precisely what the State hopes to achieve by promoting the creation and perpetuation of a subclass of illiterates within our boundaries, surely adding to the problems and costs of unemployment, welfare, and crime.[175]

One way to understand these cases is to see the Burger Court as recognizing that resident immigrants, no matter what their status, have or will become participating members in the social and economic life of the state. In these areas, the fact of their alienage was irrelevant to the overall functioning of the state. In contrast, the Court granted the states wide latitude to exclude aliens from political functions, where noncitizenship appeared directly related to interests of the state.[176]

In a parallel but less noticed development, the Burger Court recognized constitutional rights of residents in the territories. The Court made clear that pretty much any right fundamental enough to be applied to the states would also be deemed to limit the actions of territorial governments. Like the state alienage cases, these decisions were framed in terms of personal rights, not citizenship.[177] (The full range of cases necessary to bring the Bill of Rights to the states was not necessary in the territorial context because Congress, in exercise of its plenary power, had generally imposed such rights[178]—or, as in the case of Puerto Rico, had affirmed the commonwealth's recognition of such rights in its constitution.)[179]

Perhaps the zigging and zagging here is, in the end, too messy to put into a coherent schema.[180] But it is clear that the concept of citizenship plays a minor role. Citizenship surely cannot explain the alienage cases, nor is it the language of the territory cases. In areas where equal citizenship might have been invoked to extend protections, the Burger Court backed away. Most significant was the Court's decision in *Rostker v. Goldberg,* which upheld the all-male military draft registration.[181] Given the historical link of military service to citizenship, as well as the benefits and preferences made available to veterans, *Rostker* presented the Court with a powerful opportunity to press forward the equal citizenship agenda.[182] Yet the Justices went AWOL. The need for "military flexibility" overrode the right to equal treatment.

Throughout this period, the Burger Court left congressional power regarding Indians, immigrants, and the territories as it found it—virtually unchecked. Although *Graham* held unconstitutional most state discrimination against aliens, the Court applied no such rule to federal statutes that drew distinctions based on alienage.[183] In important cases, the Court stoutly reaffirmed the Congress's plenary authority over immigration and its power to "make rules [for aliens] that would be unacceptable if applied to citizens."[184] Congress's authority over the territories was described in similar terms.[185] And the Burger Court's Indian cases, even when recognizing inherent tribal authority, affirmed a superior plenary power in Congress.[186]

The coexistence of congressional plenary power and *Wheeler* and *Plyler* is not wholly mysterious. A regime of nested sovereignties and overlapping associations arguably needs national and supreme membership rules that can resolve disputes among the constituent parts. The Burger Court was willing to let Congress make those fundamental decisions. (Such decisions could be explicit or implicit: relevant to the Court in *Plyler* was the federal government's "lax enforcement of the laws barring entry into this country" and its "failure to establish an effective bar to the employment of undocumented aliens.")[187] Once the definitions and rules governing insiders and outsiders were established, the Court permitted a broad role for groups—from states to tribes—to govern themselves.

Richard Nixon and the Multicultural 1970s

Although it is commonly taken for granted that exercises of Congress's plenary power will be exclusionary and restrictive, the political branches' freedom to act has given them room to craft inclusionary policies as well. In the 1970s, Congress and the Nixon administration adopted a range of programs that, from the perspective of the 1980s and 1990s, appear surprisingly progressive. Had the term been in vogue at the time, we might well have labeled the overall approach "multicultural."

Front and center in these efforts were race-conscious programs aimed at overcoming the historical exclusion of African-Americans in the economic sphere. President Kennedy had first used the term "affirmative action" in a 1961 executive order that required federal contractors to "take affirmative action to ensure that applicants are employed and that employees are treated during employment, without regard to their race."[188] The message here was nondiscrimination, not race consciousness; that is, contractors had to take positive steps to ensure that all qualified applicants would receive consideration for employment. Following passage of the 1964 Civil Rights Act, President Johnson extended the equal employment opportunity mandate to construction contracts undertaken by recipients of federal financial assistance.[189] Pursuant to the order, the Office of Federal Contract Compliance of the Department of Labor issued regulations in 1968 requiring every major contractor and subcontractor to produce a written "affirmative action compliance program" that would "provide in detail for specific steps to guarantee equal employment opportunity keyed to the problems and needs of members of minority groups."[190]

During the Nixon administration the OFCC regulations were rewritten several times, shifting the emphasis from guaranteeing equal opportunity to correcting "underutilization" of protected groups. Thus, the 1971 version mandated that employers prepare written affirmative action programs establishing "goals and timetables" to correct "deficiencies" in the "utilization of minorities."[191] "Underutilization" was defined as "having fewer minorities in a particular job classification than would reasonably be expected by their availability."[192]

President Nixon's Labor Department also prescribed strong medicine for federal construction contractors. The so-called Philadelphia Plan required that bidders on federal construction contracts include an affirmative action plan with "specific goals for the utilization of minority manpower" in six skilled crafts (which traditionally had had low minority participation owing to discriminatory hiring hall practices). The plan withstood a court challenge as beyond the authority of the executive power to impose.[193]

The Labor Department regulations were limited to federal contractors. Title VII of the 1964 Civil Rights Act was far more expansive, generally prohibiting discrimination in private employment.[194] Again, it was the Nixon administration that first issued regulations requiring validation of employment tests and practices that disproportionately disqualified members of minority groups.[195] (The Supreme Court found these rules consistent with congressional intent in the landmark case of *Griggs v. Duke Power Co.*)[196]

In 1970 Nixon's Department of Health, Education, and Welfare recognized bilingual education as a necessary element in providing equal educational opportunity for non–English-speaking children in public schools. Guidelines implementing Title VI of the 1964 Civil Right Act mandated that

> [w]here inability to speak and understand the English language excludes national-origin minority group children from effective participation in the educational program offered by a school district, the district must take affirmative steps to rectify the language deficiency in order to open its instructional program to these students.[197]

In 1974 the Supreme Court relied on these guidelines in holding that San Francisco had violated Title VI by taking no significant steps to deal with the language deficiency of some 1,800 pupils attending public schools who could not speak, understand, read, or write English.[198]

The affirmative action and bilingualism regulations were justified in terms of providing "equal opportunity." But in practice they required race- and national origin–based measures aimed at achieving more equal outcomes.[199] This commitment to substantive non–color-blind results was paralleled in the Nixon administration's abrupt shift in Indian policy. Declaring that the termination program was "morally and legally unacceptable" and "produces bad results," Nixon asked Congress in 1970 to pass a concurrent resolution that would "expressly renounce, repudiate and repeal the termination policy."[200] The resolution would

> explicitly affirm the integrity and right to continued existence of all Indian tribes and Alaska native governments, recognizing that cultural pluralism is a source of national strength . . . [S]uch a resolution would reaffirm for the Legislative branch—as I hereby affirm for the Executive branch—that the historic relationship between the Federal government and the Indian communities cannot be abridged without the consent of the Indians.[201]

Nixon's statement declared that the federal government's special relationship with the tribes was not an "act of generosity toward a disadvantaged people" but rather "the result . . . of solemn obligations which have been entered into by the United States Government."[202] Pursuing this view, the administration proposed and saw enacted the Indian Self-Determination Act of 1975, which directed the secretary of the interior to turn over, at a tribe's request, the administration of certain federal programs and services.[203]

The Carter administration and a Democratic Congress extended and deepened the Nixon administration's commitment to race consciousness and policies that promoted tribal self-determination. In 1977 Congress enacted legislation mandating a 10 percent set-aside for minority business enterprises in some federally funded construction projects.[204] A year later the Federal Communications Commission issued regulations that provided preferences to minority broadcasters in proceedings granting or transferring television and radio station licenses.[205]

Most striking, perhaps, was enactment of the Indian Child Welfare Act of 1978 (ICWA). In the 1970s, concern was expressed about the large numbers of Indian children being adopted by non-Indian families. Although states maintained that such actions were taken in the best interests of children—and sometimes at the request of Indian parents—the tribes saw out-adoptions as threatening tribal survival and also argued that state courts operated from stereotypes that were unfriendly toward Indian culture. ICWA took dramatic steps on behalf of the tribes. In the act, Congress recited findings that "there is no resource that is more vital to the continued existence and integrity of Indian tribes than their children";[206] that "an alarmingly high percentage of Indian families are broken up by the removal, often unwarranted, of their children from them by nontribal public and private agencies"; and that an "alarmingly high percentage" of these children are placed in non-Indian homes and institutions.[207] Accordingly, the statute gave tribal courts exclusive jurisdiction in child custody cases involving an Indian child domiciled or residing with the reservation of the child's tribe. In cases involving tribal children domiciled elsewhere, state courts were required, in the absence of good cause to the contrary, to transfer such cases to a tribal court upon the petition of either parent or the tribe. Tribes were also given a right to intervene in state cases involving foster care placement and termination of parental rights. Stating as federal policy the placement of Indian children in foster or adoptive homes "which will reflect the unique values of Indian culture,"[208] the statute mandated that states give preference to placement of Indian children with a member of the child's extended family, other member of the tribe, or other Indian family.[209]

Ronald Reagan, William Rehnquist, and the Return of the Citizen

The proto-multiculturalism of the political branches in the 1970s faced increasingly tough judicial scrutiny as President Reagan's appointments took their seats on the high court. The flexibility of the Burger Court gave way, under the stewardship of Chief Justice Rehnquist, to constitutional readings that protected rights in individualistic rather than group-based terms. The Rehnquist Court's sharp turn in the affirmative action cases is a paradigmatic example. In *City of Richmond v. J. A. Croson Co.*,[210] the Court struck down a city minority set-aside program fashioned after the federal statute upheld in *Fullilove.* In requiring that such programs be judged under "strict scrutiny," the Court noted that the rights secured by the Fourteenth Amendment are "'personal rights'"[211] and that

> [t]he Richmond Plan denies certain citizens the opportunity to compete for a fixed percentage of public contracts based solely upon their race. To whatever racial group these citizens belong, their "personal rights" to be treated with equal dignity and respect are implicated by a rigid rule erecting race as the sole criterion in an aspect of public decisionmaking.[212]

It is noteworthy that the Court chose to render its individualistic account in terms of *citizens'* rights. This emphasis appears not to be accidental, as it occurs elsewhere in the opinion as well: "Under Richmond's scheme, a successful black, Hispanic, or Oriental entrepreneur from anywhere in the country enjoys an absolute preference over other citizens based solely on their race."[213] Equating individual rights and equal citizenship seems natural but is hardly compelled. The Fourteenth Amendment protects "persons," not "citizens," and efforts to end "second-class citizenship" are generally put in group-based terms.[214]

With the departures of Justices Brennan and Marshall, the Rehnquist Court was at full power. Applying *Croson* to the federal government in *Adarand Constructors, Inc. v. Pena,*[215] it overturned earlier decisions upholding race-conscious federal programs.[216]

The Court's change of course on affirmative action is consistent with a significant shift in public opinion regarding race-based measures. It is as if the nation and the Court returned to the reasoning of the cases that had helped end Reconstruction a century before:

> When a man has emerged from slavery, and by the aid of beneficent legislation has shaken off the inseparable concomitants of that state, there must be some stage in the progress of his elevation when he takes the rank of a mere citizen, and ceases to be the special favorite of the laws, and when his rights as a citizen, or a man, are to be protected in the ordinary modes by which other men's rights are protected.[217]

What we see in *Croson* and *Adarand,* then, is the adoption of the Warren Court's focus on citizenship, but with a decided tilt. In an echo of Justice McReynolds's 1920s defense of individual rights as a check on social engineering,[218] the rights of citizens become a brake on an activist government. This is far from Chief Justice Warren's promotion of full citizenship as a vehicle for ending a racial caste system.

In the Rehnquist Court's conception, citizenship also undercuts claims of "special rights" that would make some citizens more equal than others.[219] Thus, the Court's race cases are of a piece with its decision in *Employment Division, Department of Human Resources of Oregon v. Smith*.[220] There, the Court rejected the claim of a Native American church that its use of peyote as part of its ritual was protected under the free exercise clause of the First Amendment. Justice Scalia's majority opinion held that a "neutral, generally applicable" law would not be invalidated simply because it collided with an individual's religious beliefs. Justice Blackmun's dissent, joined by Justices Brennan and Marshall, noted the "potentially devastating impact" of the Court's ruling on Native American religions; not surprisingly, he found *Yoder*'s protection of group-based rights relevant.[221] But the Court dismissed the analogy to *Yoder*, distinguishing it as a case involving parental rights to control the education of their children. Indeed, for Scalia, the nation's diversity was a ground not for recognizing a free exercise claim in *Smith* but rather for rejecting it. In arguing that the validity of the state law should not be tested under a "compelling state interest" test, he stated:

> [I]f "compelling interest" really means what it says . . . , many laws will not meet the test. Any society adopting such a system would be courting anarchy, but that danger increases in direct proportion to the society's diversity of religious beliefs, and its determination to coerce or suppress none of them. Precisely because "we are a cosmopolitan nation made up of people of almost every conceivable religious preference," . . . and precisely because we value and protect that religious divergence, we cannot afford the luxury of deeming presumptively invalid, as applied to every religious objector, every regulation of conduct that does not protect an interest of the highest order.[222]

Citizenship-as-individual-rights is the glue, then, that will hold an increasingly multicultural nation together.

The individualistic rendering of citizenship has carried through to the Indian cases. The Rehnquist Court has been decidedly unfriendly toward Indian tribal power exercised over nonmembers and has acted to limit tribal authority in the name of protecting the rights of citizens. Most explicit is the Court's opinion in *Duro v. Reina*[223] (discussed in detail in Chapter 5), which held that a tribe could not prosecute an Indian who had committed murder on the reservation but was not a member of the tribe. Crucial to the Court was the defendant's "status as a citizen of the United States." Noting that "Indians like other citizens" are embraced within the Constitution's protection of individual rights, the Court could not approve of tribal jurisdiction over nonmembers (whether non-Indians or members of another Indian tribe):

> Criminal trial and punishment is so serious an intrusion on personal liberty that its exercise over non-Indian citizens was a power necessarily surrendered by the tribes in their submission to the overriding sovereignty of the United States . . . We hesitate to adopt a view of tribal sovereignty that would single out another group of citizens, nonmember Indians, for trial by political bodies that do not include them.[224]

New attention to citizenship presents the old problem of the rights of aliens. In cases reaffirming the limited role of judicial review in the immigration area, the Court has rejected constitutional challenges to immigration rules that discriminate on the basis of gender and illegitimacy[225] and to practices regarding the detention of alien juveniles.[226] The Court has also refused to permit an alien to challenge his deportation proceeding based on the claim that he was being prosecuted because of his exercise of First Amendment rights.[227] (In a 2001 case that cuts against the grain, the Court recognized constitutional limits on the power of the government to detain aliens who have been ordered deported but who cannot be returned home because their countries of origin refuse to accept them back.[228] As will be discussed in Chapter 7, Justice O'Connor joined the four members of the liberal wing of the Court in invalidating what amounted to indefinite imprisonment imposed by administrative authorities.)

The Rehnquist Court's race, Indian, and immigration cases are arguably in tension with its strong and active promotion of the constitutional value of state sovereignty. One obvious distinction, however, is that the "groupness" protected in the federalism cases is not defined in ethnic, religious, or cultural terms.[229] The defense of state sovereignty has been made primarily in terms of furthering democratic accountability, not in terms of affirming diversity on a subnational level.

In sum, the Rehnquist Court has appropriated the vehicle but not the rhetoric or motivation of the Warren Court. The return of citizenship in the service of individual rights sets a very different course from a citizenship project dedicated to erasing barriers to full inclusion.

The Progressive Promise and Peril of Citizenship

There is a hint that, with President Clinton's appointees to the Court, citizenship may once again be rendered in more Warren Court–like terms. *Saenz v. Roe* provides the leading example. Decided in 1999, the case invalidated a California statute that sought to prevent settlement in the state of persons seeking its high welfare benefits.[230] *Shapiro v. Thompson,* decided thirty years before, had held that states could not require a year's residency before providing eligibility to the welfare system. Such rules were deemed an unconstitutional burdening of the "right to travel." California sought to get around *Shapiro* by providing that new residents would be eligible for welfare, but that for a year the maximum payment they could receive would be the amount that they would have received in their prior states of residence. The scheme, argued California, would not burden the right to travel. Nonetheless the Court struck down the statute. It agreed with California that the state program did not unduly burden a person's right in free interstate movement. But it concluded that another aspect of the right to travel was violated: the right of new residents to be treated like other citizens of the state. That right, the Court held, was secured by the second sentence of the Fourteenth Amendment, which provides that "[n]o State shall make or enforce any law which shall abridge the privileges or immunities of citizens of the United States."

The invocation of the privileges or immunities clause was a shocker. Ever since the Court's decision in the *Slaughter House Cases* in 1873, it had been constitutional dogma that the clause was a virtual dead letter.[231] The Court's revivification of the clause provides new avenues for assertions of rights against the state—at the same time that the Court is fortifying states against exercises of federal power. All in all, *Saenz* is a curious case, unless viewed from the citizenship perspective.[232]

Saenz would have done the Warren Court proud. Its construction of a national citizenship through the wholly unanticipated rebirth of the privileges or immunities clause raises the possibility of advancement of the Warren Court program in bold colors.[233] (In another part of the opinion the Court goes further, stating that "the protection afforded to the citizen by the Citizenship Clause of the Amendment is a limitation on the powers of the National Government as well as the States.") Yet *Saenz* also illustrates the perils of the citizenship project. The privileges or immunities clause is expressly linked to the rights of *citizens* and therefore appears to draw an indelible line between the rights of citizens and aliens.[234] Indeed, one saving grace of the earlier tortured reading of the clause was that the Court relied on the equal protection clause to expand rights, which defines its beneficiaries as "persons"—a term forever understood to include noncitizens in the United States.[235] While a statute that applied California's scheme solely to immigrants might still be invalid under the equal protection clause,[236] the language of *Saenz* suggests that the Court's commitment to full state citizenship might not include noncitizens.[237]

Saenz also has less direct but nonetheless interesting implications for Indian law. The Court identifies three separate "components" of the right to travel: "the right of a citizen of one State to enter and to leave another State, the right to be treated as a welcome visitor rather than an unfriendly alien when temporarily present in the second State, and, for those travelers who elect to become permanent residents, the right to be treated like other citizens of that State."[238] On the surface, there is nothing here about the authority of Indian tribes to deny political and other rights to non–tribe members living on a reservation. Indeed, such measures would not discriminate against out-of-staters in favor of state residents. But the deeper structure of the analysis echoes the Court's concerns expressed in *Duro v. Reina* that tribal sovereignty in effect treats U.S. citizens on reservations as aliens. As I have noted, the Court states elsewhere that the citizenship clause limits federal powers as well as state powers. Might the Court hold, in the name of national citizenship, that similar limits apply to the tribes?

Thus, if the current Court is interested in extending the Warren Court's work on behalf of citizenship, it faces the same limitations inherent in that approach that restricted the power of the Warren Court's analysis. Citizenship remains an exclusive and excluding concept.

The twentieth century ended with conflicting trends. As Nathan Glazer has conceded, to some degree "we are all multiculturalists now."[239] But it is a soft multiculturalism, similar to the cultural pluralism of the 1930s and quite distinct from the black, brown, and red nationalist programs of the 1960s and the race consciousness of the 1970s and 1980s. The Supreme Court has erected tough limits on race-based programs, rendering the equal protection clause a sanctuary for individual rights rather than a means for eradicating vestiges of caste in American society.

Administrations continue to describe self-determination as the goal of federal Indian policy, and the tribes seem economically and politically stronger today. But tribal sovereignty has not appeared to advance in material respects, and the Court's recent statements show no inclination to expand tribal power over nonmembers.[240]

In 1996 Congress adopted the harshest anti-immigrant legislation in decades. The lurch toward nativism appeared to have subsided—in no small measure owing to the recognition that immigrants' co-ethnics are frequently citizens who exercise their right to vote. But the events of September 11, 2001 brought another round of tough new laws directed at immigrants.

If there is something new as the new century begins, it is the ascendancy of citizenship. Valuing citizenship is seen as a strategy for holding an increasingly multiethnic society together. It is a conceptual common ground. It thus differs dramatically from the ethnic and cultural basis for unity asserted at the close of the nineteenth century. This is the move from understanding the United States as a nation-state to understanding it as a citizen-state. The Warren Court showed that the ideal of citizenship could be a powerful tool in the extension of rights, the ending of second-class citizenship, and the inclusion of previously subordinated and marginalized groups. The current rendering of citizenship, however, is more defensive, a circling of the wagons to protect a threatened state from subnational and supranational forces. The Court (*Saenz* being, perhaps, a significant counter-example) has not taken up citizenship as a program for furthering the goals of the Constitution's preamble. Nor has the concept been used creatively, say, to support programs that help immigrants integrate or naturalize. George W. Bush's inaugural address was noteworthy for its repeated references to citizenship,[241] both an echo of and a moving beyond John Kennedy's "ask not . . ." But Bush's appeals were for civil society to do more,[242] rather than proposals for a public commitment to fostering more robust citizenship rights and participation. Citizenship has become, oddly, a private affair, a vehicle for the assertion of private rights, more akin to consumerism than the construction of community.

The one constant appears to be the plenary power doctrine, which was hardly weaker at the close of the twentieth century than it was at the beginning. Constitutional developments of the past several generations have dramatically reoriented our fundamental law. But the territorial, Indian, and immigration cases stand largely untouched. Congress's full and complete power in these areas remains. In the following chapters I examine constitutional arguments that might provide purchase for the overthrow of the plenary power doctrine as well as policy arguments that suggest a wiser use of Congress's power.

CHAPTER 4

Commonwealth and the Constitution: The Case of Puerto Rico

The United States acquired the island of Puerto Rico from Spain in 1898. In the Commonwealth's centennial year, the people of Puerto Rico went to the polls to indicate their preference on the political status of the island and its relationship to the United States. On the ballot were the options of statehood, independence, a continuation of the current commonwealth arrangement, and "free associated status" (a treaty-based relationship with the United States that purports to grant Puerto Rico full sovereignty and does not guarantee U.S. citizenship to persons born in Puerto Rico). Of the more than 1.5 million voters who participated in the plebiscite, only *933* supported continuation of the current arrangement.[1] A fifth option—"none of the above"—won, receiving 50.4 percent of the vote. As we say in the law, *res ipsa loquitur.*[2]

The status question has dominated Puerto Rican politics for decades (the major political parties on the island are identified by their preferred alternative), yet has received surprisingly little attention on the mainland and almost no attention in constitutional law treatises, casebooks, or courses.[3] This omission is not a good measure of the significance of the issues. If Puerto Rico were to achieve statehood, it would be the twenty-third most populous state in the Union, sending two senators and perhaps six representatives to Congress. The island, once proclaimed the "showcase for democracy" and the alternative to Cuban-style socialism, is now the American "gateway" to the developing Caribbean basin.

The current commonwealth status was put in place in the 1950s.

Commonwealth was a new and novel form of territorial government. It did not, like earlier home rule arrangements for territories, presuppose eventual Puerto Rican statehood; it was seen as responding to Puerto Rico's desire to remain part of the United States while retaining a distinct culture and language.[4] It was argued at the time that the establishment of commonwealth represented an act of self-determination by the people of Puerto Rico and constituted an end to the island's status as a colony of the United States. It is recognized today, however, that commonwealth—at least in its 1950s form—is not a permanent solution to the status question. Decolonization of Puerto Rico remains a work in progress.

Other territories acquired from Spain have worked out different governing arrangements with the federal government. The Philippines became independent in 1946; Guam, still an "unincorporated territory" of the United States, is involved in status negotiations that focus on rights of the indigenous Chamorro people, the presence of the U.S. military, and control over immigration. Persons born on American Samoa are "nationals" but not "citizens" of the United States. Pacific islands over which the United States attained trustee status following World War II have entered into compacts with the federal government establishing "free associated status."

These arrangements raise a host of constitutional questions regarding the continuing scope of federal power. They also open up broader themes of citizenship, the divisibility of sovereignty, and cultural nationalism, all of which are of increasing salience in the United States and the world.[5] I investigate these issues by focusing on Puerto Rico—by far the largest of the "possessions." As the previous chapters make clear, I am deeply skeptical of the regime of "plenary power" that continues to dominate the legal debate over status; of equal concern are easy, but untenable, claims about the Constitution that have intruded into the self-determination discussion.

"Plenary" Federal Power over the Territories

The Constitution grants Congress power to make "all needful rules and regulations respecting the Territory . . . belonging to the United States."[6] Perhaps the best-known construction of the territory clause is Justice Taney's tortured reasoning in *Dred Scott,* holding that the clause authorized congressional rule only of those territories held by the federal government at the time of the founding (Taney located congressional power to regulate after-acquired territories in the Constitution's provision authorizing Congress to admit new states).[7] But that reading was inconsistent both with earlier statements of John Marshall and with congressional practice,[8] and the Court in the *Insular Cases* made clear that the territory clause is the source of congressional power over U.S. possessions acquired by purchase, conquest, treaty, or war.[9] That power, as detailed in Chapter 2, was described as "plenary."

Theoretically, the existence of Congress's plenary power is a sword of Damocles hanging over Puerto Rican self-government. What Congress has granted, the argument runs, it may always take away. The Eleventh Circuit stated this position in the baldest terms: "Congress may unilaterally repeal the Puerto Rican Constitution . . . and replace [it] with any rules or regulations of its choice."[10] Yet despite the existence of this broad power, Congress has granted Puerto Rico increasing degrees of home rule. Under the Organic Act of 1900 (the Foraker Act), Puerto Rico was ruled by a governor appointed by the president of the United States; the governor served as commander in chief of the militia and had the power to veto legislation adopted by the locally elected legislative assembly and to appoint lower-court judges.[11] The 1917 Jones Act extended U.S. citizenship and a bill of rights to residents of Puerto Rico and provided for popular election of both houses of the legislature. In 1947 Puerto Ricans were granted the right to elect their governor. Three years later Congress started the process to fuller self-rule by adopting "an Act to provide for the organization of a constitutional government by the people of Puerto Rico." The 1950 statute (Public Law 600) declared:

> Whereas the Congress of the United States by a series of enactments has progressively recognized the right of self-government of the people of Puerto Rico; and
>
> Whereas under the terms of these congressional enactments an increasingly large measure of self-government has been achieved: Therefore,
>
> *Be it enacted* . . . [t]hat, fully recognizing the principle of government by consent, this Act is now adopted in the nature of a compact so that the people of Puerto Rico may organize a government pursuant to a constitution of their own adoption.[12]

Under the procedures provided by Public Law 600, an island-wide referendum was held, approving a call for a constitutional convention. The draft produced by the convention was adopted by the people of Puerto Rico[13] and formally approved by the Congress in 1952, with one exception[14] and two provisos.[15] The constitutional convention of Puerto Rico acted immediately to amend the constitution as mandated by the Congress, and the Constitution of Puerto Rico took effect after a formal proclamation of the governor on July 25, 1952.

It has been strongly argued that the establishment of commonwealth status ended Congress's "plenary power" under the territory clause. Under this reasoning, Congress lost general power to regulate the internal affairs of Puerto Rico or to amend the "compact" without Puerto Rican consent—much as Congress has no power to legislate for the now independent Philippines or territories that have become states.[16] (Congress could, of course, still adopt laws under other powers that applied in Puerto Rico, just as federal laws adopted under the commerce power, for example, have effect throughout the states.)

Despite some early lower court opinions (and dicta in more recent cases) suggesting that commonwealth status has fundamentally altered congressional power under the territory clause,[17] neither the Supreme Court nor the executive branch has accepted the claim.[18] Interestingly, statehood supporters and *independentistas* alike have argued that Congress lost nothing by authorizing Puerto Rican self-rule; from either perspective, the conclusion that congressional power has not been limited by commonwealth supports a move to a legal status that would clearly terminate "plenary power"—either statehood or independence.[19]

Even if one were to conclude that Congress had not alienated its power under the territory clause, it would not necessarily mean that the exercise of such power is unlimited.[20] Two sorts of limits are conceivable. First, it might be argued that Congress may not discriminate against Puerto Ricans simply on the basis of residence in the Commonwealth. Second, the Bill of Rights and other explicit limits on congressional power might apply to federal regulation of Puerto Rico.

Differential Treatment of Residents of Puerto Rico

For most federal regulatory and criminal statutes, Puerto Rico is treated as if it were a state.[21] There are, however, some important exceptions. Individuals in Puerto Rico pay no federal income taxes (although this permits Puerto Rico to set local taxes at significantly higher levels).[22] Furthermore, residents of Puerto Rico receive less favorable treatment than mainland residents under a number of major federal benefits programs. For citizens of Puerto Rico, federal payments under welfare and Medicaid programs are made at lower levels and are subject to an overall cap.[23] The Supplemental Security Income (SSI) program (aid to the aged, blind, and disabled) does not apply to Puerto Rico; rather, through continuation of an earlier, similar program, benefit levels for Puerto Ricans are capped and made at lower levels than SSI payments to eligible persons residing in the states.[24] According to a 1990 study by the Congressional Budget Office, treating Puerto Rico as a state under these programs would have increased federal transfers to the commonwealth by some $1.7 billion in fiscal year 1995.[25] It is generally agreed that, because of high levels of poverty on the island and a low average income,[26] the dollars lost owing to unfavorable treatment under the federal benefit programs substantially exceed the dollars lost to the U.S. Treasury because of the tax exemption on Puerto Rican taxpayers.[27]

The Supreme Court has given short shrift to claims that the disadvantageous treatment of Puerto Rico violates the Fifth Amendment's equal protection guarantee. In *Harris v. Rosario*,[28] the Court upheld the disparate treatment of Puerto Ricans under the then-existing federal welfare program in a page-and-a-half per curiam opinion issued without full briefing or oral argument. The summary disposition, joined by six members of the Court, stated that under the territory clause, Congress "may treat Puerto Rico differently from States so long as there is a rational basis for its actions."[29] Referring to an earlier per curiam opinion upholding the exclusion of Puerto Rico from the federal SSI program,[30] the Court identified three grounds for concluding that the differential treatment of Puerto Rico was rational: "Puerto Rican residents do not contribute to the federal treasury; the cost of treating Puerto Rico as a State under the statute would be high; and greater benefits could disrupt the Puerto Rican economy."[31]

Harris is a startling and troubling example of the Court's unwillingness to give any serious scrutiny—indeed, any serious thought—to congressional exercises of power over the territories. The Court's summary treatment of the complex issues is no doubt aided by its general unwillingness to review federal welfare programs.[32] But the reasons assigned by the Court for finding the statute rational (which are simply lifted verbatim from an earlier case and would seem to authorize virtually any discrimination against Puerto Rico residents in federal programs) suggest that something else is at work other than hostility to constitutional claims brought by poor people.

The Court is surely correct that residents of Puerto Rico pay no federal income tax and that funding Puerto Rico at the level of the states would cost the federal treasury more. Moreover, it is certainly arguable that higher welfare payments "*could* disrupt the Puerto Rican economy." To this extent, the arguments supplied in support of the statute are rational by not being crazy.

Nevertheless, the Court's finding of a rational means-end relationship is not unassailable. The second and third justifications would seem to apply equally to every state, rather than distinguishing the Commonwealth from the states: welfare payments cost money and may affect local economies by influencing decisions to work; and the more welfare recipients in a state, the higher the costs. Yet Congress had not provided for reduced reimbursement levels or overall caps for states with large numbers of welfare recipients.[33] Nor does the first justification—that Puerto Ricans pay no federal taxes—take us very far. The welfare program did not in any way link federal subventions to states to the amount that state taxpayers contribute to federal tax coffers.[34] And the fact of tax exemption says little about the fairness of reduced benefits to island residents, since the taxpayers and recipients of federal aid would be largely distinct classes of Puerto Ricans.[35]

Doctrinally, one might expose the thinness of the justification through the imposition of a higher level of judicial scrutiny. This was Justice Marshall's suggestion in his dissent from the summary disposition in *Harris*.[36] But it is not clear, under prevailing equal protection doctrine, how heightened scrutiny might be triggered. Rather, *Harris* exposes a deeper issue. Even assuming that the justifications provided by Congress are "rational" (as we understand that term in constitutional analysis), what is not explained is why they are *permissible*. The distinction drawn by Congress is one based simply on residence in a territory; it is grounded, when all is said and done, not on different facts but on status of place. If Congress were truly interested in saving money or not unduly interfering in local economies, it could draft legislation accomplishing those ends with classifications that do not distinguish territories from states. Furthermore, it is curious that under federal welfare laws, *place of residence* might count for more than *citizenship:* at the time of *Harris,* permanent resident aliens residing in the states received the same level of payments as U.S. citizens residing there; U.S. citizen residents of Puerto Rico did not.[37]

In short, the "reasoning" of *Harris* is that Puerto Rico is not a state, and that Congress is entitled to draw lines between territories and states in the disbursement of federal funds. But constitutional law ought to demand more than judgment by definition. Some set of justifications beyond those currently indulged in by the Court is demanded when Congress acts to disadvantage a class of the poorest American citizens, who, by place of residence, are not entitled to participate in the federal political system.[38]

Indeed, that lack of participation itself needs to be seriously scrutinized. In the course of the twentieth century, the territories were gradually given the power of self-government (as an act of, and subject to, the plenary power of Congress). But formal participation at the national level has not been achieved. The territories are permitted only nonvoting delegates to Congress, and cases brought by territorial residents claiming a right to vote in presidential elections have been dismissed by federal courts of appeal.[39] Justifying the denial of political rights was a primary motivation behind the *Insular Cases:* it was precisely the idea that the residents of the newly acquired territories were "alien races" for whom "the administration of government and justice, according to Anglo-Saxon principles, may for a time be impossible."[40] Of course, the racist language of the *Insular Cases* is absent from today's debates; the legal arguments against national political rights rely on constitutional provisions that key congressional representation and electoral votes to "states" ("The House of Representatives shall be composed of Members chosen . . . by the People of the several states").[41] Furthermore, many members of Congress appear genuine in their willingness to begin the process of admitting Puerto Rico as a state, should the people of the island support statehood in a referendum. Nonetheless, the current arrangement continues to appear to embrace colonial assumptions: Puerto Ricans can be permitted to govern themselves (with federal supervisory power in the wings) but are not yet ready to participate in crafting rules for the national state.

Fundamental Rights and Federal Regulations of the Territories

In the *Insular Cases,* the Court weighed in on the question of the constitutional status of the territories—an issue that received sustained national attention at the turn of the twentieth century.[42] Although there was little doubt that Congress possessed broad power to establish governments for the new acquisitions, an issue sparking heated political and legal controversy was whether the residents of the new "possessions" were entitled to the protections of the federal Constitution. Some argued that direct application of the Constitution would needlessly hinder congressional flexibility in carrying out the Empire project. Others thought that the Constitution must apply wherever the federal government acts—in the phrase of the day, "the Constitution followed the flag."[43] Interestingly, this latter claim was sometimes pressed by anti-imperialists, not with the intent of ensuring that Filipinos or Puerto Ricans in fact possessed U.S. constitutional rights, but rather to put obstacles in the way of Empire. Few Americans thought that the residents in the newly acquired territories were "civilized" enough to participate in American political institutions. Thus, a conclusion that they were entitled to full constitutional protections (and perhaps representation in Congress) would provide Congress with a strong incentive to cast off the territories.[44]

In the *Insular Cases,* the Court compromised. Unwilling to throw water on the imperialist fires burning in the nation, the Court ensured that the Constitution would not be read to unduly limit congressional options.[45] The doctrinal innovation here was the newly minted distinction between "incorporated" and "unincorporated" territories. For those territories "incorporated" into the United States by congressional and executive branch action and deemed to be on the road to statehood (such as Alaska), the Constitution applied in full. "Unincorporated" territories, such as Puerto Rico, Guam, and the Philippines, faced different constitutional rules. In the possessions, the Constitution was "operative," but this did not mean that every provision was "applicable."[46] For example, because unincorporated territories were held not to be part of the United States in a constitutional sense, the requirement that taxes "be uniform throughout the United States"[47] did not apply. More important, residents of the "unincorporated" territories were guaranteed only those rights held by the Court to be "fundamental."[48] This latter rule held whether or not the territorial population had been granted U.S. citizenship.[49] As Secretary of War Elihu Root quipped after the Court's decisions, "[A]s near as I can make out the Constitution follows the flag—but doesn't quite catch up with it."[50]

The *Insular Cases* concluded that Puerto Rico was not an "incorporated" territory of the United States, a holding that persists to this day. Accordingly, application of the Bill of Rights to the laws governing the island was not automatic, as was made clear by Chief Justice Taft's opinion for a unanimous Court in *Balzac v. Porto Rico.*[51] In *Balzac,* a newspaper editor was charged with criminal libel, a misdemeanor under Puerto Rican law. The island's code of criminal procedure did not provide for jury trial in such cases, and Balzac claimed that the law violated his rights under the Sixth Amendment. Taft concluded that, absent evidence of clear congressional intent, the Court would not hold that Puerto Rico had been incorporated into the United States; accordingly, the Sixth Amendment did not automatically apply to criminal proceedings in Puerto Rico. And under the particular circumstances of the territory, application of the jury right would be inappropriate:

> The jury system needs citizens trained to the exercise of the responsibilities of jurors. In common-law countries centuries of tradition have prepared a conception of the impartial attitude jurors must assume. The jury system postulates a conscious duty of participation in the machinery of justice which it is hard for people not brought up in fundamentally popular government at once to acquire. One of its greatest benefits is in the security it gives the people that they, as jurors, actual or possible, being part of the judicial system of the country can prevent its arbitrary use or abuse. Congress has thought that a people like the Filipinos, or the Porto Ricans, trained to a complete judicial system which knows no juries, living in compact and ancient communities, with definitely formed customs and political conceptions, should be permitted themselves to determine how far they wish to adopt this institution of Anglo-Saxon origin, and when.[52]

Balzac is a curious decision for a number of reasons. First, the Court's holding was not affected by the fact that citizens of Puerto Rico had been granted U.S. citizenship in 1917. Arguably, the earlier cases might have been distinguished on such a ground, or the granting of citizenship might have suggested that Puerto Rico had been "incorporated" into the United States.[53] Second, Puerto Rican legislation had provided for jury trial in felony cases since 1901.[54] Thus, the subtext of the opinion—that Puerto Ricans were not prepared to operate Anglo-Saxon institutions—appears weak.[55] Finally, because Puerto Ricans were citizens of the United States, they could freely travel to the mainland and be called to serve on juries in the state or federal courts, despite being "trained to a complete judicial system that knows no juries."

Athough *Balzac* has never been overturned,[56] it is of little consequence today. By statute, Puerto Ricans are guaranteed a jury trial in both commonwealth and federal prosecutions consistent with prevailing constitutional rules.[57] Beyond the right to jury trials, federal statutes and the Puerto Rican Constitution establish that the Bill of Rights applies in the Commonwealth. The 1950 legislation initiating the commonwealth process specifically mandated that any constitution drafted by Puerto Rico "shall include a bill of rights";[58] and the bill of rights subsequently included in the 1952 constitution, and approved by Congress, includes all the federal guarantees that apply to the states[59] (and more).[60] Equal protection also receives explicit mention.[61]

These legal provisions ensure that, as a matter of Puerto Rican law, governmental actions will be subject to scrutiny under prevailing constitutional norms. But they do not establish that the conduct of Puerto Rican authorities will be subject to federal constitutional review. (To see the difference, consider a state statute that is challenged as a violation of the guarantee of free speech. The state constitution may prohibit abridgments of speech, thereby permitting a state constitutional challenge to the law. This is a different question than whether a challenge may be brought in federal court.)[62]

In a number of cases the Supreme Court has made clear that the conduct of the Puerto Rican government is challengeable on federal constitutional grounds, but it has deliberately avoided saying why. Thus, in *Torres v. Puerto Rico,* the Court considered the constitutionality of a search by Puerto Rican authorities of luggage arriving in the Commonwealth from the United States. The Court found the search invalid under the Fourth Amendment; but it expressly noted that it had "no occasion to determine whether the Fourth Amendment applies directly or by operation of the Fourteenth Amendment."[63] The Court appears uncertain whether such rights apply by extension of the *Insular Cases* (whereby certain of the Bill of Rights are deemed fundamental and therefore applicable in the territories) or by analogy to the cases that apply the Bill of Rights to the states by way of the due process clause of the Fourteenth Amendment.

In sum, no matter the confusion over the source of the applicable norms, it seems clear that the conduct of the Puerto Rican government will be examined under prevailing constitutional standards.[64] It is important to see, however, that these developments do not necessarily establish that the Constitution applies in full to *federal* regulation of the territories. On a "geographical" reading of the *Insular Cases* these are the same issues: the Constitution is deemed to extend (or not) to a particular location; thus it would not matter if the regulation under challenge in the territory had been adopted by the local or the national government. (The *Insular Cases* do not address the issue because at that time the local regulation could be directly attributed to the national government.) Alternatively, it might be that the Constitution applies to commonwealth law in a manner similar to incorporation of the Bill of Rights against the states, but that less rigid norms apply at the national level because of Congress's need for flexibility in crafting governing arrangements for the territories.

Even if the latter view were adopted—that different constitutional norms might apply to the acts of the federal government than to the acts of the territorial government—strong arguments might nonetheless support a robust set of limits on federal power. Modern constitutional law could easily conclude that the Constitution has finally caught up with the flag.[65] Given the provenance of the *Insular Cases,* their thorough repudiation would mark the triumph of constitutionalism over racism. But before concluding that the Constitution applies to federal action vis-à-vis territories in precisely the same manner as it applies to other federal powers, consider the following two scenarios. Under the terms of the 1976 Convenant to Establish a Commonwealth of the Northern Mariana Islands in Political Union with the United States of America, one house of CNMI's legislature is required to provide equal representation for "each of the chartered [NMI] municipalities."[66] Because the municipalities vary in size by a ratio of nearly 20 to 1, the covenant expressly calls for a malapportioned chamber in the legislature. The provision is an obvious parallel to the United States Senate, but it plainly runs afoul of one-person-one-vote strictures placed on the states.[67] In defense of the provision, the CNMI argued in court that the municipalities of Rota and Tinian would not have joined the commonwealth without the guarantee.[68]

The second example is a provision in the CNMI constitution that restricts the acquisition of permanent and long-term interests in real property to "persons of Northern Marianas descent."[69] The provision was adopted pursuant to a section of the covenant that authorized such limits on land alienation "in view of the importance of the ownership of land for the culture and traditions of the people of the Northern Marianas Island, and in order to protect them against exploitation and to promote their economic advancement and self-sufficiency."[70]

Neither of these policies would be sustainable under prevailing constitutional norms if adopted by a state, nor could the federal government authorize a state to adopt such policies.[71] And both appear to be at war with the citizenship paradigm of the Rehnquist Court.[72] In the interest of burying the plenary power doctrine, should they not now be declared beyond the pale? I don't think so. There is an important difference between denying rights to a people based on assumptions of their inferiority and taking into account in the definition of rights the considered judgments of a people interested in preserving their political and cultural distinctiveness.[73]

The federal courts that examined the CNMI policies did so under the rubric of the *Insular Cases* and upheld them both.[74] (The challenged actions were grounded in the U.S.-CNMI covenant; they were thus directly attributable to the federal government and raised classic *Insular Cases* issues.) The court, in the land case, reaffirmed that the Constitution applied in full in "incorporated" territories, but that only "fundamental" constitutional rights applied in the unincorporated territory of the CNMI.[75] Phrasing the question this way is unfortunate. It is peculiar in this day and age to label any constitutional right not "fundamental." Moreover, continued adherence to the concept of incorporation authorizes Congress to decide the applicability of the Constitution.

Nonetheless, the courts reached the proper results in sustaining the covenant and its implementing legislation. It is of real significance that both policies were subject to negotiation and agreement between the

Congress and the CNMI; they were not unilaterally imposed by the federal government. In contrast, then, to earlier colonial policies, they are likely to embody values important to the people of the Commonwealth. Thus the court noted "the vital role native ownership of land plays in the preservation of NMI social and cultural stability" and that the political union of the United States and the Commonwealth could not have been accomplished without it. In language significantly in tension with the "citizenship" cases discussed in Chapter 3, the court declared that the "bold purpose" of the Bill of Rights was "to protect minority rights, not to enforce homogeneity." It added: "Where land is so scarce, so precious, and so vulnerable to economic predation, it is understandable that the islanders' vision does not precisely coincide with mainland attitudes toward property and our commitment to the ideal of equal opportunity in its acquisition."[76] This kind of reasoning, from the perspective of the residents of the Commonwealth, stands in marked contrast to the underlying concern of the *Insular Cases*—whether "natives" were civilized enough for participation in Anglo-Saxon institutions.

Modifying constitutional norms in response to cultural diversity raises hard questions and hypotheticals. What if a territorial government sought to exclude women from political participation, seeking to justify the policy by pointing to traditional cultural practices? Or suppose a territory sought to establish a traditional religion and deny freedom of religion to dissenters? Are we left with the answer of the *Insular Cases*—that, after all, some rights are more fundamental than others? Rather than going down this road, I would suggest a multi-factor test that begins with a baseline of international human rights law. It would be peculiar, to say the least, for the United States to seek to hold foreign states to norms that it is unwilling to impose on polities within its own territory. Even without a full analysis here, it is plain that the exclusion of women[77] and the suppression of religion would not be consistent with international human rights norms (although an established state religion does not offend prevailing norms).[78] The courts upholding the CNMI policies implicitly nodded in this direction. In the districting case, the court noted that "[s]everal countries that are considered to have 'free government' have a bicameral legislative in which one house is malapportioned. Amongst them is the United States."[79] And in the land case, the court stated:

> In the territorial context, the definition of a basic and integral freedom must narrow to incorporate the shared beliefs of diverse cultures. Thus, the asserted constitutional guarantee against discrimination in the acquisition of long-term interests in land applies only if this guarantee is fundamental in this *international* sense.[80]

In the end, there can be no simple standard for deciding these cases. There are competing principles at stake. We are more likely to find a solution of accommodation than one of theoretical precision.[81] In seeking that accommodation, a court ought to examine the centrality of the challenged practice to the particular values of self-determination and cultural autonomy being asserted, against the backdrop of evolving norms of international human rights. Also relevant would be whether the persons injured by the challenged action are adequately represented in either the federal or local political process.[82] I would hazard the guess that in most cases the asserted constitutional right would be sustained. But where strong claims can be made on behalf of the people of a territory and the practice is consistent with human rights norms, rigid application of constitutional standards derived in other contexts should be resisted.[83]

The Constitutionality of "Enhanced" Commonwealth Status

As mentioned at the opening of the chapter, the option of "none of the above" won in the Puerto Rico status plebiscite of 1998. The result should not be read as a victory for political nihilism; rather it shows the strength of the pro-commonwealthers who argued that the options crafted by the ruling pro-statehood party did not adequately reflect their preferences. Those favoring commonwealth seek more than affirmation of the 1950s political solution (recall that only a virtual handful of voters in the 1998 plebiscite supported continuation of the current arrangement). Rather, they seek an "enhanced" commonwealth status that would increase Puerto Rican autonomy vis-à-vis the federal government.[84] Over the years, a number of "enhanced commonwealth" plans have been proposed, ranging from the powerful (declaring an end to federal plenary power, granting Puerto Rico a veto over the application of federal laws to the island, and authorizing a vote in presidential elections and representation in Congress)[85] to the supplemental (requiring a "clear statement" by Congress that general legislation is to apply to Puerto Rico).

Supporters of statehood have generally condemned these plans as either unconstitutional or inherently insecure. They argue that no such arrangement can derogate from Congress's plenary power to revoke or alter any arrangement; and an attempt to limit congressional power—for example, by declaring that changes can occur only with the mutual consent of the parties—is not constitutional.

These debates were vetted in the early 1990s as Congress considered a fairly mild version of "commonwealth-plus" status. Draft legislation authorized a referendum on status and spelled out the three options in some detail. Regarding a new commonwealth status, the bill declared:

> The Commonwealth of Puerto Rico is a unique juridical status, created as a compact between the People of Puerto Rico and the United States, under which Puerto Rico enjoys sovereignty, like a State, to the extent provided by the Tenth Amendment to the United States Constitution and in addition with autonomy consistent with its character, culture and location. This relationship is permanent unless revoked by mutual consent.[86]

The legislation would have strengthened Puerto Rico's hand in federal decision making regarding the commonwealth in several respects. It provided that, should the legislature of Puerto Rico pass a resolution recommending that a particular federal law no longer apply to Puerto Rico, the recommendation could be adopted by a joint resolution of the Congress.[87] In addition, it mandated that federal agencies promulgating regulations pay appropriate respect to the special status of Puerto Rico and respond specifically to objections raised by the governor of Puerto Rico that a proposed regulation is inconsistent with the status.[88] The bill also included a number of other minor "enhancements," including provisions aimed at increasing federal consultation with the Commonwealth on matters of interest to Puerto Rico and bringing Puerto Rican participation in federal benefit programs closer in line with that of the states.[89]

The legislation did not purport to provide the Commonwealth with a veto over the application of federal law to the island. Nor did it permit Puerto Rican constitutional guarantees to trump federal statutes.[90]

It did not conceptualize commonwealth as a status with more autonomy from federal intervention than states enjoy. The thrust of the legislation was, in effect, to make Puerto Rican home rule similar to that of the states of the Union (including a guarantee—currently applicable to the states—that that status could not change without consent of the people of Puerto Rico). Arguably, the provisions requiring Congress and the federal agencies to take notice of Puerto Rican claims that federal law impinged on commonwealth status put Puerto Rico in a favored position vis-à-vis the states. But these measures may also be viewed as modest attempts to remedy what states have but Puerto Rico does not: representation in Congress and votes in the electoral college.[91]

It is thus somewhat surprising that the attorney general of the United States told Congress that the "enhanced commonwealth" status proposed in the legislation was unconstitutional.[92] Testifying before the Senate in 1991, Attorney General Richard Thornburgh stated that the provisions declaring that Puerto Rico "enjoys sovereignty, like a State, to the extent provided by the Tenth Amendment" and that the relationship could be revoked only "by mutual consent" were "totally inconsistent with the Constitution." He elaborated as follows:

> Under the Territory Clause of the Constitution . . . an area within the sovereignty of the United States that is not included in a State must necessarily be governed by or under the authority of Congress. Congress cannot escape this constitutional command by extending to Puerto Rico the provisions of the Tenth Amendment, which by its terms provides only [for] the relationship between the Federal Government and states.
>
> We also doubt that Congress may effectively limit, by a statutory mutual consent requirement, its constitutional power under the Territory Clause to alter Puerto Rico's status in some respect in the future. Not even the so-called "enhanced commonwealth" can ever hope to be outside of this constitutional provision.[93]

The attorney general offered little support for his interpretation of the territory clause, a reading that conflicted with an opinion of the Department of Justice issued by an earlier Republican administration concluding that Congress had the power to enter into an irrevocable compact.[94] It is somewhat peculiar to see the executive branch more concerned than the Congress about protecting congressional prerogatives.[95]

The attorney general's reasoning seems to be this: the United States Constitution knows only the mutually exclusive categories of "State" and "Territory." States are full and equal members of the Union, but territories are subject to plenary federal power. Such plenary power may be surrendered only by moving outside the territory clause by granting statehood or independence. To recognize congressional power to create new categories—such as "enhanced commonwealth" —violates the structure of the Constitution and potentially weakens the position of the states (if a commonwealth can be granted powers not available to states).

But the territory clause provides no blueprint for territorial government. In rather plain language, it empowers Congress to make "all needful Rules and Regulation." John Marshall described this power in the broadest terms: under the territory clause, "we find Congress possessing and exercising the absolute and undisputed power of governing and legislating for [territories]."[96] There may well be structural limits on this broad power. For example, it would be hard to make a persuasive argument that Congress could give territories representation in the Senate.[97] But nothing in "enhanced commonwealth" threatens the power of the states. Congressional practice in the creation and regulation of territories is populated with novel arrangements. The infamous *Insular Cases* recognized the need for congressional flexibility in handling the unanticipated situation of Empire. When that flexibility is now, by mutual consent of capital and former colony, exercised to restore dignity and self-government, why should congressional power suddenly be read narrowly?[98]

The attorney general's answer to the question is formalistic. It is that the territory power may not be alienated. Or, to put the point in the form of an old constitutional chestnut, a sitting Congress may not bind a future Congress.[99] Of course, this is hardly an absolute rule. The granting of neither statehood nor independence may be revoked, nor may land grants or other "vested interests" be called back by a subsequent Congress.[100] Furthermore, as I explore at length in Chapter 6, a plausible argument can be crafted in support of the constitutionality of a "mutual consent clause" that limits congressional authority to alter unilaterally tribal governing arrangements established by an agreement between a tribe and the federal government.[101]

To my mind, it is not the "inalienability" point that is really doing the theoretical work in the attorney general's testimony. Rather, it is an undisclosed and unanalyzed set of assumptions about the nature of sovereignty. We have inherited constitutional understandings of sovereignty that demand neat boxes and hierarchies. To be a sovereign nation means to exercise full and final authority over a piece of territory—authority that may not be challenged from without or within. Were it otherwise, the nation would run the risk of anarchy or external domination.[102] In this tidy nineteenth-century conceptual world, there is no room for "enhanced" commonwealth if it bestows a form of sovereignty that takes away from congressional plenary power.

Is this notion of sovereignty appropriate for our twenty-first-century world? In an insightful essay, Neil MacCormick examines strongly expressed concerns in the United Kingdom that membership in the European community threatens traditional conceptions of parliamentary sovereignty.[103] "A different view," he suggests, "would be that sovereignty and sovereign states, and the inexorable linkage of law with sovereignty and the state have been but the passing phenomena of a few centuries, that their passing is by no means regrettable, and that current developments in Europe exhibit the possibility of going beyond all that."[104] "It seems obvious," MacCormick argues, that today no state in western Europe is, in a classical sense, sovereign: "None is in a position such that all the power exercised internally in it, whether politically or legally, derives from purely internal sources."[105] But to say that no state is sovereign is not to say that there must therefore be a sovereign super-state (such as the European Union): "We must not envisage sovereignty as the object of some kind of zero sum game, such that the moment X loses it Y necessarily has it. Let us think of it rather more as of virginity, which can in at least some circumstances be lost to the general satisfaction without anybody else gaining it."[106] The challenge is to imagine a world in which "our normative existence and our practical life" exist in various institutional systems, "each of which has validity or operation in relation to some range of concerns, none of which is absolute over all the others, and all of which, for most purposes, can operate without serious mutual conflict in areas of overlap."[107]

Consideration of the status of Puerto Rico brings these issues stateside. If, as MacCormick argues, "from a jurisprudential point of view, there is no compulsion to regard 'sovereignty,' or even hierarchical relationship of superordination and subordination, as necessary to our understanding of legal order,"[108] the question is whether we can think ourselves into notions of sovereignty that permit overlapping and flexible arrangements attuned to the complex demands of enhanced autonomy within a broader regulative system of generally applicable constitutional and human rights norms. With "enhanced" commonwealth, Congress may lose a bit of its sovereignty (though certainly less than it loses whenever it admits a state to the Union), but Puerto Rico does not thereby become "sovereign" over the United States. Federal law would still be supreme over Puerto Rican law, and the U.S. Constitution would remain supreme over both. The only significant change in sovereign relations would be that amendment of the compact establishing commonwealth would require the consent of both parties.

MacCormick acknowledges that successful practical application of his understanding of sovereignty would "depend on a high degree of relatively willing co-operation and a relatively low degree of coercion in its direct and naked forms."[109] These background conditions appear satisfied in the case of Puerto Rico. There are strong economic links between the island and the mainland (approximately 40 percent of Puerto Ricans live in the states), and travel between the states and the commonwealth is unfettered. Enhanced commonwealth, should it come to pass, would be established with the consent of both Congress and the people of Puerto Rico and would operate within a larger legal culture of shared constitutional values.

A new understanding of sovereignty—as overlapping rather than hierarchical, as diminished but not necessarily depreciated—may appear to be precisely the wrong move in a world currently being torn apart by violent assertions of self-determination and nationalism. Yet it is rarely recognized that it is largely the older understanding of sovereignty (and not more "postmodern" conceptions) that are contributing to instability and bloodshed. "Nations" are demanding "states"; "states" are fighting for more territory over which to exercise "sovereignty." It may in fact be arrangements that finesse the issue of sovereignty that present the best chance for peace (the political settlement in Northern Ireland and the impossibly complex political arrangements in Bosnia being only recent examples). If both the Congress and the people of Puerto Rico seek to establish a new relationship that recognizes space within the American constitutional system for "autonomous" entities, it ill behooves either the executive branch or the judiciary to set such efforts aside in the name of nineteenth-century conceptions of sovereignty.

"'Colonialism,'" writes federal district judge José Cabranes, "is a harsh word to American ears."[110] It is also a word that seems anachronistic. With the end of empire in Africa several decades ago and in the Soviet Union more recently, claims of self-determination more frequently involve dissolution of multinational states than the liberation of a homeland from a distant and alien power. Yet, according to Cabranes, "no word other than 'colonialism' adequately describes the relationship between a powerful metropolitan state and an impoverished overseas dependency disenfranchised from the formal lawmaking processes that shape its people's daily lives."[111]

Decolonization is a political and an economic process. It is also symbolic. Supporters of each of the various status options, though they define it differently, all seek a more perfect realization of *dignidad* for the people of Puerto Rico.[112] It has been the independence movement that has pushed the "decolonization" claim with the most vigor and conviction.[113] But in the 1998 plebiscite the independence option garnered little support. More than 98 percent of those who voted expressed a preference for some kind of continued association with the United States. The fact of the plebiscite itself weakens the *independentista* claim, to the extent that the vote represents an exercise of the right of self-determination for which the movement stands.[114]

Advocates of statehood will continue to push forward, despite the results of the 1998 plebiscite. Commonwealth proponents scored points in a 1993 referendum debate by arguing that statehood would require abandonment of cultural distinctiveness. Indeed, as part of their campaign, the commonwealthers solicited and broadcast statements of conservative Republican members of Congress suggesting that it would be difficult to obtain congressional approval of statehood if Puerto Rico sought to "come in the Union with two official languages."[115] The statehood forces were quick to challenge these assertions, knowing that maintenance of Spanish is both a practical necessity and a nonnegotiable aspect of cultural self-determination for the people of Puerto Rico.[116] The argument for the equality implicit in statehood may attain majority status in the years ahead. If so, it will force the nation to confront directly deep questions of assimilation and multiculturalism. In these times of divisive and deadly ethnic nationalism, it would be an important statement for the United States to welcome as a full and equal member in the Union a polity that cherishes its cultural and linguistic difference from the mainland majority.

Commonwealth, as always, represents a place between statehood and independence. It promises, as its supporters claimed in the plebiscite debate, "the best of both worlds": maintaining United States–Puerto Rican political and cultural society. The victory of "none of the above" in 1998 was a vote to keep the "enhanced" commonwealth option alive.

As the debate continues, the Constitution has an important role to play. Decolonization requires new understandings of both powers and rights. The *Insular Cases,* tainted by racial and religious intolerance, were bad law at the beginning of the twentieth century; they should not control the twenty-first. Residents of Puerto Rico, if they are to be full members of the American polity, should not be subject to discriminatory federal legislation. Equally important, the political relations between the federal government and the people of Puerto Rico cannot be subject to plenary (read: unilateral) federal control. The relationship must evolve in the manner in which it was initiated in the 1950s—with the mutual consent of both parties. Finally, the Constitution should not be read—out of fear and loathing of new understandings of sovereignty—to prevent promising power-sharing arrangements that provide a space for political and cultural autonomy. Neither Puerto Rican statehood nor enhanced commonwealth puts the nation at risk. (Nor do accommodations in the CNMI that affirm central political and cultural values.) Rather, the Constitution is large enough, and strong enough, to affirm a multinational America that embraces its peoples as its people.

CHAPTER 5

The Erosion of American Indian Sovereignty

Just a few months before the framers of the Constitution gathered in Philadelphia in 1787, Congress adopted the Northwest Ordinance—a statute providing for the organization of territories that would eventually become the states of Illinois, Indiana, Michigan, Ohio, and Wisconsin. The Northwest Ordinance embodied principles that have resonated throughout American history. Chief Justice Taney's opinion in *Dred Scott*[1] holding that Congress was not empowered to prohibit slavery in the territories had to come to grips with the fact that Congress had done precisely that in the ordinance.[2] And current debates in some localities about granting the right to vote to settled immigrants have led to the reexamination of provisions in the ordinance that did not limit the franchise to citizens.[3] Thus, immigrants apparently participated in the conventions that drafted the initial constitutions of states carved out of the Northwest Territory.

A number of Indian nations were located within the geographic boundaries of the Northwest Territory. Some had resided there long before the arrival of European settlers in North America; others had been pushed there in the course of white settlement of the continent. The Northwest Ordinance provided the following:

> The utmost good faith shall always be observed towards the Indians; their land and property shall never be taken from them without their consent; and in their property, rights and liberty, they never shall be invaded or disturbed, unless in just and lawful wars authorized by Con-

> gress; but laws founded in justice and humanity shall from time to time be made, for preventing wrongs being done to them, and for preserving peace and friendship with them.[4]

The history of federal policy toward American Indians is a betrayal of just about every clause of this initial commitment.[5] Whether policies have sought removal or assimilation, tribal self-government or tribal termination, domination and destruction or malign neglect, Indian land has been taken without consent, treaty rights have been disregarded, and tribal sovereignty has been eroded.

We have now entered an era of federal policy that purports to support tribal self-determination and the economic development of the reservations. But these policies are put in place against a far less supportive constitutional backdrop. The plenary power doctrine—seemingly at war with any plausible conception of Indian sovereignty—remains very much the *Grundnorm* of federal Indian law. The Supreme Court has dealt a double blow to American Indian sovereignty. It has refused to adopt meaningful limits on the plenary power doctrine, and it has concomitantly restricted the scope of Indian governmental authority. The Court conceives of the tribes, in essence, as membership organizations—more than private clubs but less than nations—empowered to regulate the conduct of their members and entry onto tribal land, but little else. It has been willing to recognize self-rule without sovereignty.

In this chapter I examine constitutional norms regarding federal, tribal, and state authority over Indian reservation residents and land. I suggest that the Court's crabbed and, to my mind, mistaken conclusions about tribal authority are linked to its concerns about race-based policies and its defense of individual rights in the name of U.S. citizenship. Possible limits on the plenary power doctrine and bases for a new federal-tribe relationship are the topics of the next chapter.

Current Doctrine on Indian Sovereignty

The sovereignty of the tribes preceded the Constitution. As Patrick Macklem has noted, "The legitimacy of Indian government is not based on the mere fact that indigenous people were prior occupants of the continent, but on the fact that they were prior sovereigns."[6] The

Constitution recognized the separateness of tribes in explicit terms in several provisions,[7] and in a set of decisions by Chief Justice John Marshall, the Supreme Court initially gave serious content to the concept of the tribes as "nations."[8] In *Worcester v. Georgia,* Marshall forcefully declared that "[t]he Cherokee nation . . . is a distinct community, occupying its own territory . . . in which the laws of Georgia can have no force."[9] As discussed in earlier chapters, however, by the late 1800s few tribes exercised anything approaching full sovereignty, and Marshall's description of the tribes as "domestic" and "dependent" took on a different sense. In Marshall's usage, this relationship meant that the federal government assumed responsibility for the external affairs of the tribe. Half a century later, it justified complete federal regulation of the tribes.

The twentieth century witnessed a new commitment to Indian "self-determination" in Congress and the executive branch. But modern constitutional law is apparently uneasy with what Felix Cohen identified as "perhaps the most basic principle of all Indian law": the principle "*that those powers which are lawfully vested in an Indian tribe are not, in general, delegated powers granted by express acts of Congress, but rather inherent powers of a limited sovereignty which has never been extinguished.*"[10] The range of descriptions in U.S. constitutional history, then, runs the gamut: tribes are pre- or extraconstitutional, like foreign states; they are limited sovereigns, like states; or their powers are subject to federal extinguishment, like territories. In this section I briefly review the current doctrine regarding federal, tribal, and state sovereignty over reservation activities and residents.

In the 1975 case of *United States v. Mazurie,* the Supreme Court stated that "Indian tribes are unique aggregations possessing attributes of sovereignty over both their members and their territory . . . Cases such as *Worcester* and *Kagama* surely establish the proposition that Indian tribes within 'Indian country' are a good deal more than 'private, voluntary organizations.'" This language may be taken as a strong affirmation of tribal sovereignty, written, no less, by then-Justice Rehnquist.[11] But the pairing of *Worcester* and *Kagama* flashes a warning sign.[12] These cases read as polar opposites: *Worcester* (the Marshall decision) stands for true inherent sovereignty;[13] *Kagama* stands for the plenary power doctrine. In *Worcester,* the Court bars state regulation of the Indian "nations"; in *Kagama,* it describes tribes as "wards of the nation" whose very "weakness and helplessness" make federal regulation a virtual necessity.[14] One can make the cases fit by triangulating: Indians have sovereignty *(Worcester)*, protectable and trumpable by the federal government *(Kagama)* and immune from regulation by the states *(Worcester)*. If one adds a federal trust responsibility with bite,[15] then federal plenary power is a one-way ratchet for the protection of Indian sovereignty. This was the harmonization of doctrine that provided a foundation for the revival of tribal self-determination—Marshall ascendant and *Kagama* domesticated.[16]

But neither the Court nor Congress has played out these principles in this fashion. Despite the language in *Mazurie,* the case law taken as a whole exhibits only the semblance of sovereignty, creating a set of limits more than powers. Tribes are "sovereign" over tribal land and tribe members, in much the same way that a private organization has property rights and can adopt rules governing its members' conduct and access to its property.[17] But tribes face significant limits in regulating nonmembers on reservations, and state regulation frequently penetrates reservation boundaries.

Tribal sovereignty, then, is generally more limited than state sovereignty, which is understood to extend to all residents and over all land within state borders. Further, while Congress has authority to establish and alter reservation boundaries and regulate tribal civil and criminal jurisdiction, state borders and governmental processes are largely immune from direct federal control.[18] But tribes also possess authority not recognized in the states, such as the power to determine membership rules (which deny political participation to non-tribal residents of a reservation) and to regulate access to reservation territory.

Nor are tribes analogous to governments in U.S. territories. Indian sovereignty is to some degree more expansive: it is deemed inherent, while territorial governmental power is a product of congressional delegation.[19] Furthermore, the Constitution does not directly apply to tribal actions; under the *Insular Cases,* however, territorial residents receive the protection of some "fundamental" constitutional rights.[20] But tribal sovereignty is also less comprehensive than the power conferred on territorial governments, which are delegated authority to regulate all persons within their boundaries. And territories are plainly outside the borders of U.S. states. (California may not purport to apply its law in Guam.) Reservations, however, may be subject to regulation by the states in which they are located.

These comparisons among states, tribes, and territories evince the complicated permutations of sovereignty that coexist on U.S. soil. They represent a range of understandings of governmental power, membership, and relations with the federal government. These have been and remain dynamic concepts and relationships. For the tribes, it has largely been a story of declension.

Land and Regulation

Indian land—"Indian country," as it is known in American folklore and federal law[21]—is at the core of the controversy over Indian sovereignty. First came the issue of finding a legal basis for European occupation of Indian territory. John Marshall disposed of that problem in his difficult and disturbing opinion in *Johnson v. M'Intosh.*[22] Through discovery and conquest, the European powers attained absolute title to Indian lands, which passed to the United States at the time of independence. Indians maintained a "right of occupancy," but they lost the authority to transfer title of the lands on which they lived. "However this restriction may be opposed to natural right, and to the usages of civilized nations," Marshall wrote, "yet, if it be indispensable to that system under which the country has been settled, and be adapted to the actual condition of the two people, . . . [it] certainly cannot be rejected by Courts of justice."[23] But even the limited right of occupancy (and the principle that Indians are "to be protected, . . . while in peace, in the possession of their lands")[24] fell prey to realpolitik. By 1830, Congress put into law what Andrew Jackson had earlier put into practice: the removal of Indians from the eastern United States.

Indians were forced west—promised land west of the Alleghenies, west of the Mississippi, west of wherever whites wanted to settle next. Indians in the West living on lands valued for their minerals, water, or agriculture were the victims of vicious depredations and forced relocations. For many tribes (as for nationalist groups around the globe), land was not a fungible resource. It frequently represented ancestral homelands, burial grounds, and sacred places.[25]

In the mid-1800s the federal government embarked on its reservation policy. At the time, few whites lived in places "reserved" for the tribes; indeed, treaties establishing the reservations typically provided for "absolute and undisturbed use and occupation" and that "no persons except those herein so authorized . . . shall ever be permitted to pass over, settle upon, or reside in" reservation territory.[26] In this way, tribes were self-governing nations, ruling over land and the tribal members who constituted the citizenry of the nation.[27] The boundaries, however, were neither impermeable nor permanent. Whites' encroachment on reservation land and war against the tribes led to new treaties, less land, and defeat for most of the tribes. By the late 1880s, reservation life was frequently bleak, and Indian government was impoverished. This state of affairs undergirds the Supreme Court's decision in *Kagama,* basing plenary federal power on the tribes' "weakness and helplessness."[28]

The Indian allotment acts—most prominently the General Allotment Act of 1887[29]—broke open the reservations to white settlement. The acts permitted Indians eventual fee title to plots of land, which could then be alienated to whites. More significantly, huge portions of territory were deemed "surplus" land and made available to white purchasers. The result was a dramatic decline in reservation territory and an increase in the number of non-Indians living within reservation boundaries. Reservations today are thus a combination of tribal land (held in trust by the federal government), land owned privately by Indians and non-Indians (known as "fee land"),[30] state land, and federal land.[31]

By introducing significant non-Indian settlement within reservation boundaries, the allotment acts have been a primary source of the current conundrums regarding sovereignty. Tribes, relying on a commonsense notion of sovereignty, claim authority to regulate all reservation residents. But states generally recognize tribal authority only over tribe members or tribal land; they thus assert regulatory authority over non-Indians living on privately owned land located in Indian country. Such is the "legacy of allotment."[32] Although the policies of ending the reservations and assimilating Native Americans were officially abandoned during the New Deal, allotment nonetheless casts a long shadow over current discussions of sovereignty because of its creation of "checkerboard" settlement patterns on many remaining reservations.[33]

The Supreme Court has considered a remarkable number and variety of cases concerning the conflicts among federal, state, and Indian laws. At the risk of significant oversimplification, one can distill several general guidelines from the Court's decisions: tribal authority is strongest when regulations pertain to tribe members on reservations (including determinations of tribal membership) and to non–tribe members on tribal land;[34] tribal regulation of non–tribe members on privately owned land is far less likely to be sustained. States have little general regulatory power over reservations (unless granted by federal statute), but may regulate non-Indians. The federal government retains plenary power to distribute power among itself, the tribes, and the states as it deems appropriate.

Tribal Regulation of Members and Congressional Plenary Power

The Supreme Court recognizes that Indian tribes "retain their inherent power" to punish tribal offenders, determine tribal membership, regulate domestic relations among members, and prescribe rules of inheritance for members.[35] Tribal courts have exclusive jurisdiction over reservation-based civil suits in which both parties are tribe members. Federal treaties and statutes have gone further, recognizing tribal court jurisdiction in cases brought by a non-Indian against a tribe member for on-reservation activities[36] and divesting state courts of jurisdiction in child custody proceedings involving an Indian child born to reservation parents.[37] Tribes are also recognized to possess sovereign immunity.[38] In these respects, Felix Cohen's 1942 restatement of Indian law remains true:

> Indian self-government . . . includes the power of an Indian tribe to adopt and operate under a form of government of the Indians' choosing, to define conditions of tribal membership, to regulate domestic relations of members, to prescribe rules of inheritance, to levy taxes, to regulate property within the jurisdiction of the tribe, to control the conduct of members by municipal legislation, and to administer justice.[39]

But what the pro-sovereignty worship of Cohen sometimes ignores is Cohen's explicit recognition of congressional power to trump exercises of sovereignty even as to "internal" tribal matters. That is, while Cohen's work carves in granite the concept that Indian sovereignty is inherent—that it is not based on a delegation from Congress—it does not provide a shield against the exercise of federal power over tribes. At most, his analysis demands a kind of clear statement rule—that congressional regulation of internal matters be "express"[40]—and suggests constitutional limits on congressional power.[41] Thus, there are no cases that construct for the tribes the kind of limits on federal power that the Court has recognized on behalf of the states throughout American constitutional history.[42]

This bitter-with-the-sweet approach is regularly reflected in the cases, even those that are seen as core to the modern sovereignty position. A good example is *United States v. Wheeler*,[43] which held that federal criminal prosecution of a tribe member following prosecution in a tribal court did not violate the Fifth Amendment's double jeopardy clause. The Court rejected the defendant's claim that tribes were merely instrumentalities of the federal government: "[T]he power to punish offenses against tribal law committed by Tribe members, which was part of the Navajos' primeval sovereignty, has never been taken away from them, either explicitly or implicitly, and is attributable in no way to any delegation to them of federal authority."[44] *Wheeler* is frequently cited as an inherent sovereignty landmark.[45] But the Court makes clear that it is the plenary power doctrine—not inherent sovereignty—that is the foundational principle. After reaffirming the existence of inherent tribal sovereignty, the Court immediately states:

> The sovereignty that the Indian tribes retain is of a unique and limited character. It exists only at the *sufferance* of Congress and is subject *to complete defeasance* . . . In sum, Indian tribes still possess those aspects of sovereignty not withdrawn by treaty or statute, or by implication as a necessary result of their dependent status.[46]

Under this power, Congress has made significant inroads into tribal jurisdiction even in cases involving tribal members or tribal land. Under laws dating from the nineteenth century and still on the books, the federal government must consent to dispositions of tribal land and to contracts entered into by the tribe.[47] Prosecution of crimes is significantly restricted: the Major Crimes Act, enacted in 1885,[48] gives federal courts jurisdiction over serious criminal offenses committed by Indians on reservations; and the Indian Civil Rights Act of 1968 prohibits tribal courts from imposing punishments greater than one year's imprisonment or a $5,000 fine.[49] So, too, Congress is recognized to have virtually unrestricted authority to alter the boundaries of reservations,[50] terminate the recognition of tribes,[51] limit the scope of tribal powers,[52] and impose general federal mandates on the activities of tribal governments.[53]

Federal statutes are frequently enacted to restrict state jurisdiction over the reservations.[54] But the federal government has also used its plenary power to authorize state regulation. For example, states are authorized to conduct health inspections on reservations, to enforce state waste disposal legislation, and to tax some on-reservation Indian activities.[55] Perhaps most significant is the statute known as Public Law 280, adopted in 1953 at the height of the termination program. The statute extended, *without tribal consent,* state criminal and civil jurisdiction over reservations in California, Nebraska, Wisconsin, and (with some exceptions) Minnesota and Oregon.[56] The remaining states were given the option of assuming similar jurisdiction over reservations.[57]

Tribal Regulation of Non-Indians and Non-Indian Land on Reservations

It is a supposed given in Indian law that tribes have the authority to regulate egress and residence on reservation land.[58] But most non-Indians living on reservations are there by dint of the allotment policies and not through the exercise of, as it were, Indian immigration regulations. Whites may live or conduct businesses on scattered privately owned plots, or they may constitute the bulk of the population in small towns and cities within reservation boundaries. The Court has struggled with issues regarding the tribes' power to regulate non–tribal members (Indian and non-Indian) on reservation land.

There is language in some of the cases that might suggest a *geographically based* concept of sovereignty.[59] Thus, in *Mazurie* the Court states that tribes have sovereignty over "their members and their territory." In *Williams v. Lee,*[60] a case finding exclusive tribal court jurisdiction in a suit brought by a general store owner against tribe members who had bought goods on credit, the Court noted that the plaintiff "was on the Reservation and the transaction with an Indian took place there. The cases in this court have consistently guarded the authority of Indian governments over their reservations."[61] And in *Merrion v. Jicarilla Apache Tribe,*[62] the Court upheld as "an essential attribute of Indian sovereignty" the power of the tribe to impose a severance tax on a non-Indian corporation engaged in mining on the reservation.[63] But subsequent cases have made clear that *membership,* not geography, is a more important determinant of the extent of Indian power. The cases, in effect, draw a distinction between self-rule and sovereignty.

"The general proposition" announced by the Court in the 1981 case *Montana v. United States* is that "the inherent sovereign powers of an Indian tribe do not extend to the activities of nonmembers of the tribe."[64] This rule is subject to some qualification. As the Court noted in *Montana,* tribes—like any landowner—can regulate hunting and fishing by nonmembers on tribal or trust land.[65] Furthermore, in an attempt to hold harmless prior cases that had recognized tribal civil authority over nonmember activities, the Court established two categories of exceptions: tribes could regulate (1) activities of nonmembers "who enter consensual relationships with the tribe or its members, through commercial dealings, contracts, leases, or other arrangements" and (2) the conduct of non-Indians on privately owned lands "when that conduct threatens or has some direct effect on the political integrity, the economic security, or the health or welfare of the tribe."[66]

The second exception potentially can be quite broad. One can imagine an analogy to the Court's interpretations of the federal commerce power permitting congressional regulation of intrastate activities that affect interstate commerce. On this view, many activities conducted on non-Indian land within the reservation—hunting and fishing, water use, development—might well have a "direct effect" on the welfare of the tribe. This would seem particularly so if, as in commerce clause analysis, one examines the cumulative impact of activities carried out across private land.

But the current Court has shown no inclination to read the *Montana* exception broadly in favor of Indian regulation of nonmembers.[67] Consider the facts of a 1997 case, *Strate v. A-1 Contractors.*[68] Two vehicles collided on a state highway that traversed the Fort Berthold Indian Reservation in North Dakota. Neither driver was a member of the tribe. When one driver brought suit in the reservation tribal court, the defendant went to federal court, seeking a declaration that the tribal court had no jurisdiction over the action. A federal court of appeals concluded that the tribal court lacked jurisdiction and the Supreme Court affirmed. Justice Ginsburg, writing for the Court, found no express congressional authorization for tribal court jurisdiction; she thus analyzed the issue under the *Montana* exception. In answer to the straightforward argument that safety on reservation roads has a direct effect on tribal welfare, Justice Ginsburg stated that "if *Montana*'s second exception requires no more, the exception would severely shrink the rule."[69] Then in cursory fashion she concluded that "[n]either regulatory nor adjudicatory authority over the state highway accident at issue is needed to preserve 'the right of reservation Indians to make their own laws and be ruled by them.'"[70] The analysis looks to the impact of the non-Indian land activity on tribal *self-rule,* not to the general power of the tribe to regulate activities taking place on the reservation. A limited reading of the *Montana* exception means that tribes will generally have to look to federal delegation in order to sustain tribal regulation of nonmember conduct on reservations. This requirement of a positive grant of authority is more than a restriction on Indian sovereignty; it is a denial of sovereignty. (To see the difference, consider a plausible alternative default rule: that tribes have regulatory power unless denied it by federal statute.) *Strate*'s reading of *Montana,* in short, moves the tribes in the direction of the federal territories—exercising delegated, not inherent, power.[71]

The trend toward a restricted reading of tribal civil jurisdiction over nonmembers continued in *Nevada v. Hicks.*[72] Decided in 2001, the case considered the jurisdiction of tribal courts to entertain an action against a state game warden who had searched the house of a tribal member on the Fallon Palute-Shoshone Reservation for evidence of an off-reservation crime. The state official had obtained a search warrant from the tribal court, but Floyd Hicks alleged that the search of his home had exceeded the bounds of the warrant and that the officers had damaged his personal property. Hicks brought suit in the tribal court, asserting common law and civil rights violations.

Writing for the Court, Justice Scalia began with the proposition—established in the *Strate* case—that tribal court jurisdiction could run only so far as tribal regulatory authority. In the case at hand the tribe could have no civil jurisdiction because "tribal authority to regulate state officers in executing process related to the violation, off reservation, of state laws is not essential to tribal self-government or internal relations."[73] This categorical application of the *Montana* exception in effect creates immunity from tribal jurisdiction for state officials enforcing state law on reservations.[74]

Hicks, supported by the U.S. Department of Justice, had argued that the tribal court had jurisdiction over the state officers since Hicks's home was on tribe-owned land on the reservation. The centrality of land-ownership was surely a legitimate inference from the prior cases. But the Court held that "ownership status of land . . . is only one factor to consider in determining whether regulation of the activities of non-members" brings the non-member within the *Montana* exception—and in this case, the tribal ownership of the land was outweighed by the importance of state law enforcement.[75] This downplaying of the importance of land-ownership, of course, is fully consistent with the Court's focus on membership. The basic rule of *Montana* holds that the inherent sovereign powers of an Indian tribe do not extend to the activities of nonmembers of the tribe.[76]

Hicks, nominally a case about tribal court authority over nonmembers, ends up being more about state jurisdiction over tribal members. Tribal court jurisdiction is rejected because state officers must have unfettered authority to pursue state law violators, lest reservations become "an asylum for fugitives from justice."[77] Moreover, permitting suits against state officers would produce costly, vexatious litigation, subjecting them—according to Justice Souter's concurring opinion—to trials in courts different from state and federal courts "in their structure, in the substantive law they apply, and in the independence of their judges."[78]

The *Montana* line of cases concern civil authority of the tribes over nonmembers. The Court has adopted a similar membership-based approach to the criminal jurisdiction of the tribes. The power of a polity to punish violations of its lawful edicts might be viewed as a core attribute of sovereignty. Yet prevailing constitutional norms significantly limit tribal criminal jurisdiction, and federal statutes have further limited it. Earlier on, the Court held that states, not tribes, had authority to prosecute a non-Indian charged with the murder of a non-Indian on a reservation.[79] It was not until 1978, however, in *Oliphant v. Suquamish Indian Tribe,*[80] that the Court ruled on tribal power to try a non-Indian who commits a crime against a tribal member. Tribal authorities had arrested Oliphant, a non-Indian, for assaulting a tribal officer and resisting arrest. Another non-Indian had been arrested after a high-speed chase over reservation highways ended when his car collided with a tribal police vehicle. One might suppose that, to borrow the later language from the *Montana* exception, these cases had a direct effect on the health and welfare of the tribe.

But that was not the test applied by the Court in *Oliphant.* Writing for the Court, then-Justice Rehnquist used language that included no exceptions: "Indians do not have criminal jurisdiction over non-Indians absent affirmative delegation of such power by Congress."[81] Rehnquist's opinion focuses primarily on the overriding sovereignty of the United States that placed "inherent limitations on tribal powers." The reasoning of the opinion comes down to the following none-too-clear four sentences:

> Protection of territory within its external political boundaries is, of course, as central to the sovereign interests of the United States as it is to any other sovereign nation. But from the formation of the Union and the adoption of the Bill of Rights, the United States has manifested an equally great solicitude that its citizens be protected by the United States from unwarranted intrusions on their personal liberty. The power of the United States to try and criminally punish is an important manifestation of the power to restrict personal liberty. By submitting to the overriding sovereignty of the Untied States, Indian tribes therefore necessarily give up their power to try non-Indian citizens of the United States except in a manner acceptable to Congress.[82]

This is all a muddle. It is far from obvious why, by "submitting to the overriding sovereignty of the federal government" (a phrase hardly friendly to the idea of inherent tribal sovereignty), tribes *necessarily* gave up power to try non-Indians who commit crimes against tribal members on the reservation. No one doubted that Congress could remove Indian jurisdiction in such cases, but the idea of "overriding sovereignty" does not entail a default rule of "everything that is not granted is denied." States, too, submitted to the overriding sovereignty of the United States by signing on to a Constitution that included a supremacy clause, but they are not understood to have surrendered their authority to try any person (except, perhaps, a foreign diplomat) who commits a crime within their boundaries.

The Court saw *Oliphant* as the mirror image of *Ex Parte Crow Dog,*[83] an 1883 case that denied federal jurisdiction over crimes committed by Indians against Indians. In *Crow Dog,* the Court commented that for a federal court to try Indian defendants would have been to subject them to trial "not by their peers, nor by the customs of their people . . . [but by a] different race, according to the law of a social state of which they have an imperfect conception."[84] This unflattering nod toward Indian sovereignty returns in *Oliphant,* where Rehnquist argues that "these considerations . . . speak equally strongly against the validity of respondents' contention that Indian tribes, although fully subordinated to the sovereignty of the United States, retain the power to try non-Indians according their own customs and procedures."[85] Thus, what seems to be doing the work in Rehnquist's opinion are two related factors: concern over tribal criminal process and the right of U.S. citizens not to be prosecuted in what the Court apparently views as alien courts.[86]

Twelve years later the Court considered an issue left open in *Oliphant:* whether tribes had power to prosecute non-tribal Indians who committed crimes against tribe members. In *Duro v. Reina,*[87] the Court answered no. The case involved the shooting death of a fourteen-year-old boy on the Salt River Indian Reservation, home of the Pima-Maricopa Indians. The defendant, Albert Duro, was a resident of the reservation but a member of the Torres-Martinez band of Cahuilla Mission Indians. (The victim was a member of a third tribe.) The Court rejected the jurisdiction of the Pima-Maricopa Indian Community Court to try Duro. Justice Kennedy, writing for the majority, held that "[i]n the area of criminal enforcement . . . , tribal power does not extend beyond internal relations among members."[88]

Duro displays none of Rehnquist's repeated invocation in *Oliphant* of the subordinated status of the tribes. What is central in *Duro,* though, is the significance of nonmembership and the rights of U.S. citizens: "Petitioner is not a member of the Pima-Maricopa Tribe, and is not now eligible to become one," Kennedy wrote.[89] "Neither he nor other members of his Tribe may vote, hold office, or serve on a jury under Pima-Maricopa authority."[90] From this perspective, Duro's "Indianness" was irrelevant; as a nonmember, he stood in the same shoes as the non-Indians in *Oliphant.*

In the American legal system, criminal jurisdiction usually turns on geography, not membership. As the dissent in *Duro* noted, states have authority to prosecute nonresidents who commit crimes within their jurisdictions, and the federal government can prosecute resident aliens.[91] For the majority, tribal jurisdiction is grounded in different considerations: "Retained criminal jurisdiction over members is accepted by our precedents and justified by the voluntary character of tribal membership and the concomitant right of participation in a tribal government, the authority of which rests on consent."[92]

It is not clear how much work the concept of "consent" is supposed to do here—or can do. Philip Frickey has pointed out that Duro was a resident of the reservation and therefore might well have been deemed to consent to the application of the jurisdiction's laws.[93] Perhaps more important is a second theme that weaves through the majority opinion: Duro's status as a United States citizen. As a citizen, the Court states, Duro is protected against "unwarranted intrusions on [his] personal liberty."[94] *Oliphant* had concluded that criminal prosecution is so serious an intrusion that the tribes "necessarily surrendered" to the United States their power to try non-Indians. The Court was thus hesitant "to adopt a view of tribal sovereignty that would single out another group of citizens, nonmember Indians, for trial by political bodies that do not include them."[95] Thus, the category of citizenship did double work: it linked Duro with the non-Indian defendants in *Oliphant,* and it made problematic the assertion of authority by a club that the citizen cannot join. Such associations may have authority to deal with the wrongdoing of their own members, but that authority comes from the "consent of its members."[96]

Duro reads very differently from *Oliphant.* The Court's characterization of tribal courts is not that they are primitive or foreign but that they are private and exclusionary. In *Oliphant,* the Court said in effect that Americans cannot be prosecuted in the courts of third world countries. In *Duro,* it said that Americans cannot be prosecuted by the Rotary Club.[97]

State Regulation of On-Reservation Activities

States may seek to extend a variety of policies over reservation territory. Environmental and land use rules, hunting and fishing regulations, and many other policies may, in the state's view, require uniform application within state boundaries.[98] Not surprisingly, states would like to subject reservation businesses and residents to taxation—both to raise revenue and to ensure that reservation activities (such as cigarette and gasoline sales and gaming) do not have a competitive advantage over off-reservation businesses that pay state taxes.[99] And states may seek to prevent activities—such as high-stakes gambling—that are thought to impose negative externalities on neighboring state territory.[100]

Under current doctrine, membership concepts dominate. States are generally understood to have the authority to regulate (and tax) the activities of non-Indians on reservations; activities of the tribe and tribal members are generally exempt from state regulation. The categories cannot be hard-and-fast. Surely some regulation of non-Indians may have significant impacts on core tribal interests, and some regulation of Indians may serve compelling state goals and only modestly burden the tribes. Thus, the Court has recognized some flexibility at the margins.[101] What has been most important in the drawing of these boundaries has been federal policy in the area under scrutiny. The Court has recognized Congress's complete authority to distribute tribal and state regulatory authority as it sees fit.

This analysis, of course, differs significantly from principles of federalism and comity that underlie relationships among the states and between states and the federal government. A citizen of Montana who ventures to Wyoming is fully subject to Wyoming civil and criminal jurisdiction, and federal power cannot generally provide Montanans immunity from Wyoming courts for a crime committed in Cheyenne (even if the victim of the crime is also an out-of-state resident). Nor can New Yorkers owning land in Vermont assert that they are subject to New York and not Vermont zoning laws. American constitutional law does not treat these as difficult questions. The physical integrity of the states is constitutionally secured,[102] and their geographical jurisdiction is assumed. The Constitution protects against discrimination against out-of-staters[103] but does not condemn state regulation that applies equally within the state to state citizens and citizens from other states. While Congress is given authority to ensure that the court judgments of one state are respected in another state[104] (and is even recognized to have the power to authorize state discrimination against out-of-state commercial interests), it does not have any obvious authority to permit state X to regulate ordinary civil and criminal matters in state Y or to deny state Y authority to apply its law to citizens of state X present in state Y.

We are today a long way from John Marshall's conceptualization of the tribes as extraterritorial to the states in which they were located. By 1973 the Court had developed a decidedly different understanding. In *McClanahan v. Arizona State Tax Commission,*[105] the Court reached a pro–tribal sovereignty result, invalidating a state income tax levied on income earned on reservations by tribe members. But Justice Thurgood Marshall, as strong an advocate for tribal sovereignty as the modern Court has seen, noted that

> the trend has been away from the idea of inherent Indian sovereignty as a bar to state jurisdiction and toward reliance on federal pre-emption . . . The modern cases thus tend to avoid reliance on platonic notions of Indian sovereignty and to look instead to the applicable treaties and statutes which define the limits of state power.[106]

Tribal sovereignty was relevant, then, "not because it provides a definitive resolution of the issues in [a] suit, but because it provides a backdrop against which the applicable treaties and statutes must be read."[107]

Indian sovereignty appeared to drop another notch in *California v. Cabazon Band of Mission Indians,* which involved the state's attempt to regulate reservation high-stakes bingo games.[108] The Court stated that "[o]ur cases . . . have not established an inflexible *per se* rule precluding state jurisdiction over tribes and tribal members in the absence of express congressional consent."[109] Rather, the Court identified the controlling test as "whether state authority is pre-empted by the operation of federal law" and held that preemption would be found where state jurisdiction "interferes or is incompatible with federal and tribal interests reflected in federal law, unless the state interests at stake are sufficient to justify the assertion of state authority."[110] Ultimately the Court ruled for the tribe, striking down the state regulation. Despite the Court's assertion that "the inquiry is to proceed in light of traditional notions of Indian sovereignty," it is clear that what carried the weight was a federal policy of promoting tribal gambling enterprises as important to economic development and tribal self-determination. (The Court cursorily noted that "[t]he Tribes' interests obviously parallel the federal interests.") This is a preemption test *cum* balancing test, albeit one that places a finger on the scale on behalf of federal policy in support of the tribes. Thus, Indian sovereignty is reduced to an interest, defeasible by federal policy and possibly outweighed by important state interests.[111]

There is as yet no indication that the Court would adopt this sort of balancing test in areas at the core of tribal sovereignty. For example, there is no reason to believe that the Court would overrule its per se rule against state taxation of tribes and tribal members (absent congressional authorization).[112] And a majority of the Court has not accepted Justice Stevens's invitation to adopt a rule that state regulation of reservation activities is permissible unless and until Congress indicates otherwise.[113] This increasing reliance on preemption analysis underscores the central role of congressional "plenary power."

The cases also show the important conceptual shift from *Worcester*'s geographical approach to one based primarily on membership. This is apparent in the *Strate* decision discussed earlier. There, the Court held that a tribal court had no jurisdiction in a case involving a car accident between non-Indians on a state road that ran through the reservation. In the earlier case of *Williams v. Lee,*[114] the Court had found tribal jurisdiction in a suit brought by a non-Indian merchant against an Indian purchaser to whom he had extended credit on the reservation. Noting that it was "immaterial" that the merchant was not an Indian, the Court had stated that "exercise of state jurisdiction . . . would undermine the authority of the tribal courts over Reservation affairs and hence would infringe on the right of the Indians to govern themselves."[115] *Williams* is given short shrift in *Strate,* as Justice Ginsburg's opinion for a unanimous Court repeatedly stresses that the defendant in the suit was not a member of the tribe.[116] *Strate* does not explicitly adopt a full-scale membership test. For example, Justice Ginsburg notes that the Court's decision expresses "no view on the governing law or proper forum when an accident occurs on a tribal road within a reservation."[117] The opinion also states that "tribes retain considerable control over nonmember conduct on tribal land." (The modifier "considerable" appears carefully chosen and is not a good sign for advocates of tribal sovereignty.)[118] But surely the "infringement" test of *Williams*—which focused on the authority of the tribes "over Reservation affairs"—has been significantly weakened.

Justice Scalia's majority opinion in *Nevada v. Hicks* explicitly marks the decline and fall of *Worcester.* "State sovereignty," Scalia writes, "does not end at a reservation's border. Though tribes are often referred to as 'sovereign entities,' it was 'long ago' that 'the Court departed from

Chief Justice Marshall's view that "the laws of [a State] can have no force" within reservation boundaries.'"[119] In a telling footnote, he adds that "[o]ur holding in *Worcester* must be considered in light of the fact" that in that case there was a federal treaty guaranteeing that the Cherokee nation would not be subject to state jurisdiction.[120]

The doctrine I have described does not form a coherent whole. It is the product of more than two centuries of case law, over which time relations among the federal government, the states, and the tribes have changed dramatically. There is little doubt that cases now viewed as foundational might well be decided differently if they came before the Court for the first time today. But constitutional law is frequently more sediment than theory,[121] and Indian law is no exception.

If there is an organizing principle that dominates the legal landscape today, it is the concept of membership.[122] Criminal law principles are closely tied to membership: tribes have inherent authority to prosecute tribal members but may not prosecute non-Indians or Indians who are members of a different tribe (absent congressional authorization to do so). Tribes have somewhat more civil jurisdiction over nonmembers on reservation land but generally may not regulate non-Indians on privately owned land. Increasingly, tribal courts are denied jurisdiction over suits arising on reservations in which the parties are non-Indians. But membership is not the whole story. Tribes will continue to be able to tax non-Indians on reservations and to regulate the activities of nonmembers on tribal land—including the power to exclude nonmembers altogether. One can attempt to explain the exercise of these powers in terms of the *consent* of the regulated; that is, by carrying out activities on the reservations, non-Indians agree to pay taxes and conduct themselves according to tribal law.[123] That concept, however, seems to prove too much: why have non-Indian residents of reservations not consented to tribal criminal jurisdiction?[124]

Perhaps the metaphor of tribes as private associations comes closer to the mark: tribes can determine their membership rules and exclude nonmembers from association property but cannot generally regulate the affairs of nonmembers.[125] But, as is typical with Indian matters, no analogy is perfect: tribes are plainly more than private associations to the extent that they exercise sovereign power to enact laws, punish lawbreaking members, determine property rights, and decide domestic relations law cases.

The Court may view its work as fully consistent with the goal of tribal self-rule—a concept that turns on notions of membership and provides a basis for the protection of tribal property rights. I have tried, however, to show that self-rule is not the same as territorial sovereignty. To a degree unimaginable for states, tribal governments lack control over much land and many activities within reservation borders. Furthermore, the Court has increasingly come to rely on federal Indian policy in distributing powers among the tribes and the states. This reliance on federal law—and the concomitant downplaying of tribal sovereignty—in effect reverses Felix Cohen's "first principle" of Indian law that tribal powers are inherent, not delegated.

Why Membership?

John Marshall's opinion in *Worcester* notes time and again that the Indian "nations" had always been considered "distinct, independent, political communities,"[126] and that the relationship of the United States to the Indian tribe was thus established by treaty. "The words 'treaty' and 'nation,'" Marshall wrote, "are words of our own language, selected in our diplomatic and legislative proceedings, by ourselves, having each a definite and well-understood meaning. We have applied them to Indians, as we have applied them to the other nations of the earth; they are applied to all in the same sense."[127] And just as states had no jurisdiction in foreign nations, so too "[t]he treaties and laws of the United States contemplate the Indian territory as completely separated from that of the states."[128] As Milner Ball has noted, John Marshall's view was that tribal land was "extraterritorial" to the states.[129]

This view is obviously at odds with the Rehnquist Court's membership perspective, which limits tribes to self-rule and tolerates state jurisdiction on reservations. How far the Court has come is clear in how it phrases the issue of state regulation in the modern cases: "[W]e must 'reconcile the plenary power of the States over residents within their borders with the semi-autonomous status of Indians living on tribal reservations.'"[130]

History, in part, accounts for this shift. By 1871, when Congress ended treaty-making with the tribes, Justice McLean's dictum in *Worcester*—that state regulation might be proper if the tribe "shall become so degraded and reduced in numbers, as to lose the power of self-government"[131]—appeared closer to the truth than Marshall's depiction of the tribes as "distinct political communities, having territorial boundaries, within which their authority is exclusive."[132] But allotment and termination policies have been roundly repudiated; presidents from Nixon to Clinton (including Ronald Reagan) have proclaimed policies of Indian "self-determination." Why, then, hasn't the Court returned to the Marshallian view—as has been frequently urged by scholars and advocates?[133]

The answer, I believe, is grounded on three concerns of the Court. The first I label the "democratic deficit." The second is based on the ethno-racial basis of tribal membership. The third turns on the importance the Court attaches to citizenship in an increasingly multicultural United States. As I hope to make clear, these concerns are interrelated and mutually supporting.

The term "democratic deficit" is borrowed from discussions of the political theory of the European Union (EU), where it serves as a critique of structural arrangements that delegate significant power to largely unaccountable EU administrators.[134] My meaning here is closer to "no taxation without representation." Simply put, large number of non-Indians live within reservation boundaries, yet they are not eligible for tribe membership and cannot vote in tribal elections, run for tribal office, or serve on tribal juries.[135]

The Court made this concern explicit in *Duro v. Reina*,[136] noting that Duro "is not now eligible to become" a member of the Pima-Maricopa tribe and that "[n]either he nor other members of his Tribe may vote, hold office, or serve on a jury under Pima-Maricopa authority."[137] These considerations led the Court to "hesitate to adopt a view of tribal sovereignty" that would permit the trial of nonmembers by "political bodies that do not include them."[138]

Such considerations cannot, by themselves, secure the democratic deficit claim. "Nonmembership" alone is not usually considered a bar to the exercise of sovereign power. As the dissent in *Duro* notes, no one doubts that states have jurisdiction over crimes committed within their boundaries, whatever the citizenship or residence of the alleged perpetrator. Generally, presence on the sovereign's territory—and not the right to vote—is deemed to constitute adequate consent to the exercise of civil and criminal jurisdiction.[139] A resident of Florida (or a citizen of France) who commits a crime in Colorado is subject to prosecution in Colorado courts.[140] Indeed, without recognition of this principle, Congress's "plenary power" over immigrants in the United States could not exist.

For the Court, however, it is not the mere presence of nonvoting residents that is the problem. It is that they cannot readily become voting members. Unlike in states, where new residents are immediately deemed citizens eligible to vote in state elections,[141] residency on a reservation is not a basis for tribal membership (nor do tribes generally initiate "naturalization" proceedings by which long-term residents can attain tribal status). The idea of a class of residents permanently excluded from political participation is clearly of concern to the Court.[142] This concern is magnified by demands for greater tribal self-determination. So long as tribes are largely regulating their members' conduct, the Court may well give them a wide berth.[143] But as self-determination begins to look like territorial sovereignty, policies that exclude some territorial residents from political power take on a different cast.[144]

For those who view the tribes as "nations," such membership rules are hardly extraordinary. They are the kinds of immigration and citizenship regulations that all sovereign nations are recognized as empowered to adopt. The Court's answer cannot be that tribes are more analogous to state and local governments (which cannot limit membership) than nations; that would admit a geographical sovereignty that the Court has denied tribes. Rather, in its reconceptualization, tribes are not political communities generally sovereign over their territory; they are voluntary organizations whose power over members rests on consent.[145] From this perspective, the recognized authority of tribes to construct membership rules—and to keep nonmembers from participating in decision making—is wholly ordinary; it is how PTAs, unions, religious orders, philately clubs, and the American Bar Association operate. Criminal prosecution of a nonmember would take an association beyond its legitimate power of regulating association members.

There is an additional element to the democratic deficit concern: minority rule. Many reservations include significant numbers of non-Indian residents.[146] At times, the numbers can be startling. For example, in *Oliphant* the Court noted that only fifty members of the Suquamish tribe lived on the reservation and that nontribal residents outnumbered tribal residents by 60 to 1.[147] From the tribe's perspective, this is insult added to injury: the repudiated federal policies of allotment and termination that dramatically reduced reservation size and increased non-Indian populations now supply the basis for concerns about tribal sovereignty. But the Court in several cases has made specific mention of Indian and non-Indian population figures,[148] suggesting that a preference for majoritarianism plays a role in its approach to the issues.

The second major area of concern for the Court is that tribal membership rules are primarily blood-based.[149] Again, from the perspective of nationhood this might not be troubling. Children almost universally acquire the citizenship of their parents at birth. (To be sure, tribes do not follow the principle of *jus soli* inscribed in the Fourteenth Amendment; such a policy would give membership to all persons born on the reservation.) And even some voluntary associations—most notably, religions—have descent-based membership norms. But the ethno-racial basis of tribal membership has no parallel in subnational political communities in the United States. Citizens may take up residence in any state (or territory) and by doing so acquire full membership rights.[150]

The Court has not recently[151] put its objections in these terms. To do so would be to indict much federal Indian law, which still includes provisions that regulate based on the quantum of Indian blood.[152] Indeed, the Court has expressly held that classifications based on tribal membership are "political rather than racial in nature."[153] Furthermore, an objection to Indian sovereignty owing to the tribes' blood-based membership rules would conflict with the Court's conceptualization of the tribes as consent-based. But an underlying concern about descent-based membership is consistent with the strong objections registered by the Court to race-conscious distributions of political power[154] and economic opportunities.[155] On this view, whites on reservations become "discrete and insular" minorities, permanently locked out of political power based on their race.

Unwilling to take on the issue of race head-on, the Court has instead talked culture. Permitting tribal courts to try non-Indians is to subject litigants to an "unfamiliar court"[156] and to trial "not by their peers, nor by the customs of their people."[157] In *Duro,* the Court described the "special nature" of tribal courts:

> While modern tribal courts include many familiar features of the judicial process, they are influenced by the unique customs, languages, and usages of the tribes they serve. Tribal courts are often "subordinate to the political branches of tribal governments," and their legal methods may depend on "unspoken practices and norms." It is significant that the Bill of Rights does not apply to Indian tribal governments. The Indian Civil Rights Act of 1968 provides some statutory guarantees of fair procedure, but these guarantees are not equivalent to their constitutional counterparts.[158]

There are important empirical questions here that the Court does not feel bound to resolve. How, in fact, do tribal courts operate? Is the justice they dispense materially different from state court proceedings? What impact has the Indian Civil Rights Act (ICRA) had on tribal courts? There is, moreover, a deeper unaddressed issue. *Assuming* that tribal courts are influenced by "unique customs, languages, and usages," why do those differences lead the Court to restrict Indian sovereignty? The comparison with the Court's views on state power is instructive. It is commonplace in discussions of American federalism to celebrate—or at least respect—the diversity of state structures and procedures. States are seen as laboratories, as political bodies closer to the people they govern, and as bulwarks against the possible tyranny of the federal government. In recent years, the Court has acted in dramatic fashion to revivify federalism limits on congressional power.[159] In this jurisprudence of devolution, why have not the tribes similarly benefited? The answer, I believe, turns on the fact that states are not identified with any particular racial or ethnic group.[160] Thus, to affirm state power is to affirm governance closer to the people, not governance by a particular group of people. For the Court, Indian sovereignty represents devolution to a racial or ethnic group; it is multiculturalism with political power. As such, it undercuts an individualistic, non–race-based constitutionalism that lies at the heart of much of the current Court's work[161]—a core concept of which, as I have tried to show in Chapter 2, is citizenship. Citizenship provides a nonethnic, nonracial basis for commonality, and it suggests the possession of individual rights and a guarantee of equality before the law.

Duro makes this clear on the face of the opinion. The section of the majority opinion that discusses sovereignty begins: "Whatever might be said of the historical record, we must view it in light of petitioner's status as a citizen of the United States."[162] Being a citizen, Duro is protected against "unwarranted intrusions" on his personal liberty, and criminal trial and punishment is "so serious an intrusion on personal liberty that its exercise over non-Indian citizens was a power necessarily surrendered by the tribes in their submission to the overriding sovereignty of the United States."[163] This is the holding of *Oliphant*. The Court then extends *Oliphant* to deny tribal jurisdiction over an Indian who is not a member of the prosecuting tribe because to recognize jurisdiction would be to "single out another group of citizens, nonmember Indians, for trial by political bodies that do not include them."[164]

There is something to the Court's equal protection–like analysis. As the Court states later in the opinion, "[T]he tribes are not mere fungible groups of homogenous persons."[165] Thus, if *Oliphant* is good law, it is hard to construct a persuasive argument that tribes may not try non-Indians but may try Indians from another tribe.

Under established constitutional norms, however, it is not the common possession of citizenship that makes nonmember Indians and nonmember non-Indians similar. The due process and equal protection clauses speak of "person[s]," and they have repeatedly been held to protect aliens in the United States.[166] (Aliens are also subject to state criminal processes even though they can neither vote nor serve on juries.) Furthermore, as the dissent in *Duro* points out, the Court would surely sustain a federal statute that granted tribal courts jurisdiction over nonmembers who commit reservation crimes.[167] This can hardly be squared with the Court's reasoning that the citizenship of Indians removes them from tribal jurisdiction to which they did not consent.

These weaknesses in the opinion would not have escaped the Justices who signed the majority opinion. Thus, *Duro* should be read as a strong case—one grounded in deep concerns about the ways in which a perceived democratic deficit and political multiculturalism undercut the ideal of equal citizenship.[168]

Indeed, it is sometimes argued that Indians possess "special rights" that make them more equal than other citizens.[169] Critics assert that tribes are permitted to hunt and fish where and when others cannot, to operate businesses exempt from state taxation, and to exclude non-Indians from reservation land.[170] Consider the statement of a resident of Illinois concerned about a lawsuit brought by the Miami Indians laying claim to 2.6 million acres of Illinois under treaties signed in 1795 and 1805: "We're not racists. We're looking for equal rights for all, and creating new separate little Indian nations with their own rights and own sovereignty isn't the equal rights that Lincoln fought for."[171]

The "special rights" claim is also made in terms of political participation. Full territorial sovereignty for the tribes, it has been said, would establish an asymmetry between U.S. citizens who belong to tribes and those who do not. In his dissenting views to the 1977 final report of the American Indian Policy Review Commission, Congressman Lloyd Meeds (who served as vice chairman of the commission) noted the inclusion of tribe members in state political processes but the exclusion of nonmembers from tribal governance:

> Reservation Indians would be citizens of the State but be wholly free of State law and State taxation even though they participate in the creation of State law and State taxing schemes. In short, reservation Indians would have all the benefits of citizenship and none of its burdens. On the other hand, non-Indian citizens of the State would have no say in the creation of Indian law and policy on the reservation, even if they were residents of the reservation, and yet be subject to tribal jurisdiction. In short, non-Indians would have all the burdens of citizenship but none of the benefits.[172]

Today the argument against "special rights" takes added strength from the success of casino gambling on reservations. States object sometimes on moral grounds, but generally on fiscal grounds, to Indian gaming. As with on-reservation cigarette and tobacco sales, but on a much larger scale, reservation gambling is seen as draining millions of tax dollars from state coffers—both because state enterprises lose business and because the tribal activities are exempt from state taxes. The numbers here are significant. The National Gambling Impact Study Commission reported in 1999 that tribes operated 260 gambling facilities in a total of thirty-one states. From 1988 to 1997, tribal gaming revenues increased from $212 million to $6.7 billion.[173] The Foxwoods Casino of the Mashantucket Pequot tribe is reportedly the most profitable casino in the United States, with annual profits of between $300 and $600 million.[174]

Indian advocates are saddened but not surprised by what they view as the hypocrisy of these arguments. The "special rights" argument is usually spurious; frequently the rights asserted are guaranteed by treaty,[175] and casino gambling is permissible under federal law only in states that permit similar types of gambling enterprises.[176] Nonetheless, the belief behind the claim is that Indians (who have been U.S. citizens since 1924) are receiving better treatment than ordinary citizens.

This is a rather remarkable rhetorical turn. For years the reservations have been criticized as economic wastelands. The standard of living on reservations—measured by poverty and unemployment rates, child mortality and life expectancy, and alcohol abuse—is, on average, far below the national norm. Yet the fact that some tribes are now beginning to achieve (preliminary and partial) success is being used by opponents of tribal sovereignty to undercut tribal self-determination. States have increasingly relied on huge lottery programs to fund basic governmental services; that is, the lotteries have been seen as supporting the exercise of sovereign power. It is not obvious why Indian gaming operations should be viewed differently.[177] Indeed, it was the Reagan administration that first supported gaming as an important element in economic development.[178]

Those who see Indian gaming as antithetical to traditional Indian culture misunderstand the meaning of self-determination, which is the right to choose one's goals and means within a set of community values,[179] not the duty to preserve traditional practices (perhaps for the cultural enrichment of non-Indians).[180] This is a different conception of citizenship—not as leveling but as empowering. More republican than liberal, more Aristotelian than Lockean, it stresses public deliberation about the kind of community citizens want to create, maintain, and pass on. In the Indian cases, the Court wields citizenship as a sword, cutting down what it views as undemocratic, race-based, rights-denying assertions of tribal power over nonmembers. The solution for the Court is to limit Indian self-determination to authority over tribal members.

At one time in American history, tribes were understood as preexisting sovereigns, whose relations with the U.S. government were set by treaty. But the nineteenth century's plenary power doctrine, combined with the twentieth century's conception of citizenship, has narrowly confined Indian sovereignty. Tribes now have (limited) power only over their own members and whatever other power the Great White Father grants them. Any broader idea of sovereignty, according to the Supreme Court, is likely to trample on the rights of We the People.

CHAPTER 6

Indian Tribal Sovereignty beyond Plenary Power

The existence of federal plenary power over Indian tribes does not necessarily condemn tribes to domination and subjugation—just as plenary power over immigration does not mandate a regime of closed borders. Indeed, in recent decades Congress has constructed a fairly robust regime of tribal self-rule. Under the Indian Self-Determination and Education Assistance Act of 1975, Congress placed the administration of important reservation programs in tribal hands.[1] These policies were furthered by the Tribal Self-Governance Act of 1994.[2] Tribes have also been given a significant role in the implementation of federal environmental regulations on reservations.[3] And, as previously mentioned, tribes have established gaming operations under the Indian Gaming Regulatory Act that have brought large resources to reservation communities.

The executive branch has concurred in these developments. Presidents from Nixon forward have declared "tribal self-determination" to be the core of federal policy. President Clinton's 1994 memorandum on the "government-to-government relationship with federally recognized Native American tribes" underscored his administration's commitment to building "a more effective day-to-day working relationship reflecting respect for the rights of self-government due the sovereign tribal governments."[4] The Environmental Protection Agency has worked to advance tribal environmental regulation,[5] and other federal agencies have entered into novel arrangements, such as granting the tribes a role in the management of national parks.[6]

Reservation population is on the rise, increasing by 18 percent (from 370,125 to 437,431 residents) between 1980 and 1990 (almost twice the rate of overall U.S. population growth),[7] and, in a somewhat surprising development, the number of persons counted as Indian by the 1990 census was 43.4 percent greater than the number in the 1980 census (from 1.3 million to 1.9 million respondents)[8]—an increase credited more to patterns of self-identification than to a rise in births.[9] The 2000 census reported further sustained growth in the 1990s. Almost 2.4 million persons identified themselves as American Indian or Alaska Native, and a total of 4.1 million listed those categories either alone or in combination with other racial categories.[10]

When one adds examples of tribal economic development to these trends,[11] one can chart significant advance on the reservations.[12] All told, Vine Deloria and Clifford Lytle, in the preface to the 1998 edition of their important book *The Nations Within,* could conclude that "the future looks brighter than it has in decades."[13]

Tribal political and economic development has cut two ways on the sovereignty issue. Advocates of tribal sovereignty note the increasing responsibilities tribes now take on and the concomitant development of tribal institutions. The maturation of tribal government is said to demonstrate the capability of tribes for fuller sovereignty rights. For others, the increasing wealth and sophistication of the tribes argue for their assimilation and the ending of special Indian programs. To adopt the language of the late nineteenth century, Indians no longer need the guardianship of the federal government.

Thus, some in Congress have urged the adoption of further restrictions on Indian sovereignty, such as the termination of tribal sovereign immunity from suit[14] and repeal of preferences given to tribal Indians for employment with the Bureau of Indian Affairs and in government contracting.[15] Whether or not proposals such as these gain traction,[16] their constitutionality is scarcely in doubt. That is, whatever the current state of federal policy, the plenary power doctrine gives Congress complete power to revise and amend. And the past century and a half of federal Indian policy shows nothing if not Congress's willingness to change course dramatically every twenty years or so.

It is possible to envision uses of plenary power to further enhance tribal sovereignty: tribes *could* be given fuller (or full) civil and criminal jurisdiction within reservation borders; legislation *could* be enacted entitling tribes to elect delegates to Congress; state authority over non-Indian activities on reservations *could* be limited. I suppose we could attempt to assess the odds of any of these measures being introduced or adopted. Not surprisingly, many advocates for tribal sovereignty seek something a bit more certain and more permanent than new policy proposals from the federal political branches. Rather than taking their chances on future Congresses, they seek to protect and support tribal authority by limiting federal plenary power and by expanding understandings of inherent tribal sovereignty.

How might this be done?

Tribes as Foreign States

The most direct challenge to plenary power is the claim pressed by sovereignty advocates that tribes are foreign states—conquered and colonized, but nonetheless still sovereign. Starting with the text of the Constitution, a strong case can be made that the framers envisioned congressional authority to deal with the tribes as of a piece with federal authority to regulate foreign affairs. The commerce clause endows Congress with power to regulate commerce "with foreign Nations, and among the several States, and with the Indian tribes."[17] No one supposed that the power to regulate trade *with* England included authority to enact federal laws *for* England. The separateness of the tribes was made equally clear by language in Article I that apportioned representatives among the states based on population exclusive of "Indians not taxed."[18] By earlier practice, relations with the tribes were regulated by treaties,[19] a course of conduct that the framers understood would continue under the new Constitution; and reference in the supremacy clause to "all Treaties *made*, or which shall be made, under the Authority of the United States"[20] kept in force compacts with the tribes executed under the Articles of Confederation. Note may also be taken of the two provisions in the Constitution that specifically authorize Congress to adopt governing rules for territories and the District of Columbia.[21] No similar clause endows Congress with power to regulate the internal affairs of Indian tribes.

It is this understanding of federal relations with the tribes that was at work in Marshall's opinions in the Indian trilogy. In words well worth rereading today, Marshall is clear-eyed in seeing that the tribes existed as sovereign nations prior to white settlement, that their power demanded a state-to-state relationship with England and subsequently the United States, and that federal treaties recognized "the pre-existing power of the nation to govern itself."[22] In later cases, the Supreme Court ruled that Indians born within tribes were not citizens of the United States under the Fourteenth Amendment,[23] that tribes—like foreign nations—had sovereign immunity from suit,[24] and that the Bill of Rights did not apply to tribal governments.[25]

Examining the text and the history, scholars have declared that, despite years of congressional action to the contrary, Congress in fact has no power to regulate the internal affairs of the tribes.[26] From this perspective, the Navajo Nation stands in the same relationship to the United States as does Canada: the federal government may enter into negotiations and conclude agreements with both governments, but it may not exercise authority over the domestic affairs of either. The upshot of the analysis is that Title 25 of the United States Code is wholly unconstitutional.[27]

The tribes-as-foreign-nations position is also said to gain strength from emerging international law principles on the rights of indigenous peoples. Those norms, it has been claimed, guarantee a right of tribes to determine freely their political status and their relationship to the United States.[28]

Thus, an interpretation of the Constitution denying Congress power to regulate the internal affairs of tribes (absent a treaty) has plausibility. But there is virtually no chance that the Supreme Court will adopt it.[29] In every era, the Justices have been willing to find congressional authority. Usually the larger context of constitutional law decides the favored source of the day. In the late nineteenth century, "plenary power" was invoked—consistent with the language of the alienage and territories decisions. When twentieth-century sensibilities balked at the demeaning words of the earlier cases, the broad modern commerce power and treaty power have been invoked to justify federal authority.[30] These sources of federal power—read expansively in the modern era—can readily be relied on as a source for most congressional legislation regulating the tribes.

A review of the international legal materials does not establish that tribes are immune from regulation by the states in which they are located. The draft United Nations Declaration on the Rights of Indigenous Peoples establishes important benchmarks for political, economic, and cultural self-determination and enjoins state parties to take "effective and appropriate measures" to give full effect to its guarantees.[31] But the declaration stops short of any statement of the nonapplicability of the laws of the state in which indigenous peoples reside. Indeed, it implicitly endorses continuing state legal authority by declaring that indigenous peoples have the right to participate "in devising legislative or administrative measures that may affect them."[32]

Constitutional Limits on Plenary Power

The conclusion that Congress possesses power to regulate the tribes does not, of course, establish that such power is unconstrained. On the contrary, it is a constitutional commonplace that Congress's powers are limited by express and implied constitutional principles. The argument for constitutional limits parallels debates in the immigration field (which will be discussed in the next chapter). The structure of these arguments is that the Constitution both establishes a government and sets limits on that government, that the idea of delegated and limited powers was of prime importance to the framers, and that the notion of a rule of law in modern days rebels at assertions of unlimited, unreviewable federal powers. International human rights law advances the claim by establishing that rights trump blanket assertions of state sovereignty.

In an important article, Nell Jessup Newton suggests a number of constitutional limits that might be imposed on the plenary power doctrine. She reasons that the factors on which the Court has relied to justify strict scrutiny in other areas ought to apply with equal force in evaluating congressional regulations of Indian tribes. Among other proposals, she argues that the Fifth Amendment imposes restrictions on congressional power to extinguish aboriginal title and to take title to tribal land held in fee.[33]

The concept of the federal government's trust responsibility toward Indians provides additional grounds for restricting plenary power.[34] Although frequently cited with more contempt than praise (owing to its source in *Kagama* and other cases now seriously criticized), the trust doctrine arguably puts a burden on Congress to show that its regulation of the tribes advances tribal interests.[35] And the Court has indicated, to mixed reviews,[36] that the trust responsibility can occasionally have constitutional bite.[37]

Subconstitutional norms may also aid in the domestication of plenary power. Indian law posits an array of canons of statutory and treaty interpretation that favors the tribes. For example, the Court reaffirmed in 1999 that "Indian treaties are to be interpreted liberally in favor of the Indians" and that "any ambiguities are to be resolved in their favor."[38] So, too, the Court has required that Congress make clear its intent to abrogate a prior treaty before a statute will be given such effect.[39] Philip Frickey has argued that, like the treaties themselves, these norms have been breached in recent years.[40] But they remain available to jurists interested in producing a kinder and gentler plenary power doctrine. Likewise, the trust doctrine is regularly invoked in aid of statutory interpretation favorable to the tribes and to provide a basis for judicial review of federal administrative power.[41] Christina Wood has made a powerful case for a reinvigorated trust doctrine that would recognize the duty of the federal government to protect native separatism and tribal sovereignty.[42]

Together, these (and other)[43] strategies could be mobilized by the Court to limit the plenary power doctrine. If successful, it would mean that federal power over Indians would take its place among other federal powers that are "plenary" in the sense that they apply to the entire subject matter but that are not exempt from usual constitutional limits. The results would not be trivial. Under a constitutionally secured trust doctrine, for example, legislation regulating the tribes (including federal statutes authorizing state regulation) would be scrutinized to ensure that they materially advance tribal interests.[44] Or perhaps associational rights might be grounds for challenging diminution of reservations or termination of tribes.

But subjecting congressional exercises of power to constitutional limits may not, in the end, get to the nub of the sovereignty issue. A fully "decolonized"[45] Indian law requires more than limits on federal power. It must secure self-determination in the deeper sense of protecting a tribe's authority to structure its form of government and to choose means to pursue tribally determined ends. As James Anaya has suggested, self-determination for indigenous peoples occurs on two levels: it involves the development and implementation of day-to-day policies that are the normal stuff of government (what Anaya terms *on-*

going self determination), and it also includes decisions on *constitutive* arrangements, such as governmental structure and membership rules.[46]

Exercises of congressional plenary power have historically operated on both levels. While federal action on the day-to-day level may be a significant intrusion on tribal self-determination, it is commonplace in our constitutional structure: federal policies frequently displace state policies regulating private conduct.[47] What is distinct about Indian law is the insecurity of tribal decisions on the constitutive level. Here, Congress has taken actions that would seem truly extraordinary if applied to the states. It has unilaterally reduced the size of reservations (and, correspondingly, the reach of tribal sovereignty), extended state civil and criminal jurisdiction over reservations, mandated that constitutions established under the Indian Reorganization Act be agreed to by the secretary of the interior,[48] and required federal administrative approval of tribal contracts and land dispositions. Most remarkably, Congress has simply terminated tribes altogether and dispersed their landholdings.

The Court has given its imprimatur to these actions. The 1979 case of *Washington v. Confederated Bands and Tribes of the Yakima Indian Nation*[49] considered the constitutionality of Public Law 280, under which the state of Washington asserted partial criminal and civil jurisdiction over the reservation. The tribe argued that the unilateral imposition of state authority violated its right to self-government and was beyond the power of Congress. The Court quickly disposed of the constitutional claim, finding that the tribe had no "fundamental right" to self-rule that would mandate special judicial protection. It was "well-established," it noted, "that Congress, in the exercise of its plenary power over Indian affairs, may restrict the retained sovereign powers of the Indian tribes."[50] Even Justice Marshall's opinion in *Santa Clara Pueblo v. Martinez,* frequently cited as near the apex of pro-sovereignty decisions, makes reference to the legal principle that "Congress has plenary authority to limit, modify or eliminate the powers of local self-government which the tribes otherwise possess."[51]

That Indian sovereignty is expressly secured by treaty is no bar to subsequent congressional defeasance, and, most egregiously, Congress remains free to abrogate treaty rights and structures unilaterally even in violation of a provision requiring tribal consent for such action. The controlling precedent here is *Lone Wolf v. Hitchcock.*[52] Article 12 of an

1868 treaty between the United States and the Kiowa and Comanche tribes prohibited cessions of reservation land unless approved by three-fourths of adult male tribe members.[53] In 1892 the government secured an agreement that called for the allotment of tribal land, in effect terminating the reservation.[54] Subsequent investigation established that the agreement had been procured by fraud and, despite representations of the federal agent to the contrary, had not been ratified by three-fourths of the tribe.[55] Nonetheless, Congress adopted legislation in 1900 that essentially imposed the agreement on the tribe.[56] Citing doctrine established in the foreign affairs area that subsequent statutes can abrogate prior treaties, the Supreme Court upheld the 1900 legislation.[57] The Court recognized that "of course, a moral obligation rested upon Congress to act in good faith in performing the stipulations entered into on its behalf," but no legal norm restricted "the legislative power . . . [to] pass laws in conflict with treaties made with the Indians."[58] In any event, said the Court, the claims of fraud could not be inquired into by the Court since such matters were "solely within the domain of the legislative authority, and its action is conclusive upon the courts."[59] "If injury was occasioned" by the 1900 legislation, "relief must be sought by an appeal to . . . [Congress] for redress and not to the courts."[60] In short, violation of Article 12 of the 1867 treaty was nonjusticiable. *Lone Wolf* thus represents plenary power at the meta-level. Not only may Congress take action inconsistent with substantive provisions in treaties (there, protecting the existence of the reservation), but it may also violate constitutive rules regulating amendment of the treaty.

Can a constitutional case be made that constitutive aspects of Indian self-determination receive significant protection in the courts; or does Congress, as the plenary power doctrine holds, truly have unfettered discretion to limit, rearrange, and terminate tribal sovereignty?

One of the *Lone Wolf* roadblocks to judicial scrutiny is today out of the way. The Court no longer holds that federal regulations governing the tribes present "political questions" beyond the competence of the courts. In *Delaware Tribal Business Committee v. Weeks,* the Court repudiated *Lone Wolf* on this point, noting that the prior case "has not deterred this Court, particularly in this day, from scrutinizing Indian legislation to determine whether it violates the equal protection component of the Fifth Amendment."[61]

Assuming, then, that burdens on Indian sovereignty are not wholly immune from judicial scrutiny, the question remains whether such sovereignty receives any substantive protection. Protection might be afforded (1) if tribal sovereignty is a protectable interest secured by the Constitution, or (2) if federal legislation creates a "vested right" whose abridgment would warrant judicial scrutiny of congressional justifications.

Self-Government as a Constitutionally Secured Interest

As to the first argument, that tribal sovereignty is secured by the Constitution, Russel Barsh and James Henderson have suggested that Indian self-government might be asserted as a fundamental right protected by the Ninth Amendment,[62] and Dean Newton has urged advocates to press the claim that tribal sovereignty is secured under the due process clause's protection of liberty.[63] Under both analyses, the constitutional text cited serves as a placeholder for substantive rights whose source is outside the text.

There are a bundle of constitutional values in self-governance and protection of culture that have been recognized in the Court's cases. The First Amendment's free speech clause protects the associational rights of groups to undertake collective political and cultural action.[64] The amendment's guarantee of religious exercise protects dissenting groups that seek to preserve a traditional form of association in the face of state demands for acculturation,[65] and the due process clause has long been understood to protect family decisions on child raising and schooling.[66] To the extent that these cases establish a kind of group privacy right to be free from governmental efforts aimed at "foster[ing] a homogeneous people,"[67] they complement the Court's reconceptualization of the tribes as private voluntary organizations.[68]

It has been argued that the constitutional values implicit in the cases can be cobbled together to provide protection for tribal self-government.[69] If so, then federal legislation that infringes on sovereignty—particularly sovereign arrangements secured by treaty—would presumably receive close judicial scrutiny.[70] The associational rights argument, however, has yet to coalesce for the courts. Constitutional norms might well protect tribes against state laws that seek to regulate religious practices,[71] tribal membership,[72] and decisions regarding the education of children, but that is a long way from a constitutional right to exercise civil and criminal jurisdiction over tribe members and nontribal residents. As the constitutional claims on behalf of the tribes move from the protection of culture to a power of "jurisgenesis,"[73] the Court is likely to grow increasingly concerned.[74]

There is another cluster of constitutional values that may be more fruitfully invoked in a search for principles protecting tribal sovereignty.[75] The Court has, in recent years, provided strong protection for state processes from direct federal regulation.[76] The "commandeering" of state officials for federal duties is held to be an unconstitutional intrusion into local decision making, frustrating local democracy and subverting accountability.[77] The idea that Congress could restructure state governments is well beyond the pale.[78] What is at stake in these cases is not the substantive regulation of matters of local concern; as the Court concedes, Congress retains authority to preempt state regulation of private conduct on most matters. Rather, it is Congress's impact on the structure of local government—that is, infringement on the constitutive level—that concerns the Court. At the core of the federalism cases is a conceptualization of state sovereignty—not as a nonenumerated right of a group of people, but rather as an underlying structural assumption of the constitutional order.[79]

Tribal governing structures are not currently conceived of as part of that order. But it is not hard to see how the justifications for protection of state governments would translate to tribal sovereignty. Tribal sovereignty, like state sovereignty, is neither created by federal delegation nor established by the Constitution. It precedes, and receives recognition in, the Constitution.[80] The preestablished sovereignty of the tribes is reflected in the commerce clause, which lists three kinds of political communities that do not owe their existence to ratification of the Constitution: states, foreign nations, and Indian tribes.[81] Tribes may not be foreign nations, for which Congress has no power to regulate internal affairs, but why might they not at least receive the same kind of protection as states—that is, that their structure of government is for their citizens, and not for Congress, to decide?

The values usually associated with federalism—accountability, experimentation, and local diversity—apply in spades to tribal governments. Whatever displacement of local choice occurs through preemptive national legislation, it is far less intrusive than the wholesale restructuring of territory and governance that Congress can impose on the reservations; and whatever merit remains of Herbert Wechsler's description of the political safeguards of federalism,[82] it is hard to argue that the tribes are structurally represented in Congress or the electoral college.[83] Furthermore, tribal cultural and political choices contribute at least as much to American diversity as do the activities of states, which appear more and more to be mere local representations of national political and cultural trends.

By analogy to the federalism cases, then, the Court could well hold that constitutive tribal arrangements receive constitutional protection.[84] The received wisdom that Congress has plenary authority to rearrange or extinguish Indian sovereignty would be overturned just as was the post–New Deal assumption that state sovereignty imposed no limits on plenary federal powers. To be sure, this would work a dramatic change in the law. Perhaps Congress would retain power to recognize tribes, but once recognized, tribes would be free to structure their governments as they deem appropriate without federal supervision (short of a showing of a compelling federal interest). Accordingly, current statutory provisions requiring approval by the secretary of the interior of amendments to tribe constitutions might well be unconstitutional,[85] and because tribal sovereignty is so closely linked with territory, congressional diminution or termination of reservations would not be permissible without tribal consent. So too limitations on tribal criminal jurisdiction would be problematic. Were this the law, legislation of the kind at issue in *Lone Wolf* would be invalid. These conclusions seem radical when applied to Indian law, but imagine how the Court would respond to federal regulation of state constitutions or to federal legislation purporting to decrease the territory of a state.

Tribal Sovereignty as a Statute-Based or Treaty-Based Interest

In the preceding section I canvassed arguments that tribal sovereignty is a protectable constitutional interest. An alternative approach would attempt to locate a protectable interest of Indian sovereignty in the federal statutes that affirm the tribes and their governing laws. The analogy here is to the important line of cases holding that federal (and state) laws may create entitlements that cannot be taken away without due process of law.[86]

It is unlikely that statutory recognition of tribal authority alone is enough to establish a "right" to self-governance. Not only does the plenary power doctrine undercut a claim to entitlement to current governance structures, but also, more important, the procedural due process cases establish rights to fair process, not substantive rights to a continuation of the entitlement program.[87] Although Congress cannot mandate that a flip of a coin determines one's eligibility for welfare, it may—as recent history demonstrates—set a time limit on eligibility no matter the harm imposed on the person who loses benefits.

Suppose, however, that Congress sought to guarantee the continuation of tribal sovereignty by stating in legislation that governing arrangements could not subsequently be altered without tribal consent. Would such a guarantee be deemed to create a substantive entitlement to the sovereignty provided in the statute? This, of course, is just a different form of the question in *Lone Wolf,* where the Court concluded that a mutual consent clause in a treaty was not binding on a subsequent Congress, but it is past time for a serious reconsideration of *Lone Wolf.*

As noted in Chapter 4, the usual constitutional answer is that a sitting Congress may not bind a future Congress. Borrowing language from constitutional debates, it would be said that the first Congress may not *entrench* tribal sovereignty so as to limit a subsequent Congress's power to arrange matters differently (or terminate sovereignty altogether). Julian Eule[88] has grounded the anti-entrenchment principle in the concept of a temporal legislature, elected for a term of years with limited power to control the future (or the past).[89] A Congress that can bind future legislatures, in effect, denies the democratic rights of electors of the subsequent Congress. Permitting entrenchment as an ordinary practice would also likely have disastrous consequences for the congressional process. Members of Congress facing electoral loss would seek to lock in long-term benefits for constituencies, and subsequent Congresses would be under heavy pressure to do the same for their favored groups. The utilitarian arguments against such practices—particularly in a quickly changing world—provide a strong supplement to the democratic theory concerns.[90]

This is a foundational—if generally unexamined—assumption of constitutional law, applied by the Court at the state[91] and federal level.[92] There are, to be sure, recognized exceptions to the principle.

Congress may not declare that land granted to a person by a prior Congress shall revert to the federal government, nor may it repeal a contract made by an earlier Congress.[93] The prior acts are deemed to have established vested rights, and infringements of those rights will call forth judicial remedies. Although seen as exceptions to the anti-entrenchment rule, the vested rights cases in fact help define the rule. Many things done by one Congress will affect subsequent Congresses. An aircraft carrier purchased at time *T* cannot be handed back at time *T* plus 1; wages paid today to government employees are not recallable tomorrow. This is simply the application of a higher-level (constitutional) norm that protects property rights.

Indian law has affirmed this vested right principle to some extent, thereby undercutting a reading of *Lone Wolf* as permitting Congress to take recognized tribal land at will. In the landmark 1980 *Sioux Nation* case, the Court held that Congress's taking of the Black Hills in violation of the 1868 Fort Laramie Treaty could be challenged and that compensation was due the tribe because the federal government could not demonstrate that the abrogation of the treaty was an appropriate measure for protecting and advancing tribal interests (a violation of the federal government's trust responsibility).[94] But the Court has shown no general inclination to rethink the broader doctrine that a subsequent statute can abrogate a treaty. In Indian law, the most that tribes can benefit from is a canon of interpretation that Congress's intent to abrogate must be express.[95] The trust doctrine/vested right limit on the anti-entrenchment rule, then, is not available under current doctrine to protect constitutive agreements between Congress and the tribes.[96] There is no reason to believe that a federal statute with a mutual consent clause would be treated differently.

To say that treaties and statutory consent clauses do not protect governing arrangements from subsequent change is not to say that tribal sovereignty might not be entrenched under another theory. The argument I want to press is that Congress and the tribes should be able to put constitutive arrangements beyond the reach of unilateral congressional action by establishing the relationship in a manner that resembles not ordinary politics but higher lawmaking. The result of such processes may be said either to constitute a limited exception to anti-entrenchment principles or to constitute "mid-level lawmaking"—higher than normal lawmaking but below constitutional politics.[97]

This no doubt sounds foreign, but there are examples readily at hand. In the twentieth century, a number of territories of the United States established new relationships with Congress that may not be unilaterally altered: the Philippines was granted independence, and Hawaii and Alaska were admitted as states. These actions were not taken through the simple enactment of a statute. Each case involved a multiyear process, with actions by the people of the territories as a whole (not just their legislatures). Hawaiian statehood was the product of lengthy deliberation and bipartisan support. More than twenty congressional hearings over a twenty-five-year period considered the issue, and statehood legislation, originally introduced in 1919, passed the House in 1947, 1950, and 1955. Both the Eisenhower and Truman administrations supported statehood for Hawaii. The process for admission required congressional approval of a constitution drafted by the territory. Hawaii had convened a constitutional convention in 1950, whose members were popularly elected. The convention's draft constitution was submitted by plebiscite to the people of the territory, who approved the constitution by more than a 3-to-1 margin. Congress proposed several minor amendments to the constitution,[98] and the document was again submitted to the people of Hawaii for approval.[99] Following a favorable vote in the territory, Hawaii was admitted to the Union.

Philippine independence was secured in a similar fashion. From the beginning of U.S. authority over the Philippines in 1898, it was understood that independence was the ultimate goal. Following federal legislation in 1934, the Philippine legislature provided for the election of delegates to a constitutional convention which drafted a Constitution for the Commonwealth of the Philippine Islands. The constitution was approved by President Roosevelt and by popular plebiscite. Commonwealth was to be established for ten years to provide a transition to independence. Although Japanese occupation during World War II interrupted the process, the Philippines gained independence on July 4, 1946. The admission of Hawaii (and Alaska) as states and the independence of the Philippines were products of federal legislation, but no one supposes that the political changes wrought by the legislation could be undone by a subsequent Congress.

Arrangements with the tribes seem somehow less permanent than either admitting states or granting independence to territories. Just as entry as an immigrant is commonly seen as a way station to the full membership of citizenship, and territorial governments have been viewed as preparing a territory for eventual statehood, so too the "dependent sovereignty" of the tribes might be seen as a status leading ultimately toward something more permanent.[100] In the early days of Indian policy, the "solution" was removal of the tribes to areas beyond white settlement (or extermination); in later days it was the breakup of the reservations and assimilation. There is, however, no obvious reason why a formal agreement recognizing self-determination should be viewed as an inappropriate long-term arrangement between the tribes and the federal government—except that we are accustomed to thinking in other categories.

If such arrangements are the product of deliberative and consensual processes, the values protected by the anti-entrenchment doctrine are not at risk. Consider how an agreement between the tribes and the government might be reached: the parties negotiate a compact that recognizes the sovereignty of the tribe within designated boundaries; any limits on tribal authority are made explicit; the tribe and Congress expressly approve the agreement; and the agreement provides that it cannot be altered without the consent of both parties. Under such circumstances, unilateral abrogation of the agreement would undermine the democratic self-rule the agreement is designed to establish. Moreover, the ratification of the agreement by the people of the tribe moves the agreement out of the category of ordinary legislation.[101] The act of the people signifies a higher form of lawmaking, similar to the ratification of a constitution.

The framers of the U.S. Constitution understood the importance of popular ratification. The Constitution drafted in 1787 went far beyond the terms under which the Philadelphia Convention had assembled. Moreover, it included provisions that would encroach on existing state prerogatives. Madison recognized that a "higher Sanction than the Legislative authority" would be necessary if the Constitution and ensuing federal laws were to be viewed as legitimate and superior to state laws.[102] Popular ratification could supply that "sanction." According to historian Jack Rakove, Madison believed that "[p]opular ratification provided more than a symbolic affirmation of popular sovereignty; it promised to render the constitution legally superior to ordinary acts of government that also expressed popular consent through mechanisms of representation."[103] Ultimately, the Constitution drafted in

Philadelphia included a self-referential provision stating that it would come into force when approved by "Conventions of nine states"—a formulation that expressly rejected other proposals that state legislative approval could suffice.[104] Rakove concludes that

> the resort to popular sovereignty . . . marked the point where the distinction between a constitution and ordinary law became the fundamental doctrine of political thinking.
>
> . . . Whatever else might be said about the legality or illegality of [the] process, it produced a completely unambiguous result that ensured that the Constitution would attain immediate legitimacy.[105]

Tribal ratification is not a precise analogue because it involves popular participation by only one of the parties. It may therefore be argued that whatever meaning it has for the tribe, it cannot provide an exception to the nonentrenchment doctrine that would bind the people of the United States. The argument would carry weight if we were to reduce entrenchment to a specific formula—for example, that it can occur only if approved in a particular manner by the electorate and elected representatives. But it is unclear where such particular rules would come from. The claim here is less rigid: it is that certain constitutive arrangements, when adopted in a manner that goes beyond simple lawmaking on behalf of a people who expressly approve the structure, can establish binding commitments.

Furthermore, the agreement is likely to be the product of a careful and lengthy negotiation, perhaps involving the actions of several Congresses. Because the negotiations are over constitutive arrangements, the risk that "ins" would attempt to lock in particular policies (self-serving or not) seems minimal. This is not to deny that long-term structural policies could be viewed in partisan terms (consider statutes attempting to entrench rules on campaign contributions or voting requirements), but it is hard to see partisan considerations playing an important role in the negotiation of federal government–tribe agreements that define a form of government for the tribe.

There is an additional consideration that removes constitutive arrangements from the usual kind of legislation subject to the anti-entrenchment rule. Sovereign arrangements demand a certain security if the governments they establish are to flourish. (This idea receives recognition in Article V of the Constitution, which establishes a difficult-to-mobilize amendment process.) Long-term planning—for economic growth, resource management, and education—and public participation may both suffer if governing structures are subject to alteration by another authority. In repudiating the termination policy, the Nixon administration recognized that "the mere threat of termination tends to discourage greater self-sufficiency among Indian groups[.]"[106] This point may be generalized. Meaningful self-determination needs a fence around constitutive arrangements, providing a spatial and temporal independence that can inculcate commitment and long-term vision within a *demos.*

It is therefore not surprising that the compacts with the Federated States of Micronesia and the Commonwealth of the Northern Mariana Islands include provisions stating that the agreements cannot be modified without the consent of both parties.[107] That these provisions be understood as binding is of significant importance to the populations of the polities recognized by the agreements. In earlier days, the executive branch took the position that the mutual consent provisions were binding on the federal government; and two opinions issued by the Justice Department's Office of Legal Counsel (OLC) took a similar position. (One of the opinions was issued by then–Assistant Attorney General William Rehnquist.)[108]

More recently, OLC has opined that mutual consent provisions are not outside the general rule of nonentrenchment. The issue has arisen in the negotiations with Guam over a new commonwealth status. A draft Guam Commonwealth Act included two such provisions: one declaring that the act would not be amendable without the consent of both governments, the other stating that no federal laws or regulations adopted after enactment of the act would be applied to Guam without the mutual consent of Guam and Congress. A 1994 OLC opinion concluded that the provisions were unenforceable and that their inclusion in the act could create "illusory expectations that might . . . mislead the electorate of Guam about the consequences of the legislation."[109] With wooden logic and language, the opinion adopts a categorical approach: "The plenary authority of Congress over a non-state area persists as long as the area remains in that condition and terminates only when the area becomes a State or ceases to be under United States sovereignty. There is no intermediary status as far as the Congressional power is concerned."[110] The ground for this conclusion is nearly an *ipse dixit:* it is declared that the power of Congress to delegate governmental powers to "non-state areas" is "contingent on the retention by Congress of its power to revise, alter, and revoke that legislation." This conclusion is said to be "but a specific application of the maxim that one Congress cannot bind a subsequent Congress."[111]

The opinion does not reason to this result. It does not consider alternative formulations or the possibility that constitutive arrangements might call forth a different rule. The Justice Department recognizes that Congress's power to amend earlier legislation is limited by the Constitution's contracts and due process clauses but holds that these guarantees do not apply because "a specific political relationship" cannot be considered a form of protected property. That may well be correct, but it hardly ends the discussion. The question is whether there are good grounds for holding that governing arrangements—popularly ratified—are not subject to the nonentrenchment doctrine. That question is not answered by a conclusion that such arrangements are not "property."

Whatever merit the OLC opinion may have as to territories, it would have even less force if applied to tribal governments. As noted, the inherent authority of the tribes is not a product of congressional delegation; recognition of tribal sovereignty was thus not—in the words of the OLC opinion—accompanied by a reserved power of Congress to revoke or amend. Such reserved authority might be justified if territorial government is viewed as inherently nonpermanent (though I questioned this claim in Chapter 4), but that reasoning cannot apply to tribal sovereignty in the era of self-determination. James Anaya has summarized the evolving international law norms on constitutive arrangements for indigenous peoples:

> The world community now holds in contempt the imposition of government structures upon people, regardless of their social or political makeup . . . Today, procedures toward the creation, alteration or territorial extension of governmental authority normally are regulated by self-determination precepts requiring minimum levels of participation on the part of all affected peoples commensurate with their respective interests.[112]

It is time to take stock. I have examined a range of arguments for constitutional limits on Congress's plenary power over Indian tribes, including claims that the right of self-government is constitutionally protected. I have attempted to provide an additional argument as to how and why constitutive arrangements—which are the product of deliberative processes and tribal popular approval—might be protected against subsequent congressional alteration. If the argument is persuasive, it would supply a limit on congressional plenary power, even if other constitutionally based claims prove unsuccessful. One might well question the efficacy of my claim on the ground that, since 1871, Congress has regulated the tribes by way of legislation. What good, then, is an argument that certain kinds of treaty provisions are outside the scope of the anti-entrenchment principle? In the next section I take up that question, suggesting that a government-to-government relationship is best pursued through the negotiation and ratification of *binding* agreements between the tribes and the federal government. That is, for that relationship to have force and legitimacy, the rule of *Lone Wolf* must be abandoned.

New Arrangements: Beyond Plenary Power

Whether or not the Supreme Court establishes constitutional protection for tribal sovereignty, Congress retains the power to advance Indian self-determination. As has been noted, federal policy over the past several decades has promoted self-determination. What is missing is the architecture to maintain and promote this relationship.

Compacts

A number of scholars have proposed that federal-tribal relations be established primarily through negotiated compacts.[113] A compact between a tribe and the federal government securing tribal sovereignty over designated land shifts the axis in federal government–Indian relations. It makes clear that tribes are not subjects of federal regulation, but rather polities able to structure their place within American federalism.[114] Robert Williams has written eloquently of the function and meaning of treaties to the tribes in the early days of encounter with European settlers. From the Indians' perspective, the treaties represented bonds of trusts, of shared humanity, in a world of diversity and conflict. "According to this American Indian treaty vision of law and peace," Williams writes, "human solidarity is achieved by a constitutional tradition of imagining the possibilities of different peoples linking arms together."[115]

The suggestion of a return to a treaty relationship may appear odd, to say the least, but the problem is not the vehicle; it is that shifting congressional policies and the plenary power doctrine make government-to-government agreements insecure. I have argued that constitutive arrangements ratified by the tribe and the Congress ought to be viewed as outside the usual nonentrenchment doctrine and that agreements with mutual consent clauses ought to be held enforceable against unilateral congressional legislation that violates the agreement. If the argument is persuasive, it supplies the limit on plenary power required to make compact arrangements a plausible basis for tribal sovereignty.[116]

Scholars have made sensible suggestions regarding principles and frameworks for federal government–Indian compacts.[117] Clearly, given the great variety of tribes and prior histories, there can be no one-size-fits-all answers. Indeed, for smaller tribes with no significant land base, novel approaches will be necessary.[118] What is crucial is the fundamental redefinition of federal government–to–tribe relations that would be brought about by ending congressional dictation of policy via statute. Robert Clinton aptly notes the "considerable difference between managing affairs *with* the Indian tribes . . . and managing the affairs *of* the Indian tribes and their members."[119] It is the difference between a regime of plenary power and of treaty relations "explicitly recognizing the national character" of the tribes "and their right to self-government."[120]

A regime of compacts would not prevent the federal government from providing incentives for certain tribal activities. The federal government could continue to provide funds and attach conditions that further national interests. It could also enforce generally applicable federal health, labor, and environmental legislation.[121] In these respects, a compact regime would differ substantially from treaty relations with foreign states; in the latter case, the federal government has no power to impose legal rules within foreign borders. The tribes are not foreign states, however; they *have* been incorporated into the United States, and all Indians born in the United States are citizens at birth. But a compact regime would remove the federal government's power to make unilateral changes in tribal governance and territory and to dictate day-to-day tribal policies.[122]

The idea here is not to turn the tribes into mini-states.[123] Unlike the states, tribes would not have voting representation in Congress, and they would not, without a substantial change in current doctrine, have complete territorial sovereignty. (I will shortly address proposals on these issues.) They would also possess powers that states do not have, such as the authority to regulate admission and residence on reservations and to craft membership rules.[124] In this way, they would function more as foreign states—fashioning, in effect, immigration policies. It is this in-betweenness that makes the political position of the tribes appear anomalous, but it is anomalous only if one seeks a perfect analogy between the tribe and some other political community (domestic state or foreign state). As international law is coming to recognize, indigenous peoples have a distinct set of rights and a distinct relationship with the states in which they are located. Histories of conquest and colonialism over preexisting sovereignties make their situations sui generis. Rather than seeking an analogy, we must come to terms with the sovereignty questions in their own right.

And yet our disquiet over in-betweenness is not easily allayed. I have suggested why that might be so: recognizing tribal sovereignty appears to affirm political power for exclusionary, race-based groups—in marked contrast to state sovereignty, which is exercised over heterogeneous populations whose entry and residence cannot be controlled by state authorities.[125] It is now time to address this concern head-on.

In thinking this through, it is important that we start with a distinction between "Indianness" and membership in a tribe that has political authority over a reservation. The first may well be primarily a racial designation. Thus, federal statutes and regulations to this day incorporate "blood quantum" metrics.[126] A Bureau of Indian Affairs employment preference for Indians—upheld in *Morton v. Mancari*[127]—is available to persons who are "one-fourth or more degree Indian blood and . . . a member of a Federally recognized tribe."[128] Regulations pertaining to Indians *qua* Indians, whether or not they are members of tribes, might be justified in the same way as other race-based measures: to remedy past discrimination, to overcome current barriers to equal opportunity, and to serve diversity goals. Whether such programs can survive the strict rules now applied to race-conscious programs[129] is an open question,[130] but it is important not to confuse these kinds of programs and their justifications with efforts to bolster tribal sovereignty.

Tribal membership is not strictly a racial concept.[131] Although tribal laws define membership primarily in "blood" terms,[132] tribal constitutions generally include a provision authorizing the tribal councils to "enact ordinances . . . governing future membership and the adoption of new members." In the nineteenth century, tribal adoption (what might be termed naturalization) was widely practiced; Felix Cohen could report in 1942 that nearly all tribal constitutions provided for adoption through special action of the tribe. Interestingly, the Supreme Court cases examining these issues referred to adoption as establishing tribal "citizenship," not membership.[133] Cohen further noted a trend away from "the older notion" that membership rights "run with Indian blood" and toward the view that membership in a tribe is "a political relation rather than a racial attribute."[134] In this, Cohen proved to be mistaken. Current tribal membership rules frequently bar adoption[135] and still predominantly define membership in blood quantum terms.[136] These changes have several sources. Constitutions drafted for tribes by the BIA under the 1934 Indian Reorganization Act generally included blood quantum requirements in membership provisions.[137] An explicit racial definition is also consistent with political events in the 1960s and 1970s that sought to organize an Indian movement in step with the race consciousness of some civil rights strategies. Furthermore, a definition that turns primarily on blood also facilitates return to the reservation by establishing membership for off-reservation Indians whose parents may not have been enrolled in the tribe.

Even with the changes in membership rules, however, tribal membership is not the same as racial identity. Significantly, persons may relinquish tribal membership (a prospect much more problematic for members of racial minorities), and they may be "disenrolled" by the tribe. And many persons who classify themselves as Indians (based on blood) are not members of enrolled tribes.[138] Although the Supreme Court's decision in *Morton v. Mancari* may be criticized for its lack of craftsmanship, the Court's understanding of tribal membership as a *political*—not a racial—classification is plausible and important.[139]

Some have found this reasoning specious.[140] If blood is a sine qua non of tribal membership, it might be argued that it is senseless to claim that membership is not conceived in racial terms. Take, for example, the Navajo Nation Code, which defines as members persons "born to any enrolled member of the Navajo Nation . . . provided they are at least one-fourth degree Navajo blood."[141] But there is another way to see these rules. Blood quantum rules are based on birth. They are thus akin to the laws of virtually all states that permit transmission of citizenship to children born to citizens. Interestingly, some tribal membership rules expressly require birth to a tribal member in addition to a blood quantum.[142] (Such citizenship-by-descent is generally referred to as *jus sanguinis* citizenship.) Although United States citizenship laws do not adopt blood quantum rules as explicit as those relied on by tribes, federal statutes provide a number of avenues for establishing the transmission of citizenship to children born to U.S. parents overseas—depending on whether the child has one U.S. parent or two, whether the child was born in or out of wedlock, and other circumstances.[143]

There are some noteworthy differences between tribal membership rules and U.S. citizenship rules. U.S. citizenship cannot be "watered down" through marriage to a noncitizen; that is, children born to the couple are not "one-half" U.S. citizens who may face different rules for transmitting U.S. citizenship to their children (although other restrictions on citizenship by descent exist; for example, children born overseas cannot transmit citizenship to their children unless they establish residence in the United States prior to the child's birth). Furthermore, tribal membership rules usually refer to blood quantum, not birth to tribal members. This means that although membership is based on descent, parents need not be tribal members to confer membership on their children, and in this respect they differ from usual *jus sanguinis* rules. But the citizenship policies of some foreign states look quite similar to the typical tribal rules. For instance, under Irish law, a person can claim Irish citizenship if one of his or her grandparents was an Irish citizen—whether or not the person's parents were ever registered as citizens.[144]

The point here is that the membership-by-descent rules of tribes look more like national state membership rules than is usually supposed. Both tribes and national states are ongoing human associations in which membership is primarily determined by birth but is also ultimately voluntary. From this perspective, to permit the exercise of tribal political authority is not to legitimize political power based on race; it is to understand tribes as intergenerational polities. It is not without reason that tribes have forever been referred to as *nations.*

Finally, demographic trends are likely to put pressure on blood quantum membership rules. Because of significant levels of intermarriage, the vast majority of Indians can presently claim membership in another racial group. If current intermarriage rates continue, blood quantum requirements will become harder to satisfy.[145] Furthermore, the growing multiracialism of the Indian population—and the U.S. population as a whole—is likely to make blood requirements appear increasingly archaic. These developments may result in conceptions of membership defined primarily by political and cultural indicia; or, if descent-based rules continue to dominate, they may be reconstructed in classic *jus sanguinis* terms (membership based on birth to a member) rather than blood quantum terms.

Territorial Sovereignty

Sovereignty cannot, in this day and age, mean unfettered state power over all persons within a state's territory, but it must at least begin with the assumption that all persons within the sovereign's borders are subject to its jurisdiction.[146] The civil and criminal jurisdictional patchwork present today on most reservations is arbitrary and unworkable. For example, the inability of tribes to try non-Indians who commit major offenses on reservations is unparalleled at the international level[147] and in other domestic jurisdictions.[148]

Because the tribes vary greatly in population and resources, a flat rule extending sovereignty for all purposes over all persons on reservation land is not sensible. But geographic sovereignty could be an aspiration toward which compacts could advance the tribes. Such arrangements would have a dramatic effect on current legal practices, but they would not require any new constitutional principles.[149] There are two possible routes. The first would be a broad reading of the so-called *Montana* exception[150] that permits tribes to regulate the conduct of nonmembers on reservations when it has a "direct effect on the political integrity, the economic security, or the health or welfare of the tribe." The second would be by way of federally delegated power. The first route appears unlikely, as evidenced by the Court's decision in the *Strate* and *Hicks* cases (described in the previous chapter). The more feasible approach is a negotiated compact under which the federal government delegates regulatory authority. This route is not barred by previous Court holdings denying tribal power: even though the Court has deemed some exercises of tribal power to be "inconsistent" with a tribe's "dependent status,"[151] it has also made clear that Congress has the authority to authorize tribal jurisdiction in such cases if it reaches a different conclusion.[152] (This is precisely what Congress did following the *Duro* case.) To be sure, relying on federal power to extend tribal sovereignty may appear problematic, unless such delegations can be made secure. This may be accomplished, however, if compacts are deemed subject to change only with the mutual consent of the parties. I have already tried to sketch a plausible version of that claim.

The unanswered question is whether Congress has the political will to enter into binding agreements authorizing territorial sovereignty for tribes. A significant problem here is the "democratic deficit." "Legalities aside," Charles Wilkinson has written, "many fair-minded observers believe that the complaints of non-Indians raise legitimate policy questions" about tribal exercise of authority over nonmembers.[153]

Understanding tribes as descent communities—as nations—may help allay concerns about race-based governance, but it only puts the democratic deficit claim in bolder relief. For nations, nonmembers are aliens. Nonmembers may be granted permission to enter and reside, and may be afforded certain privileges, but they have no right to participation in governance. Furthermore, a nation's preference for its nationals over nonmembers is rarely viewed as problematic.[154] This is standard stuff in international law, but it presents difficulties as applied to tribes because tribal nonmembers are also (in the main) U.S. citizens. Bedrock constitutional principles establish the right of citizens to enter and reside in any state or territory in the Union and to take up political rights therein almost immediately.[155] But the "nationness" of tribes effectively turns some U.S citizens into aliens on U.S. soil, permitting tribes to deny them political rights in the reservation's governing body—even if they own land within reservation boundaries.

One answer here may be that other arrangements can and should substitute for political rights. Canadians visiting San Francisco and New Yorkers vacationing in Palm Springs have no "right" to vote in California elections. But should nonresidents be prosecuted for criminal offenses in California, they are entitled to an array of rights that guarantee due process. Why should the situation of non–tribal members on reservations be any different? In earlier days, one could perhaps respond that the absence of effective court systems and the nonapplicability of the Bill of Rights to tribal governments rendered rights protections precarious. But these concerns are far weaker today, with the development of tribal courts and thirty years of practice under the Indian Civil Rights Act (ICRA) (which applies most of the Bill of Rights to the tribes).[156] Nonetheless, this cannot be a complete answer because the democratic deficit is a claim raised on behalf of settlers, not sojourners. It is the claim of the New Yorker who *moves* to Palm Springs.[157]

We should, however, hesitate before leaping to this analogy. The political status of the tribes is not analogous to that of states, and federal policy affirms tribal interests in self-government and cultural self-determination that differ dramatically from the usual protections afforded the state under theories of federalism. For Charles Wilkinson, the "settled principles of preconstitutional and extraconstitutional tribal status, coupled with the promise of a viable, evolving separatism in the treaties and treaty substitutes, justify race-based tribal governments without political representation by nonmembers."[158] This does not mean that nonmember settlers are without rights. Indeed, Wilkinson suggests a reexamination of the rule that claims for violations of ICRA are not generally cognizable in federal courts—a rule that is "perceived as a fundamental barrier to a just legal process in Indian country by creating the specter of tribal powers that cannot be checked outside of the tribe."[159]

I would press a bit further. Our current models of membership are too binary: one is either a citizen or an "alien." The first status is accompanied by full membership rights,[160] the second by only those political and social rights that a beneficent sovereign grants to its guests. More textured understandings of membership, however, are gaining currency, as western democracies come to grips with several decades of high levels of immigration. It is increasingly suggested that lawful residents who participate in and contribute to the social and economic life of a community should be recognized, to some degree, as members of that community entitled to a set of rights and a guarantee of fair treatment.[161] I will adopt the label "denizenship" to describe this membership status of resident "aliens."[162]

The concept of denizenship opens up a number of possible political arrangements between full voting rights and total political exclusion.

For example, nonmember residents could be permitted to select a nonvoting delegate to the tribal council (much as U.S. territories elect delegates to Congress), or tribes could establish informal advisory boards on which nonmembers could serve.[163] Tribes may even want to experiment with nonmember voting. Several U.S. localities permit immigrants to vote in local elections, and the European Union (EU) guarantees the right of citizens of member states living in another EU state to vote in local elections.[164] Under these policies, voting rights do not constitute citizenship. So, too, a right to vote in tribal elections need not be equated with tribal membership (in the sense, for example, of being able to transmit membership to children). Whether any of these proposals makes sense would have to be judged within the context of a particular reservation and tribe. And the argument is not that representational rights for nonmembers is a sine qua non for full territorial sovereignty. Rather, the point is that conceiving of resident nonmembers as denizens suggests accommodations of political arrangements that can undercut the democratic deficit claim.

Others have pressed even further. Barsh and Henderson have argued for a constitutional amendment that would establish tribes on the model of states. They would reserve the tribes' powers over membership, which "has proved necessary, for the time being, to their political and economic stability." They suggest, however, that "[o]nce better established and able to support larger populations, tribes will probably conclude that traditional restrictions on entry and the political franchise tend to chill further growth, and will abolish them."[165] Canada has carried out much of the Barsh and Henderson program in establishing the new territory of Nunavut. Carved out of the Northwest Territory, Nunavut is intended to secure self-determination for the Inuit people. The territory is endowed with general governmental powers within its borders, much like any Canadian territory. At the end of the twentieth century, the Inuit constituted 85 percent of the population and were securely in control of the political apparatus;[166] but movement into Nunavut, and the franchise, are open to all Canadians.[167] This model of government, according to a report of the Canadian Royal Commission on Aboriginal Peoples, "expresses self-determination through an Aboriginal-controlled public government rather than an Aboriginal-exclusive form of self-government."[168]

Perhaps the Navajo Nation, located on more than 16 million acres spanning three states and with a population of about 150,000 (95 percent of whom are Indians), could at some point adopt the Nunavut model—and thereby make a very strong claim to full territorial sovereignty. For most tribes, however—as Barsh and Henderson note—membership rules and voting rights cannot be made open without severe risks to tribal cultural and political self-determination.[169] Unilateral federal imposition of such norms would be the final victory of the allotment strategy of the nineteenth century, allowing the dominant society to take first the lands and then the governing structure of indigenous peoples.

Indeed, a stronger case might well be made for explicit *Indian* representation at the *national* level, so that tribal voices may be heard as Congress crafts Indian policies. Permitting tribes to send delegates to Congress is an idea that dates from some of the earliest treaties with the tribes,[170] and such rules have more recently been adopted for indigenous populations elsewhere.[171] It could be an important route to ensuring the promise made by the Continental Congress in the Northwest Ordinance: that laws dealing with American Indians be "founded in justice and humanity."[172]

Tribes are both *in* and *of* the United States. For tribal advocates, this relationship may be too close for comfort. But it represents the situation of most indigenous peoples around the world. International law distinguishes between colonies outside the territorial borders of a state and once sovereign peoples located within a state. The former may be entitled to independence, under the guarantee of a people's right of self-determination, but international law does not recognize the right of indigenous peoples to create their own independent state out of the territory of the state in which they reside—a doctrine known as the "blue water thesis," meaning that decolonization is required only where the colony is across an ocean.[173] The doctrine's apparent hypocrisy can be explained by its source in an international regime dedicated to the preservation of states. Indigenous peoples living within states established by their conquerors are part of that state. Indeed, a draft U.N. Declaration on the Rights of Indigenous Peoples expressly guarantees indigenous peoples the right "to participate fully, if they so choose, in the political, economic, social and cultural life of the

State."[174] Indians are citizens of the United States, entitled to vote in state and federal elections. They serve in the U.S. armed forces, travel on U.S. passports, and participate on U.S. Olympic teams. They pay federal income taxes (residents of Puerto Rico do not). Indians living on reservations may move freely throughout the United States and settle where they choose. About one-half of all Indians live outside the reservations, and those who do have the same rights and obligations as other U.S. citizens.

Within this complicated relationship there is room for economic and cultural self-determination for the tribes and for the political arrangements necessary to secure them. A robust concept of U.S. citizenship is not inconsistent with tribal governance and should not be used by the courts or Congress to undermine tribal territorial sovereignty. While it is unlikely that the Supreme Court will deny Congress the power to regulate the tribes, new political arrangements with the tribes can provide needed limits on the plenary power doctrine. Tribes, as the Court used to say but has apparently forgotten, are more than private, voluntary associations. They are polities that have somehow survived and continue to flourish against great odds.

CHAPTER 7

Plenary Power, Immigration Regulation, and Decentered Citizenship

Let me start with two propositions regarding rights and citizenship in the American constitutional system: (1) the background norm of U.S. constitutional law is that noncitizens are, in the main, entitled to all the constitutional protections conferred upon citizens; and (2) lines drawn on the basis of alienage, in the main, demand special justification from the government. The first proposition is an accurate statement of current law; the second is half right: state, but not federal, policies that discriminate against immigrants are generally subject to "strict scrutiny" by the courts. These two partially descriptive, partially normative claims stand for the broader proposition that I will defend in this chapter: the constitutional rights of persons residing in the United States are not, in the main, based on the possession of national state membership (citizenship).[1]

What, then, is the hue and cry about the plenary power doctrine? The doctrine does two things. First, it largely immunizes from constitutional scrutiny federal regulations of immigration and naturalization. Thus, although aliens (even undocumented aliens) arrested in the United States for crimes are entitled to all the usual protections afforded criminal defendants (a jury trial, government-provided counsel, *Miranda* warnings), and aliens in the United States may claim the protection of the First Amendment's guarantees of free speech and free exercise of religion in their everyday lives,[2] congressional decisions as to who may enter and reside in the United States and the procedures for determining entry and residence are not subject to the usual constitutional restraints.[3] Second, the plenary power doctrine ratchets down the level of judicial scrutiny given to federal statutes and policies that draw lines based on alienage. Thus, while the Supreme Court has held invalid under the equal protection clause most *state* laws that deny settled immigrants social and economic benefits[4] (going so far as to deny states the power to exclude undocumented children from public schools),[5] *federal* laws restricting benefits to citizens have been routinely upheld.

In this chapter I describe and critique justifications usually offered for the nonapplication of constitutional norms to immigration and naturalization regulations and minimal scrutiny of federal policies that discriminate on the basis of alienage. I argue that underlying the offered justifications is the Court's concern about intrusion into matters it believes better left to the political branches. That is, the plenary power doctrine acts as a vehicle for institutional deference. I suggest that such deference is, today, misplaced and that the Supreme Court has already taken a significant step away from the plenary power doctrine. Abandoning plenary power in the immigration field will not undermine American sovereignty. The analysis will show, I hope, that overruling the plenary power doctrine would be a short trip over a well-marked trail.

I will also try to shed light on the background premises that have provided support for the Court's doctrinal approach to regulation of immigration and immigrants. I argue that the Court's constitutional rules reflect an understanding of national membership that makes citizens full members and noncitizens less than full, or non-, members. (I label this approach citizenship-as-membership). I attempt to build as strong a case as I can for citizenship-as-membership and then suggest a different approach, one that recognizes the membership of settled immigrants (here the word "denizen" will reappear).[6] This claim will raise the question of what significance citizenship might have in a United States where immigrants enjoy constitutional rights equally with citizens. I conclude by suggesting an understanding of citizenship that *decenters* the concept; citizenship describes not a core set of rights holders but rather those understood to *belong to* America.

Plenary Power in Immigration and Naturalization Law

For more than a hundred years, constitutional reasoning about immigration law has been dominated by the plenary power doctrine. Justice Frankfurter's mid-century characterization of the doctrine shows both its strength and its potential harshness: "[T]he underlying policies of what classes of aliens shall be allowed to enter and what classes of aliens shall be allowed to stay, are for Congress exclusively to determine even though such determination may be deemed to offend American traditions."[7]

Congress acts largely free from any Court-imposed constitutional limits when it defines the categories of aliens entitled to enter,[8] designates categories of excludable aliens,[9] establishes admissions and detention procedures at the border,[10] authorizes the deportation of aliens residing in the country,[11] denies resident aliens benefits[12] and federal employment,[13] permits the interdiction on the high seas of aliens seeking to come to the United States,[14] and defines classes of aliens ineligible for U.S. citizenship.[15] (The Court has applied constitutional norms of due process in deportation proceedings,[16] but because deportation is held not to constitute "punishment," substantive grounds of deportation may not be challenged as cruel and unusual punishment, ex post facto laws, or bills of attainder.)[17]

The Court's immigration cases bristle with language that sounds anachronistic to the modern constitutional lawyer: "Congress regularly makes rules [under its immigration power] that would be unacceptable if applied to citizens."[18] "Our cases 'have long recognized the power to expel or exclude aliens as a fundamental sovereign attribute exercised by the Government's political departments largely immune from judicial control.'"[19] These are not the words of a bygone era. Government litigators continue to describe congressional power in the broadest possible terms. In a brief filed in 1997, the solicitor general of the United States told the Supreme Court that "[d]eferential review of legislation concerning immigration and nationality is not a relic of the legal past";[20] the plenary power doctrine is appropriate because immigration regulation is "a necessary and inherent attribute of national sovereignty" and "uniquely political in character."[21]

These statements stand in marked contrast to the constitutional protections afforded immigrants outside of the context of immigration regulation. And they are dramatically out of step with broader constitutional developments over the past half-century. What is their source and the strength of their staying power?

Bases of the Plenary Power Cases

I described in Chapter 2 the late-nineteenth-century Supreme Court decisions that announced Congress's "plenary power" to regulate immigration.[22] Consistent with the categorical judicial style of the day,[23] the Court's opinions purported to distinguish separate spheres for the judiciary and the political branches. The judiciary would police those boundaries, but it would not intrude into issues squarely within the province of the nonjudicial branches. Such issues were labeled "political"—meaning appropriate for resolution by the political branches. In calling a question "political," the Court had already concluded that Congress or the executive was operating within constitutional or statutory limits and that no further substantive judicial review of the challenged conduct was therefore warranted.[24]

Thus, in *Fong Yue Ting v. United States,* the Court noted that, in exercising the power of judicial review, "it behooves the court to be careful that it does not undertake to pass upon *political questions,* the final decision of which has been committed by the Constitution to the other departments of the government."[25] In more modern terms, we would say that the nineteenth-century Court would not second-guess the legislature or executive branch on issues of policy. That this is the Court's meaning is made clear later in the same opinion:

> The question whether, and upon what conditions, these aliens shall be permitted to remain within the United States being one to be determined by the political departments of the government, the judicial department cannot properly express an opinion upon the wisdom, the policy or the justice of the measures enacted by Congress in the exercise of the powers confided to it by the Constitution over this subject.[26]

In this case the Court concluded, as a matter of substantive constitutional law, that the Constitution had not been violated either because the Constitution did not speak to the question or because the exercise of authority was clearly within the legitimate domain of the legislature or executive.[27]

The modern cases are structured quite differently, though they cite and quote the late-nineteenth-century cases. The Court's categorical reasoning has been replaced by twentieth-century discussions of the appropriate level of scrutiny to be applied to the immigration or nationality regulation at issue. The Court thus talks not about matters being confided to the final judgment of the political branches but rather of "the need for special judicial deference"[28] and the appropriateness of "narrow standard of review of decisions made by the Congress or the President in the area of immigration and naturalization."[29]

There are two possible foundations for the extraordinary deference shown by the courts. The first is that *different substantive constitutional norms* apply to immigration and naturalization regulations than apply to other congressional powers. On this account, for example, the general norms against discrimination based on gender and illegitimacy would not apply with the same force to immigration rules.[30] A second basis is focused on the Court's understanding of its *institutional role:* judicial intervention in the decisions of Congress and the executive branch regarding immigration policy is inappropriate. Institutional deference might have two sources. A court may conclude that such deference is constitutionally mandated, or it may exercise judicial restraint for nonconstitutional institutional reasons.[31] Significantly, this justification for the plenary power doctrine is not based on a claim that the Constitution establishes substantive norms for evaluating immigration and naturalization laws that are different from those applied outside the immigration context. That is, the usual constitutional norms may in fact be applicable to immigration regulations; the Court, however, will not bring them fully to bear.[32] The institutional deference account, then, does not free Congress from any constitutional restraints. Indeed, it may impose special burdens on Congress to consider the constitutionality of its laws, if it knows that the Court—for institutional reasons—is unlikely to do so.[33]

Institutional Deference: The Model

Most of the scholarship in the immigration field has adopted a "substantive norms" interpretation of the plenary power cases. To some extent this characterization of the cases may be part of a strategic effort to persuade the courts to abandon the substantive double standard: the idea that the Constitution would not condemn, say, race-based exclusion laws seems so foreign to modern constitutionalism that to assert that the doctrine does so is to undermine it. This reading of the cases finds footing in some of the rather extreme language that the Court has used over the years. What, after all, does one make of the statements that "[w]hatever the procedure authorized by Congress is, it is due process as far as an alien denied entry is concerned"[34] and "an alien seeking initial admission to the United States requests a privilege and has no constitutional rights regarding his application"?[35] The substantive norm interpretation has also been aided by an obiter dictum in *Mathews v. Diaz*.[36] In the course of noting that the Constitution does not automatically condemn all distinctions between citizens and aliens—hardly a startling conclusion—Justice Stevens wrote that "[i]n the exercise of its broad power over naturalization and immigration, Congress regularly makes rules that would be unacceptable if applied to citizens."[37]

But there is less to these hints than meets the eye. First, Justice Stevens's comment in *Diaz* has been dramatically overread in support of classifications that discriminate against aliens.[38] As Justice Stevens makes clear in a sentence that immediately follows the oft-cited proposition, he is referring not to regulations that draw distinctions based on alienage but rather to Congress's power to exclude and remove aliens—a power that Congress presumably cannot exercise over citizens.

Second, the statements by the Court in the past half-century that most strongly support the substantive norm explanation are primarily found in cases involving the rights of persons arriving at the border for the first time.[39] This exception at the border has a long, if controversial, history in immigration law. It is founded on the fiction that an alien at a port of entry is not inside the territory of the United States and therefore the Constitution does not apply. Decades of scholarship have decried the fiction. As scholars from Henry Hart to Gerald Neuman have forcefully shown, the claim that the Constitution has nothing to say when the government expels persons who are seeking to enter our territory cannot be squared with the idea of a rule of law.[40] Reversal of these cases is thus long overdue. In any event, they add no obvious support to a substantive norm position with respect to aliens inside the border.[41]

These weaknesses suggest that something else is the engine that drives the plenary power train. An alternative explanation—the institutional deference reading—receives strong support in the one modern case in which the Court actually seeks to supply a rationale in support of low-level scrutiny. In *Diaz,* Justice Stevens, writing for the Court, provided the following analysis:

> For reasons long recognized as valid, the responsibility for regulating the relationship between the United States and our alien visitors has been committed to the political branches of the Federal Government. Since decisions in these matters may implicate our relations with foreign powers, and since a wide variety of classifications must be defined in the light of changing political and economic circumstances, such decisions are frequently of a character more appropriate to either the Legislature or the Executive than to the Judiciary . . . Any rule of constitutional law that would inhibit the flexibility of the political branches of government to respond to changing world conditions should be adopted only with the greatest caution. *The reasons that preclude judicial review of political questions also dictate a narrow standard of review of decisions made by the Congress or the President in the area of immigration and naturalization.*[42]

The language here is not of a separate set of substantive norms for immigration and nationality cases but rather of the need for judicial caution and attention to role. Particularly revealing is the concluding sentence's reference to the "political question" doctrine—signaling concerns of justiciability rather than the presence of an applicable (lower than normal) substantive constitutional norm. As the Court has noted, "In invoking the political question doctrine, a court acknowledges the possibility that a constitutional provision may not be judicially enforceable. Such a decision is of course very different from determining that specific congressional action does not violate the Constitution."[43]

Justice Stevens is careful to reason by analogy to the political question doctrine rather than to invoke it fully. A conclusion that immigration cases involve nonjusticiable political questions is not consistent with applying even a low level of scrutiny. But Justice Stevens's description of immigration and nationality policies as "decisions . . . [that] may implicate our relations with foreign powers" is an obvious reference to congressional and executive branch actions that have typically been found to constitute nonjusticiable political questions.[44] Reference to the political question doctrine also provides a linkage—albeit in the form of a pun—to the nineteenth-century decisions that saw immigration cases as raising "political questions." As I have noted, that terminology in the early cases referred to matters of policy appropriate for congressional resolution, not to the modern political question doctrine of nonjusticiability nor to the deferential standard of review applied in the modern plenary power cases. But Justice Stevens makes the most of the play on words, using the word "political" four times in the quoted paragraph. In sum, the Court in *Diaz* based the application of low-level scrutiny on an understanding of the appropriate role of the courts, invoking the spirit but not the full force of both the nineteenth-century cases and the modern political question doctrine in crafting a rule of institutional deference.

To be sure, the cases are not examples of ringing clarity on the question of the source of low-level scrutiny. In the important case of *Fiallo v. Bell,*[45] for instance, the Court's opinion quotes from the nineteenth-century cases, refers to the "political character" of the immigration power, cites *Diaz* and other modern deference cases, and concludes with a quotation from Justice Frankfurter that immigration matters are "solely for the responsibility of the Congress and wholly outside the power of this Court to control."[46] With this kind of ordnance, the result in the case is, so to speak, overdetermined. And *Diaz* itself can be read as a substantive norm case, despite the Court's invocation of a quasi–political question doctrine. There, the Court held that the rule of strict scrutiny for state laws that deny welfare benefits on the basis of alienage is not applicable to federal laws that do the same. One might see in *Diaz,* then, the application of a substantive norm that regulations disfavoring aliens, when adopted by Congress, are not unconstitutional when viewed as an exercise of the immigration power. On this reading, the Court has not refused for prudential reasons to apply the usual nondiscrimination norm; it has crafted a different (fully enforced) nondiscrimination norm for federal laws.[47]

In the end, however, the institutional deference has significant plausibility. One can make the decisions fit the substantive law position, but it does not seem to get to the core of the cases. Consider *Fiallo.* At issue in the case was a provision in the immigration code that permitted out-of-wedlock children to enter the United States based on a relationship with a U.S. citizen or permanent resident-alien mother, but not a U.S. citizen or permanent resident-alien father. The plaintiffs argued that the "double-barreled discrimination" (sex and illegitimacy) rendered the statute plainly unconstitutional under prevailing law.[48] A majority of the Justices disagreed. The Court adopted a standard of virtual judicial abdication—that the statute will be sustained if based on a "facially legitimate and bona fide reason."[49] But it did not do so by announcing a substantive norm for immigration cases; it did not make arguments that discrimination on these bases was less offensive in the immigration area, that immigrants may not invoke equal protection principles, or that those principles must be differently interpreted when applied to immigrants. Instead, the Court reiterated several times the premise that it had "no judicial authority to substitute our political judgment for that of the Congress."[50] This is the language of institutional deference, not the rendering of a substantive judgment on the meaning of equal protection in immigration cases.[51]

Institutional Deference: The Critique

The institutional deference reading has two important implications. First, it means that whatever the courts' diffidence in enforcing constitutional norms on the political branches, those norms are nonetheless fully binding on the legislative and executive branches.[52] This obligates decision makers to measure governmental action against the norm—and not to forgo such analysis on the ground that the courts will not enforce it.[53]

Second—and more important for present purposes—abandonment of the plenary power doctrine would not require a dramatic new reading of the Constitution. Rather, it requires a rethinking of the judicial role. Just how strong are the reasons for judicial modesty in the field of immigration and nationality regulation today?

As noted earlier, the Court has explained its stance of deference in terms that borrow from the "political question" cases.[54] As others have shown,[55] however, it takes little more than a glance at the factors identified in the leading political question decision, *Baker v. Carr,*[56] to recognize their inapplicability to most constitutional questions involving immigration and naturalization. These areas of federal power are no more or less demonstrably committed to another branch than other federal powers such as the commerce or tax and spending powers. (Indeed, the immigration power is not specifically mentioned anywhere in the Constitution.) When the challenges are based on the due process and equal protection clauses (as most are), there is no basis for finding a lack of judicially discoverable or manageable standards; these are mainstays of modern constitutional law. Nor it is likely that a court decision invalidating an immigration or naturalization classification or procedure would "[express] [a] lack of respect due coordinate branches" or unduly create "the potentiality of embarrassment from multifarious pronouncements by various departments on one question"[57]—at least no more than a holding that an exercise of the commerce power exceeds Congress's authority.[58]

Immigration regulations are frequently said to implicate the foreign relations of the United States, an area that courts have largely left to the political branches. But *Baker* properly notes that "it is error to suppose that every case or controversy which touches foreign relations lies beyond judicial cognizance."[59] As Stephen Legomsky has sensibly suggested, nothing would prevent a court from staying its hand in a case that truly called for application of the political question doctrine,[60] for example, a declaration by the president barring entry to the United States by citizens of a country with which the United States is at war.[61]

A variant of the quasi–political question ground for institutional deference focuses on the nature of immigration and nationality regulations as "membership decisions." As the government has argued in briefs to the Supreme Court:

> [P]olicies toward the admission to this country, and most especially to full citizenship therein, of those not born here are uniquely political in character, dealing as they do with the threshold question of who is entitled to any share in the benefits, protections, and responsibilities of the democratic compact that the Constitution represents.[62]

Further:

> The judiciary has an unquestioned role in protecting rights accorded under the Constitution to citizens and to those aliens who have been allowed to become legal residents of this country, but it has *no role to play* in adopting the policies for determining which foreign-born persons should be permitted to become members of our society in the first place.[63]

Michael Walzer has similarly argued that admission policies "suggest the deepest meaning of self-determination," helping to constitute "historically stable, ongoing associations of men and women with some special commitment to one another and some special sense of their common life."[64] To some degree these statements are true, but there are substantial risks in using the immigration power to define "ideal members" of a national community. Membership decisions may display virulent intolerance based on race, political opinion, or lifestyle.[65] The Alien and Sedition Acts and Chinese exclusion laws, as well as ideological exclusion grounds currently in force, should serve as cautionary examples to those who urge that the immigration power be left unconstrained by the Constitution in order to promote the maintenance of "communities of character."

Happily, "self-definition" has rarely been a central aspect of immigration regulation. The vast majority of immigration decisions are not club membership rules carefully crafted to preserve a particular group identity. They are much closer to university admission policies than to rules regulating religious conversions. The classification of aliens and the establishment of procedures for their entry and removal constitute decisions that are grounded in everyday judgments about family ties, efficiency, fraud and crime prevention, and economic impact. The immigration power is thus roughly analogous to the commerce power. It is an important instrument for channeling and controlling economic and social development and for pursuing humanitarian goals (such as the admission of refugees). Like the commerce power, it has significant implications for our relations with foreign nations. To be sure, such policies have important social, economic, and political consequences for the United States. But so do a host of other federal regulations that the Court would not hesitate to analyze under prevailing constitutional norms.[66]

The institutional deference claim, then, is not persuasive. Applying the usual constitutional norms to immigration regulations will neither unduly intrude the judiciary into political matters, nor will it leave the United States weak, unprotected, or vulnerable. For nearly a century the Supreme Court has applied due process norms to procedures for the removal of aliens.[67] There is no evidence that these rulings have hobbled federal efforts at enforcement of the immigration laws.

The most recent example comes in a case that may ultimately prove to have been the beginning of the end for the plenary power doctrine. In *Zadvydas v. Davis,* the Supreme Court considered the legality of the indefinite detention of aliens who had been ordered deported but could not be removed because they were stateless or their home countries would not accept them back.[68] (That these detainees are commonly referred to as "lifers" by immigration officials shows how bleak the prospects are that they face.) The INS had instituted a review policy under which detained aliens could be released if they were deemed not likely to abscond or to pose a significant threat to public safety. The Court, in a 5-to-4 decision, held that an alien who has been ordered deported must be released after six months in detention if it is shown that "there is no significant likelihood of removal in the reasonably foreseeable future."[69]

As a technical matter, the Court's decision was one of statutory interpretation. But what clearly does the work in the majority opinion are underlying constitutional values that censure indefinite detention. The Court noted that its prior cases had established that preventive detention of dangerous persons in civil proceedings is unconstitutional unless "the dangerousness rationale [is] accompanied by some other special circumstance, such as mental illness, that helps to create the danger."[70] Such a special circumstance was found lacking in the immigration context. Moreover, not only was the detention potentially indefinite, but also it was imposed in administrative proceedings without the possibility of significant judicial scrutiny. In order to avoid the serious constitutional issue that would be raised by interpreting the statute to permit indefinite detention, the Court read the statute to permit detention only for the purpose of removing the alien: when it has become clear, after a reasonable period of time, that deportation is not likely, the alien must be released.

As noted by the dissent, the majority's opinion has significant consequences. Individuals convicted of serious crimes who have no legal right to enter or reside in the United States will now be released from INS detention if their home countries are unwilling to accept them back.[71] Perhaps more important, however, is the majority's treatment of the plenary power doctrine.

In its brief to the Court, the government relied on the long line of plenary power precedents in arguing that "the political Branches must have broad latitude in fashioning policies concerning the detention or release of aliens who are ordered removed from the United States, and . . . courts must give great deference to Congress in enacting laws governing detention and to the Executive in implementing those laws."[72] Justice Scalia's dissent, citing the *Chinese Exclusion Case,* accepted the government's position that an alien in detention who had been ordered deported is in the same position as an alien seeking initial entry to the United States: "Insofar as a claimed legal right to release into this country is concerned, an alien under final order of removal stands on an equal footing with an inadmissible alien at the threshold of entry: He has no such right."[73] But noticeably absent from Justice Breyer's majority opinion is the usual list of plenary power cases and quotations to their language of extreme deference. The detention issue is analyzed under the usual constitutional norms applied outside the immigration context. Noting that "[t]he Government . . . looks for support to cases holding that Congress has 'plenary power' to create immigration law, and that the judicial branch must defer to executive and legislative branch decisionmaking in that area," the majority opinion responded—as if the proposition were not controversial—"[b]ut that power is subject to important constitutional limitations."[74]

This quick dismissal of plenary power would be a rather remarkable way to announce the end of a century-old doctrine. Thus, it is hard to read the Court's opinion as stating that henceforth all immigration rules will be subject to normal constitutional scrutiny. Perhaps *Zadvydas* will be limited to cases of indefinite detention, or put in the category of cases that apply due process to deportation proceedings,[75] without disturbing congressional authority to determine classes of admissible aliens, the conditions of their stay, or the grounds for their removal. Words of qualification in Breyer's opinion leave this impression. He noted that the indefinite detention cases do not "require us to consider the political branches' authority to control entry into the United States."[76] Furthermore, Justice O'Connor, who provided the crucial fifth vote for the majority, seemed to adhere to the continuing vitality of *Fiallo v. Bell.* Dissenting in another case decided the same term as *Zadvydas,* O'Connor quotes with apparent approval *Fiallo*'s plenary power language.[77]

How far the current Court is willing to let the ripples of *Zadvydas* run is unclear. If nothing else, the case provides a revealing glimpse of our immigration landscape without plenary power.[78] In so doing, *Zadvydas* must mean that at present a majority of the Court believes that our nation's defenses will not crumble if the Constitution is deemed applicable to—at least some—immigration regulations.

In earlier days it was argued that the Court's intervention in the "political thicket"[79] of reapportionment would be improvident and unwise. History now tells a different story. Democratic norms have been promoted without any diminution of respect for the Court.[80] Chief among the naysayers was Felix Frankfurter, whose dissent in *Baker v. Carr* is a monument to the perils of dire predictions. His call for judicial nonintervention in the reapportionment cases echoes his statements in the immigration cases. The utterances, which still figure prominently in the Court's decisions and in government briefs, seem increasingly sterile as the years pass. In a concurring opinion in *Harisiades* (which no other member of the Court joined), he declared that regulation of immigration is a matter "solely for the responsibility of the Congress and wholly outside the power of this Court to control."[81] Thus, "whether immigration laws have been crude and cruel, whether they may have reflected xenophobia in general or anti-Semitism or anti-Catholicism," it is up to Congress, not the courts, to correct them.[82] Three years later Justice Frankfurter wrote the majority opinion in *Galvan v. Press,*[83] a case upholding the retroactive application of a deportation statute that ordered the removal of any person who at any time after entry had been a member of the Communist Party. Had he been "writing on a clean slate," Justice Frankfurter reported, he might have concluded that the law violated the due process and ex post facto clauses.[84] The slate, however, was not clean: "[T]hat the formulation of these [immigration] policies is entrusted exclusively to Congress has become about as firmly embedded in the legislative and judicial tissues of our body politic as any aspect of our government."[85] These words were written in the same year that *Brown v. Board of Education* invalidated the deeply ingrained legal and social system of segregation. The Court took the right turn in *Baker*, laying Justice Frankfurter's rhetoric to the side. It is time to do the same in the immigration cases.

Citizenship-as-Membership

Before 1996, permanent resident aliens were generally eligible for federal means-tested social benefit programs on equal terms with U.S. citizens. The 1996 welfare legislation eliminated immigrant eligibility for such programs, both for future immigrants and (egregiously) for immigrants already in the United States and receiving aid. These cuts provided an estimated $23 billion with which to finance the welfare legislation, more than 40 percent of the funds estimated to be necessary for the "reforms."[86] President Clinton announced strong opposition to the alien provisions, yet signed the bill into law. Sustained efforts by advocacy groups led to the restoration of some benefits to immigrants already present in the United States at the time of the legislation's enactment. The prospective bars, however, remain.

Some defenders of the legislation argued that the alien provisions were consistent with long-standing policies that excluded from admission aliens "likely to become a public charge."[87] During the floor debate, Congresswoman Marge Roukema expressed it this way:

> While the exclusion for legal aliens has received quite a bit of criticism, I want to make sure that everyone realizes an often-overlooked, but essential component of our immigration laws—for decades, our immigration laws have required immigrants to stipulate that they will be self-sufficient once they arrive in America, as a condition of their being allowed to immigrate in the first place. Consequently, receiving welfare has been grounds for deportation for these very same immigrants for generations.[88]

This is not quite right. The deportability ground for welfare usage allows removal of an alien who "within five years after the date of entry, has become a public charge *from causes not affirmatively shown to have arisen since entry.*"[89] That is, the deportability ground enforces the inadmissibility ground. Significantly, it does not provide that any immigrant who goes on welfare is deportable.

Nonetheless, lower courts have had no trouble upholding the 1996 exclusion of permanent resident aliens from federal means-tested programs,[90] and the Supreme Court has so far denied further review of the cases.[91] The lower courts have relied on a 1976 decision of the Supreme Court, *Mathews v. Diaz,*[92] that applied a relaxed standard of review to federal laws discriminating on the basis of alienage. At challenge in the case was a provision in the Medicare statute that conditioned eligibility for immigrants on five years in permanent residence status in the United States. The plaintiffs had invoked an earlier Supreme Court case (*Graham v. Richardson*) that had invalidated under the equal protection clause alienage discrimination in a *state* welfare program; the Court had applied "strict scrutiny" to the statute—a standard that doomed the provision. Since the time of the school desegregation cases, it has been generally understood that constitutional nondiscrimination norms applicable to states apply with equal force to the federal government.[93] Thus, it was argued that the rule in *Graham* should control the result in *Mathews.* But the Supreme Court disagreed: while a state may have no apparent justification for distinguishing aliens from citizens, such a classification by the federal government is "a routine and normally legitimate part of its business."[94] In other words, the Congress's immigration power supplied a reason for the differential treatment; it also justified a "narrow standard of review." The Court went on to sustain the statute, "declin[ing] the invitation" to substitute our judgment for that of Congress."[95]

The cases upholding the 1996 welfare law leave no doubt about the impact of the plenary power doctrine. Normally the federal courts would view with great suspicion such singling out of a politically vulnerable group. But the judges who have assessed the constitutionality of the law have permitted Congress to deny assistance to immigrants as a class to save money ("In effectuating the governmental goal of cost savings, Congress had to start somewhere");[96] they have credited the goal of providing an incentive to naturalization (even though that was plainly not a purpose of the statute); they have accepted the goal of promoting self-sufficiency (despite termination of assistance to those receiving SSI benefits owing to age or disability); and they have found that the statute was "rationally related to the legitimate governmental goal of discouraging immigration that is motivated by the availability of welfare benefits"[97] (despite its application to persons already in the country). The over- and underinclusiveness of the provisions, which would have proved fatal under any heightened form of scrutiny, did not fail the rational basis standard.

The Theory

Once the Court determined that low-level scrutiny applied to federal regulation of aliens, the results in such cases have been foregone conclusions,[98] as amply demonstrated by the lower court's validation of the 1996 welfare legislation. What needs to be explored, however, is the ease with which the plenary power doctrine has been applied to alienage discrimination and immigration regulations. The underpinnings of the doctrine, I have argued, is a stance of judicial deference based on concerns about court intrusion into "political" matters. Perhaps that concern—plus the weight of precedent—is enough to explain the Court's approach. But, as noted, the usual arguments offered (foreign policy, the need for flexibility, membership) are so inadequate that it may be worth looking for a deeper set of premises that make the current doctrine appear unobjectionable.

A glimpse at the background assumptions that make the current doctrine untroubling, I believe, is provided in the words of a member of Congress who spoke in support of the 1996 welfare law. Said Congressman Frank Riggs, "[T]he message that we are sending here, and we are clearly stating to our fellow citizens [is] that we really are going to put the rights and the needs of American citizens first."[99] This view—that Congress has the power, perhaps even the duty, to prefer citizens to aliens—is grounded in common enough notions of membership: citizens are full members, noncitizens are something less than full members, and membership has its privileges. I call this conception "citizenship-as-membership."[100]

Citizenship-as-membership has a long past that resonates with deep understandings about the nature of American sovereignty and democracy. In 1875 Chief Justice Waite wrote for the Court, "[Citizenship] convey[s] the idea of membership of a nation, and nothing more";

"There cannot be a nation without a people."[101] Fourscore years later, in a case holding that citizenship could not be lost without the consent of the citizen, Justice Black exclaimed, "[The] citizenry is the country and the country is its citizenry."[102]

These statements understand citizenship as membership in a *national community*—one that asserts the power to rule over a geographical area and the people residing therein.[103] It is here that the link between citizenship and the Constitution becomes understandable. Because the Constitution is seen as providing a legal framework for our national community, it seems reasonable to view the document as primarily concerned with the members of the national community—that is, citizens. (I will argue that this does not logically follow.) This link is made explicit in the oath required of new citizens. To obtain naturalization, an alien does not pledge allegiance to the American people or to the land mass of the United States. Rather, he or she must promise to "support and defend the Constitution" and "to bear true faith and allegiance to the same."[104] Becoming a citizen means joining a national political association—one founded by, dedicated to, and united around the Constitution.

A nation is organized in order to act on behalf of, and in the interests of, its members. It is self-consciously instrumental, as the Preamble to the Constitution makes clear ("in Order to form a more perfect Union, establish Justice, insure domestic Tranquility, provide for the common defence, promote the general Welfare, and secure Blessings of Liberty to ourselves and our Posterity"). To quote Chief Justice Waite again, "The very idea of a political community, such as a nation is, implies an association of persons for the promotion of their general welfare."[105] The crucial word in this quotation is "their"; it reminds us that nations are not eleemosynary associations established for the benefit of nonmembers. The concept of national membership is thus doubly exclusive. It designates nonmembers by defining members. It also recognizes an association that is expected to exercise power in the interests of members with less concern for the interests of nonmembers.

Citizenship-as-membership might at first glance seem inconsistent with the premises of liberal democracy. What, after all, justifies those living in a society (largely by accident of birth) denying equal concern and respect to other human beings?[106] Laws excluding permanent resident aliens from political participation or government benefits are dramatically over- and underinclusive if they are justified in terms of loyalty, competence, or identification with "American values." Alienage, in these situations, appears not to be a proxy for any other characteristic, but rather seems to provide a difference by definition. One might expect a liberal democracy to demand functional, not definitional, differences before denying persons opportunities and benefits.

The explanation, I believe, can be traced to the underlying political theory of a liberal democracy: the notion of popular sovereignty. In a monarchy, sovereignty (in the form of the king or queen) is external to the subject and alien alike. In a sense, every alien and every citizen faces the sovereign on a one-to-one basis. But in a democracy, sovereignty is something shared by citizens and citizens alone. Without a notion of citizenship, sovereignty has no home. In *Cabell v. Chavez-Salido,* a case upholding a state requirement that probation officers be citizens, the Supreme Court stated this understanding of citizenship in bold terms:

> The exclusion of aliens from basic governmental processes is not a deficiency in the democratic system but a necessary consequence of the community's process of political self-definition. Self-government . . . begins by defining the scope of the community of the governed and thus of the governors as well: Aliens are *by definition* those outside of this community.[107]

The Court does not mean that aliens are not "governed" when they reside here; of course they are subject to our laws. It means that a political system in which the people rule must begin with a concept of "The People." For the Court, the Constitution starts precisely that way, and in so doing, it defines outsiders.[108] On this view, citizenship-as-full-membership is not the shoal on which liberal democracy founders; it is the rock on which it is founded.

It is important to note that the American immigration system does not impose permanent outsiderness on aliens.[109] Immigrants who meet congressional prerequisites for naturalization may attain citizenship and thus full membership. Resident aliens who choose not to do so are viewed as selecting themselves out.[110] Justice Jackson's majority opinion in *Harisiades v. Shaughnessy* illustrates the criticism or suspicion that may ensue. The case rejected various constitutional challenges to a federal law ordering the deportation of aliens who had been former members of the Communist Party. Jackson began his constitutional analysis with the following observations:

> For over thirty years each of these aliens has enjoyed such advantages as accrue from residence here without renouncing his foreign allegiance or formally acknowledging adherence to the Constitution he now invokes. Each was admitted to the United States, upon passing formidable exclusionary hurdles, in the hope that, after what may be called a probationary period, he would desire and be found desirable for citizenship.[111]

Thus, the aliens' lack of full membership—making them subject to deportation—was a self-inflicted wound. Those who seek a place in the inner circle of constitutional protections may, if they follow the rules and have the characteristics that a polity is entitled to require, attain it. This consent-based approach to membership is plainly at home with traditional principles of liberalism.[112]

Can citizenship-as-membership account for the proposition with which I began the chapter: that aliens inside the United States enjoy most of the constitutional rights afforded citizens? This conundrum has been with us since the start. The international law doctrines that supplied the basis for the nineteenth-century "plenary power" cases also recognized that aliens, once admitted, were entitled to protections normally afforded citizens of the admitting state.[113] Similar understandings pervade the common law. Duties of care toward guests are imposed on landowners even though landowners have broad authority to choose their guests and to require guests to leave. Just as the imposition of obligations on a host does not change the status of a guest, so too can citizenship-as-membership recognize duties of care toward resident aliens without thereby transforming them into full members. Yet it may be that the various doctrines are not part of a coherent whole but rather reflect conflicting strands in our constitutionalism: one concerned with affirming the importance of membership in a national community and the other concerned with pursuing a notion of fundamental human rights that protects individuals regardless of their status.[114] Or perhaps, as I explore below, recognition of the norm that immigrants possess rights can provide critical purchase for reorienting the Court's current model of membership.

The Critique

Chief Justice Rehnquist has argued that "the Constitution itself recognizes a basic difference between citizens and aliens."[115] That distinction, he asserts, "is constitutionally important in no less than 11 instances in a political document noted for its brevity."[116] He relies on these data in concluding that classifications based on alienage are not "suspect" (and thus should not be subjected to "strict scrutiny"). But the textual references to citizenship can be read two ways. Either the framers thought that their Constitution was really about citizens, and therefore regularly reminded us of that, or they thought that their document was primarily about persons, and therefore mentioned citizens in particular situations as a special case. Current membership theory is closer to the first approach, consigning aliens to outsiderness, but much can be said for the latter perspective.

The Bill of Rights seems consciously to avoid the word "citizen."[117] In places where "citizen" or "citizens" could have been used, the amendments adopt terms like "person" or "the accused." Frequently, the beneficiary of the provision is simply not identified (for example, "Congress shall make no law" and "Excessive bail shall not be required . . . nor cruel and unusual punishments inflicted"). The phrase "the people" does occur a number of times and could be understood to mean "citizens"—particularly given the first three words of the Preamble. It has never been suggested, however, nor has the Court ever held, that such enumerated rights apply only to citizens. For example, the Fourth Amendment states that "[t]he right of the people to be secure in their persons, houses, papers . . . shall not be violated." Yet it is well established that aliens (even aliens who enter unlawfully) are entitled to Fourth Amendment protection.[118] Perhaps most dramatic is section 1 of the Fourteenth Amendment. It begins with a definition of citizenship, yet subsequent clauses pointedly provide protection to "persons."[119] Aliens also figure in other important provisions of the Constitution. Apportionment of representatives is based on the "whole number of persons"—a formulation that has forever been understood to include aliens. The definitions of the military and taxing powers conspicuously avoid limiting Congress's authority to burden noncitizens. Not surprisingly, draft and taxation measures (with certain exceptions) have regularly applied to resident aliens. Nonenumerated rights too—such as the "right of privacy"—have never been limited to citizens. When the Court identifies such rights, it simply seems to assume that they apply to all persons within the territorial limits of the United States.

When read in this manner, the Constitution reflects quite a different theory of membership. Rather than seeing citizens as the general case and aliens as the special case (the outsider), we can understand the document as being primarily about "persons"—a category that includes aliens and citizens as subsets.

This is not to deny that the Constitution treats citizens as special for some purposes. The president and members of Congress must be citizens, and only citizens are protected in the amendments extending the franchise. Nothing necessarily makes possession of the franchise a test of membership, however. For most of our constitutional history, large groups of citizens have been denied the right to vote. Moreover, in the nineteenth century, aliens were allowed to vote in a number of states.[120] Of course, our polity now operates on the principles of universal (citizen) suffrage, and it is probably fair to say that today we view possession of political rights as the central significance of citizenship. But the definition of a special subset of electors and elected does not entail that persons outside the subset are nonmembers. That is, one can understand constitutional membership as extending to all persons within the jurisdiction of the United States even if the document privileges citizenship in certain respects.

A notion of constitutional membership beyond citizenship provides a firm base for the current understanding that the Bill of Rights applies to resident aliens. It also helps us understand an aspect of our constitutional tradition. For more than a hundred years it has been accepted that children born to aliens (even undocumented aliens) in the United States are citizens of the United States. Such a conclusion may not be surprising given the words of the Fourteenth Amendment,[121] but it seems difficult to square with an understanding of citizenship-as-full-membership because it gives aliens the power to "create" members.

Citizenship-as-membership is also surprisingly out of touch with the current reality of the immigration process. If citizenship constitutes full membership, the theory should predict a naturalization process that carefully screens candidates acceding to the inner circle. (Consider how much more seriously many faculties and law firms take tenure and partnership decisions in comparison to initial hiring.) In actual practice, however, the immigration system makes its most careful membership decision at the time of entry, not at naturalization. Gaining admission to the United States is extraordinarily difficult. Numerical quotas and detailed grounds of inadmissibility disqualify the vast majority of the world's population from entering the United States, but for aliens who attain admission and seek citizenship, naturalization is usually a matter of course.

Furthermore, the citizenship-as-membership perspective dramatically misrepresents the integration and incorporation of immigrants into the daily life of the United States. Permanently residing aliens live and function much like citizens. They hold jobs, attend churches, send their children to school, and pay taxes. Children they give birth to in the United States are American citizens. From this perspective, the fact that aliens are not required by law to apply for citizenship is not surprising; in day-to-day terms, permanently residing aliens and citizens are already largely indistinguishable. These considerations expose the weakness of current equal protection doctrine which tolerates federal laws that discriminate on the basis of alienage.[122]

The Court, in its better moments, seems to recognize this. In *Graham v. Richardson,*[123] the Court struck down statutes that excluded permanent resident aliens from state welfare programs. Justice Blackmun's majority opinion found the state laws doubly bad. By effectively denying aliens "entrance and abode," the state laws conflicted with federal immigration policy.[124] This holding is at home in membership theory: the states cannot upset the terms of the federal government's invitation. The other ground of the decision, however, ran quite counter to citizenship-as-membership. Justice Blackmun, with virtually no analysis, designated aliens "a discrete and insular minority," thereby triggering strict scrutiny of laws that discriminate against them.[125] Labeling aliens "discrete and insular" is an effective way, under prevailing equal protection analysis, to invalidate unfriendly laws. Justice Blackmun's invocation of the phrase, however, glides too readily past serious analytical difficulties.[126]

The last paragraph of Blackmun's discussion of the equal protection claim seems to take a different turn, one that appears to recognize admission for permanent residence as establishing membership:

> We agree with the three-judge court . . . that the "justification of limiting expenses is particularly inappropriate and unreasonable when the discriminated class consist of aliens. Aliens like citizens pay taxes and may be called into the armed forces . . . [A]liens may live within a state for many years, work in the state and contribute to the economic growth of the state." There can be no "special public interest" [justifying the exclusion of aliens from state programs] in tax revenues to which aliens have contributed on an equal basis with the residents of the State.[127]

Although Blackmun does not appear to recognize the tension this paragraph creates for his opinion, in these lines he actually flips the justification for invalidating discriminatory state laws. The statutes in *Graham* should be invalidated not because aliens are a defenseless group needing judicial protection, but rather because—at least from the state's perspective—they are indistinguishable from other residents of the state. State laws excluding aliens from opportunities should be seen as no more legitimate than laws excluding redheads. Both would be invalid, not because such groups are downtrodden but because the state can offer no legitimate reason for singling them out.[128]

This reading of *Graham* links up with the discussion of "denizenship" in Chapter 6. The claim is that lawful, settled members of a polity are entitled to consideration from, and perhaps participation in, the political system that exercises power over them.[129] Congress retains authority to regulate ingress, establishing—subject to the usual constitutional rules—categories and numerical limits. But once an immigrant is admitted and takes up permanent residence in the United States, discrimination on the basis of alienage alone begins to appear arbitrary.

Living without the Plenary Power Doctrine

Casting aside the plenary power doctrine would open up a number of significant immigration policies to close judicial scrutiny. Cases refusing to apply due process to aliens at U.S. borders would be overturned.[130] Detention policies permitting indefinite incarceration of inadmissible aliens would be condemned as violations of liberty.[131] Naturalization regulations requiring applicants to disclose all groups of which they are members would be deemed to violate the right of association.[132] Ex post facto application of removal grounds would be subject to serious challenge.[133] And immigrants would be able to raise the claim that they had been singled out for removal proceedings because of speech protected by the First Amendment.[134] That this list charts an expansive agenda may give some judicial decision makers pause. But one might approach it from the other direction as well. It shows how strong the plenary power doctrine has been in immunizing immigration law from norms that courts apply every day to exercises of federal power.

If citizenship-as-membership is rejected as an implicit principle of our constitutionalism, then regulations distinguishing resident aliens from citizens are likely to be harder to sustain. Examples exist both inside and outside the immigration system. First, consider the application of deportability grounds to long-term permanent resident aliens. Under citizenship-as-membership, because permanent resident aliens have not become full members, their insecurity in the United States is not troubling. Indeed, their failure to naturalize can be taken as an indication that their loyalty lies elsewhere and thus provides a basis for differential treatment.[135] Broadening our membership horizon to include resident aliens puts things in a different light, however. Permitting the removal of some long-term members of our communities on the basis of their immigration status begins to appear arbitrary. Deportation shifts from a self-inflicted wound ("you chose not to naturalize") to a punishment—one that we could not impose on citizens.[136]

U.S. immigration law also discriminates in favor of citizens regarding rights to sponsor in family members. The alien spouses and minor children of U.S. citizens are not subject to a numerical limitation and thus face no waiting list when seeking entry to the United States. The spouses and children of permanent resident aliens, however, are subject to a limit and face a waiting list several years long.[137] What sustains this distinction, which trenches on a fundamental constitutional interest that protects family?[138] One argument might be that the family of a U.S. citizen is more likely to remain in the United States for the long haul, but that the permanent resident alien—who has already changed residence once—might decide to leave. Perhaps the thinking is that "reunification" can occur over there as well as here and that the permanent resident alien would face less of a hardship moving overseas than the U.S. citizen. A final justification might be that the distinction provides an incentive to naturalize.

The problem with all these explanations is that they are obviously (and woefully) under- and overinclusive, true for some but not all citizens and some but not all aliens. The ill fit between means and ends is not troubling under citizenship-as-membership; indeed, the difference in status is theoretically enough by itself to justify the difference in treatment. If we approach the question from the ground up, however, from real people fully participating in U.S. social and economic life who seek to live with their closest family relatives, the ill fit of the scheme approaches irrationality.

Finally, let us return to the example with which we began: the 1996 welfare law's exclusion of permanent resident aliens from most means-tested federal benefit programs. As a constitutional matter, the Supreme Court has made clear that the exclusion of persons from social programs cannot be based on "a bare congressional desire to harm a politically unpopular group."[139] Congress must assert some permissible basis for distinguishing included from excluded groups.[140] Citizenship-as-membership supplies that distinction; a broader view of membership that encompasses permanently residing immigrants quite clearly calls it into question. Justifications for the exclusion might be more persuasive if they could be linked more closely to Congress's power to regulate immigration. One argument might be that Congress has the authority to deny impecunious migrants entry to the United States, so denying immigrants in the United States welfare is a way to strengthen the exclusion of the poor. But denying means-tested benefits to immigrants who have fallen on hard times after years of gainful employment in the United States is not rationally related to the goal of excluding poor immigrants up front.[141] (The argument that denial of benefits might provide an incentive to naturalize is surely not what motivated Congress.) Conceivably, the denial of welfare to long-term residents might be justified as a "kinder" form of immigration regulation than denial of entry or deportation—granting entry to U.S. territory but not access to the U.S. welfare state—but this just restates the initial question whether U.S. policy ought to treat immigrants differently from citizens. To label that different treatment "immigration regulation" is not to answer the question. Nothing other than "membership" seems to provide a meaningful distinction between the two groups.

Decentering Citizenship

Abandoning the plenary power doctrine would bring noncitizens more fully into the constitutional fold and make distinctions drawn by the federal government between citizens and settled immigrants quite problematic. Some commentators fear that erasing differences between immigrants and citizens would drain the category of citizenship of meaning.[142] Indeed, the Supreme Court has justified exclusion of aliens from state political positions in part on the ground that it is important that we not "obliterate all the distinctions between citizens and aliens, and thus deprecate the historic value of citizenship."[143] As an initial matter, there is something distasteful—if not unconstitutional[144]—about imposing disabilities on one group to make another group feel special. More important, however, I want to challenge the deep structure of the argument that extending rights to immigrants would undercut the concept of citizenship.

The argument for "necessary differences" is based on a conceptualization of membership as a set of concentric circles. The different levels of membership are also understood to correlate with different degrees of rights.[145] Citizens, occupying the center ring, are full members and are entitled equally to full membership rights.[146] Aliens occupy other circles, depending on their status (permanent, temporary, undocumented, outside the United States), and are afforded rights and benefits calibrated to their position in the set of circles. The Supreme Court has expressed it this way: an alien is "accorded a generous and ascending scale of rights as he increases his identity with our society."[147] Naturalization is induction into the inner circle, demonstrating the kind of commitment that merits full rights.

This account is based on the right premise—that citizenship does and should matter—but it gets the metaphor wrong. Although we tend to link the concept of citizenship with rights, I believe it connotes two other meanings that have little to do with rights and much to do with the idea of belonging. The first meaning arises from an international regime of national states. In Rogers Brubaker's phrase, citizenship is "an international filing system, a mechanism for allocating persons to states."[148] Designation of such membership is useful, perhaps necessary, at a global level,[149] and persons who are stateless or who are refugees are in a perilous condition, warranting special international norms and agreements to find them protection, if not a home.

A second meaning of citizenship is the status and sentiment of belonging to the land and people of a national state; it is a sense of identification, the sense of being "an American." The idea of belonging[150] is, in important ways, intergenerational. One is a citizen of an ongoing historical project that looks back to the settlement of the continent, the creation of the nation, and seminal events in the past. No matter when their ancestors arrived in the United States, Americans can claim the Founding Fathers as their own without a sense of irony. A people's pride in its history and achievements can give rise to what John Rawls has termed a "proper patriotism."[151] Rawls has reminded us of John Stuart Mill's definition of nationality as a people united by "common sympathies," caused most strongly by "identity of political antecedents; the possession of a national history; and consequent community of recollections; collective pride and humiliation, pleasure and regret, connected with the same incidents in the past."[152] The project also looks forward. Today's citizens generally believe that their nation is worth preserving for future generations, and the practice of birthright citizenship makes that commitment a personal one.

What is important to see is that neither of these accounts of citizenship requires or depends on keeping constitutional rights from other occupants of national territory. A national state does not necessarily honor its past (or future) by discriminating against noncitizens; indeed, it may dishonor it.[153] T. H. Marshall's famous formulation of the stages of citizenship—proceeding from civil to political to social rights[154]—is an inadequate description of American history and practice because immigrants have shared in this evolutionary process as well. Legislation enacted after the Civil War protecting such civil rights as the right to contract, to sue, and to give evidence in court applied to immigrants;[155] and early on the Supreme Court held that aliens were protected by the Fourteenth Amendment's guarantee of equal protection against unfriendly state legislation.[156] The programs of the Great Society that expanded the social rights of citizens were available to permanent resident aliens as well. Even as to political rights, where exclusion of immigrants from voting and officeholding is now taken as a given, history shows that suffrage for white male immigrants actually preceded the enfranchisement of women and African-Americans. (Today, a small movement is pushing for voting rights for immigrants in local communities. Proponents of such measures do not wish to efface all distinctions between immigrants and citizens; rather, they recognize that local voting by immigrants does not drain citizenship of meaning.)[157] More important, the First Amendment's protections on speech and assembly protect aliens as well as citizens,[158] and recent scholarship describes an increasing interest in, and sophistication of, immigrant political organizing in the United States.[159]

Our image should not be one of concentric circles with citizens in the center, possessing rights and opportunities not generally available to others. Rather, we should see a picture of overlapping circles, one constituted by citizens who "belong to America" and another that includes persons who are the subjects of sovereign U.S. power and the beneficiaries of rights under the laws and Constitution of the United States.[160] This conception does no harm to the idea of popular sovereignty, as advocates of citizenship-as-membership model might assert. James Madison argued long ago that an understanding of citizens as the authors of the Constitution does not entail denial of rights to noncitizens. In his attack on the Alien and Sedition Acts of 1798 he wrote:

> [I]t does not follow, because aliens are not parties to the constitution, as citizens are parties to it, that whilst they actually conform to it they have no right to its protection. Aliens are not more parties to the laws than they are parties to the constitution; yet it will not be disputed, that, as they owe on one hand a temporary obedience, they are entitled in return, to their protection and advantage.[161]

The aim of this analysis is not to "deconstruct" citizenship. I am not claiming that we have entered a postnational world where, as Yasemin Soysal has argued, the legitimacy of the nation-state is grounded on its conformance with international human rights principles rather than on popular sovereignty.[162] The perspective I am sketching *decenters* citizenship—an approach under which citizenship retains crucial significance in the international sphere and, perhaps more important, serves as a form of identification with and commitment to a national state and its future.[163]

Some may object to this rendering of citizenship as a kind of nationalism that inevitably ends up as exclusionary. Indeed, it might be asserted that the move to citizenship in the twentieth century was precisely a way to overcome Anglo-Saxonism or other exclusionary definitions of Americanism. This argument would parallel defenses of color blindness in race law as a way to overcome the harmful use of race in political, economic, and social spheres. Moreover, it could be claimed that a rights-based understanding of citizenship need not leave aliens rightless: the increasing recognition of human rights can be brought to bear on how national states treat noncitizen residents.

As I have argued elsewhere, I do not find the human rights movement advanced enough to protect immigrants adequately in the United States.[164] Nor can I agree that affirming a sense of belonging presents a serious risk, today, of fostering an intolerant nationalism.

To see this, compare the Tall Ships celebration described at the beginning of Chapter 1 (commemorating the five-hundredth anniversary of Columbus's landing in the Western Hemisphere) with Henry James's reactions to New York upon his return to the United States in 1906.[165] In *The American Scene,* James presents his impressions of his rediscovered country of origin after a stay of more than two decades in England and the European continent. Like the Tall Ships a century earlier and ninety years later, James travels around New York City on the water—on a train-bearing barge that connected railroad lines running between Washington and Boston.

James visits Ellis Island, "the first harbour of refuge and stage of patience for the million or so of immigrants annually knocking at our official door."[166] He is struck by the "poignant and unforgettable" drama that goes on "without a pause, day by day and year by year[—]this visible act of ingurgitation on the part of our body politic and social, and constituting really an appeal to amazement beyond that of any sword-swallowing or fire-swallowing of the circus."[167] The scene is overpowering, as if the observer had "seen a ghost in his supposedly safe old house," because it brings home to him "the degree in which it is his American fate to share the sanctity of his American consciousness, the intimacy of his American patriotism, with the inconceivable alien."[168] For James, "the *idea of the country* itself underwent something of that profane overhauling through which it appears to suffer the indignity of change."[169]

I would guess that most readers are troubled today by James's conception of the "inconceivable alien" destroying an American "national consciousness." It was wrong in its day; the immigrants James saw entering the United States helped build and defend modern America.

More important, whatever the prevailing view at the time James wrote, the United States is no longer figured in exclusionary ethno-racial terms. Today's immigrants—again, perhaps a million a year—are entering an America whose national narrative is multiculturalism,[170] even as its national motto remains *E Pluribus Unum.* And they are naturalizing in record numbers. To see citizenship as dedication to this modern American project does not run the risk of a return to the imperialist nationalism of a century ago. It can represent a "proper patriotism" not linked to a denial of rights to noncitizens.

CHAPTER 8

Reconceptualizing Sovereignty: Toward a New American Narrative

For more than a century, American constitutional law has pursued intertwined themes of congressional plenary power and the meaning of national membership. The plenary power doctrines were initially propounded by the Supreme Court as the nation faced "the other" overseas, at U.S. borders, and on Indian reservations. At that time, membership was not figured as citizenship. Citizenship neither guaranteed women the right to vote nor offered effective protection to African-Americans in the enjoyment of civil or political rights. Grants of citizenship to Puerto Ricans and Indians did not guarantee them full constitutional protection. And until the end of the first quarter of the twentieth century, immigrants were enfranchised in a number of states. Membership at the time was largely seen in ethno-racial terms, as the plenary power doctrines aided the United States' self-conception as a *nation-state.*

Over time, the incorporation of whites from northern and western, and then eastern and southern, Europe moved America beyond Anglo-Saxonism (the Irish, Italians, and Jews became "white"). Race became more a matter of skin color and less a matter of national origin.[1] Post–World War II attempts to breach the race line fixed on the overarching and high-minded concept of citizenship. The Warren Court and a Second Reconstruction Congress took dramatic steps against the second-class citizenship of blacks; efforts on behalf of women followed. U.S. immigration law was overhauled: the national origins quota system was repealed and racial bars to naturalization were finally removed.

The American *citizen-state* of the late twentieth century could tolerate, even celebrate, a soft cultural pluralism. Indeed, social and political movements for multiculturalism and indigenous rights gained traction in the political branches. Affirmative action blossomed in the 1970s; the executive branch entered into new negotiations with Puerto Rico, Guam, and other dependencies over sovereignty; and the federal government embraced tribal self-government as the goal of Indian policy.

To the extent that these programs and policies fell into areas dominated by the plenary power doctrines, the Supreme Court left Congress largely unchecked. Legal claims asserting broad inherent tribal sovereignty or constitutional limits on the federal immigration power received increasingly stern answers from the Court. A constitutional strategy crafted to end the second-class citizenship of groups discriminated against on the basis of immutable characteristics could not easily come to grips with other sorts of membership issues. It had a difficult time making sense of the claims of Puerto Ricans and Indian tribes to greater autonomy, and discrimination based on alienage seemed to be a wholly acceptable ground for distinguishing members from nonmembers. In the context of present day concerns about an overall decline in national state sovereignty owing to globalization, the power of supranational legal institutions, and large migration flows, the plenary power doctrines take on added strength as important redoubts of congressional authority to preserve the national state.

I have argued in the preceding chapters against these prevailing norms and understandings of sovereignty and membership. The question before us is how to refashion doctrine and scholarship to bring the sovereignty cases out of the backwaters of constitutional law. I do not contend that the national state is about to, or should, depart from the world stage; to my mind, postnationalism is a long way away. I do suggest, however, that both sovereignty and membership need to be reconceptualized in less rigid terms if we are to establish a political regime that overcomes historical subordination and justly rules over the territory and inhabitants of the United States. An America open to such flexibility will bespeak a (typically American) resilience and optimism appropriate for the new century.

Abandoning Plenary Power

The more offensive language of the plenary power cases is not usually quoted today, even as the cases themselves are regularly cited.[2] Nonetheless, the cases remain monuments to nineteenth-century conceptions of nation and membership. It is a vision wholly out of step with modern constitutional law and the reality of our world today. The cases continue to support results that degrade the best of our constitutionalism. On what grounds today can it be asserted that courts should apply no constitutional scrutiny to the procedures that Congress establishes for the selection and entry of immigrants?[3] How can the Constitution have nothing to say when Congress unilaterally abrogates rights guaranteed in a treaty that solemnly promises not to abrogate those rights without tribal consent?[4] On what plausible basis can it be claimed that the Puerto Ricans living in New York are eligible for federal benefits that Puerto Ricans living in San Juan are not?

In the previous chapters I have argued that the plenary power cases should be abandoned, their doctrine replaced by modern norms of due process, equal protection, and individual rights. In the area of immigration regulation, this would mean that the courts (and Congress) would see immigrant admissions policies in the same way that they view regulations of commerce: Congress would be understood to have plenary power in the sense of possessing full authority to regulate such matters, but any exercise of power would be judged by generally applicable external constitutional limits such as the First Amendment protections and due process. As I have argued in Chapter 7, this doctrinal shift would be facilitated by understanding the plenary power immigration cases as instances of judicial deference rather than as explications of substantive constitutional norms. So too we must recognize that the Constitution embodies a concept of membership broader than citizenship.

Perhaps it is not too hard to imagine a day when immigration procedures are subject to well-established norms of due process, but it may be more difficult to envision the Court announcing that norms of fair treatment condemn discrimination against immigrants in the provision of federal benefits. Here again citizenship-as-membership appears to support the current constitutional regime. I have argued that lines drawn between settled immigrants and citizens begin to appear arbitrary once we shift perceptual lenses. The broadest claims for the rights of immigrants are grounded on international human rights,[5] but this would be a long leap for U.S. constitutionalism.[6] My claim is more limited: it is that a requirement of equal treatment follows from the conceptualization of permanently residing immigrants (denizens) as already being members.

The plenary power cases have made a mockery of the Constitution in Indian law. The sovereignty of the tribes hangs by a thread, secured only by the good graces of Congress. The Court's vision of sovereignty largely restricts tribes to regulating the conduct of their members. It is not a sovereignty that can resist federal power to alter reservations or fundamental governance structures. Nor does it recognize general tribal authority over non–tribe members who reside on reservations. I have suggested that the current Court's narrow reading has much to do with its concerns expressed elsewhere in constitutional law. For the Court, tribal authority epitomizes the problem of race consciousness: a racially defined group exercising governmental authority on behalf of its members at the expense of members of other racial groups.[7] Tribal power is rendered even more suspect in the Court's eyes because resident nonmembers—who are U.S. citizens—are not able to participate in reservation governance.

The plenary power cases in Indian law stand on dubious constitutional reasoning and a repugnant ideology of white supremacy. Enhancing tribal sovereignty would be about far more than making "reparations" for past wrongs. It would be a recognition that the nationhood of tribes ought to be fostered because indigenous peoples have a right to preserve and construct their cultures and because they contribute to an American pluralism that benefits all the residents of the United States. To restore a proper respect for Indian sovereignty, the federal government ought to reintroduce a relationship based on negotiated agreements, not unilateral statutes. This can be successful, however, only if the Court abandons its view that Congress is free to abrogate treaties and only if the Court affirms the binding status of provisions that bar changes in treaties without the consent of both parties.[8] Constitutional law must grasp that "our federalism" embraces relationships between and among three sovereignties, not two.

The territories cases present similar opportunities for reining in the plenary power doctrine. The *Insular Cases* were poor constitutional law when written, and their broadest readings no longer persuade the Court. As has been suggested for the Indian cases, the Court ought to hold that "mutual consent" provisions in territorial covenants are enforceable.[9] This would disavow the current position of the executive branch that Congress has the power to alter unilaterally the governing structures in Puerto Rico, Guam, or the Virgin Islands.

The territories present an opportunity for a more nuanced understanding of sovereignty appropriate for this new century. Perhaps a rigid understanding of sovereignty is a predictable stance in a world that is witnessing challenges to the national state from supra- and transnational institutions asserting sovereignty from beyond state borders and from subnational groups demanding increased autonomy within state borders; but governments that seek to rally the nation around hard notions of state sovereignty may find the concept ultimately too brittle. Today's world is full of arrangements and accommodations that make it clear that national states do not, need not, and should not cling to nineteenth-century conceptions of sovereignty. International human rights norms, humanitarian interventions, autonomy in the West Bank, the political status of Catalonia, devolution in Scotland, federalism in Canada, the evolution of the European Union, and the political settlement for Bosnia all show that sovereignty is a relative, not an absolute, concept—layered and shared and complicated. The United States can experiment with political arrangements that recognize forms of autonomy for political communities (other than states) without undermining its sovereignty on the world stage. Thus we should be quite skeptical of claims that the Constitution prohibits a more robust form of commonwealth for Puerto Rico or novel governing structures in other territories.

My argument against automatic, wooden application of constitutional norms may sound to some like an echo of the *Insular Cases,* but it in fact turns the *Insular Cases* on their head. Instead of the federal unilateralism of earlier days (grounded in racism and paternalism), I have proposed negotiated, bilateral compacts that provide space for political and cultural diversity sought by the people of the subnational polities. Thus the attack on the plenary power cases here diverges from the critique of the immigration cases. In the latter cases full application of prevailing constitutional norms is appropriate because immigrants generally seek inclusion and nondiscrimination, not self-governing areas within the United States.[10]

Different strategies might also be appropriate regarding the inclusion of newcomers in the territories, non–tribal members on Indian reservations, and immigrants. The first group has always been treated similarly to new residents in states: the establishment of residence entitles one to full rights. This should remain the rule no matter what form the status of Puerto Rico takes (other than the unlikely choice of independence). It is significant that Puerto Rico has never asserted an ethnic basis for membership, even as it has promoted Spanish language and a set of cultural traditions. Moreover, there is little risk of a kind of massive immigration of citizens from the mainland that would radically alter the Puerto Rican population.[11] This is not the case for Indian reservations. Indeed, on many reservations, the number of nonmembers exceeds the number of tribal members. Here, immediate inclusion would seriously affect any sort of self-determination for the tribe—a result that runs counter to long-standing federal policy. Thus, other methods of inclusion (as briefly surveyed in Chapter 6) might be considered.[12]

Inclusion of immigrants presents a third model. Aliens have no claim to automatic citizenship upon arrival (as do Americans in the territories), but neither will their residence and participation put self-determination of full members at risk (as might be the case for extending rights to non–tribe members on reservations). Although immigrants have frequently settled in neighborhoods with other immigrants and co-ethnics, immigrant groups, as noted, have not sought the establishment of autonomous governance structures.[13] I have argued that settled immigrants should be treated on terms equal to citizens for most purposes, on the basis of their participation in American society and on a reading of the Constitution that does not confine membership or rights to citizens. Including immigrants in most social and economic programs is also likely to speed integration and build commitment to their place of residence. Recent sociological studies suggest that exclusionary policies can result in a "boomerang" (counterassimilatory) effect: immigrants who perceive themselves as being treated as outsiders increasingly identify by their national origin or as members of a pan-ethnicity rather than as "American" or as "hyphenated" Americans.[14]

Across all these areas, stronger notions of democracy ought to take hold. Residents of the territories have no effective voice in the federal government that exercises plenary power over them. In earlier days, localities and states granted immigrants the right to vote. Measures might also be taken by Indian tribes to permit some form of representation for nonmembers living on reservations. Once we can see beyond citizenship-as-membership, a number of routes become available for affirming the principle that people have a right to participate in the governing of those institutions that govern them.

Objections

Recognizing permutations of sovereignty may look frightening in today's world, particularly when linked to claims of preserving culture and language. Arguably, one strength of American federalism is that it has recognized sovereignty in subnational units that are not based on racial, religious, or ethnic characteristics. The cultural nationalisms tearing apart other countries are unknown in the United States. We have no Québec here. So some of the proposals I have sketched, it could be argued, would take us in precisely the wrong direction—toward versions of a political multiculturalism that will lead toward a "disuniting of America."[15]

To be sure, history substantiates the possibility that the presence of competing nationalisms within a single state can have tragic consequences. The term "balkanization" has a real-world referent. The American Civil War, on some accounts, provides another painful example. But surely we misuse history if we think it shows that recognizing an added measure of political authority for Indian tribes or the territories, or applying constitutional limits to federal regulations of immigration, risks cracking the foundation of the republic. As a sovereign nation, the United States has never been stronger—economically, militarily, and culturally. The claim that abandoning plenary power doctrines strikes a blow to the exercise and practice of U.S. sovereignty simply cannot be taken seriously.

Moreover, several considerations should help allay concerns about granting greater autonomy to subnational groups (such as Indian tribes or commonwealth governments). Although it is not frequently acknowledged, these groups themselves are widely diverse.[16] Puerto Ricans may be largely united in their support of the Spanish language, but they are deeply divided along classic U.S. political lines. The island has a dynamic and open political system in which competing parties have regularly gained and lost the governorship and other top political posts. Indian tribes are far from monolithic. Members frequently disagree on political and cultural issues, such as the wisdom of various forms of economic development (including gaming).[17]

Furthermore, autonomy in governance can be accompanied by the guarantee of fundamental individual rights. The Puerto Rican constitution incorporates the Bill of Rights,[18] and tribes are bound by the Indian Civil Rights Act, which applied most of the guarantees of the Bill of Rights to tribal governmental action.[19] Surely such rights could receive explicit protection in agreements reached between the federal government and subnational communities.[20]

Perhaps the fear of disunion is more about narrative than rights. That is, the claim might be that what links Americans is a commitment to a common story, a shared understanding of a shared past. Differentiated forms of citizenship and multiculturalism may so undermine that commonality as to threaten national solidarity. But critics would need to point to something more than a plurality of narratives to make the disuniting claim persuasive. Competing narratives have been present from the start;[21] and Americans have generally (later) regretted attempts to compel conformity. The shift from Anglo-Saxonism to cultural pluralism can only have been the product of a new narrative challenging an established understanding. Moreover, U.S constitutionalism is firmly committed to freedoms of conscience and religion that virtually guarantee a range of deeply held—and sometimes mutually exclusive—beliefs. This diversity, reflected in where people worship, whom they marry, how they raise their children, what holidays they celebrate, and what food they eat, has not been seen as destructive of a common American narrative; indeed, it is an important part of that narrative.

So the "disuniting of America" claim cannot sensibly be about the ability of the United States to project power at home or abroad, or the risks that subnational autonomy poses to rights or to a single American narrative. I fear that what in fact lies beneath concerns about American balkanization is what has forever been "the ghost in the machine"[22] of American history: race. Simply put, most Puerto Ricans and Indians, as well as the vast majority of today's immigrants, are nonwhite. Their presence and political power do not threaten U.S. sovereignty; they threaten European-American dominance. The invocation of citizenship purports to establish a level playing field and to eliminate the use of categories that have oppressed in the past. But it can also provide cover for policies and constitutional judgments that, ultimately, preserve the power of white European-Americans. I am not asserting that the concept of citizenship is always employed for this reason; I am arguing that what gives the "disuniting" claim the purchase it has is the race of the "others" now seeking power or self-determination.

In earlier times, race was the boundary of exclusion: heathens of color—Indians, new immigrants, indigenous peoples of the territories—had to be subjected to white rule for their own good. Because they were not yet ready to participate fully in western institutions or governance, it was necessary to remove them or "civilize" them. The post–World War II civil rights era promised inclusion through a different sort of racial exclusion: the category had to be overcome and made invisible in order to eradicate its harmful uses. The rhetoric of citizenship moved that project forward. As I argued in Chapter 3, however, inclusion through color blindness was no less a strategy for the "whitening" of America. As nonwhite groups began to assert claims to color-conscious, multicultural rights, citizenship was mobilized as the great leveler, cutting down "special rights" that were seen as being based on categories that had been used to exclude in the earlier period.[23]

The Supreme Court's decision in *Rice v. Cayetano*[24] is emblematic of the approach. The case involved the constitutionality of voting rules for the selection of trustees of the Office of Hawaiian Affairs (OHA), an agency established by the Hawaiian state constitution for the betterment of conditions of descendants of aboriginal peoples. The OHA administers programs funded by a share of the revenue from 1.2 million acres of land granted by the United States to Hawaii at the time of statehood and from other federal and state appropriations made for the benefit of indigenous Hawaiians. By statute, the class of persons eligible to vote for the nine-member OHA board of trustees was restricted to "any descendant of the aboriginal peoples inhabiting the Hawaiian Islands which exercised sovereignty and subsisted in the Hawaiian Islands in 1778 [the date of Captain Cook's arrival], and which peoples thereafter have continued to reside in Hawaii."[25]

Hawaii defended the voting eligibility rule as being closely related to purposes of the agency. It cited Indian law and other decisions by the Court that had permitted restriction of the franchise in special-purpose district elections. Justice Stevens in his dissenting opinion argued that "there is simply no invidious discrimination present in this effort to see that indigenous peoples are compensated for past wrongs, and to preserve a distinct and vibrant culture that is as much a part of this Nation's heritage as any."[26] This conclusion, according to Stevens, received support from the fact that the challenged statute had been approved by a majority of the Hawaiian people:

> Our traditional understanding of democracy and voting preferences makes it difficult to conceive that the majority of the State's voting population would have enacted a measure that discriminates against, or in any way represents prejudice and hostility toward, that self-same majority. Indeed, the best insurance against that danger is that the electorate here retains the power to revise its laws.[27]

But the Court rejected the analogy to the Indian cases on the ground that the elections selected state officials, not officials "of a separate quasi-sovereign."[28] It also ignored Stevens's process-based arguments. For the majority, the case was about race discrimination, pure and simple: "All citizens, regardless of race, have an interest in selecting officials who make policies on their behalf, even if those policies will affect some groups more than others. Under the Fifteenth Amendment voters are treated not as members of a distinct race but as members of the whole citizenry."[29] Rather than crediting the benign purpose of the statute, the majority found that it rested "on the demeaning premise that citizens of a particular race are somehow more qualified than others to vote on certain matters."[30]

The term "citizen" appears repeatedly in the majority opinion, from its opening sentence ("A citizen of Hawaii comes before us claiming that an explicit, race-based voting qualification has barred him from voting in a statewide election") to the concluding sentence of the penultimate paragraph ("The Constitution of the United States, too, has become the heritage of all the citizens of Hawaii").[31] For the Court, citizenship does double work: it wields a sword against political rights based on ancestry, and it provides a common currency for a multicultural society. This last point is made implicitly in a paragraph of the majority opinion that states that "[t]he other important feature of Hawaiian demographics to be noted is the immigration to the islands by people of many different races and cultures"; labor demands on sugar plantations brought "successive immigration waves" of Chinese, Portuguese, Japanese, and Filipinos to Hawaii.[32] "Each of these ethnic and national groups has had its own history in Hawaii, its own struggles with societal and official discrimination, its own successes, and its own role in creating the present society of the islands."[33] The Court makes no use of this demographic information in its opinion, but its import seems clear. Many (perhaps most) groups in society can make claims for special treatment based on past disadvantage, and such claims can lead to divisive arguments about comparative victimhood. What unites us is our common (race-blind, ethnicity-blind) citizenship. Indeed, for the Court, citizenship does not just trump ethnic identification, it supplants it. The majority describes Rice as "a citizen of Hawaii and thus himself a Hawaiian in a well-accepted sense of the term."[34] The move here is linguistic alchemy, changing an indigenous people and a multicultural society to colorlessness.

Rice shows something more as well. It demonstrates how citizenship works to solidify the link between "the people" and the "nation-state." This asserted relationship—let me call it the Congruency Thesis—is rendered most explicit in Justice Black's declamation for the Court in *Afroyim v. Rusk* that "[c]itizenship in this Nation is part of a cooperative affair. Its citizenry is the country and the country is its citizenry."[35] The view is echoed a quarter-century later in Justice White's majority opinion in *Cabell v. Chavez-Salido:* "Self-government . . . begins by defining the scope of the community of the governed and thus of the governors as well: Aliens are by definition those outside of this community."[36] In this conception, citizenship is the meeting ground of sovereignty and democracy: sovereignty is located in the citizenry (the *demos*) that selects those who will captain the ship of state. The Congruency Thesis provides a tight fit: all citizens, but only citizens, possess sovereignty, they possess it equally, and they are entitled to equal rights within the sovereign state they constitute. The Congruency Thesis thus sets its face against special rights for some citizens (such as the Native Hawaiians in *Rice*) and supports federal power to discriminate against immigrants (such as the permanent resident aliens in *Cabell*).

As an initial matter, it is hard to make sense of this on the rhetorical level. "The country" is plainly more than the "citizenry" of the United

States. Currently, more than 10 percent of the United States population—some 28 million persons—is foreign-born,[37] the population of California is 25 percent foreign-born,[38] and the population of New York City is 40 percent foreign-born.[39] These persons help constitute "the country" in any reasonable understanding of that term, and they are surely part of the "community of the governed." More important, as I have argued in previous chapters, the Congruency Thesis is a dubious reading of our Constitution (which generally includes immigrants under its umbrella of protection),[40] and neither the extension of rights nor novel political arrangements at the local level pose a risk to the robustness of national U.S. sovereignty.

One might reject the Congruency Thesis and still believe that citizenship is a respectable principle for uniting a diverse nation, providing a kind of "social glue"[41] far more benign than race, ethnicity, or religion. I do not disagree, provided we have the proper conception of citizenship in view. That conception, I have argued in Chapter 7, portrays citizenship as an ongoing intergenerational narrative, with an invented past and a commitment to a better future. This is a "thick" conception of citizenship—thicker than the notion that what unites us is our attachment to a set of abstract liberal values that hover above and outside our disparate groups and associations.[42] Citizenship is both more than a commonly held set of rights and less than a common culture. It is an important joint venture, on a defined piece of territory, to which people contribute from their particular circumstances (of faith, gender, occupation, race, region, and ethnicity).

I describe this perspective as "decentering" citizenship, contrasting it with the Court's model of citizenship as a package of rights shared by persons in the innermost ring of a set of concentric circles of membership. Under the Court's model, privileging citizens over immigrants (who occupy outer rings) appears wholly natural. But a decentered perspective is oblique to the question of extending rights to noncitizens, and it does not condemn subnational self-determination as a violation of the equal citizenship of those in a favored center ring. Less emphasis on citizenship as a rights-bearing status may actually do more to help construct a community of citizens. Consider again *Rice v. Cayetano.* Which was more inclusionary and more supportive of community building and healing: the state policy (which had been approved by a majority of the state population and whose purpose was to make amends for historical wrongs) or the Court's ruling in the name of citizenship that struck down the state policy?

The American Narrative

The "sovereign nation-state," writes E. J. Hobsbawm, "has entered an era of uncertainty, perhaps of retreat."[43] This rise of supranational pressures on the state—from economic, political, and social forces—has been well chronicled. Europe is evolving before our eyes. Who, a generation ago, would have imagined that the euro would retire the deutschemark and the franc? The World Trade Organization and the International Criminal Court represent dramatic new developments on the world stage. Humanitarian intervention in Kosovo is deemed by the NATO states to have been morally justified—if not entirely legal—under traditional international law norms. Products labeled as made in one state frequently include component parts from others and are assembled in factories with a foreign labor force. International money markets and domestic economies can be roiled by the manipulations of private speculators. The state is also being pressured from within, as demands for self-determination and devolution increase.

But the international regime of national states is not about to collapse. National sovereignty may be somewhat less secure these days, but it is still the strongest game in town. It is important that it be so. As Hobsbawm notes, the state remains "the main mechanism for social transfers, that is to say for collecting an appropriate fraction of the economy's total income . . . and redistributing it among the population according to some criterion of public interest, common welfare and social needs."[44] It is also "the best unit we have . . . from the point of view of democratic politics, for which supranational, transnational and global authorities provide little or no real space."[45]

Support for democratic institutions and redistributive policies requires a commitment of a state's population to something other than individual self-interest or the interest of one's group.[46] Citizenship can play a central role, providing dedication to, and membership in, a national project. Such dedication does not come easily. It requires a faith in the project that may demand, at times, huge personal sacrifice.[47] The role of citizenship, then, is not to identify a set of rights holders who benefit from policies promoting justice and equality; rather, it is to establish a commitment to that political organization most efficacious in carrying out such policies in today's world. Citizenship does not guarantee a common culture for Americans; it provides the common calling of being American.

This vision of American citizenship connotes a sense of nationality (and nationalism) not tied to race or ethnic affiliation. In its ideal form, I would add an element of dynamism. As noted in Chapter 7, Henry James was amazed and troubled by the impact of the "ingurgitation" of immigrants from new lands in the early twentieth century. Describing the class of new immigrants as "the inconceivable alien," he found them presumptuous for readjusting the very idea of America. "The combination there of their quantity and their quality," he wrote, "operates, for the native, as their note of settled possession, something they have nobody to thank for; so that *un*settled possession is what we, on our side, seem reduced to."[48] James longed instead for "the fond alternative vision" and the "imagination . . . of the ideal," which is to say "the luxury of some such close and sweet and *whole* national consciousness as that of the Switzer and the Scot."[49]

Randolph Bourne, writing a decade later, painted a different picture of America and a different "fond alternative vision." Where James saw dispossession and a spinning apart, Bourne saw reinvigoration and the excitement of things new. He described a "transnational America"—one very much in the making and to which new immigrants groups would contribute.[50] For Bourne, Anglo-Saxonism was not *the* American culture; it was merely the culture of the first immigrants. His transnationalism staked out a position between assimilation and essentialism. It was dynamic, future-oriented, and optimistic:

> As long as we thought of Americanism in terms of the "melting-pot," our American cultural tradition lay in the past. It was something to which the new Americans were to be moulded. In the light of our changing ideal of Americanism, we must perpetrate the paradox that our American cultural tradition lies in the future. It will be what we all together make out of this incomparable opportunity of attacking the future with a new key.[51]

Bourne's description of America as being in flux is surely no less apt today.[52] Some fear or dread this uncertainty, but I think Bourne's optimistic reading gets it about right. And two considerations provide both sail and anchor. First, new groups, as much as the old, want the project to succeed, for them and their children. Second, the vision is not one of a new set of Americans imposing a new concept of America; rather, it is one in which newcomers join those here in advancing a tradition. To move that tradition forward, our constitutional law needs to shed the dead weight of the nineteenth-century plenary power cases. Nuanced and flexible understandings of sovereignty and membership are appropriate tools for "attacking the future with a new key."

NOTES

INDEX

Notes

1. Introduction

1. Robert D. McFadden, "A Quiet Majesty Sails the Hudson with Tall Ships," *N.Y. Times,* July 5, 1992, at A1.
2. Id.
3. Id.
4. See Catharine A. MacKinnon, *Feminism Unmodified: Discourses on Life and Law* 166–74 (1987); Mari Matsuda et al., *Words That Wound: Critical Race Theory, Assaultive Speech, and the First Amendment* 12–13, 79 (1993).
5. See Werner Sollors, "Americans All: 'Of Plymouth Rock and Jamestown and Ellis Island'; or Ethnic Literature and Some Redefinition of 'America,'" <http://www.nyupress.nyu.edu/americansall5.html>; Roger Daniels, "No Lamps Were Lit for Them: Angel Island and the Historiography of Asian American Immigration," 17 *J. of Am. Ethnic History* 3 (Fall 1997); Ronald Takaki, *Strangers from a Different Shore: A History of Asian Americans* xi–xii (1998).
6. Ernest Renan, a French philosopher-nationalist, famously said at a conference at the Sorbonne in 1882 that "[g]etting its history wrong is part of being a nation." E. J. Hobsbawm, *Nations and Nationalism since 1870: Programme, Myth, and Reality* 12 (1990).
7. Randolph S. Bourne, "Trans-National America," in *War and the Intellectuals: Essays, 1915–1919* at 107, 108 (1964) (paraphrasing Mary Antin). It is noteworthy that it is the Plymouth landing that commands our attention rather than the earlier Spanish settling of what became Florida.
8. This phrase is borrowed from David A. Hollinger, *Postethnic America: Beyond Multiculturalism* 68 (1995).

9. Board of Trustees of the University of Alabama v. Garrett, 121 S.Ct. 955 (2001); United States v. Morrison, 120 S.Ct. 1740 (2000); City of Boerne v. Flores, 521 U.S. 507 (1997); Printz v. United States, 521 U.S. 898 (1997); United States v. Lopez, 514 U.S. 549 (1995); New York v. United States, 505 U.S. 144 (1992).
10. For many scholars, the Court has failed to provide a persuasive or coherent account. See Larry D. Kramer, "Putting the Politics Back into the Political Safeguards of Federalism," 100 *Colum. L. Rev.* 215 (2000); Vicki C. Jackson, "Federalism and the Uses and Limits of Law: *Printz* and Principle," 111 *Harv. L. Rev.* 2180 (1998); Edward L. Rubin and Malcolm Feeley, "Federalism: Some Notes on a National Neurosis," 41 *U.C.L.A. L. Rev.* 903 (1994). For example, the Court's doctrine prohibits Congress from imposing even minor duties on state or local officials yet tolerates broad federal preemption of state regulatory authority, a seemingly far greater intrusion into local governing prerogatives.
11. Texas v. White, 74 U.S. (7 Wall.) 700, 725 (1868).
12. The updated version of a constitutional law casebook authored by Paul Brest, Sanford Levinson, J. M. Balkin, and Akhil Reed Amar, *Processes of Constitutional Decisionmaking: Cases and Materials* (4th ed. 2000), is a welcome exception. The text devotes considerable attention to sovereignty issues, including the federal immigration power, the status of Native Americans, and the *Insular Cases.* There is also a large and important body of scholarship on Indian sovereignty, which, despite the depth of the scholarship and the significance of the issues, is largely ignored by constitutional casebooks and remains virtually unknown to most constitutional scholars.
13. For a noteworthy exception, see Gerald L. Neuman, *Strangers to the Constitution: Immigrants, Borders, and Fundamental Law* (1996).
14. See F. H. Hinsley, *Sovereignty* 26 (2d ed. 1986) (calling sovereignty "the idea that there is a final and absolute political authority in the political community . . . 'and no final and absolute authority exists elsewhere'").
15. I am thus using "state" in the sense normally employed by international lawyers. The meaning here is closer to "polity" than to the meaning of "state" as government apparatus (used in the "state-society" distinction).
16. Cf. Hinsley, *Sovereignty* at 158 ("The idea that there is a sovereign authority within the community carries with it . . . the idea that this authority is one among other authorities ruling in other communities in the same sovereign way: a state which claims to be free of limit and control within its community is bound in logic to concede the same freedom to other states in theirs").

17. W. Rogers Brubaker, *Citizenship and Nationhood in France and Germany* ch. 1 (1992).
18. Jamin Raskin, "Legal Aliens, Local Citizens: The Historical, Constitutional, and Theoretical Meaning of Alien Suffrage," 141 *U. Pa. L. Rev.* 1391 (1993); Gerald Rosberg, "Aliens and Equal Protection: Why Not the Right to Vote?" 75 *Mich. L. Rev.* 1092 (1977).
19. *Chinese Exclusion Case* (Chae Chan Ping v. United States), 130 U.S. 581 (1889); Fong Yue Ting v. United States, 149 U.S. 698 (1893); United States v. Kagama, 118 U.S. 375 (1886); Downes v. Bidwell, 182 U.S. 244 (1901). See also In re Ross, 140 U.S. 453 (1891).
20. Eric J. Hobsbawm, "The Future of the State," 27 *Dev. & Change* 267, 269 (1996).
21. David Scobey, "The Specter of Citizenship," 5 *Citizenship Studies* 11, 24 (2001); Anne-Marie Slaughter, "The Real New World Order," *Foreign Affairs* (September–October 1997) at 184.

2. The Sovereignty Cases and the Pursuit of an American Nation-State

1. Other scholars have noted the connections among these cases. See Sarah H. Cleveland, "The Plenary Power Background of *Curtiss-Wright,* 70 *Colo. L. Rev.* 1127 (1999); Sarah H. Cleveland, "Powers Inherent in Sovereignty: Indians, Aliens, Territories, and the Nineteenth-Century Origins of Plenary Power over Foreign Affairs" (unpub. ms.); Philip P. Frickey, "Domesticating Federal Indian Law," 81 *Minn. L. Rev.* 31 (1996); Angela P. Harris, "Equality Trouble: Sameness and Difference in Twentieth-Century Race Law," 88 *Cal. L. Rev.* 1923, 1943–57 (2000).
2. It should be recalled that the most famous dictum of Mr. Dooley—the fictitious saloon-keeper—referred to the Court's decisions in the *Insular Cases.* In talking of the status of the territories acquired in the Spanish-American War, Mr. Dooley said, "[N]o matter whether th' constitution follows th' flag or not, th' supreme court follows th' iliction returns." Finley Peter Dunne, *The World of Mr. Dooley* 89 (1962).
3. Matthew Frye Jacobson, *Whiteness of a Different Color: European Immigrants and the Alchemy of Race* 91–109 (1998).
4. Gender-based citizenship laws were also repealed during this period. In several statutes in the 1920s, Congress repealed provisions of federal law that terminated the citizenship of a woman U.S. citizen who married a noncitizen; and in 1934 Congress amended birthright citizenship rules that had, since 1790, granted only male U.S. citizens the right to transmit citizenship to children born outside the

United States. See Candice Lewis Bredbenner, *A Nationality of Her Own: Women, Marriage, and the Law of Citizenship* (1998); Nancy F. Cott, "Marriage and Women's Citizenship in the United States, 1830–1934," 103 *Am. Hist. Rev.* 1440 (1998).

5. 130 U.S. 581 (1889) [hereinafter the *Chinese Exclusion Case*].
6. Minor immigration legislation of 1875 and 1882 prohibited entry of criminals, prostitutes, idiots, lunatics, and persons likely to become a public charge. See Act of Aug. 3, 1882, ch. 376, 22 Stat. 214; Act of March 3, 1875, ch. 141, 18 Stat. 477. Chinese exclusion legislation is considered in detail in Chapter 2.
7. See Act of Oct. 1, 1888, ch. 1064, 25 Stat. 504.
8. *Chinese Exclusion Case,* 130 U.S. at 603.
9. Id. at 603–4.
10. Id. at 606.
11. Id. at 606. The imagery of the "vast hordes" continues to haunt judicial opinions. See Jean v. Nelson, 727 F.2d 957, 977 n.28 (11th Cir. 1984) (en banc), modified, 472 U.S. 846 (1985).
12. See The Antelope, 23 U.S. (10 Wheat.) 66, 122 (1825) ("No principle of general law is more universally acknowledged, than the perfect equality of nations"); Schooner v. McFaddon, 11 U.S. (7 Cranch) 116, 136 (1812) ("The jurisdiction of the nation within its own territory, is necessarily exclusive and absolute . . . Any restriction upon it, deriving validity from an external source, would imply a diminution of its sovereignty, to the extent of the restriction, and an investment of that sovereignty, to the same extent, in that power which could impose such restriction").
13. American Banana Co. v. United Fruit Co., 213 U.S. 347, 355 (1909).
14. Underhill v. Hernandez, 168 U.S. 250, 252 (1897); see Anne-Marie Burley, "Law among Liberal States: Liberal Internationalism and the Act of State Doctrine," 92 *Colum. L. Rev.* 1907 (1992).
15. *American Banana Co.,* 213 U.S. at 357; see Larry Kramer, "Vestiges of Beale: Extraterritorial Application of American Law," 1991 *Sup. Ct. Rev.* 179, 185–86.
16. Slater v. Mexican Nat'l R.R. Co., 194 U.S. 121, 126 (1904) (citation omitted).
17. Whether neat or not, Beale's solution was rejected by courts and scholars within a generation. See Daniel C. K. Chow, "Rethinking the Act of State Doctrine: An Analysis in Terms of Jurisdiction to Prescribe," 62 *Wash. L. Rev.* 397 (1987). The "vested rights" analysis was condemned as too much of an abridgement of the sovereignty of the forum state. See id. at 412 n.89.

18. 159 U.S. 113 (1895).
19. See id. at 227–28.
20. A 1907 expatriation statute attempted to resolve problems of dual nationality. See Expatriation Act of 1907, Pub. L. No. 59–193, ch. 2534, 34 Stat. 1228.
21. More specifically, he might have derived authority from the commerce clause, the naturalization clause, or the migration clause. See T. Alexander Aleinikoff, David Martin, and Hiroshi Motomura, *Immigration and Citizenship: Process and Policy* ch. 1 (4th ed. 1998).
22. See Cleveland, "Powers Inherent in Sovereignty."
23. *Chinese Exclusion Case,* 130 U.S. at 606.
24. See Stephen H. Legomsky, "Immigration Law and the Principle of Plenary Congressional Power," 1984 *Sup. Ct. Rev.* 255.
25. See Oceanic Steam Navigation Co. v. Stranahan, 214 U.S. 320, 339 (1909) ("[O]ver no conceivable subject is the legislative power of Congress more complete than it is over [the admission of aliens]").
26. *Chinese Exclusion Case,* 130 U.S. at 606. Similar ideas are repeated in *Underhill:* "Redress of grievances" by the injured party "must be obtained through the means open to be availed of by sovereign powers as between themselves." 168 U.S. at 252.
27. I will explore in Chapter 7 various formulations of this prong of the plenary power doctrine. It turns out that the usual rendering (that the Constitution does not apply to immigration regulation) is wrong. Rather, the Court—as a matter of judicial prudence—"underenforces" constitutional norms.
28. This opposing view was adopted in Chief Justice Fuller's dissents in the sovereignty cases. See Fong Yue Ting v. United States, 149 U.S. 698, 763–64 (1893) (Fuller, J., dissenting), and Downes v. Bidwell, 182 U.S. 244, 358–59 (1901) (Fuller, J., dissenting); cf. Gerald L. Neuman, "Whose Constitution?" 100 *Yale L. J.* 909, 953–57 (1991).
29. See United States ex rel. Knauff v. Shaughnessy, 338 U.S. 537 (1950). The Court has latterly drawn a distinction between first-time entrants and returning residents at the border. See Landon v. Plasencia, 459 U.S. 21 (1982).
30. See Yamataya v. Fisher, 189 U.S. 86 (1903).
31. 149 U.S. 698 (1893).
32. See In re Ross, 140 U.S. 453, 464 (1891) ("The Constitution can have no operation in another country"). Gerald L. Neuman discusses territorial approaches to application of the Constitution in ch. 5 of *Strangers to the Constitution: Immigrants, Borders, and Fundamental Law* (1996).

33. See Johnson v. M'Intosh, 21 U.S. (8 Wheat.) 543, 590 (1823) ("But the tribes of Indians inhabiting this country were fierce savages, whose occupation was war, and whose subsistence was drawn chiefly from the forest. To leave them in possession of their country, was to leave the country a wilderness").
34. The phrase was coined in Cherokee Nation v. Georgia, 30 U.S. (5 Pet.) 1, 17 (1831).
35. See, e.g., Alaska v. Native Village of Venetie Tribal Gov't, 522 U.S. 520, 531 (1998); Oklahoma Tax Comm'n v. Potawatomi Tribe, 498 U.S. 505, 509 (1991).
36. Santa Clara Pueblo v. Martinez, 436 U.S. 49, 71 (1978); McClanahan v. Arizona Tax Comm'n, 411 U.S. 164, 173 (1973).
37. Worcester v. Georgia, 31 U.S. (6 Pet.) 515, 559 (1832); see also Elk v. Wilkins, 112 U.S. 94, 99 (1884).
38. U.S. Constitution, Art. I, §2.
39. See Nell Jessup Newton, "Federal Power over Indians: Its Sources, Scope, and Limitations," 132 *U. Pa. L. Rev.* 195, 200–205 (1984).
40. See Act of March 3, 1871, ch. 120, 16 Stat. 544, 566 ("[N]o Indian nation or tribe within the territory of the United States shall be acknowledged or recognized as an independent nation, tribe, or power with whom the United States may contract by treaty").
41. See Francis Paul Prucha, *American Indian Treaties: The History of a Political Anomaly* ch. 12 (1994).
42. See Robert Berkhofer, Jr., *The White Man's Indian: Images of the American Indian from Columbus to the Present* 170 (1978).
43. United States v. Kagama, 118 U.S. 375, 383–84 (1886). The guardianship analogy had been used in earlier cases, but there it had a more legal sense: the federal government was charged with protecting the tribes against predatory state regulation. See, e.g., *Worcester,* 31 U.S. (6 Pet.) at 561 ("The Cherokee nation, then, is a distinct community, occupying its own territory, with boundaries accurately described, in which the laws of Georgia can have no force, and which the citizens of Georgia have no right to enter, but with the assent of the Cherokees themselves, or in conformity with treaties, and with the acts of congress"). By the late nineteenth century, "ward" had a more pejorative meaning; Indians were helpless people, dependent on the federal government "largely for their daily food." *Kagama,* 118 U.S. at 384.
44. Id. at 384.
45. 187 U.S. 553 (1903).
46. Id. at 565–66 (citations omitted).
47. Id. at 568.

48. Id.
49. See 112 U.S. 94, 99 (1884).
50. See id. at 102.
51. Id. at 106–7; see also United States v. Rickert, 188 U.S. 432, 443 (1903) ("Indians are in a state of dependency and pupilage, entitled to the care and protection of the government. When they shall be let out of that state is for the United States to determine without interference by the courts or by any state").
52. See, e.g., United States v. Celestine, 215 U.S. 278 (1909); see generally David E. Wilkins, *American Indian Sovereignty and the U.S. Supreme Court* 119–36 (1997) (discussing impact of citizenship grants under the allotment acts of the nineteenth century and the 1924 statute conferring citizenship on all Indians born in the United States).
53. See *Downes,* 182 U.S. at 286, 300; Late Corp. of the Church of Jesus Christ of Latter-Day Saints v. United States, 136 U.S. 1, 42 (1890) ("The power of Congress over the Territories of the United States is general and plenary, arising from and incidental to the right to acquire the Territory itself, and from the power given by the Constitution to make all needful rules and regulations respecting the Territory or other property belonging to the United States. It would be absurd to hold that the United States has power to acquire territory, and no power to govern it when acquired") [hereinafter the *Mormon Church Case*]; National Bank v. County of Yankton, 101 U.S. (11 Otto) 129 (1879).
54. See Neuman, *Strangers to the Constitution* at 79–83. Despite severe criticism of Justice Taney's opinion in *Dred Scott,* the Court generally held to Taney's view that the Constitution applied to congressional regulation of the territories. See id. at 80–81.
55. The label *Insular Cases* refers to a set of cases decided by the Supreme Court in 1901: Downes v. Bidwell, 182 U.S. 244 (1901); Dooley v. United States, 182 U.S. 222 (1901); De Lima v. Bidwell, 182 U.S. 1 (1901); Armstrong v. United States, 182 U.S. 243 (1901); and Dooley v. United States, 183 U.S. 151 (1901). Other cases decided over the next several years take up similar issues, e.g., Hawaii v. Mankichi, 190 U.S. 197 (1903); Kepner v. United States, 195 U.S. 138 (1904); Dorr v. United States, 195 U.S. 138 (1904); and Rassmussen v. United States, 197 U.S. 516 (1905). This list is adopted from Owen M. Fiss, *Troubled Beginnings of the Modern State, 1888–1910* [vol. 8 of the Oliver Wendell Holmes Devise, *The History of the Supreme Court of the United States*] 226 n. 1 (1993).
56. *Downes,* 182 U.S. at 247. *Downes* will be explored in Chapter 4.

57. *Dorr,* 195 U.S. at 142.
58. See id. at 142–43.
59. *Rassmussen,* 197 U.S. at 523; see also Hawaii v. Mankichi, 190 U.S. 197 (1903). *Mankichi* held that there was no jury trial right in Hawaii prior to a 1900 federal statute that formally organized the territory. According to Justice White, "[T]he mere annexation not having effected the incorporation of the islands into the United States, it is not an open question that the provisions of the Constitution as to grand and petit juries were not applicable to them." *Mankichi,* 190 U.S. at 220 (White, J., concurring).
60. See Balzac v. Porto Rico, 258 U.S. 298, 306 (1922); *Dorr,* 195 U.S. at 143.
61. *Dorr,* 195 U.S. at 146–47 (quoting the *Mormon Church Case,* 136 U.S. at 44).
62. *Dorr,* 195 U.S. at 148.
63. *Downes,* 182 U.S. at 373 (Fuller, J., dissenting). The same term is used later by Justice Harlan. See id. at 391 (Harlan, J., dissenting).
64. *Dorr,* 195 U.S. at 148.
65. *De Lima,* 182 U.S. at 220 (McKenna, J., dissenting).
66. *Downes,* 182 U.S. at 286.
67. Significantly, as in the Indian cases, acquisition of citizenship by territorial inhabitants did not, in the Court's view, change the constitutional calculus. Thus in 1922 the Court held that despite the fact that Congress had bestowed U.S. citizenship on Puerto Ricans in 1917, Puerto Rico remained an "unincorporated" territory; hence, failure to provide for jury trials in criminal cases did not violate the Constitution. See *Balzac,* 258 U.S. at 309. This produced the curious result that aliens in the continental United States were entitled to federal jury trials, while citizens in Puerto Rico were not.
68. *Downes,* 182 U.S. at 278.
69. It was dissenting Justice Field in *Fong Yue Ting* who said that "[t]here is a great deal of confusion in the use of the word 'sovereignty' by law writers." 149 U.S. at 757–58 (Field, J., dissenting). Field criticized the majority for making "loose observations" about sovereignty and for making citations that "d[id] not touch upon the question" and were "not strictly accurate." Id. at 756–57 (Field, J., dissenting). Unlike the majority, Field believed that "[s]overeignty or supreme power is in this country vested in the people, and only in the people. By them certain sovereign powers have been delegated to the government of the United States and other sovereign powers reserved to the States or to themselves . . . When, therefore, power is exercised by Congress, au-

thority for it must be found in express terms in the Constitution, or in the means necessary or proper for the execution of the power expressed. If it cannot be thus found, it does not exist." Id. at 758 (Field, J., dissenting).

70. In cases of the same era involving state statutes that regulated shipping lines bringing foreign passengers to the United States, the Court considered whether the state laws interfered with Congress's power to regulate foreign commerce. E.g., Henderson v. New York, 92 U.S. (2 Otto) 259 (1876) (discussing earlier cases). For plausible textual bases for a federal power to regulate immigration, see Aleinikoff et al., *Immigration and Citizenship* at 185–91.
71. 198 U.S. 45 (1905). So Martin Sklar's account of the Progressive Era—corporate liberalism, with the courts protecting private rights—can only be a partial account, ignoring the experiences of Indians, African-Americans, aliens, and citizens in the territories. See Martin J. Sklar, *The Corporate Reconstruction of American Capitalism, 1890–1916: The Market, The Law, and Politics* (1988).
72. For discussions of the racialized conception of immigrants, see Jacobson, *Whiteness of a Different Color* ch. 2; Shaare Tefila Congregation v. Cobb, 481 U.S. 615 (1987) (Jewish congregation whose synagogue was defaced by anti-Semitic slogans could bring a 42 U.S.C. §1983 claim because Jews were considered a race when the section was passed, even if such a characterization would not be accepted today); St. Francis College v. Al-Khazraji, 481 U.S. 604 (1987) (plaintiff could assert racial discrimination under 42 U.S.C. §1981 because Arabs and Caucasians were considered separate races in the late nineteenth century).
73. Rudyard Kipling, "White Man's Burden," *McClure* (February 1899) at 12. As Sarah Cleveland reminds us, Kipling's famous lines were written in regard to the United States' relationship with the Philippines. See Cleveland, "Powers Inherent in Sovereignty" at 216.
74. See Muller v. Oregon, 208 U.S. 412 (1908).
75. *Al-Khazraji* discusses in some detail Congress's understanding of race in 1870. According to the Court, Congress conceived of as "races" such groups as Scandinavians, Chinese, Latin, Spanish, Anglo-Saxons, Mexicans, blacks, Mongolians, Gypsies, Germans, Prussians, French, and Irish. See 481 U.S. at 612–13.
76. John Higham, *Send These to Me: Immigrants in Urban America* 46 (rev. ed. 1984).
77. Rogers M. Smith, *Civic Ideals* 349–57 (1997).
78. See Reginald Horsman, *Race and Manifest Destiny: The Origins of American Racial Anglo-Saxonism* 5–6 (1981).

79. Id. at 2.
80. Id. at 297.
81. The expansionist policies of the day were fed in part by an optimism and sense of adventure—typified by Theodore Roosevelt—but also by a deep anxiety that gripped the United States in the 1890s. The turn-of-the-century decades witnessed the nationalization of the economy, the staggering depression of the 1890s, the rise of labor militancy and left-wing politics, and the belief that the settlement of the continental United States was complete. The "civic frustrations of the era," Richard Hofstadter has argued, "created . . . a restless aggressiveness" and jingoism born of the "desire to be assured that the power and vitality of the nation were not waning." Richard Hofstadter, *The Paranoid Style in American Politics and Other Essays* 158 (1965). Foreign conflict provided a safe site for displacement of such national feelings. See id. at 159.
82. Nell Irvin Painter, *Standing at Armageddon: The United States, 1877–1919* at 168 (1987); see also Thomas F. Gossett, *Race: The History of an Idea in America* 310–38 (1963).
83. Josiah Strong, *Our Country* 216–17 (Jurgen Herbst, ed., 1963). On Strong's popularity, see Walter LaFeber, *The New Empire: An Interpretation of American Expansion, 1860–1898* at 72–80 (1963).
84. Painter, *Standing at Armageddon* at 147.
85. Id.
86. Id. Proponents of the moderate expansionist position—that the "heathens" should be educated for self-government—resisted the label of imperialism. According to Whitelaw Reid, a Republican vice presidential candidate, an editor of the *Herald Tribune,* and one of the commissioners who negotiated the Treaty of Paris that ended the war with Spain, "It is not Imperialism to take up honestly the responsibility for order we incurred before the world, and continue under it, even if that should lead us to extend the civil rights of the American Constitution over new regions and strange peoples. It is not Imperialism when duty keeps us among these chaotic, warring, distracted tribes, civilized, semi-civilized, and barbarous, to help them, as far as their several capacities will permit, toward self-government, on the basis of those civil rights." Whitelaw Reid, *Problems of Expansion: As Considered in Papers and Addresses* 180 (1900) (speech delivered at Princeton University, 1899). The idea that inhabitants of the Philippines could be reasonably incorporated into the American people was beyond Reid's imagination. In a March 1900 speech to the Massachusetts Club in Boston, he described the American "republican institutions" as "the most successful in the history of the world" and also "the most complicated"—

so complicated that they "tax the intelligence, the patience, and the virtue of the highest Caucasian development." Id. at 208–9. It was thus a system "absolutely unworkable by a group of Oriental and tropical races, more or less hostile to each other, whose highest type is a Chinese and Malay half-breed, and among whom millions, a majority possibly, are far below the level of the pure Malay." Id. at 209.

87. The Chinese were initially welcomed on the West Coast, as they were recognized as representatives of an ancient culture and as hard workers. But with completion of the railroad, migration of Chinese immigrants was seen as a threat to "American" labor and culture. As Ronald Takaki has noted, the Chinese laborers were described in derogatory terms (morally inferior, savage, childlike, lustful, and a threat to white racial purity) that had previously been assigned to blacks. The ideological intent and effect was the same as for African-Americans: to constitute the Chinese as a racial caste inferior to whites. See Ronald Takaki, *Strangers from a Different Shore: A History of Asian Americans* 100–101 (1989). President Hayes made the link explicit. He found that the U.S. experience "in dealing with the weaker races—the Negroes and Indians . . .—is not encouraging"; thus he "would consider with favor any suitable measures to discourage the Chinese coming to our shores." Id. at 103.

88. Immigration and Naturalization Service, *1996 Statistical Yearbook of the Immigration and Naturalization Service* (1997), table 2:

Italian immigration: 1871–1880: 55,759
1881–1890: 307,309
1891–1900: 651,893
1901–1910: 2,045,877

Russian immigration: 1871–1880: 39,284
1881–1890: 213,282
1891–1900: 505,290
1901–1910: 1,597,306

Austria-Hungarian immigration: 1871–1880: 72,969
1881–1890: 353,719
1891–1900: 592,707
1901–1910: 2,145,266

89. See Kristin A. Hansen and Carol S. Faber, *Census Bureau, U.S. Department of Commerce, Current Population Reports: The Foreign-Born Population, 1996* at 1 (Series P20–494, March 1997) (available on-line at <http://www.census.gov/prod/2/pop/p20/p20–494.pdf>).

90. Robert H. Wiebe, *The Search for Order, 1877–1920* at 54 (1967); see also Higham, *Send These to Me* at 43–58.
91. See Eric Hobsbawm, "Mass-Producing Traditions: Europe, 1870–1914," in *The Invention of Tradition* 263, 279–80 (Eric Hobsbawm and Terence Ranger, eds., 1983) (discussing the simultaneous rise of patriotism in the United States and Europe).
92. See Wiebe, *The Search for Order* at 57; see also Hobsbawm, "Mass-Producing Traditions" at 279–80; Werner Sollors, "Americans All: 'Of Plymouth Rock and Jamestown and Ellis Island'; or Ethnic Literature and Some Redefinitions of 'America,'" <http://www.nyupress.nyu.edu/americansall.html>.
93. Sollors, "Americans All" at 3.
94. See id.
95. Id.
96. Twain continued in his 1881 comment: "O my friends, hear me and reform! . . . Oh, stop, stop, while you are still temperate in your appreciation of your ancestors! Hear me, I beseech you; get up an auction and sell Plymouth Rock!" Id. at 6.
97. Desmond King provides a detailed study of immigration restrictionism in the early decades of the twentieth century in *Making Americans: Immigration, Race, and the Origins of the Diverse Democracy* (2000). For more on the "Americanization" movement, see John Higham, *Strangers in the Land: Patters of American Nativism, 1860–1925* at 234–63 (1978).
98. See Act of Feb. 5, 1917, ch. 29, 39 Stat. 874.
99. See Act of May 19, 1921, 42 Stat. 5.
100. See Berkhofer, *The White Man's Indian* at 25–31.
101. E.g., Ex Parte Crow Dog, 109 U.S. 556, 570 (1883).
102. Charles C. Painter, "Our Indian Policy as Related to the Civilization of the Indian," in *Americanizing the American Indians: Writings by the "Friends of the Indian," 1880–1900* at 66, 70 (Francis P. Prucha, ed., 1973). In the same vein are comments by Merrill E. Gates:

> While we profess to desire their civilization, we adopt in the Indian reservation the plan which of all possible plans seems most carefully designed to preserve the degrading customs and the low moral standards of heathen barbarism. Take a barbaric tribe, place them upon a vast track of land from which you carefully exclude all civilized men, separate them by hundreds of miles from organized civil society and the example of reputable white settlers, and having thus insulated them in empty space, doubly insulate them from Christian civilization by surrounding them with

> sticky layers of the vilest, most designingly wicked men our century knows, the whiskey-selling whites and the debased half-breeds who infest the fringes of our reservations, men who have the vices of the barbarian plus the worst vices of the reckless frontiersman and the city criminal, and then endeavor to incite the electrifying, life-giving currents of civilized life to flow through this doubly insulated mass.

Merrill E. Gates, "Land and Law as Agents in Educating Indians," in Prucha, *Americanizing the American Indians* at 45, 52–53. Gates was at one time president of Rutgers and Amherst colleges and was appointed by President Chester A. Arthur to the Board of Indian Commissioners in 1884.

103. See Act of Feb. 8, 1887, ch. 119, 24 Stat. 388. The allotment policy was part of a three-pronged assimilation program of education, citizenship, and land-ownership. See Frederick Hoxie, *A Final Promise: The Campaign to Assimilate the Indians, 1880–1820* at 42–81 (1984).
104. In 1948 a review of the allotment policy by the Indian Task Force of the Hoover Commission on government reorganization concluded that the program "proved to be chiefly a way of getting Indian land into non-Indian ownership. . . . The rationalization behind this policy is so obviously false that it could not have prevailed so long a time if not supported by the avid demands of others for Indian lands." Angie Debo, *A History of the Indians of the United States* 283 (1970).
105. Henry L. Dawes, "Solving the Indian Problem," in Prucha, *Americanizing the American Indians* at 27, 28.
106. Act of Feb. 8, 1887, §1, 24 Stat. at 388.
107. Excess reservation land not needed for allotments would be purchased by the federal government from the tribe. The proceeds of the sales would be held in trust for the "education and civilization of such tribe or tribes of Indians or the members thereof." Id. at 390.
108. Id.
109. William Strong, "Remarks on Indian Reform," in Prucha, *Americanizing the American Indians* at 38, 39.
110. Id. at 39.
111. See Hoxie, *A Final Promise* at 239–44.
112. The Mormon cases displayed equally unflattering characterizations. See, e.g., *Mormon Church Case,* 136 U.S. at 49 ("The organization of a community for the spread and practice of polygamy is, in a measure, a return to barbarism. It is contrary to the spirit of Christianity and of the civilization which Christianity has produced in the Western

world"). This case upheld Congress's repeal of the church's charter and the seizure of its property.

113. *Chinese Exclusion Case,* 130 U.S. at 606.
114. 149 U.S. at 743 (Brewer, J., dissenting).
115. Hawaii and Alaska are the exceptions that prove the rule. By the time of the U.S. annexation of Hawaii in 1898, the indigenous peoples constituted less than 25 percent of the total population. Through decades of settlement and U.S. corporate penetration, the islands had become predominantly Christian, and whites exerted political and cultural control:

> Since 1847 [the Hawaiian islands] had enjoyed the blessings of a civilized government, and a system of jurisprudence modelled largely upon the common law of England and the United States. Though lying in the tropical zone, the salubrity of their climate and the fertility of their soil had attracted thither large numbers of people from Europe and America, who brought with them political ideas and traditions which, about sixty years ago, found expression in the adoption of a code of laws appropriate to their new conditions. Churches were founded, schools opened, courts of justice established, and civil and criminal laws administered upon substantially the same principles which prevailed in the two countries from which most of the immigrants had come.

Mankichi, 190 U.S. at 211. See generally Roger Bell, *Last among Equals: Hawaiian Statehood and American Politics* (1984); Lawrence H. Fuchs, *Hawaii Pono: A Social History* (1961). Hawaii was deemed economically and culturally close enough to be incorporated into the United States, yet the racial composition of the population was troubling enough to southern members of Congress that they opposed statehood until the 1950s. Alaska, which was virtually uninhabited and open to U.S. frontier activities, posed no threat to the cultural and racial images of the United States in the nineteenth century.

116. *Downes,* 182 U.S. at 287.
117. *Ex parte Crow Dog,* 109 U.S. at 569.
118. Id. at 571.
119. Id.
120. See Seven Crimes Act of March 3, 1885, ch. 341, §9, 23 Stat. 362, 385. The act, which was later expanded to include thirteen crimes, is now commonly referred to as the Major Crimes Act.
121. 118 U.S. 375 (1886).
122. 140 U.S. 453 (1891).

123. Id. at 465.

124. Id. at 480.

125. Id. Other cases of the era demonstrate the influence of the Court's assumptions about "civilized" and "uncivilized" cultures and states. The traditional international law norms urging mutual respect for the acts of equal and independent nation-states did not apply to "uncivilized" legal systems. See, for example, *Slater,* 194 U.S. at 129, where Justice Holmes wrote that "[t]he case is not one demanding extreme measures like those where a tort is committed in an uncivilized country," and *Hilton,* 159 U.S. at 205, where Justice Gray deemed comity appropriate when a foreign judgment is rendered by a competent court whose proceedings "are according to the course of a civilized jurisprudence."

126. Of course, *Plessy v. Ferguson,* 163 U.S. 537 (1896), is an important part of this story too, as is the Court's tolerance of the disenfranchisement of African-Americans at the turn of the century.

127. Arguably, *United States v. Wong Kim Ark,* 169 U.S. 649 (1898), provides a counterexample to the theme of this chapter. In that case, the Court held that children born in the United States to Chinese resident aliens were, by virtue of the Fourteenth Amendment, citizens of the United States. The result is somewhat startling, given the Court's holding in *Elk v. Wilkins,* 112 U.S. 94 (1884), that Indian children were not citizens and that federal statutes prohibited the alien parents from naturalizing. One might well have supposed that the congressional decision to exclude the parents from full U.S. membership would have persuaded the Court to hold that children born to such parents (and born subjects of China) were not "within [the] jurisdiction" of the United States within the terms of the Fourteenth Amendment. Yet several aspects of *Wong Kim Ark* should be noted. First, the majority opinion is grounded firmly in the territorial model to the extent that it adopts *jus soli* principles—"the fundamental rule of citizenship by birth within [a country's] sovereignty." *Wong Kim Ark,* 169 U.S. at 674. Indeed, not to recognize the citizenship of U.S.-born children of aliens would be to permit the aliens' foreign sovereign, through extraterritorial application of its law, to intrude into the sovereign authority of the United States over its territory. Second, it might be presumed that children born in the United States—no matter the status of their parents—would successfully be socialized by dominant (white) American institutions and assimilated into U.S. culture in the same way as children of citizens. In this respect the children in *Wong Kim Ark* are closer to the residents of Hawaii (deemed "incorporated" because of

the white domination of culture and economy) than to children of Indians born and raised in distinct tribal cultures. Third, a contrary rule—as the Court notes in a quick and buried paragraph—"would be to deny citizenship to thousands of persons of English, Scotch, Irish, German, or other European parentage, who have always been considered and treated as citizens of the United States." Id. at 694. Fourth, American racism offered curious support for the *Wong Kim Ark* holding. As the "friends of the Indians" had pointed out in urging citizenship for Indians, the nation had extended citizenship to African-Americans; on what plausible argument, then, could it be denied other nonwhites? See also Rogers M. Smith, *Civic Ideals: Conflicting Visions of Citizenship in U.S. History* 440–42 (1997) (noting liberal consequences of the Court's decision, but locating it within the "ascriptive nationalism" of the day).

128. See Act of Nov. 15, 1861, Art. III, 12 Stat. 1191, 1192. That is, certain Indians who "adopted the habits of civilized life" were able to obtain citizenship. Id.
129. See Act of June 2, 1924, ch. 232, 43 Stat. 253.
130. See Act of March 2, 1917, ch. 145, §5, 39 Stat. 951, 953.
131. Section 16 of the Voting Rights Act of 1870 guaranteed "all persons" the same right "to make and enforce contracts, to sue, be parties, give evidence, and to the full and equal benefit of all laws and proceedings for the security of person and property as is enjoyed by white citizens." Act of May 31, 1870, ch. 114, §16, 16 Stat. 140, 144 (codified at 42 U.S.C. §1981(a) (1994)). Use of the phrase "all persons"—rather than "all citizens"—was intended to bring Chinese aliens within the law's protection. See Charles J. McClain, Jr., "The Chinese Struggle for Civil Rights in Nineteenth-Century America: The First Phase, 1850–1870," 72 *Cal. L. Rev.* 529, 566 (1984).
132. The term is used intentionally here.
133. See Gunnar Myrdal, *An American Dilemma: The Negro Problem and Modern Democracy* (1962).
134. Phillip C. Garrett, "Indian Citizenship," in Prucha, *Americanizing the American Indians* at 61–62.
135. See *Plessy*, 137 U.S. at 537.
136. Woodrow Wilson, "Address to Several Thousand Foreign-Born Citizens, after Naturalization Ceremonies, Philadelphia, May 10, 1915," reprinted in 1 *The Public Papers of Woodrow Wilson: The New Democracy* 318, 319 (Ray S. Baker and William E. Dodd, eds., 1926): "You cannot become thorough Americans if you think of yourselves in groups. America does not consist of groups. A man who thinks of himself as belonging to a particular national group in America has not yet be-

come an American, and the man who goes among you to trade upon your nationality is no worthy son to live under the Stars and Stripes."

137. W. E. B. DuBois, "The Conservation of the Races," reprinted in *Writings* 815, 820 (Nathan I. Huggins, ed., 1986) (destiny of the Negro people is not "a servile imitation of Anglo-Saxon culture but a stalwart originality which shall unswervingly follow Negro ideals").
138. Horace Kallen, "Democracy versus the Melting Pot," 100 *Nation* 190, 217 (February 18 and 25, 1915).
139. Id. at 218. DuBois and Kallen are discussed in Higham, *Send These to Me* at 204–14.
140. Randolph Bourne, "Trans-National America," 118 *Atlantic Monthly* 86, 95, 96 (1916).
141. Especially severe were those in East St. Louis (July 1–2, 1917) and Chicago (July 27–29, 1919), in each of which dozens were killed and hundreds wounded. See *Report of the National Advisory Commission on Civil Disorders* 101–2 (1968).
142. See Higham, *Strangers in the Land* chs. 8, 10.
143. Id. at 301.
144. See King, *Making Americans* ch. 7.
145. See Ashley Montagu, *Man's Most Dangerous Myth: The Fallacy of Race* (1942); Franz Boas, "This Nordic Nonsense," 74 *Forum* 502, 507 (1925) ("We must clear our minds of the erroneous concept of a biologically determined racial behavior"). Boas (at 505) noted it was "quite impossible to show that certain constitutions are confined to definite races. On the contrary, every constitutional type is found in all races, at least so far as the European types are concerned."
146. Ruth Benedict, *Patterns of Culture* 11 (1934). Benedict noted that the mix of cultures brought on by immigration to the United States had been met with the unfortunate response of "nationalism and racial snobbery." Modern anthropology, through the study and appreciation of other cultures, could provide an alternative. Indeed, she wrote, "There has never been a time when civilization stood more in need of individuals who are genuinely culture-conscious, who can see objectively the socially conditioned behaviour of other peoples without fear or recrimination." Id. at 10.
147. Robert E. Park and Herbert A. Miller, *Old World Traits Transplanted* 296–308 (1921; reprinted 1969).
148. See generally John Collier, *The Indians of the Americas* (1947).
149. His 1920s phrase. Horace M. Kallen, *Culture and Democracy in the United States: Studies in the Group Psychologies of the American Peoples* 42–43 (1924).
150. Lawrence H. Fuchs, *The American Kaleidoscope: Race, Ethnicity, and the*

Civic Culture ch. 3 (1990); see Higham, *Send These to Me* at 213 (the idea of cultural pluralism is itself one of the products of the American melting pot).

151. Truman called the harsh measure "utterly unworthy" of American "traditions and . . . ideals." Veto of Bill to Revise the Laws Relating to Immigration, Naturalization, and Nationality, 1952 *Pub. Papers* 441, 443 (1952).
152. Act of June 27, 1952, ch. 477, §212(a)(28)(D), 66 Stat. 163, 185.
153. The act did, however, finally repeal racial bars to naturalization. See Ian F. Haney-López, *White by Law: The Legal Construction of Race* 42–46 (1996).
154. The report on the legislation of the Senate Judiciary Committee noted:

> Without giving credence to any theory of Nordic Superiority, the subcommittee believes that the adoption of the national origins formula was a rational and logical method of numerically restricting immigration in such a manner as to best preserve the sociological and cultural balance in the population of the United States. There is no doubt that it favored the peoples of the countries of northern and western Europe over those of southern and eastern Europe, but the subcommittee holds that the peoples who had made the greatest contribution to the development of this country were fully justified in determining that the country was no longer a field for further colonization, and henceforth, further immigration would not only be restricted but directed to admit immigrants considered to be more readily assimilable because of the similarity of their cultural background to those of the principal components of our population.

155. Robert E. Park, "Social Assimilation," in *Encyclopaedia of the Social Sciences* 282 (Edwin R. A. Seligman and Alvin Johnson, eds., 1930).
156. See Roger Daniels, *Asian America: Chinese and Japanese in the United States since 1850,* at 96 (1988); Takaki, *Strangers from a Different Shore* at 99–112.
157. Act of June 18, 1934, 48 Stat. 984 (1934).
158. See Charles F. Wilkinson and Eric R. Biggs, "The Evolution of the Termination Policy," 5 *Am. Indian L. Rev.* 139, 140 (1977).
159. H.R. Con. Res. 108 (1953). The policy was also motivated by conservative interest in cutting the postwar federal budget, and concerns of some liberals that special laws for Indians seemed to be the kind of race-based distinctions that America had fought a war to end. See Vine

Deloria, Jr., and Clifford M. Lytle, *American Indians, American Justice* 16–17 (1983).

160. Wilkinson and Briggs, "Evolution of the Termination Policy."
161. Act of Aug. 15, 1953, 67 Stat. 588 (1953).
162. *Knauff,* 338 U.S. at 544; Shaughnessy v. United States ex rel. Mezei, 345 U.S. 206, 212 (1953) (quoting *Knauff*).
163. Galvan v. Press, 347 U.S. 522, 531 (1954) ("[T]hat the formulation of [immigration policies] is entrusted exclusively to Congress has become about as firmly imbedded in the legislative and judicial tissues of our body politic as any aspect of our government"). See also Marcello v. Bonds, 349 U.S. 302 (1955).
164. Harisiades v. Shaughnessy, 342 U.S. 580 (1952).
165. Id. at 590; see also Hines v. Davidowitz, 312 U.S. 52 (1941) (Pennsylvania law requiring registration of aliens preempted by federal regulatory scheme; Court notes that "it is of importance that this legislation is in a field which affects international relations, the one aspect of our government that from the first has been most generally conceded imperatively to demand broad national authority"). Id at 68.
166. Felix S. Cohen, *Handbook of Federal Indian Law* ch. 5 (U.S. Department of Interior, 1942).
167. Id. at 90: "Reference to the so-called 'plenary' power of Congress over the Indians . . . becomes so frequent in recent cases that it may seem captious to point out that there is excellent authority for the view that Congress has no constitutional power over Indians except what is conferred by the commerce clause and other clauses of the Constitution."
168. Id. at 96. Cohen stated that a taking of tribal land or individually owned land would give rise to a claim for compensation (which was, unfortunately, "imperfect" until Congress authorized suit against the United States), and he took note of cases suggesting that the federal role of guardian required that federal rules not be purely arbitrary.
169. David E. Wilkins provides an in-depth analysis of several of the cases of this era in his study *American Indian Sovereignty and the U.S. Supreme Court* at 119–65. See also Northwestern Band of Shoshone Indians v. United States, 324 U.S 335 (1945) (rejecting claim for compensation for taking of 15 million acres, based on finding that treaty had not recognized tribal rights in the land); Sizemore v. Brady 235 U.S. 441 (1914) (Creek Indians are "wards of the United States, which possessed full power, if it deemed such a course wise, to assume full control over them and their affairs, to ascertain who were members of the tribe, to distribute the lands and funds among them, and to terminate tribal government"). An important counterexample is United States v.

Alcea Band of Tillamooks, 329 U.S. 40 (1946), which permitted recovery in the Court of Claims for a taking of "original Indian title" (the right of the tribe to occupy land). Chief Justice Vinson's opinion stated that "[t]he power of Congress over Indian affairs may be of a plenary nature; but it is not absolute." Id. at 54. *Tillamooks,* however, was effectively abandoned nine years later in Tee-Hit-Ton Indians v. United States, 348 U.S. 272 (1955) (distinguishing *Tillamooks* as based on federal statute authorizing recovery). See Wilkins, *American Indian Sovereignty and the U.S. Supreme Court* at 179–80; Nell Jessup Newton, "At the Whim of the Sovereign: Aboriginal Title Reconsidered," 31 *Hastings L. J.* 1215 (1980).

170. Cincinnati Soap Co. v. United States, 301 U.S. 308, 323 (1937). See also Inter-Island Steam Nav. Co. v. Territory of Hawaii, 305 U.S. 306, 314 (1938).
171. See Chapter 4.
172. H. Doc. 435, 82d Cong., 2d Sess. 4 (1952), quoted in José Trías Monge, *Puerto Rico: The Trials of the Oldest Colony in the World* 115 (1997).
173. H. Rep. 1832, 82d Cong., 2d Sess. 15 (1952).

3. The Citizen-State

1. 347 U.S. 483, 493.
2. For a rare intervention, see Schneiderman v. United States, 320 U.S. 118 (1943).
3. See José Trías Monge, *Puerto Rico: The Trials of the Oldest Colony in the World* 76 (1997); Angie Debo, *A History of the Indians of the United States* 335 (1970).
4. State of the Union Address, January 11, 1944, *Public Papers of the Presidents of the United States: Franklin D. Roosevelt, 1944* at 41.
5. William Forbath has pointed out, however, that the citizenship talk during the New Deal was not about entitlement to minimum welfare benefits but rather about substantive economic rights, democracy, and social justice. See William E. Forbath, "Caste, Class, and Equal Citizenship," 98 *Mich. L. Rev.* 1 (1999).
6. See Kenneth L. Karst, "Foreword: Equal Citizenship under the Fourteenth Amendment," 91 *Harv. L. Rev.* 1, 48 (1977) (two harms result from stigma: harm to self-respect and cumulative consequences); see also Paul Brest, "Foreword: In Defense of the Antidiscrimination Principle," 90 *Harv. L. Rev.* 1 (1976).
7. U.S. Constitution, Amend. XIV, §1. As the Court would make clear in

the 1970s, the equal protection clause extends significant rights to immigrants. See Graham v. Richardson, 403 U.S. 365 (1971). This was recognized early on, when discrimination against aliens was perpetrated as race discrimination. See Yick Wo v. Hopkins, 118 U.S. 356 (1886).

8. 60 U.S. (19 How.) 393 (1857).
9. Strauder v. West Virginia, 100 U.S. 303 (1879). The Fourteenth Amendment embraces "[an] exemption from legal discriminations, implying inferiority in civil society, lessening the security of [the colored race's] enjoyment of the rights which others enjoy, and discriminations which are steps towards reducing them to the condition of a subject race." Id. at 308. See also Harlan's dissent in Plessy v. Ferguson: the state law "proceed[ed] on the ground that colored citizens are so inferior and degraded that they cannot be allowed to sit in public coaches occupied by white citizens[.]" 163 U.S. 537, 560. See T. Alexander Aleinikoff, "Re-reading Justice Harlan's Dissent in *Plessy v. Ferguson,*" 1992 *U. Ill. L. Rev.* 961.
10. Karst, "Foreword: Equal Citizenship" at 21. The Court also protected citizenship rights outside the Fourteenth Amendment context. The major First Amendment opinions of the Warren Court protected political speech. See Brandenburg v. Ohio, 395 U.S. 444 (1969); Tinker v. Des Moines Indep. Cmty. Sch. District, 393 U.S. 503 (1969); New York Times v. Sullivan, 376 U.S. 254 (1964); NAACP v. Alabama, 357 U.S. 449 (1958). But see United States v. O'Brien, 391 U.S. 367 (1968). Karst, to my mind, stretches a bit to make the privacy case fit within the equal citizenship rubric (31–32). This is not to say that the Warren Court viewed rights only through the citizenship lens. The cases protect aliens and many have no obvious link to citizenship (e.g., criminal rights).
11. Others have noted the equality motif in the work of the Warren Court. See Philip B. Kurland, *Politics, the Constitution, and the Warren Court* (1970); Robert M. Cover and T. Alexander Aleinikoff, "Dialectical Federalism: Habeas Corpus and the Court," 86 *Yale L. J.* 1035 (1977).
12. See Baker v. Carr, 369 U.S. 186 (1962); Reynolds v. Sims, 377 U.S. 533, 561–62 (1964) ("[T]he right of suffrage is a fundamental matter in a free and democratic society [and] is preservative of other basic civil and political rights[;] any alleged infringement of the rights of citizens to vote must be carefully and meticulously scrutinized"); Gray v. Sanders, 372 U.S. 368 (1963); Wesberry v. Sanders, 376 U.S. 1 (1964) (one person, one vote); Harper v. Virginia State Bd. of Elections, 383 U.S. 663 (1966) (invalidating poll tax); Kramer v. Union Free Sch. Dis-

trict, 395 U.S. 621 (1969) ("Statutes granting the franchise to residents on a selective basis always pose the danger of denying some citizens any effective voice in the governmental affairs which substantially affect their lives").

13. See Shapiro v. Thompson, 394 U.S. 618 (1969) (invalidating state laws requiring waiting periods for new residents applying for welfare): "[T]he nature of our Federal Union and our constitutional concepts of personal liberty unite to require that all citizens be free to travel throughout the length and breadth of our land." Id. at 629.
14. See Douglas v. California, 372 U.S. 353 (1963); Griffin v. Illinois, 351 U.S. 12 (1956).
15. As will be discussed, the equality movement did not extend to immigrants' rights. No significant cases involving discrimination based on alienage were decided during the Warren Court, although extraordinary protection was ordered for United States citizenship. See Afroyim v. Rusk, 387 U.S. 253 (1967); Schneider v. Rusk, 377 U.S. 163 (1964). It is the Burger Court that extends "strict scrutiny" to alienage classifications. See Graham v. Richardson, 403 U.S. 365 (1971).
16. See Perez v. Brownell, 356 U.S. 44, 64–65 (1958).
17. See *Schneider,* 377 U.S. 163.
18. See Kennedy v. Mendoza-Martinez, 372 U.S. 144 (1963).
19. See *Afroyim,* 387 U.S. 253.
20. See *Mendoza-Martinez,* 372 U.S. at 159.
21. *Perez,* 356 U.S. at 64 (Warren, C. J., dissenting). Warren's dissent becomes the law ten years later in *Afroyim,* 387 U.S. 253 (1967).
22. Here the Court relies on Hannah Arendt. See *Mendoza-Martinez,* 372 U.S. at 161.
23. See *Afroyim,* 387 U.S. at 268: "The very nature of our free government makes it completely incongruous to have a rule of law under which a group of citizens temporarily in office can deprive another group of citizens of their citizenship."
24. See Miranda v. Arizona, 384 U.S. 436 (1966); Massiah v. United States, 377 U.S. 201 (1964); Mapp v. Ohio, 367 U.S. 643 (1961).
25. See Goldberg v. Kelly, 397 U.S. 254 (1970); Sniadach v. Family Fin. Corp. of Bay View, 395 U.S. 337 (1969).
26. See Reynolds v. Sims, 377 U.S. 533 (1964); Baker v. Carr, 369 U.S. 186 (1962).
27. See Brandenburg v. Ohio, 395 U.S. 444 (1969); New York Times v. Sullivan, 376 U.S. 254 (1964).
28. See Katz v. United States, 389 U.S. 47 (1967); Griswold v. Connecticut, 381 U.S. 479 (1965).

29. See also Kent v. Dulles, 357 U.S. 116, 129 (1958) (secretary of state had no authority to deny passport based on U.S. citizen's membership in Communist Party: "Where activities or enjoyment, natural and often necessary to the well-being of an American citizen, such as travel, are involved, we will construe narrowly all delegated powers that curtail or dilute them").
30. 83 U.S. (16 Wall.) 36 (1873).
31. See *The Constitution of the United States of America* 965 (Edward S. Corwin, ed., 1953); Philip B. Kurland, "The Privileges or Immunities Clause: 'Its Hour Come Round at Last?'" 1972 *Wash. U. L. Q.* 405. See also Saenz v. Roe, 526 U.S. 489 (1999).
32. See Fiske v. Kansas, 274 U.S. 380 (1927) (free speech); Cantwell v. Connecticut, 310 U.S. 296 (1940) (religion); see also Wolf v. Colorado, 338 U.S. 25 (1949) (Fourth Amendment).
33. Among the most significant: Duncan v. Louisiana, 391 U.S. 145 (1968) (Sixth Amendment's jury trial right); Benton v. Maryland, 395 U.S. 784 (1969) (Fifth Amendment's prohibition on double jeopardy); Gideon v. Wainright, 372 U.S. 335 (1963) (Sixth Amendment's right to counsel); Robinson v. California, 370 U.S. 660 (1962) (Eighth Amendment's cruel and unusual punishment clause); Mapp v. Ohio, 367 U.S. 643 (1961) (exclusionary rule under Fourth Amendment's protection against unreasonable searches and seizures).
34. 354 U.S. 1 (1957).
35. Id. at 6 (opinion of Black, J.). The ruling also rejected the government's contention that Article I, section 8, clause 14 granted Congress power to provide for trial in military courts of civilian spouses charged with capital offenses. Id. at 19.
36. Reid v. Covert, 351 U.S. 487 (1956).
37. See Chapter 2.
38. Justice Black called *Ross* "a relic from a different era." 354 U.S. at 12.
39. Recall that full constitutional protection is afforded residents in incorporated territories—at that time, Alaska and Hawaii. See Rassmussen v. United States, 197 U.S. 516, 520–21 (1905).
40. *Reid,* 354 U.S. at 14.
41. Mexican-Americans were also recognized as a protected class. *Hernandez v. Texas,* 347 U.S. 475 (1954), appears in the same volume as *Brown.*
42. See Mary Dudziak, "Desegregation as a Cold War Imperative," 41 *Stan. L. Rev.* 81 (1988); see Derrick Bell, "*Brown* and the Interest-Convergence Dilemma," in *Shades of* Brown 90 (Derrick Bell, ed., 1980).
43. See Brest, "In Defense of the Antidiscrimination Principle."

44. See Frank Michelman, "On Protecting the Poor through the Fourteenth Amendment," 83 *Harv. L. Rev.* 7 (1969).
45. Civil Rights Act of 1964, 78 Stat. 241.
46. Act of April 11, 1968, 82 Stat. 73.
47. Civil Rights Act of 1964; Voting Rights Act of 1965, Pub. L. No. 89–110, 79 Stat. 437.
48. Civil Rights Act of 1964, tit. II.
49. Civil Rights Act of 1964, tits. IV and VI.
50. See Heart of Atlanta Motel v. United States, 379 U.S. 241 (1964) (commerce clause); Katzenbach v. McClung, 379 U.S. 294 (1964) (commerce clause); Katzenbach v. Morgan, 384 U.S. 641 (1966) (section 5 of the 14th Amendment).
51. See Jones v. Alfred H. Mayer, 392 U.S. 409 (1968); United States v. Guest, 383 U.S. 745 (1966); United Stated v. Price, 383 U.S. 787 (1966).
52. See Brown v. Louisiana, 383 U.S. 131 (1966) (per curiam); Loving v. Virginia, 388 U.S. 1 (1967); Gayle v. Browder, 352 U.S. 903 (1956).
53. See Gomillion v. Lightfoot, 364 U.S. 339 (1960).
54. See Coleman v. Alabama, 389 U.S. 22 (1967); Arnold v. North Carolina, 376 U.S. 773 (1964).
55. See Evans v. Newton, 382 U.S. 296 (1966); Burton v. Wilmington Parking Authority, 365 U.S. 715 (1961); Pennsylvania v. Bd. of Dir. of City Trusts of Philadelphia, 353 U.S. 230 (1957).
56. See Bell v. Maryland, 378 U.S. 226 (1964); Peterson v. Greenville, 373 U.S. 244 (1963).
57. See T. H. Marshall, "Citizenship and Social Class," in Thomas H. Marshall and Tom Bottomore, *Citizenship and Social Class* (1992). See also William E. Forbath, "Caste, Class, and Equal Citizenship," in *Moral Problems in American Life: New Perspectives on Cultural History* 167 (Karen Halttunen and Lewis Perry, eds., 1998).
58. See Marshall, "Citizenship" at 8. Defining citizenship as "a status bestowed on those who are full members of a community," Marshall traced the development of citizenship through three stages: the recognition of civil rights ("rights necessary for individual freedom," such as freedom of speech, right to own property and conclude contracts, right to due process, and access to court), political rights (rights to vote and hold office), and social rights. Marshall, in telling Great Britain's story, assigned the formative period for the three elements to three successive centuries.
59. Gunnar Myrdal, *An American Dilemma* (1944).
60. Id. at 575, 576; see also Charles L. Black, Jr., "The Lawfulness of the

Segregation Decisions," 69 *Yale L. J.* 421 (1960) ("[E]veryone knew who the laws were equal against").

61. Myrdal, *American Dilemma* at 642.
62. 163 U.S. 537 (1896). "The object of the [fourteenth] amendment was undoubtedly to enforce the absolute equality of the two races before the law, but in the nature of things it could not have been intended to abolish distinctions based upon color, or to enforce social, as distinguished from political equality, or a commingling of the two races upon terms unsatisfactory to either. . . If the two races are to meet upon terms of social equality it must be the result of natural affinities, a mutual appreciation of each other's merits, and a voluntary consent of individuals." Id. at 544, 551.
63. Equality could yield substantive as well as formal results. When those in power seek to preserve the resources and opportunities they enjoy, a requirement of equality can promise similar benefits to the less well off. This was signaled in the slogan of some integrationists that "green [money] follows white."
64. See, e.g., Economic Opportunity Act of 1964, Pub. L. No. 88–452, 78 Stat. 508; Food Stamp Act of 1964, Pub. L. No. 88–525, 78 Stat. 525; Housing Act of 1964, Pub. L. No. 88–560, 78 Stat. 769; Act of Oct. 13, 1964, Pub. L. No. 88–641, 78 Stat. 1042; Social Security Amendments of 1965, Pub. L. No. 89–97, 79 Stat. 286; Housing and Urban Development Act of 1965, Pub. L. No. 89–117, 79 Stat. 451.
65. *Public Papers of the Presidents of the United States: Lyndon B. Johnson, 1965,* 635, 636 (June 4, 1965).
66. Id.
67. Forbath, "Caste, Class, and Equal Citizenship" at 194.
68. See Martin Luther King, Jr., *Where Do We Go from Here: Chaos or Community?* (1967), Appendix: Programs and Prospects.
69. The vehicle was the "fundamental interest" prong of equal protection analysis. See Michelman, "On Protecting the Poor."
70. See, e.g., "Developments in the Law: Equal Protection," 82 *Harv. L. Rev.* 1065, 1183–92 (1969).
71. Alexander M. Bickel, *The Morality of Consent* (1975).
72. For a thoughtful examination of *Reid v. Covert* and the issue of the constitutional rights of U.S. citizens outside U.S. borders, see Gerald L. Neuman, *Strangers to the Constitution: Immigrants, Borders, and Fundamental Law* chs. 5 and 6 (1996).
73. In *Reid v. Covert,* four Justices limited *In re Ross* to its time. 354 U.S. at 12 (opinion of Black, J.).

74. Shaughnessy v. United States ex rel. Mezei, 345 U.S. 206 (1953); United States ex rel. Knauff v. Shaughnessy, 338 U.S. 537 (1950).
75. Henry M. Hart, Jr., "The Power of Congress to Limit the Jurisdiction of Federal Courts: An Exercise in Dialectic," 66 *Harv. L. Rev.* 1362, 1396 (1953).
76. 354 U.S. at 5–6.
77. 347 U.S. 522, 531 (1954).
78. Boutilier v. INS, 387 U.S. 118 (1967). Warren joined the six-person majority; Brennan, Douglas, and Fortas dissented on the issue of statutory interpretation but expressed no view on the constitutional issue.
79. *Boutllier,* 387 U.S. at 123–24. See also Leng May Ma v. Barber, 357 U.S. 185, 187 (1958) (citing with favor Shaughnessy v. U.S. ex rel. Mezei).
80. Takahashi v. Fish & Game Comm'n, 334 U.S. 410 (1948); Yick Wo, 118 U.S. 356.
81. See, e.g., Katzenbach v. Morgan, 384 U.S. 641 (1966); McLaughlin v. Florida, 379 U.S. 184 (1964).
82. Number of immigrants entering the country:

    1901–1910: 8,795,386
    1951–1960: 2,515,479
    1981–1990: 7,338,062

    Immigration and Naturalization Service, *1996 Statistical Yearbook of the Immigration and Naturalization Service* (1997) at 25.
83. See Veto Message, 82d Cong., 2d Sess., H. Doc. 520.
84. See Charles D. Weisselberg, "The Exclusion and Detention of Aliens: Lessons from the Lives of Ellen Knauff and Ignatz Mezei," 143 *U. Pa. L. Rev.* 933 (1995).
85. See Chapter 7.
86. John Hart Ely, *Democracy and Distrust* 161–62 (1980).
87. See Charles L. Black, Jr., *Structure and Relationship in Constitutional Law* 64 (1969), and "The Unfinished Business of the Warren Court," 46 *Wash. L. Rev.* 3 (1970); see also Michael Perry, "Modern Equal Protection," 79 *Colum. L. Rev.* 1023, 1060–65 (1979).
88. Karst writes, "The broader principle of equal citizenship extends its core values to noncitizens, because for most purposes they are members of our society." "Foreword: Equal Citizenship" at 45. I will adopt a similar position in Chapter 7, but I do not think it is possible to make the argument based on citizenship. Stronger protections for aliens *challenges* constitutionalism built around citizenship.
89. "Remarks at the Signing of the Immigration Bill," October 3, 1965, *Public Papers of the Presidents of the United States: Lyndon B. Johnson,* 1037, 1038.

90. See Immigration and Nationality Act of 1965, §202(a), 79 Stat. 911 (codified at 8 U.S.C. §1152(a)(1)): "No person shall receive any preference or priority or be discriminated against in the issuance of an immigrant visa because of his race, sex, nationality, place of birth, or place of residence[.]" To the extent that family ties dominated the flow, the act might still appear to give preference to established immigrant groups in the United States; but by repealing the tiny quota permitted for Asian immigrants, the act opened up a large flow of immigrants from areas underrepresented in earlier years. See Gabriel J. Chin, "The Civil Rights Revolution Comes to Immigration Law," 75 *N.C. L. Rev.* 273 (1996).
91. This is not to say that the Warren Court would not have found constitutional rights applicable to aliens—see, e.g., Almeida-Sanchez v. United States, 413 U.S. 266 (1973)—but there are no decided cases.
92. 112 U.S. 94 (1884).
93. This has historically been the position of the State Department, although commentators have debated whether such children "are not citizens, regardless of Congressional action, by operation of the first sentence of the Fourteenth Amendment." Arnold H. Leibowitz, *Defining Status* 28 (1989).
94. See generally Friend v. Reno, 172 F.3d 638 (9th Cir. 1999), cert. denied, 528 U.S. 1163 (2000); Rabang v. INS, 35 F.3d 1449 (9th Cir. 1994), cert. denied, 515 U.S. 1130 (1995). Children born in the territory of Alaska were citizens at birth by dint of Article II of the Treaty of Cession (1867) with Russia. *Alaska Historical Documents since 1867,* 1, 3 (R. Lauteret, comp., 1989). The Organic Act establishing the territory of Hawaii also provided for birthright citizenship. See Act of April 30, 1900, 31 Stat. 141.
95. Residents of all territories except Samoa have obtained citizenship by congressional action. See Leibowitz, *Defining Status* at 28.
96. See Vine Deloria, Jr., and Clifford M. Lytle, *American Indians, American Justice* 221 (1983): "During this period citizenship became a ceremonial event, something akin to religious conversion. It symbolized the determination of the individual to cast aside traditions and customs and assume the dress, values, and beliefs of the larger society. One citizenship ceremony involved the man 'shooting his last arrow' and taking hold of the handles of a plow to indicate his intent to become a citizen."
97. Act of June 2, 1924, 43 Stat. 253.
98. See Trías Monge, *Puerto Rico* at 74–76.
99. Balzac v. Porto Rico, 258 U.S. 298 (1922), discussed in Chapter 4.

100. Filipinos who fought with U.S. troops in World War II were granted a statutory right to naturalize that eased some of the usual requirements (i.e., requirements of a period of residency in the United States and of literacy in English). See Second War Powers Act, Pub. L. No. 77–107, tit. IX, 56 Stat. 182. By September 1945, the U.S. government's implementation of the law had become halfhearted, if not oppositional. There is a decades-long history of litigation under the statute. See, e.g., INS v. Hibi, 414 U.S. 5 (1967) (per curiam).
101. 354 U.S. at 14 (opinion of Black, J.).
102. 163 U.S. 376 (1896).
103. 358 U.S. 217 (1959).
104. Charles F. Wilkinson, *American Indians, Time, and the Law* 1, 2 (1987).
105. 358 U.S. at 223.
106. As I discuss later on, the Rehnquist Court has exploited this tension by restricting tribal sovereignty.
107. 358 U.S. at 223.
108. See Deloria and Lytle, *American Indians, American Justice;* Wilkinson, *American Indians, Time, and the Law.* Ending programs designated especially for Indians was also part of postwar budget-cutting.
109. The American people, wrote Justice Reed, "seek to have the Indians share the benefits of our society as citizens of this Nation." Tee-Hit-Ton Indians v. United States, 348 U.S. 272, 281 (1955).
110. 358 U.S. at 220–21.
111. Also noteworthy is the early Warren Court decision in *Tee-Hit-Ton Indians v. United States,* 348 U.S. 272 (1955), which rejected a claim by an Alaskan tribe that the federal government had unconstitutionally taken timber in which it had a possessory interest. In 1951 the secretary of agriculture, pursuant to congressional authorization, had entered into a contract with a private company for timber located on 350,000 acres of land near and within the Tongass National Forest. The Tlingits argued that the sale was a compensable taking of part of their proprietary interest, which was based on their continued occupation and use of the land since time immemorial. The Court rejected the claim, holding that the tribe had no property right in the land but only a "right of occupancy" which "may be terminated and such lands fully disposed of by the sovereign itself without any legally enforceable obligation to compensate the Indians." Id. at 279. Thus, it reaffirmed established doctrine that congressional extinguishments of so-called "Indian title" (understood as mere possession, not recognized ownership) raised "political, not justiciable" issues. Id. at 281 (quoting United States v. Santa Fe Pac. R.R., 314 U.S. 339 (1941)). (The Court conceded that there would have been a compensable taking if Con-

gress had previously recognized in the tribe permanent rights to hold the land. 348 U.S. at 277–78.) In language echoing the immigration cases, the Court declared that remedies must come from the political branches: "Our conclusion does not uphold harshness as against tenderness toward the Indians, but it leaves with Congress, where it belongs, the policy of Indian gratuities for the termination of Indian occupancy of Government-owned land." Id. at 290–91. Milner Ball has persuasively argued that *Tee-Hit-Ton* wholly inverts John Marshall's opinion in *Johnson v. McIntosh.* The Court in *Tee-Hit-Ton* summarizes the Marshall decision as denying "the power of an Indian tribe to pass their right of occupancy to another." 348 U.S. at 279–80. In fact, *Johnson v. McIntosh* held only that the European discoverer/conqueror acquired an exclusive right to purchase from the native people lands in the discovered area; the Indians retained a right of occupancy and the power to dispose of their interests in the property. Milner Ball, "Constitution, Court, Indian Tribes," 1987 *Am. B. Found. Res. J.* 1, 23–29, and 44 n.190. For an in-depth discussion of *Tee-Hit-Ton,* see David E. Wilkins, *American Indian Sovereignty and the U.S. Supreme Court* 166–85 (1997).

112. 354 U.S. at 14 (opinion of Black, J.).
113. Academic defenders of the Warren Court have likewise neglected these areas. See generally Black, *Structure and Relationship;* Karst, "Foreword: Equal Citizenship."
114. Bickel, *Morality of Consent* at 54.
115. Act of March 2, 1917, Pub. L. No. 64–368, 39 Stat. 951.
116. Act of July 3, 1950, Pub. L. No. 82–600, §2, 64 Stat. 319.
117. Constitution of Puerto Rico, Art. II.
118. Guam Elective Governor Act, Sept. 11, 1968, §1, 82 Stat. 842. See Leibowitz, *Defining Status* at 342–48, for a discussion of the statute and exceptions.
119. Indian Civil Rights Act of 1968, Pub. L. No. 90–284, tit. II, 82 Stat. 73. Exceptions were made for the establishment clause and the right to a jury trial in civil cases.
120. Significantly, the statute also amended Pub. L. 280 to require tribal consent to state assumption of jurisdiction over a reservation. Indian Civil Rights Act, tit. IV, §§401(a), 402(a).
121. "Constitutional Rights of the American Indian: Hearings on S.R. 961–68, before the Senate Subcommittee on Indian Affairs," 89th Cong. 21 (1965) (statement of Frank J. Barry, Solicitor, Department of the Interior).
122. See *Hearings on S.R. 691–68* at 1–2.
123. In 1962 James Baldwin commented on the "tone of warm congratula-

tion with which so many [white] liberals address their Negro equals. It is the Negro, of course, who is presumed to have become equal—an achievement that not only proves the comforting fact that perseverance has no color but also overwhelmingly corroborates the white man's sense of his own value." James Baldwin, *The Fire Next Time* 127 (1962).

124. Civil Rights Act of 1866, 14 Stat. 27 (codified at 42 U.S.C. §§1981–82 (1994)). Note that while section 1981 guarantees rights (freedom of contract, access to courts) to "all persons," section 1982 (property rights) applies to "all citizens."
125. Congressional actions in the era made this linkage clear. It is noteworthy that much major Indian and immigration legislation in the 1960s is civil rights legislation: ICRA, enacted as part of the 1968 Civil Rights Act (known primarily for its fair housing provisions in Title VIII), would ensure Indians the rights of citizens against local governing units. The 1965 Immigration Act ending the national origins quota system was explicitly justified in color-blind terms and included typical civil rights language prohibiting the distribution of immigrant visas on the basis of race.
126. See Will Herberg, *Protestant, Catholic, Jew* (1955); Nathan Glazer and Daniel Patrick Moynihan, *Beyond the Melting Pot* (1st ed. 1963). Gender as a dividing line remained largely invisible to most mainstream social theorists.
127. Milton M. Gordon, *Assimilation in American Life: The Role of Race, Religion, and National Origins* 242 (1964). Even second-generation immigrants, although "irreversibly" on their way to full acculturation, might not necessarily achieve structural assimilation. Id. at 244.
128. Glazer and Moynihan, *Beyond the Melting Pot* at 314. The conclusion is consistent with Herberg's earlier work.
129. Nathan Glazer and Daniel Patrick Moynihan, *Beyond the Melting Pot* at xxxiii–xxxviii (2d ed. 1970). "Beyond the accidents of history, one suspects, is the reality that human groups endure, that they provide some satisfaction to their members, and the adoption of a totally new ethnic identity, by dropping whatever one is to become simply American, is inhibited by strong elements in the social structure of the United States. It is inhibited by a subtle system of identifying, which ranges from brutal discrimination and prejudice to merely naming. It is inhibited by the unavailability of a simple 'American' identity." Id. at xxxiii.
130. See Gary Peller, "Race Consciousness," 1990 *Duke L. J.* 758, 783–811.
131. Stokely Carmichael and Charles V. Hamilton, *Black Power* 54, 55 (1967).

132. Id. at 62 (citing Gordon, *Assimilation in American Life*).
133. Malcolm X, "The Ballot or the Bullet" (April 3, 1964), in *Malcolm X Speaks* 26 (1965).
134. Black, *Structure and Relationship* at 59; see also Frederick Schauer, "Community, Citizenship, and the Search for National Identity," 84 *Mich. L. Rev.* 1504 (1986).
135. Black, *Structure and Relationship* at 60.
136. Id.
137. See generally Gerald L. Neuman, "Whose Constitution?" 100 *Yale L. J.* 909 (1991).
138. See Marshall, "Citizenship and Social Class."
139. U.S. Constitution, Art. I, §9, cl. 8.
140. Marshall's political, civil, and social rights. See Marshall, "Citizenship and Social Class."
141. See Morris B. Abram, "Affirmative Action: Fair Shakers and Social Engineers," 99 *Harv. L. Rev.* 1312 (1986).
142. It is worth recalling that the substantive programs proposed and implemented to improve the conditions in which blacks lived were non–race based. They took aim at poor education and housing, a lack of jobs and medical care. Note the recommendations of the Kerner Commission, Johnson's Great Society program. National Advisory Commission on Civil Disorders, *Report,* pt. III (1968). Johnson uses the term "affirmative action" in Executive Order 11,246, but in a sense of positive action to remove barriers to equal opportunity, not as a proposal for race-based programs. Exec. Order No. 11,246, 30 Fed. Reg. 12,319, reprinted in 42 U.S.C. §2000e (1965). See also Nathan Glazer, *Affirmative Discrimination* (1975).
143. Regents of the Univ. of California v. Bakke, 438 U.S. 265, 407 (1978). See also Lyndon Johnson's recognition that equal opportunity would not be enough where blacks had been disadvantaged for centuries. "You do not take a person who for years has been hobbled by chains and liberate him, bring him up to the starting line of a race and then say, 'you are free to compete with all the others,' and still justly believe that you have been completely fair." "To Fulfill These Rights," June 4, 1965, 1965 *Public Papers* at 635, 636.
144. Nixon controlled the Court by 1972, having nominated Burger (1969), Blackmun (1970), Powell (1972), and Rehnquist (1972). These justices could form conservative majorities with Warren Court holdovers Potter Stewart and Byron White.
145. Frontiero v. Richardson, 411 U.S. 677 (1973) (gender); Reed v. Reed, 404 U.S. 71 (1971) (gender); Graham v. Richardson, 403 U.S. 365 (1971) (alienage).

146. And, of course, decided *Roe v. Wade* as well.
147. See San Antonio Indep. School Dist. v. Rodriguez, 411 U.S. 1 (1973); Dandridge v. Williams, 397 U.S. 471 (1970).
148. See Nat'l League of Cities v. Usery, 426 U.S. 833 (1976).
149. See Ingraham v. Wright, 430 U.S. 651, 662 (1977) (permitting corporal punishment in schools "as is reasonably necessary for the proper education of the child and for the maintenance of group discipline").
150. Brown v. Glines, 444 U.S. 348 (1980) (upholding against First Amendment challenge a requirement that members of the U.S. Air Force obtain approval from their commanders before circulating petitions on air force bases).
151. See, e.g., Rhodes v. Chapman, 452 U.S. 337 (1981); Bell v. Wolfish, 441 U.S. 520 (1979). Compare Robert Post's insightful analysis of the regulation by government institutions of speech within the institution. Post notes that the Supreme Court has assessed the constitutionality of such a regulation by examining whether the limitation is "necessary in order to achieve the institution's legitimate objectives." Robert C. Post, *Constitutional Domains: Democracy, Community, Management* 236 (1995).
152. Parham v. J.R., 442 U.S. 584 (1979) (formal adversary proceedings not constitutionally required before parents could place children in mental institutions); cf. In re Gault, 387 U.S. 1 (1967) (Warren Court due process case regarding juvenile proceedings).
153. See United States v. Wheeler, 435 U.S. 313 (1978).
154. Brown v. Bd. of Educ. of Topeka, 347 U.S. 483, 493 (1954).
155. Wisconsin v. Yoder, 406 U.S. 205, 221, 222, 224 (1972).
156. Id. at 241–46.
157. See, e.g., Owen M. Fiss, "Groups and the Equal Protection Clause," 5 *Phil. & Pub. Aff.* 107 (1976).
158. See Regents of the Univ. of Calif. v. Bakke, 438 U.S. 265, 359 (1978) (opinion of Brennan, White, Marshall, Blackmun, J. J.).
159. See Keyes v. School Dist. No. 1, 413 U.S. 189 (1973); Swann v. Charlotte-Mecklenburg Bd. of Educ., 402 U.S. 1 (1971); see also Norwood v. Harrison, 413 U.S. 455 (1973); J. Harvie Wilkinson, *From Brown to Bakke* (1979).
160. Milliken v. Bradley, 48 U.S. 717 (1974).
161. See *Bakke,* 438 U.S. at 362–73 (opinion of Brennan, White, Marshall, Blackmun, J. J.) (remedying effects of past discrimination); id. at 311–15 (opinion of Powell, J.) (promoting diversity in higher education).

162. 448 U.S. 448 (1980); see also Morton v. Mancari, 417 U.S. 535 (1974) (upholding employment program of Bureau of Indian Affairs giving preferences to Indians).

163. 435 U.S. 313, 330–31 (1978) ("[T]he prospect of avoiding a more severe federal punishment would surely motivate a member of a tribe charged with the commission of an offense to seek to stand trial first in a tribal court").

164. Id. at 322–23, 332.

165. 435 U.S. 191 (1978).

166. Interestingly, Burger joined Marshall's dissent. *Oliphant* is an interesting echo of *Reid v. Covert,* which noted that although improvements had been made in military justice, military courts were still not the same as Article III courts; military culture stresses the "iron hand of discipline more than it does the even scales of justice." 354 U.S. 1, 38 (1957).

167. 436 U.S. 49 (1978).

168. See Catharine A. MacKinnon, "Whose Culture: A Case Note on *Martinez v. Santa Clara Pueblo,*" in Catharine A. MacKinnon, *Feminism Unmodified* (1987); Judith Resnik, "Multiple Sovereignties: Indian Tribes, States, and the Federal Government," 79 *Judicature* 118 (1995).

169. ICRA expressly provides habeas corpus jurisdiction in criminal cases. See 25 U.S.C. §1303 (1994).

170. The Burger Court ruled for Indian tribes in several other important cases. See, e.g., United States v. Sioux Nation of Indians, 448 U.S. 371 (1980) (1877 statute effected taking of land granted to Sioux by treaty, implying obligation to make just compensation unless federal government could show measure protected or advanced tribal interests); Morton v. Mancari, 417 U.S. 535 (1974) (upholding against an equal protection challenge an affirmative action program adopted by the Bureau of Indian Affairs that gave an employment preference for positions in the bureau to "qualified Indians"); United States v. Mazurie, 419 U.S. 543 (1975) (upholding congressional delegation to tribe to regulate sale of liquor on reservation); McClanahan v. State Tax Comm'n of Arizona, 411 U.S. 164 (1973) (holding that Arizona has no power to tax the income of Indians residing on a reservation whose income derives from reservation activities).

171. 403 U.S. 365, 372 (1971). As will be discussed in Chapter 7, Justice Blackmun's reasoning is not persuasive, but the result may be justified on other grounds.

172. 457 U.S. 202 (1982).

173. See, e.g., Michael J. Perry, "Equal Protection, Judicial Activism, and

the Intellectual Agenda of Constitutional Theory: Reflections On, and Beyond, *Plyler v. Doe,*" 44 *U. Pitt. L. Rev.* 329 (1983).

174. See Peter H. Schuck, "The Transformation of Immigration Law," 84 *Colum. L. Rev.* 1, 58 (1984): in *Plyler,* the Court "seems to have begun to redefine the community to include all those whose destinies have somehow, even in violation of our law, become linked with ours."
175. 457 U.S. at 223. "By denying these children a basic education, we deny them the ability to live within the structure of our civic institutions, and foreclose any realistic possibility that they will contribute in even the smallest way to the progress of our Nation." Id. at 230.
176. See Sugarman v. Dougall, 413 U.S. 634 (1973) (invalidating a state law barring aliens from civil service jobs, but noting that a citizenship qualification would be appropriate for voting and for elected and appointed offices that participate in the formulation, execution, or review of public policy). The so-called "*Sugarman* exception" was applied by the Burger Court to uphold citizenship requirements for state troopers in Foley v. Connolie, 435 U.S. 291 (1978), teachers in Ambach v. Norwick, 441 U.S. 68 (1978), and probation officers in Cabell v. Chavez-Salido, 454 U.S. 432 (1982).
177. See Sarah Cleveland, "Powers Inherent in Sovereignty: Indians, Aliens, Territories, and the Nineteenth-Century Origins of Plenary Power over Foreign Affairs" (unpub. ms.) at 199–206. Indeed, one of the cases involved an equal protection claim by an alien residing in Puerto Rico. See Examining Bd. of Engineers, Architects, and Surveyors v. Flores de Otero, 426 U.S. 572 (1976) (exclusion of aliens from civil engineering profession). The Court applied the standard it uses to evaluate alienage discrimination by states. In Rodriguez v. Popular Democratic Party, 457 U.S. 1, 8 (1982), the right at stake—the right to vote—was, for obvious reasons, tied to citizenship.
178. See, e.g., Act of July 1, 1902, c. 1369, §5, 32 Stat. 692 (enacting bill of rights for Philippine Islands).
179. See Act of July 3, 1952, 66 Stat. 327.
180. Cf. Vincent Blasi, "The Rootless Activism of the Burger Court," in *The Burger Court: The Counter-revolution That Wasn't* 198–217 (Vincent Blasi, ed., 1983).
181. 438 U.S. 57 (1981).
182. See Kenneth L. Karst, *Law's Promise, Law's Expression: Visions of Power in the Politics of Race, Gender, and Religion* 112–13, 116–24 (1993) (women's exclusion from combat roles constitutes a denial of the Fourteenth Amendment's guarantee of equal citizenship).
183. See Mathews v. Diaz, 426 U.S. 67 (1976).

184. Id. at 80; see Cabell v. Chavez-Salido, 454 U.S. 432 (1982); Fiallo v. Bell, 430 U.S. 787 (1977). Discussed in Chapter 7.
185. See Harris v. Rosario, 446 U.S. 651 (1980).
186. See United States v. Wheeler, 435 U.S. 313. Indian sovereignty "exists only at the sufferance of Congress and is subject to complete defeasance." Id. at 323. The Burger Court also backtracked slightly from the Warren Court citizenship cases. See Vance v. Terrazas, 444 U.S. 252 (1980); Rogers v. Bellei, 401 U.S. 815 (1971).
187. 457 U.S. at 218.
188. Exec. Order No. 10,925, §301 (March 6, 1961).
189. Exec. Order No. 11,246, §301 (September 24, 1965).
190. 41 C.F.R. §60–1.40 (1969).
191. 41 C.F.R. §60–2.10 (1971).
192. 41 C.F.R. §60–2.11 (1971).
193. See Contractors Ass'n of Eastern Pennsylvania v. Secretary of Labor, 442 F.2d 159 (3d Cir. 1971), cert. denied, 404 U.S. 854 (1971).
194. Civil Rights Act of 1964, Pub. L. No. 88–352, tit. VII, 78 Stat. 241; see also 35 Fed. Reg. 12,333 (August 1, 1970), amending August 26, 1966, guidelines.
195. Discrimination was defined as the use of a test which adversely affected an employment opportunity unless the test had been validated. See 29 C.F.R. §1607.3 (1971). Evidence of possible discrimination included "higher rejection rates for minority candidates than nonminority candidates." 29 C.F.R. §1607.4(a) (1971). And "any differential rejection rates that may exist . . . must be relevant to performance on the jobs in question." Id.
196. 401 U.S. 424 (1971).
197. 35 Fed. Reg. 11,595 (1970).
198. See Lau v. Nichols, 414 U.S. 563 (1974).
199. See Nathan Glazer, *Affirmative Discrimination* (1975).
200. Richard M. Nixon, "Special Message to Congress on Indian Affairs," July 8, 1970, *Public Papers of the Presidents of the United States: Richard M. Nixon, 1970,* 564, 567.
201. Id.
202. Id. at 565. See Philip S. Deloria, "The Era of Indian Self-Determination: An Overview," in *Indian Self-Rule* 202 (Kenneth R. Philip, ed., 1986) (Nixon message seen by many as the "high point" of the era of self-determination with regard to federal policy).
203. Act of Jan. 4, 1975, 88 Stat. 2203 (1975) (now codified at 25 U.S.C. §§450, 450a). These views were also carried into the territorial sphere. In 1973, in the course of negotiations over the status of Micronesia,

then–Assistant Attorney General Rehnquist reaffirmed the Justice Department's position that so-called "mutual consent" provisions—permitting amendment of an agreement only with the consent of both parties—were legal and binding. Cited in Memorandum from Teresa Wynn Roseborough for the Special Representative for Guam Commonwealth, "Mutual Consent Provisions in the Guam Commonwealth Legislation," July 28, 1994. By barring unilateral congressional action, such provisions constitute a substantial incursion into congressional plenary power. See Chapters 4 and 6.

204. The program is upheld by the Burger Court in *Fullilove v. Klutznick*, 448 U.S. 448 (1980).

205. See Statement of Policy on Minority Ownership of Broadcasting Facilities, 68 F.C.C.2d 979 (1978). The rules were upheld in a five-to-four decision, Metro Broadcasting, Inc. v. F.C.C., 497 U.S. 547 (1990). In the majority were Justices Brennan, White, Marshall, Stevens, and Blackmun; dissenting were Chief Justice Rehnquist and Justices O'Connor, Kennedy, and Scalia. The arrival of Justice Thomas permitted the overturning of *Metro Broadcasting* in Adarand Constructors, Inc. v. Pena, 515 U.S. 200 (1995).

206. 25 U.S.C. §1901(3) (1994).

207. Id. §1901(4).

208. Id. §1902.

209. The statute received a reading strongly in favor of tribal jurisdiction in Mississippi Band of Choctaw Indians v. Holyfield, 490 U.S. 30 (1989).

210. 488 U.S. 469 (1989).

211. Id. at 493 (quoting Shelley v. Kraemer, 334 U.S. 1, 22 (1948)).

212. Id. Justice Scalia's separate opinion continues the theme: "It is plainly true that in our society blacks have suffered discrimination immeasurably greater than any directed at other racial groups. But those who believe that racial preferences can help to 'even the score' display, and reinforce, a manner of thinking by race that was the source of the injustice and that will, if it endures within our society, be the source of more injustice still. The relevant proposition is not that it was blacks, or Jews, or Irish who were discriminated against, but that it was individual men and women, 'created equal,' who were discriminated against." Id. at 527–28.

213. Id. at 508; the final paragraph of the opinion again refers twice to citizens.

214. See, e.g., Fiss, "Groups and the Equal Protection Clause"; T. Alexander Aleinikoff, "A Case for Race Consciousness," 91 *Colum. L. Rev.* 1060 (1991).

215. 515 U.S. 200 (1995).

216. Specifically, Fullilove v. Klutznick, 448 U.S. 448 (1980) and Metro Broadcasting, Inc. v. F.C.C., 497 U.S. 547 (1990).
217. Civil Rights Cases, 109 U.S. 3, 25 (1883).
218. See Pierce v. Soc'y of Sisters, 268 U.S. 510, 534–35 (1925).
219. See Peter J. Rubin, "Equal Rights, Special Rights, and the Nature of Antidiscrimination Law," 97 *Mich. L. Rev.* 564 (1998).
220. 494 U.S. 872 (1990).
221. "If Oregon can constitutionally prosecute [members of the group] for this act of worship, they, like the Amish, may be 'forced to migrate to some other and more tolerant region.'" Id. at 920 (quoting *Yoder*).
222. Id. at 888.
223. 495 U.S. 676 (1990).
224. Id. at 692–93. The Court's decision in *Mississippi Choctaw Indian Band v. Holyfield,* 490 U.S. 30 (1989), might be seen as a counterexample. There the Court upheld provisions of the Indian Child Welfare Act that vest exclusive jurisdiction in tribal courts in custody cases involving tribal children, and the act represents a clear congressional preference that Indian children be placed with Indian caregivers. But the tribal court's jurisdiction is limited to tribal children; thus *Holyfield* does not belong in the same category as *Duro.*
225. See Fiallo v. Bell, 430 U.S. 787 (1977).
226. See Reno v. Flores, 507 U.S. 292 (1993).
227. See Reno v. American-Arab Anti-Discrimination Comm., 525 U.S. 471 (1999).
228. Zadvydas v. Davis, 121 S.Ct. 2491 (2001).
229. See Vicki Jackson, "Federalism and the Uses and Limits of Law: *Printz* and Principle?" 111 *Harv. L. Rev.* 2180 (1998).
230. 526 U.S. 489 (1999).
231. The classic comment is Edward Corwin's: "Unique among constitutional provisions, the privileges and immunities clause of the Fourteenth Amendment enjoys the distinction of having been rendered a 'practical nullity' by a single decision of the Supreme Court rendered within five years of its ratification." Quoted in Kurland, "The Privileges and Immunities Clause" at 405. Why the court resuscitated the clause is not entirely clear. One answer might be that invocation of the equal protection clause in *Saenz* would have required identification of a "fundamental interest" that would trigger strict scrutiny. The Court has shown no interest in expanding this prong of equal protection, no doubt seeing such analysis as open-ended judicial lawmaking. Reliance on the privileges or immunities clause tethers the interpreter to the text of the document.
232. See Laurence H. Tribe, "*Saenz* sans Prophecy: Does the Privileges or

Immunities Revival Portend the Future—or Reveal the Structure of the Present?" 113 *Harv. L. Rev* 110 (1999) (*Saenz* decision as in step with Court's interpretative strategy of "structural inference," protecting new residents in states on the basis of a principle of equal state citizenship rather than a concern with helping the poor).

233. But see Tribe, id., distinguishing *Saenz* from the Warren Court's approach in *Shapiro* and suggesting that the rebirth of the privileges or immunities clause—while holding the promise of a new rights-furthering agenda—most likely simply reflects the current Court's interest in structural protections (of which some rights may be a part).
234. But see Ely, *Democracy and Distrust* at 24–25: the clause can be read to cover aliens by seeing "privileges and immunities of citizens of the United States" as defining a category of rights, not a class of beneficiaries. Ely seems to be alone in suggesting this reading; it has never been adopted by the Court and seems inconsistent with the decision in *Saenz.*
235. See Yick Wo v. Hopkins, 118 U.S. 356 (1886).
236. See Graham v. Richardson, 403 U.S. 365 (1971).
237. Tribe suggests the possibility of shifting substantive due process rights to a reinvigorated privileges or immunities clause. Noting that such a move would undercut protections for aliens, he argues for "redundancy" in the "tandem" use of both the due process clause and the privileges or immunities clause. Tribe, "*Saenz* Sans Prophecy" at 193 n.353. I find this approach fraught with peril. Conceptual shifts have their consequences, and the Court is likely to welcome a way out of substantive due process analysis, whatever its impact on the rights of noncitizens.
238. Saenz v. Roe, 526 U.S. 489, 500 (1999).
239. See Nathan Glazer, *We Are All Multiculturalists Now* (1997).
240. Nevada v. Hicks, 121 S.Ct. 2304 (2001); Strate v. A-1 Contractors, 520 U.S. 438, 458 (1997), discussed in Chapter 5.
241. For example: "What you do is as important as anything government does. I ask you to seek a common good beyond your comfort, to defend needed reforms against easy attacks, to serve your nation, beginning with your neighbor. I ask you to be citizens. Citizens, not spectators. Citizens, not subjects. Responsible citizens, building communities of service and a nation of character." President George W. Bush, inaugural address, January 20, 2001.
242. Id.:

> Where there is suffering, there is duty. Americans in need are not strangers, they are citizens, not problems, but priorities; and all of us are diminished when any are hopeless.

> Government has great responsibilities, for public safety and public health, for civil rights and common schools. Yet compassion is the work of a nation, not just a government. And some needs and hurts are so deep they will only respond to a mentor's touch or a pastor's prayer. Church and charity, synagogue and mosque, lend our communities their humanity, and they will have an honored place in our plans and in our laws.

4. Commonwealth and the Constitution

1. See statement of Pedro Rosselló before the Senate Committee on Energy and Natural Resources, May 6, 1999.
2. "The thing speaks for itself." A prior plebescite in 1993 had reached equally inconclusive results. With almost three-quarters of registered voters participating, just over 48 percent of the voters selected retention of commonwealth status, 46 percent preferred statehood, and 5 percent chose the independence option.
3. See Hon. José A. Cabranes, "Puerto Rico and the Constitution," 110 F.R.D. 476, 477 (1985). For a happy exception, see Paul Brest, Sanford Levinson, J. M. Balkin, and Akhil Reed Amar, *Processes of Constitutional Decisionmaking: Cases and Materials* 297–309 (4th ed. 2000).
4. See Rafael Hernández Colón, "The Commonwealth of Puerto Rico: Territory or State?" 19 *Revista del Colegio de Abogados de Puerto Rico* 207, 210 (1959).
5. I reserve for consideration at a later date the vexing matter of who should vote on the status question. Some have argued that the 2.5 million Puerto Ricans living on the mainland (about 1 million of whom live in New York City) should have been able to vote in the 1993 plebiscite. Difficulties with defining who is "Puerto Rican" and practical problems with voting procedures led the island's political parties to limit the referendum to residents of Puerto Rico. In effect, the answer sides with the view of Puerto Rico as a "proto-state" rather than an independent nation: voting turns, as it does in state elections, on residence, not "nationality." Of course, underlying much of the debate on participation by mainland Puerto Ricans were strategic political calculations of how the off-island population would vote. Legislation introduced in the 101st Congress would have authorized the government of Puerto Rico to enable persons not residing in Puerto Rico to vote in a referendum on status if they were born in Puerto Rico or had at least one parent who was born in Puerto Rico. H.R. 4765, 101st Cong., 2d Sess. §3 (1990). Supporters of independence have criticized the refusal to extend voting privileges to mainland Puerto Ricans, declar-

ing that the referendum denied these "Puerto Rican nationals" the right to vote, while enfranchising "more than 100,000 foreigners with United States citizenship [residing] in Puerto Rico." U.N. GAOR Special Comm. on the Situation with Regard to the Implementation of the Declaration on the Granting of Independence to Colonial Countries and Peoples, 1,422d meeting at 52, U.N. doc. A/AC.109/PV.1422 (1993) (statement of Juan Mari Brás); id. at 24 (statement of Carlos Noriega Rodríguez, president of the Bar Association of Puerto Rico). See generally "Puerto Rico Self-Determination Act, 1990: Hearings on H.R. 4765 before the Subcomm. on Insular and Int'l. Affairs of the House Comm. on Interior and Insular Affairs," 101st Cong., 2d Sess., pt. 1 (1990). And see Angelo Falcón, "A Divided Nation: the Puerto Rican Diaspora in the United States and the Proposed Referendum," in *Colonial Dilemma: Critical Perspectives on Contemporary Puerto Rico* 173–80 (Eguardo Meléndez and Edwin Meléndez, eds.,1993). Despite the fact that neither Congress nor the Commonwealth authorized a mainland vote, balloting was organized in New York in October 1993. Plans for votes in Chicago, New Jersey, and elsewhere were ultimately abandoned.

6. U.S. Constitution, Art. IV, §3, cl. 2.
7. Scott v. Sandford, 60 U.S. (19 How.) 393, 438–39, 443 (1856). Taney's legal conclusion permitted him to declare that Congress had no authority to prohibit slavery in territories carved out of the Louisiana Purchase without necessarily casting doubt on the Northwest Ordinance's prohibition of slavery in the Northwest Territory (which had belonged to the United States at the time of the Constitution's adoption).
8. American Ins. Co. v. Canter, 26 U.S. (1 Pet.) 511, 542 (1828); Dorr v. United States, 195 U.S. 138, 140 (1904) (quoting John Marshall's opinion in Sere v. Pitot, 10 U.S. (6 Cranch) 332, 337 (1810) (recognizing Congress's "absolute and undisputed power of governing and legislating" for territories)); Arnold H. Leibowitz, *Defining Status* 140–55 (1989).
9. E.g., *Dorr,* 195 U.S. at 146.
10. United States v. Sanchez, 992 F.2d 1143, 1152–53 (11th Cir. 1993) (holding that "dual sovereignty" doctrine does not apply in case of Puerto Rican and federal prosecutions for the same criminal conduct because "[t]he authority with which Puerto Rico brings charges as a prosecuting entity derives from the United States as sovereign"). The First Circuit had reached a contrary conclusion. United States v. Lopez Andino, 831 F.2d. 1164 (1st Cir. 1987), cert. denied, 486 U.S. 1034 (1988).

11. Foraker Act, 31 Stat. 77 §§17, 31, 33 (1900) (repealed 1917). Laws enacted by the legislative assembly could also be annulled by Congress. Id. at §31, 31 Stat. at 83. The Supreme Court of Puerto Rico and the upper house of the legislature were appointed by the president of the United States. Id. at §§18, 27, 33, 31 Stat. at 81–82, 84.
12. Act of July 3, 1950, Pub. L. No. 600, ch. 446, 64 Stat. 319 [hereinafter Public Law 600].
13. Referendum on March 3, 1952: 374,469 to 82,923. Act of July 3, 1952, Pub. L. No. 447, ch. 567, 66 Stat. 327.
14. Congress refused to approve Section 20 of Article II of the proposed constitution, which provided a list of positive "human rights" such as the rights to obtain work and to a standard of living adequate for personal and family well-being, and "the right of motherhood and childhood to special care and assistance." 66 Stat. at 327. These guarantees were thought to be incompatible with traditional understandings of a bill of rights.
15. The provisos required that the Puerto Rican constitution be amended, first, to add the following to the section guaranteeing free and nonsectarian education: "Compulsory attendance at elementary public schools to the extent permitted by the facilities of the state as herein provided shall not be construed as applicable to those who receive elementary education in schools established under nongovernmental auspices." The second proviso required the addition of the following to the article establishing an amendment procedure:

    > Any amendment or revision of this constitution shall be consistent with the resolution enacted by the Congress of the United States approving this constitution, with the applicable provisions of the constitution of the United States, with the Puerto Rican Federal Relations Act, and with Public Law 600, Eighty-first Congress, adopted in the nature of a compact.

    66 Stat. at 327.
16. Supporters of this view point to language in the preamble of the Puerto Rican constitution, which provides: "We, the people of Puerto Rico . . . do ordain and establish this Constitution for the commonwealth which, in the exercise of our natural rights, we now create within our union with the United States of America." Constitution of Puerto Rico, pmbl.; see also Art. I, §1 ("[T]he Commonwealth of Puerto Rico is hereby constituted. Its political power emanates from the people and shall be exercised in accordance with their will, within the terms of the compact agreed upon between the people of Puerto Rico and the United States of America"); Hernández Colón, "The

Commonwealth of Puerto Rico" at 254: "[T]he legal status of the commonwealth . . . [rests] on the sovereignty of the people of Puerto Rico. They created it, they empowered it, they made it sovereign . . . Congress surrendered those powers which had traditionally been exercised by the territory of Puerto Rico."

17. See United States v. Quinones, 758 F.2d 40, 42 (1st Cir. 1985):

> Thus, in 1952, Puerto Rico ceased being a territory of the United States subject to the plenary powers of congress as provided in the Federal constitution. The authority exercised by the federal government emanated thereafter from the compact itself. Under the compact between the people of Puerto Rico and the United States, Congress cannot amend the Puerto Rico Constitution unilaterally, and the government of Puerto Rico is no longer a federal government agency exercising delegated power.

See also Figueroa v. Puerto Rico, 232 F.2d 615, 620 (1st Cir. 1953); United States v. Vega Figueroa, 984 F. Supp. 71 (D. P.R. 1997) (citing cases); Leibowitz, *Defining Status* at 165–85.

18. Harris v. Rosario, 446 U.S. 651, 651–52 (1980) (per curiam); "Political Status of Puerto Rico, 1991: Hearings on S. 244 before the Senate Comm. on Energy and Natural Resources," 102d Cong., 1st Sess., 193–94 (1991) (statement of Hon. Richard Thornburgh, Attorney General); Cabranes, "Puerto Rico and the Constitution" at 483 n.26; Peter J. Fliess, "Puerto Rico's Political Status under Its New Constitution," 5 *W. Pol. Q.* 635, 643 n.29 (1952) (concerning position of government lawyers during commonwealth process), and at 644 (concluding that "[t]here can be little question that Congress' legal powers under the United States constitution and Section 9 of the Organic Act are tantamount to unilateral authority over future mainland-island relations"). For lower court decisions to the same effect, see United States v. Sanchez, 992 F.2d 1143, 1148–49 (11th Cir. 1993), cert. denied, 510 U.S. 1110 (1994); United States v. Rivera Torrez, 826 F.2d 151,154 (1st Cir. 1987); Perez de la Cruz v. Crowley Towing and Transp. Co., 807 F.2d 1084, 1088 (1st Cir. 1986), cert. denied, 481 U.S. 1050 (1987); see also United States v. Lopez Andino, 831 F.2d 1164, 1173 (1st Cir. 1987), cert denied, 486 U.S. 1034 (1988); (Torruella, J., concurring):

> [T]he legislative history of [P.L. 600] leaves no doubt that even though its passage signaled the grant of internal self-government to Puerto Rico, no change was intended by Congress or Puerto Rico authorities in the territory's *constitutional* status or in Con-

gress's continuing plenary power over Puerto Rico pursuant to the Territory Clause of the Constitution.

See generally Juan R. Torruella, *The Supreme Court and Puerto Rico: The Doctrine of Separate and Unequal* 167–200 (1985); David M. Helfeld, "How Much of the United States Constitution and Statutes Are Applicable to the Commonwealth of Puerto Rico?" 110 F.R.D. 452 (1985) [hereinafter Helfeld I]; David M. Helfeld, "Congressional Intent and Attitude toward Public Law 600 and the Constitution of the Commonwealth of Puerto Rico," 21 *Revista Juridica de la Universidad de Puerto Rico* [*Rev. Jur. U.P.R.*] 255 (1952) [hereinafter Helfeld II]. But consider the following representation made in 1953 by the United States to the United Nations' Decolonization Committee:

> The Federal Relations Act to which reference has been made has continued provisions of political and economic union which the people of Puerto Rico have wished to maintain. In this sense the relationships between Puerto Rico and the United States have not changed. It would be wrong, however, to hold that because this is so and has been so declared in Congress, the creation of the Commonwealth of Puerto Rico does not signify a fundamental change in the status of Puerto Rico. The previous status of Puerto Rico was that of a territory subject to the full authority of the Congress of the United States in all governmental matters. The previous constitution of Puerto Rico was in fact a law of the Congress of the United States, which we called an Organic Act. Only Congress could amend the Organic Act of Puerto Rico. The present status of Puerto Rico is that of a people with a constitution of their own adoption, stemming from their own authority, which only they can alter or amend. The relationships previously established also by a law of the Congress, which only Congress could amend, have now become provisions of a compact of a bilateral nature whose terms may be changed only by common consent.

Statement of the Hon. Frances P. Bolton, American delegate, before the Special Committee on the Situation with Regard to the Implementation of the Declaration of the Granting of Independence to Colonial Countries and Peoples (quoted in Torruella, *The Supreme Court and Puerto Rico* at 164 n. 624). Although commonwealth status is not deemed to have affected congressional power, the Court views the establishment of commonwealth as rendering Puerto Rico more "statelike." See Examining Bd. of Eng'rs, Architects and Surveyors v. Flores de Otero, 426 U.S. 572, 594 (1976) ("[T]he purpose of Congress in the 1950 and 1952 legislation was to accord to Puerto Rico the degree of autonomy and independence normally associated with States of the Union"). This characterization may carry weight in matters of statutory interpretation. E.g., Calero-Toledo v. Pearson Yacht Leasing Co., 416 U.S. 663, 670–76 (1974) (statutes of Puerto Rico are "state statutes" for purposes of invoking three-judge court).

19. See Carlos Romero-Barceló, "Puerto Rico, U.S.A.: The Case for Statehood," *Foreign Aff.* 60–61 (Fall 1980); Rubén Berríos Martinez, "Independence for Puerto Rico: The Only Solution," *Foreign Aff.* 566–67 (April 1977). It should be stressed that Congress has, in fact, rarely purported to intervene in local self-rule. See United States v. Figueroa Rios, 140 F. Supp. 376, 380–81 (D.P.R. 1956) (federal statute criminalizing transporting of firearm by person convicted of crime of violence in interstate commerce or within territory held not to apply to intra–Puerto Rico transportation). Most statutes that have an effect in Puerto Rico are exercises of other delegated powers. (For a counterexample, see Helfeld I at 467 n.67.)
20. See Chapter 6.
21. General Accounting Office, Pub. No. GAO/HRD-89–104FS, "Puerto Rico: Update of Selected Information Contained in a 1981 GAO Report (1989)," reprinted in 3 *Puerto Rico Political Status Referendum* 213, 246–61 (Appendix III) (1992) ("Political Status Referendum") (examining thirty major federal statutes in the areas of income support, health care, taxes, immigration, labor, environment, and trade); Helfeld I at 460.
22. David L. Brumbaugh, "Puerto Rico's Status Options and Federal Taxes (Congressional Research Service, 1990)," reprinted in 2 *Political Status Referendum* at 211, 214 ("In a very general sense . . . the effect of Federal and Puerto Rican tax laws is to substitute Puerto Rico's own income tax for the Federal").
23. See José Trías Monge, *Puerto Rico: The Trials of the Oldest Colony in the World* 186–88 (1997); House of Representatives, Committee on Ways and Means, *2000 Green Book* 767, 769. Puerto Rico is excluded from the federal food stamp program. It receives instead a separate grant, capped in advance by Congress ($1.2 billion in fiscal year 1998). *2000 Green Book* at 767.
24. S. Rep. No. 481, 101st Cong., 2d Sess., 10 (1990).
25. "Potential Economic Impacts of Changes in Puerto Rico's Status under S. 712 (Congressional Budget Office, 1990)," reprinted in 2 *Political Status Referendum* 1, 23 (1992).

26. According to 1990 census data, per capita annual income in Puerto Rico was $4,177, compared to a national average of $14,420. The figure for Mississippi, the state with the lowest per capita income, was $9,648. U.S. Dept. of Commerce, "1990 Census of Population and Housing, Summary Social, Economic, and Housing Characteristics: Puerto Rico," 1990 *C.H.*-5–53 at 191 (February 1993); U.S. Dep't. of Commerce, "1990 Census of Population and Housing, Summary Social, Economic, and Housing Characteristics: United States," 1990 *C.H.*-5–1 at 228 (November 1992).
27. Carolyn L. Merck, "Welfare and Taxes under Alternative Status Options for Puerto Rico" (Congressional Research Service, 1991), reprinted in 2 *Political Status Referendum* 291, 301–2. (This estimate does not include gains to the federal budget that would accrue from statehood owing to the repeal of tax credits to mainland corporations doing business in Puerto Rico.)
28. 446 U.S. 651 (1980).
29. 446 U.S. at 651–52.
30. 446 U.S. at 652 (citing Califano v. Torres, 435 U.S. 1 (1978) (per curiam)).
31. Id.
32. Cf. Dandridge v. Williams, 397 U.S. 471 (1970) (upholding regulation capping AFDC payment regardless of family size). The Court has made exceptions where a protected class is involved. See, e.g., Califano v. Goldfarb, 430 U.S. 199 (1977) (gender); Jimenez v. Weinberger, 417 U.S. 365 (1971) (aliens).
33. In 1991, California (with a population a bit more than eight times that of Puerto Rico) had twelve times the number of families receiving AFDC (the average family size was the same for both jurisdictions)—California: 729,170; Puerto Rico: 60,842. U.S. Dep't. of Health and Human Services, *Administration for Children and Families, Office of Family Assistance, Characteristics and Financial Circumstances of AFDC Recipients* 19, table 1 (FY 1991). The federal dollar contributions show a far larger disparity (owing to the higher level of welfare payments in California). In 1992, the federal contribution to the California AFDC program totaled about $3 billion; federal payments to the Puerto Rican program totaled $63 million. House of Representatives, Committee on Ways and Means, *1991 Green Book* 674–75 (1993).
34. Why might not it be just as reasonable to link welfare participation with service in the armed forces? Puerto Ricans, as U.S. citizens, have been subject to the draft and have fought in Operation Desert Storm as part of the volunteer armed forces.

35. Moreover, the tax exemption is not necessarily a windfall to residents of Puerto Rico. Because of the lack of a federal income tax, Commonwealth tax rates are set higher.
36. 446 U.S. at 654 (Marshall, J., dissenting).
37. The 1996 welfare statute terminated most means-tested federal aid to immigrants in the United States. Subsequent changes restored some benefits to persons already in the United States in 1996, but prospective bars on immigrants remain. See T. Alexander Aleinikoff, David Martin, and Hiroshi Motomura, *Immigration and Citizenship: Process and Policy* 538–39 550–52 (4th ed. 1998).
38. This raises the interesting question whether the federal tax exemption enjoyed by Puerto Ricans should be constitutionally suspect—a topic omitted from most commentaries criticizing the Court's conceptualization of the constitutional status of Puerto Rico. Favorable treatment may well be problematic unless it is justified as some form of a remedy for colonial treatment and absence of political rights.
39. Igartua De la Rosa v. U.S. 229 F.3d 80 (1st Cir. 2000); Igartua De la Rosa v. U.S., 32 F.3d 8 (1st Cir. 1994), cert. denied, 514 U.S. 1049 (1995).
40. *Downes,* 182 U.S. at 287.
41. U.S. Constitution, Art. I, §2, para. 1.
42. See generally Owen M. Fiss, *Troubled Beginnings of the Modern State, 1888–1910* [vol. 8 of the Oliver Wendell Holmes Devise, *The History of the Supreme Court of the United States*] ch. 8 (1993)].
43. It is usually forgotten that one of our most famous constitutional aphorisms arises from the controversies of this time. In full, Mr. Dooley's observation was: "[N]o matter whether th' constitution follows th' flag, or not, th' supreme court follows th' ilection returns." Finley Peter Dunne, *Mr. Dooley's Opinions* 26 (1906). To the dismay of its advocates, the idea that the Constitution applied in the territories echoed Justice Taney's opinion in *Dred Scott*—an irony of which members of the Court were painfully aware. See Downes v. Bidwell, 182 U.S. 244, 287–92 (1901) (White, Shiras, and McKenna, J., concurring).
44. See Hon. José A. Cabranes, "Puerto Rico: Colonialism as Constitutional Doctrine," 100 *Harv. L. Rev.* 450, 455 (1986) (book review).
45. This view is stated most directly by Justice Brown's opinion in *Downes v. Bidwell.* Because the language is extraordinarily revealing, I quote it at length:

> Patriotic and intelligent men may differ widely as to the desireableness of this or that acquisition, but this is solely a political

> question. We can only consider this aspect of the case so far as to say that no construction of the Constitution should be adopted which would prevent Congress from considering each case upon its merits, unless the language of the instrument imperatively demand it. A false step at this time might be fatal to the development of what Chief Justice Marshall called the American Empire. Choice in some cases, the natural gravitation of small bodies towards large ones in others, the result of a successful war in still others, may bring about conditions which would render the annexation of distant possessions desirable. If those possessions are inhabited by alien races, differing from us in religion, customs, laws, methods of taxation and modes of thought the administration of government and justice, according to Anglo-Saxon principles, may for a time be impossible, and the question at once arises whether large concessions ought not to be made for a time, that, ultimately, our own theories may be carried out, and the blessings of a free government under the Constitution extended to them. We decline to hold that there is anything in the Constitution to forbid such action.

182 U.S. 244, 286–87 (1901).

46. *Downes,* 182 U.S. at 292 (White, J., concurring), adopted by the Court in Dorr v. United States, 195 U.S. 138 (1904); Balzac v. Porto Rico, 258 U.S. 298 (1922). The Court thus rejected polar positions urged in the course of the debate over the status of the territories: (1) that it was fully up to Congress to determine which rights would be extended to the territories and (2) that the Constitution applies in full wherever the government of the United States acts. For a detailed description and analysis of these arguments, see Gerald L. Neuman, "Whose Constitution?" 100 *Yale L. J.* 909 (1991).
47. U.S. Constitution, Art. I, §8, cl. 1.
48. *Dorr,* 195 U.S. at 146.
49. *Balzac,* 258 U.S. at 308–10.
50. Quoted in Fiss, *Troubled Beginnings of the Modern State* at 245 n.77.
51. 258 U.S. 298 (1922).
52. Id. at 310. Would Taft's reasoning support exclusion of naturalized U.S. citizens from juries if they grew up in legal systems without juries?
53. "[U]nder the circumstances," wrote the Chief Justice, "[U.S. citizenship is] entirely consistent with non-incorporation." The granting of citizenship ensured Puerto Ricans the protection of a sovereign, but it did not automatically demonstrate a congressional intent to incorporate the territory. Id. at 308.

54. See Torruella, *The Supreme Court and Puerto Rico* at 99–100.
55. Taft's words here sound carefully chosen. He seems unwilling to join the generally held opinion of the day that Puerto Ricans simply were not "civilized" enough to understand or operate under Anglo-Saxon traditions. (Other Justices in the *Insular Cases* were less restrained. See, e.g., *Downes,* 182 U.S. at 279–80: "[I]t is doubtful if Congress would ever assent to the annexation of territory upon the condition that its inhabitants, however foreign they may be to our habits, traditions and modes of life, shall become at once citizens of the United States.") Rather, Taft sounds a note of deference in *Balzac* to local decision makers, which helps him conclude that the availability of jury trials for felonies is not determinative.
56. See Torres v. Puerto Rico, 442 U.S. 465, 475–76 (1979) (Brennan, J., concurring) (suggesting that *Insular Cases* represent the views of an earlier age); Reid v. Covert, 354 U.S. 1, 8–9 (1957) (opinion of Black, J.).
57. Constitution of Puerto Rico, Art. II, §11. For explanation of the statutory background, see Helfeld I at 458. Not all territories, however, are bound by the jury trial right. Compare King v. Andrus, 452 F. Supp. 11 (D.D.C. 1977) (Sixth Amendment jury trial right applies in American Samoa) with Northern Mariana Islands v. Atalig, 723 F.2d 682 (9th Cir. 1984), cert. denied, 467 U.S. 1244 (1984) (jury trial not required as matter of federal constitutional law).
58. Public Law 600, §2.
59. See Constitution of Puerto Rico, Art. II.
60. E.g., id. §7 (prohibiting the death penalty); §8 ("Every person has the right to the protection of law against abusive attacks on his honor, reputation and private or family life"); §10 (prohibiting wiretapping). Section 19, in looking two ways at once, shows an acute awareness of U.S. constitutional development: "The foregoing enumeration of rights shall not be construed restrictively nor does it contemplate the exclusion of other rights not specifically mentioned which belong to the people in a democracy. The power of the Legislative Assembly to enact laws for the protection of life, health and general welfare of the people shall likewise not be construed restrictively."
61. Id. §7 provides that "[n]o person in Puerto Rico shall be denied the equal protection of the laws." The congressional legislation approving the constitution required the commonwealth to amend it to include a guarantee that subsequent amendments be "consistent . . . with the applicable provisions of the Constitution of the United States." Act of July 3, 1952, ch. 567, 66 Stat. 27. The Puerto Rican Constitutional Convention formally accepted the congressionally mandated amend-

ment to the constitution's amending provision. It is interesting that the congressional proviso demands adherence to "applicable provisions of the Constitution"—suggesting continued fidelity to the principle of the *Insular Cases* that not all constitutional rights automatically apply in Puerto Rico.

62. Prior to commonwealth, it could be argued, the acts of the Puerto Rican government constituted federal action in a federal territory; hence, constitutional norms limiting federal action could be imposed on the conduct of the island's officials. But, as a number of lower court cases have suggested, the coming of commonwealth seems to have undermined the position that the Puerto Rican government may be viewed as exercising federal power. *Figueroa v. Puerto Rico,* 232 F.2d 615 (Puerto Rican constitution is not an act of Congress); Mora v. Torres, 113 F. Supp. 309 (D.P.R.), aff'd sub nom. Mora v. Mejias, 206 F.2d 377 (1st Cir. 1953) (Fifth Amendment no longer applicable to acts of Puerto Rican government: "The [Puerto Rican] government is no longer an agency of the Government of the United States nor does it exercise any longer its powers by way of delegation of the Federal Government"). Cf. *United States v. Lopez Andino,* 831 F.2d 1164 ("dual sovereignty" doctrine applies to criminal prosecution by Puerto Rico; no double jeopardy problem). But see *United States v. Sanchez,* 992 F.2d at 1150 ("Punitive authority in a territory of the United States flows directly from this plenary power. Every exercise of authority which does not proceed under a direct Congressional enactment proceeds, at least, at the sufferance of the Congress, which may override disfavored rules or institutions as will. The United States Congress is the source of prosecutorial authority for . . . the courts of United States territories" (footnote omitted)).

63. 442 U.S. 465, 471 (1979). See also Calero-Toledo v. Pearson Yacht Leasing Co., 416 U.S. 663, 668–69 n.5 (1974) (due process applies, either by way of Fifth or Fourteenth Amendment); Examining Board v. Flores de Otero, 426 U.S. 572, 600–601 (1976):

> It is clear now . . . that the protections accorded by either the Due Process Clause of the Fifth Amendment or the Due Process and Equal Protection Clauses of the Fourteenth Amendment apply to residents for Puerto Rico . . .
>
> The Court, however, thus far has declined to say whether it is the Fifth Amendment or the Fourteenth which provides the protection . . . Once again, we need not resolve that precise question because, irrespective of which Amendment applies, the statutory restriction . . . is plainly unconstitutional.

64. Four Justices in *Torres* would have held directly that the Bill of Rights applied in full to Puerto Rico: "Whatever the validity of [the *Insular Cases*] . . . in the particular historical context in which they were decided, those cases are clearly not authority for questioning the application of the Fourth Amendment—or any other provision of the Bill of Rights—to the Commonwealth of Puerto Rico in the 1970's." 442 U.S. at 475–76 (Brennan, J., concurring in the judgment).
65. This conclusion could be based on notions of territoriality or, to adopt Gerald Neuman's term, a mutuality of obligations ("[R]ights are prerequisites for justifying legal obligations"). Gerald Neuman, *Strangers to the Constitution: Immigrants, Borders, and Fundamental Law* 7–8 (1996).
66. Covenant to Establish a Commonwealth of the Northern Mariana Islands in Political Union with the United States of America, Act of March 24, 1976, Pub. L. 94–241, 90 Stat. 263, Art. II, §203(c).
67. See, e.g., Reynolds v. Sims, 377 U.S. 533 (1964).
68. Rayphand v. Sablan, 95 F. Supp. 2d 1133 (D.N. Mariana Islands 1999) (three-judge court), sum. aff'd sub nom. Torres v. Sablan, 528 U.S. 1110 (2000).
69. Constitution of the Commonwealth of the Northern Mariana Islands, Art. XII, §1.
70. Covenant, §805.
71. See Saenz v. Roe, 526 U.S. 489, 507 (1999) (Congress may not authorize states to violate Fourteenth Amendment).
72. See Chapter 3. See also Gerald L. Neuman, "Constitutional and Individual Rights in the Territories" (unpub. ms.), pt. 4.
73. See Will Kymlicka, *Multicultural Citizenship: A Liberal Theory of Minority Rights* ch. 8 (1995). See also Neuman, "Constitutional and Individual Rights in the Territories" (noting that Justice Harlan's dissent in *Downes v. Bidwell* was "assimilationist, not multicultural").
74. *Rayphand v. Sablan;* Wabol v. Villacrusis, 958 F.2d 1450 (9th Cir.), cert. denied, 506 U.S. 1027 (1992).
75. *Wabol,* 958 F.2d at 1459.
76. Id. at 1461, 1462.
77. See, e.g., International Covenant on Civil and Political Rights, Arts. 3, 25, 999 U.N.T.S. 171, 174, 179; Convention on the Elimination of All Forms of Discrimination against Women, Art. 7(a), 19 I.L.M. 33, 37 (1980); Restatement (Third) of the Foreign Relations Law of the United States § 702, cmts *l,* m (1987).
78. See, e.g., International Covenant on Civil and Political Rights, Art. 18, 999 U.N.T.S. 171, 178.
79. *Rayphand,* 95 F. Supp. 2d at 1140.

80. *Wabol,* 958 F.2d at 1460.
81. David Scobey has helped me think through these issues.
82. It is also worth noting that residents of the territories have an "exit" option: all are entitled to travel freely to the United States, where they enjoy the rights of citizens in whatever state they choose to reside. This cannot be a complete justification for differentiated rights, however, given the financial and psychological costs of leaving one's homeland.
83. See, e.g., King v. Andrus, 452 F. Supp. 11 (D.D.C. 1977) (constitutional right to jury trial in American Samoa despite claim that it would undercut preservation of traditional values and harmonious relationships).
84. A noteworthy study, issued in 1975, was conducted by the Ad Hoc Advisory Group on Puerto Rico appointed by the president of the United States and the governor of Puerto Rico. Charged with submitting recommendations on how to "develop the maximum of self-government and self-determination within the framework of Commonwealth," the group proposed a new compact "of permanent union" which would have, inter alia, (1) ended disfavorable treatment of Puerto Rican residents in federal benefit programs (§6); (2) granted Puerto Rico some degree of control over immigration to the island (§10); (3) provided for a Puerto Rican delegate in the U.S. Senate (§11); (4) provided that future federal laws would not apply in Puerto Rico unless a statute specifically referred to the island, and such laws, when objected to by Puerto Rico as inconsistent with the compact, must be essential to the interests of the United States (§12); and (5) authorized amendments to the compact only upon the mutual consent of both parties (§21). Ad Hoc Advisory Group on Puerto Rico, *Compact of Permanent Union between Puerto Rico and the United States* (October 1975). The enhanced commonwealth proposal at issue in the 1993 plebiscite included four measures: restoring and making permanent favorable federal tax treatment of corporate profits earned in Puerto Rico, extending SSI to the island, removing the cap on food assistance funds, and protecting Puerto Rican agriculture through federal tariffs. Robert Friedman, "PDP Expected to Move Cautiously in D.C.," *San Juan Star,* November 15, 1993, at 9.
85. See generally Trías Monge, *Puerto Rico* ch. 15 ("Possible Paths to Decolonization").
86. S. 244, 102d Cong., 1st Sess., §401(a) (1991).
87. S. 244, §403(a). Exempted from the procedures of the bill were statutes relating to citizenship, foreign relations, defense and national security, and legislative matters under the jurisdiction of the Senate

committees on finance (i.e., tax legislation), agriculture, nutrition, and forestry. S. 244, §403(c).

88. The agency had to respond by finding (1) that it had no discretion not to make the rule applicable to Puerto Rico, (2) that the national interest demanded that the rule apply, or (3) that the rule was not consistent with commonwealth status and therefore should not apply. S. 244, §404.

89. These included the following: S. 244, §403(d) (authorizing governor of Puerto Rico to enter into international agreements "as authorized by the President of the United States and consistent with the laws and international obligations of the United States"); §405 (federal Department of Transportation to seek advice of commonwealth when negotiating air transportation agreements that would affect air traffic to or from Puerto Rico); §§407, 415 (aiming at parity for Puerto Rico under federal benefits programs); §408 (requiring federal officials to consult with the commonwealth on appointments to federal positions in Puerto Rico); §411 (entitling "community values" by exempting from antitrust laws agreements by Puerto Rican broadcasters to develop guidelines to "alleviate the negative impact" of violence, drugs, and sexually explicit material on television).

90. Cf. *United State v. Quinones,* 728 F.2d 40 (federal statute authorizing wiretapping permits introduction of wiretap evidence in federal prosecution in Puerto Rico, despite provision in Puerto Rico's constitution prohibiting wiretaps).

91. If Congress were to accept the commonwealth's suggestion that a particular federal law not apply to the island, then it could be seen as giving the commonwealth preferred treatment (and not simply establishing Puerto Rican parity with the states). For example, it has sometimes been argued that federal environmental standards might be relaxed in Puerto Rico so as not to hinder economic development. But under the 1991 proposal (S. 244), this would have been a federal decision, not the exercise of a power to "opt out" by Puerto Rico.

92. Others have wondered whether the Republican Party's official support for statehood colored its constitutional conclusions regarding "enhanced Commonwealth." See "Puerto Rico Self-Determination Act, 1990: Hearings on H.R. 4765 before the Subcomm. on Insular and Int'l. Affairs of the House Comm. on Interior and Insular Affairs," 101st Cong., 2d Sess., pt. 2, 112–17 (1990) (statement of Jaime B. Fuster, delegate from Puerto Rico).

93. "Puerto Rico Status Referendum Act, 1991: Hearings on S. 244 before the Senate Comm. on Energy and Natural Resources," 102d Cong., 1st Sess., 190 (1991) (statement of Richard Thornburgh, Attorney Gen-

eral) ("Hearings on S. 244"). In section-by-section comments attached to the attorney general's testimony, the Department of Justice also objected to the power granted the governor of Puerto Rico to force reconsideration of federal regulations. It argued that such action would constitute "significant governmental authority under the laws of the United States" and therefore could be carried out only by a federal official appointed under the appointments clause of the Constitution. Id. at 212 (citing Buckley v. Valeo, 424 U.S. 1, 126–41 (1976)). It also opined that the requirement that the president consult with the Puerto Rican government before appointing federal officials in Puerto Rico would be an unconstitutional intrusion upon the president's appointment power. Id. at 213.

94. Letter of A. Mitchell McConnell, Jr., Acting Assistant Attorney General for Legislative Affairs, to Marlow W. Cook, Co-chairman, Ad Hoc Advisory Group on Puerto Rico, May 12, 1975. The section-by-section analysis of the Justice Department submitted with Attorney General Thornburgh's testimony stated that the earlier opinion of the department was "subject to serious question." "Hearings on S. 244" at 211. Thornburgh's view was reaffirmed by the Department of Justice during the Clinton administration in regard to the Guam status negotiations. See Memorandum from Teresa Wynn Roseborough for the Special Representative for Guam Commonwealth, "Mutual Consent Provisions in the Guam Commonwealth Legislation," July 28, 1994.
95. Perhaps such vigilance might be explained as protecting future Congresses from the current Congress.
96. Sere and Laralde v. Pilot, 10 U.S. (6 Cranch) 332, 337 (1810).
97. Difficult, but not impossible. For a plausible argument that residents of the District of Columbia ought to receive representation in the House of Representations, see Adams v. Clinton, 90 F. Supp. 2d 35, 75 (D.D.C.) (three-judge court) (Oberdorfer, J., dissenting in part and concurring in part), aff'd mem., 531 U.S. 941 (2000). The claim that residents of the territories have a constitutional right to vote in presidential elections has twice been rejected by federal courts of appeals. *Igartua De la Rosa v. United States,* 229 F.3d 80 (Puerto Rico); Attorney General of Guam v. United States, 738 F.2d 1017 (9th Cir. 1984), cert. denied, 469 U.S. 1209 (1985) (Guam).
98. Cf. Cincinnati Soap Co. v. United States, 301 U.S. 308 (1937) (upholding transfer to the Philippine Treasury of federal taxes collected on coconut oil produced in the Philippines; Court recognizes broad congressional power to structure territorial relations as it deems appropriate).
99. Even if the attorney general is correct on this point as a matter of law,

it does not follow that it is wrong for Congress to state its commitment not to alter Puerto Rican status without consent of the people of Puerto Rico. Such a congressional commitment would have strong moral and political force and would not likely be ignored by a subsequent Congress, whether or not it is legally binding.

100. Fletcher v. Peck, 10 U.S. (6 Cranch) 87 (1810); Marbury v. Madison, 5 U.S. (1 Cranch) 137 (1803).
101. Indeed, it has been suggested that the legislative history of the establishment of commonwealth in the 1950s can be read to create "an irrevocable grant of authority in local affairs with an understanding of mutual consent being required before Congress would resolve the ultimate status question or change the status of the Commonwealth." See Leibowitz, *Defining Status* at 172.
102. See Cooper v. Aaron, 358 U.S. 1 (1958), for the domestic claim; the *Chinese Exclusion Case,* 130 U.S. 581 (1889), for the foreign claim.
103. Neil MacCormick, "Beyond the Sovereign State," 56 *Mod. L. Rev.* 1 (1993).
104. Id. at 1.
105. Id.at 16.
106. Id.
107. Id. at 17.
108. Id. at 10. MacCormick elaborates:

> To escape the idea that all law must originate in a single power source, like a sovereign, is thus to discover the possibility of taking a broader, more diffuse, view of law. The alternative approach is system-oriented in the sense that it stresses the kind of normative system law is rather than some particular or exclusive set of power relations as fundamental to the nature of law. It is a view of law that allows of the possibility that different systems can overlap and interact, without necessarily requiring that one be subordinate or hierarchically inferior to the other or to some third system.

109. Id. at 17.
110. Cabranes, "Puerto Rico and the Constitution" at 481.
111. Id. at 480.
112. See Berríos Martinez, "Independence for Puerto Rico" at 583 ("Our people cannot live without freedom and dignity. Independence is the only solution"); "Political Status of Puerto Rico, Hearings before the Senate Committee on Energy and Natural Resources," 101st Cong., 1st Sess., pt. 1 at 171 (1989) (statement of Hon. Rafael Hernández Colón, Governor of Puerto Rico) (enhanced Commonwealth "will go a long

way towards updating what was a brilliant solution to the dilemma of a people seeking their place in dignity within the American constitutional system—a people unwilling to give up their identity and culture"); Romero-Barceló, "Puerto Rico, U.S.A." at 81 (advocating statehood: "A people's quest for dignity is nearing its goal . . . The goal of the Puerto Rican people is political equality within a framework which will permit our island and our nation to prosper together").

113. Independence supporters have made regular trips to the United Nations, arguing that Puerto Rico remains a colony and that international pressure should be brought to bear on the United States for decolonization. Following establishment of the commonwealth, the United Nations—at the request of the United States—removed Puerto Rico from the list of non–self-governing territories. G.A. Res. 748, U.N. GAOR, 8th Sess., Supp. No. 17 at 25–26, U.N. Doc. A/64 (1953). The resolution lifted the requirement that the United States report to the United Nations on conditions in the territory and efforts being taken to promote self-government. In 1972 the United Nations Decolonization Committee (officially, the Special Committee on the Situation with Regard to the Implementation of the Declaration of the Granting of Independence to Colonial Countries and People) put the Puerto Rican question on its agenda and has continued discussion of the island's status. The committee has regularly adopted resolutions "[reaffirming] the inalienable right of the people of Puerto Rico to self-determination and independence." In 1993 the committee appeared to be ready to close up shop. It did, however, put over the Puerto Rico question for another year. United Nations, Special Committee on the Situation with Regard to the Implementation of the Declaration of the Granting of Independence to Colonial Countries and Peoples [hereinafter Decolonization Committee]; Verbatim Record of the 1424th Meeting at 50, U.N. Doc. A/AC109/PV.1424 (August 15, 1993) (unedited transcript). Pro-decolonization groups have asked the committee to recommend to the General Assembly that it seek an opinion from the International Court of Justice defining the status of Puerto Rico under international law. Decolonization Committee, supra; Verbatim Record of the 1422d Meeting at 28, U.N. Doc. A/AC109/PV.1422 (August 9, 1993) (statement of Puerto Rican Bar Association).

114. Independence supporters attempted to answer this argument following their blistering loss in the 1993 referendum. They contended that the referendum could not constitute a genuine act of self-determination because (1) some 2 million Puerto Rican nationals living on the

mainland were not allowed to participate while nonnationals living on the island were; (2) its results were not binding on the Congress; (3) it took place within a context that subverted free exercise of the right of self-determination, namely, the exercise of U.S. authority and the presence of the U.S. military in Puerto Rico; and (4) by including the commonwealth option, the plebiscite did not guarantee an end to colonialism. Decolonization Committee, A/AC.109/PV.1422 at 23–24.

115. Robert Friedman, "Congressman Says Spanish Remains Barrier for Statehood," *San Juan Star,* October 29, 1993, at 14 (quoting Rep. Gerald B. Solomon (R.-N.Y.)). See Robert Friedman, "N.Y. Congressman Joins Status Ad Blitz," *San Juan Star,* October 28, 1993, at 16.

116. See generally Edgardo Meléndez,, "Colonialism, Citizenship, and Contemporary Statehood," in Meléndez and Meléndez *Colonial Dilemma* at 41–52 (describing "creole statehood"—i.e., protection of cultural and linguistic identity of Puerto Rico within the structure of U.S. federalism—as dominant conception of statehood movement).

5. The Erosion of American Indian Sovereignty

1. Dred Scott v. Sandford, 60 U.S. (19 How.) 393 (1856).
2. Northwest Ordinance of 1787, Art. VI, ch. VIII, 1 Stat. 50, 51 (1789) ("There shall be neither slavery nor involuntary servitude in the said territory"). Taney's opinion ruled unconstitutional similar provisions in the Missouri Compromise of 1820, but he left standing the Northwest Ordinance. The difference, Taney contended, was that the Constitution's delegation of power to Congress to make "all needful Rules and Regulations respecting the Territory . . . belonging to the United States" applied only to territory that the United States possessed at the time of the adoption of the Constitution. See *Dred Scott,* 60 U.S. at 432–36 (quoting U.S. Constitution, Art. IV, §3). The clause thus did not empower Congress to prohibit slavery in territory acquired from France in the Louisiana Purchase of 1803.
3. See Jamin B. Raskin, "Legal Aliens, Local Citizens: The Historical, Constitutional, and Theoretical Meanings of Alien Suffrage," 141 *U. Pa. L. Rev.* 1391, 1402 (1993) (arguing that the provision in the Northwest Ordinance of 1787 for rights of long-term resident aliens was not unusual, but was an attempt to increase immigration in the area northwest of the Ohio River); see also Northwest Ordinance of 1787, ch. VIII, 1 Stat. 50, 51 (1789): "So soon as there shall be five thousand free male inhabitants, of full age, in the district, upon giving proof thereof to the governor, they shall receive authority, with time and

place, to elect representatives from their counties or townships, to represent them in the general assembly . . . ; provided . . . , that a freehold in fifty acres of land in the district, having been a citizen of one of the States, and being resident in the district, or the like freehold and two years residence in the district shall be necessary to qualify a man as an elector of a representative."

4. Northwest Ordinance of 1787, Art. III, ch. VIII, 1 Stat. 50, 52 (1789).
5. Indeed, serious conflict erupted in the Northwest Territory within a matter of years, ending in the defeat of the Indians and the 1794 treaty of Greenville. As Anthony Wallace notes, the Treaty represented "the end of effective Indian resistance north of the Ohio River to the advance of white settlement into the territory between the Appalachians and the Mississippi." Anthony F. C. Wallace, *Jefferson and the Indians: The Tragic Fate of the First Americans* 174 (1999).
6. Patrick Macklem, "Distributing Sovereignty: Indian Nations and Equality of Peoples," 45 *Stan. L. Rev.* 1311, 1333 (1993). Macklem draws this conclusion from Chief Justice Marshall's statement in *Worcester v. Georgia* that "'America, separated from Europe by a wide ocean, was inhabited by a distinct people, divided into nations, independent of each other and of the rest of the world, having institutions of their own, and governing themselves by their own laws.'" Id. at 1334 (quoting Worcester v. Georgia, 31 U.S. (6 Pet.) 515, 542–43 (1832)).
7. See U.S. Constitution, Art. I, §8 (granting Congress power to regulate commerce with foreign nations, among the states, and with Indian tribes); id. §2 (excluding "Indians not taxed" for purposes of apportioning representation in the House).
8. The decisions are known as the Marshall Trilogy. They are Johnson v. M'Intosh, 21 U.S. (8 Wheat.) 543 (1823), Cherokee Nation v. Georgia, 30 U.S. (5 Pet.) 1 (1831), and Worcester v. Georgia, 31 U.S. (6 Pet.) 515 (1832).
9. *Worcester*, 31 U.S. (6 Pet.) at 561.
10. Felix S. Cohen, *Handbook of Federal Indian Law* 122 (1942 ed.) [hereinafter Cohen, *Handbook of Federal Indian Law*, 1942 ed.].
11. 419 U.S. 544, 557 (1975) (citations omitted). The broad language of *Mazurie* is in marked contrast to the language and tenor of other Rehnquist opinions, but it is explainable by the particular facts of the case. At issue was a tribal prosecution for violation of reservation liquor sale rules. The Court held that Congress had authority under the Indian commerce clause to regulate liquor transactions and that it had delegated its authority to the tribe. The statement about the inherent sovereignty of tribes answered the defendant's claim that Con-

gress had unlawfully delegated authority to a private group. Furthermore, the citation to *Kagama* is a sure reminder of Congress's plenary power over the tribes.

12. Mary Christina Wood, "Indian Land and the Promise of Native Sovereignty: The Trust Doctrine Revisited," 1994 *Utah L. Rev.* 1471, 503–5 (recognizing the differences in models as laid out in *Worcester,* which seeks a viable separatism, and in *Kagama,* which looks to assimilation).
13. Cf. Steven P. McSloy, "Back to the Future: Native American Sovereignty in the 21st Century," 20 *N.Y.U. Rev. L. & Soc. Change* 217 (1993) (asserting that the plenary power doctrine is unconstitutional given Marshall's opinion in *Worcester* that Indians are independent and sovereign).
14. 118 U.S. 375, 383–84 (1886).
15. See, e.g., Wood, "Indian Land and the Promise"; Mary Christina Wood, "Protecting the Attributes of Native Sovereignty: A New Trust Paradigm for Federal Actions Affecting Tribal Lands and Resources," 1995 *Utah L. Rev.* 109.
16. See Charles F. Wilkinson, *American Indians, Time, and the Law: Native Societies in Modern Constitutional Democracy* 3–5 (1987) (Indian law doctrines, although flawed, also provide basis for hope).
17. See Allison M. Dussias, "Geographically-Based and Membership-Based Views of Indian Tribal Sovereignty: The Supreme Court's Changing Vision," 55 *U. Pitt. L. Rev.* 1, 92–94 (1993); L. Scott Gould, "The Consent Paradigm: Tribal Sovereignty at the Millenium," 96 *Colum. L. Rev.* 809, 838–42 (1996); Joseph W. Singer, "Sovereignty and Property," 86 *Nw. U. L. Rev.* 1, 5–6 (1991).
18. See U.S. Constitution, Art. IV, §3 (no state may be created within an existing state or by joining states together without state consent); Printz v. United States, 521 U.S. 898 (1997); New York v. United States, 505 U.S. 144 (1992).
19. See United States v. Wheeler, 435 U.S. 313, 319 (1978).
20. Compare Talton v. Mayes, 163 U.S. 376 (1896), with Downes v. Bidwell, 182 U.S. 244 (1901).
21. The term "Indian country" means: "(a) all land within the limits of any Indian reservation under the jurisdiction of the United States Government, notwithstanding the issuance of any patent, and, including rights-of-way running through the reservation, (b) all dependent Indian communities within the borders of the United States whether within the original or subsequently acquired territory thereof, and whether within or without the limits of a state, and (c) all Indian allotments, the Indian titles to which have not been extinguished, including rights-of-way running through the same." 18 U.S.C. §1151 (1994).

22. 21 U.S. (8 Wheat.) 543 (1823).
23. Id. at 591–92.
24. Id. at 591.
25. See Frank Pommersheim, *Braid of Feathers: American Indian Law and Contemporary Tribal Life* 11–36 (1995).
26. Wilkinson, *American Indians, Time, and the Law* at 16 n.44 (citing treaties with the Kiowa, Comanche, Navajo and Sioux tribes).
27. Supreme Court cases of this era describe members of Indian tribes as "citizens" of Indian nations. See, e.g., Parks v. Ross, 52 U.S. (11 How.) 362, 373 (1850); United States v. Rogers, 45 U.S. (4 How.) 567, 571 (1846).
28. 118 U.S. at 375.
29. See Act of Feb. 8, 1887, ch. 119, 24 Stat. 388.
30. The phrase "fee land," a shortened version of the legalism "fee simple absolute," means land in which a person is recognized to have complete ownership and power of disposition (subject to restrictions imposed by law).
31. For example, as reported by the Court in *Montana v. United States,* land-ownership on the Crow reservation broke down as follows: 52 percent of the land is allotted to individual members of the tribe and held in trust by the United States government; 17 percent is held in trust by the government on behalf of the tribe itself; 28 percent is held in fee by non-Indians; the state of Montana owns 2 percent of the land in fee simple; and the United States government owns less than 1 percent of the land in fee simple. See 450 U.S. 544, 548 (1980).
32. See Judith V. Royster, "The Legacy of Allotment," 27 *Ariz. St. L. J.* 1 (1995).
33. See Philip P. Frickey, "A Common Law for Our Age of Colonialism: The Judicial Divestiture of Indian Tribal Authority over Nonmembers," 109 *Yale L. J.* 1, 15 (1999).
34. I will qualify this in the discussion of *Montana v. United States* and *Nevada v. Hicks,* 121 S.Ct. 2304 (2001), which follows.
35. Montana v. United States, 450 U.S. at 564.
36. Willliams v. Lee, 358 U.S. 217, 223 (1959).
37. See 25 U.S.C. §1911(a) (1994).
38. See Felix S. Cohen, *Handbook of Federal Indian Law* 324–28 (Rennard Strickland and Charles F. Wilkinson, eds., 1982) (citing cases) [hereinafter Cohen, *Handbook of Federal Indian Law,* 1982 ed.].
39. Cohen, *Handbook of Federal Indian Law,* 1942 ed., at 122.
40. Id. at 123.
41. Id. at 91.
42. See, e.g., Printz v. United States, 521 U.S. 898 (1997) (prohibiting fed-

eral government from infringing on state autonomy by obligating states to take measures to enforce the Brady Handgun Violence Prevention Act).

43. 435 U.S. 313 (1978).
44. Id. at 328.
45. Wilkinson, *American Indians, Time, and the Law* at 61–62.
46. *Wheeler,* 435 U.S. at 323 (emphasis added); see also Merrion v. Jicarilla Apache Tribe, 455 U.S. 130, 156 (1982). Although *Merrion* is a strong pro-sovereignty case, Justice Marshall still notes that "Congress, of course, retains plenary power to limit tribal taxing authority or to alter the current scheme under which the tribes may impose taxes." *Merrion,* 455 U.S. at 156. The plenary power doctrine is a kind of insurance policy, allowing the Court to give inherent sovereignty play.
47. See Act of March 3, 1871, ch. 120, §3, 16 Stat. 544, 570; Act of June 30, 1913, ch. 4, §18, 38 Stat. 77, 97; see also 25 U.S.C. §§81, 84, 85, 177 (1994).
48. See Act of March 3, 1885, ch. 341, §9, 23 Stat. 362, 385.
49. See 25 U.S.C. §1302(7) (1994). The Indian Civil Rights Act leaves open the question whether tribal courts also have jurisdiction in cases where federal courts are granted jurisdiction under the Major Crimes Act. Given the limits on penalties, however, this ambiguity may not be particularly important. See Oliphant v. Suquamish Indian Tribe, 435 U.S. 191, 203 n.14 (1978).
50. See Hagen v. Utah, 510 U.S. 399, 404 (1994); Lone Wolf v. Hitchcock, 187 U.S. 553, 567–68 (1903). Congress, however, must pay "just compensation" if it takes tribal lands recognized pursuant to treaty or statute. See United States v. Sioux Nation of Indians, 448 U.S. 371, 415 n.29 (1980).
51. See United States v. Sandoval, 231 U.S. 28, 46 (1913); cf. United States v. John, 437 U.S. 634, 652–53 (1978).
52. See Santa Clara Pueblo v. Martinez, 436 U.S. 49, 57 (1978).
53. E.g., Safe Drinking Water Act, 42 U.S.C. §300j–11 (1988).
54. See, e.g., Indian Child Welfare Act, 25 U.S.C. §§1901–63 (1994) (limiting state jurisdiction over child custody cases involving reservation Indian children); 4 U.S.C. §109 (1994) (excepting "Indians not otherwise taxed" from state sales and income taxes); Cohen, *Handbook of Federal Indian Law,* 1982 ed., at 418 (discussing preemption of state taxation of land allotted to Indians). Among the earliest federal Indian statutes are the Trade and Intercourse Acts. See Act of July 22, 1790, ch. 33, 1 Stat. 137. These acts continue to be invoked as authority for preempting state laws. See Department of Taxation and Finance

v. Milhelm Attea & Bros., 512 U.S. 61, 70–71 (1994) ("The Indian Trader Statutes and the 'apparently all-inclusive regulations' under them . . . 'would seem in themselves sufficient to show that Congress has taken the business of Indian trading on reservations so fully in hand that no room remains for state laws imposing additional burdens upon traders,'" quoting Warren Trading Post Co. v. Arizona State Tax Comm'n, 380 U.S. 685, 690 (1965)).

55. See 25 U.S.C. §231 (1994); see also Cohen, *Handbook of Federal Indian Law,* 1982 ed., at 407–12 (outlining provisions for taxation), 305–8 (outlining liquor regulations).

56. See Act of Aug. 15, 1953, Pub. L. No. 83–280, ch. 505, 67 Stat. 588. The 1953 act was amended by a 1968 act, which required consent by the tribes. See Act of April 11, 1968, Pub. L. No. 90–284, tit. 4, §§401(a), 402(a), 82 Stat. 73, 78–79.

57. See Act of Aug. 15, 1953, §7, 67 Stat. at 590. Ten states opted in. See Cohen, *Handbook of Federal Indian Law,* 1982 ed., at 28, 368–70. Moreover, the 1968 act gave the states the power to retrocede jurisdiction. See Act of April 11, 1968, §403(a), 82 Stat. at 79. Some states have. See Stephen L. Pevar, *The Rights of Indians and Tribes: The Basic ACLU Guide to Indian and Tribal Rights* 118 (1992). Congress has also expressly granted certain states criminal jurisdiction over offenses committed by or against Indians on reservations in particular states. See Act of June 8, 1940, Pub. L. No. 76–565, ch. 276, 54 Stat. 249, 249 (granting Kansas jurisdiction); Act of May 31, 1946, Pub. L. No. 79–394, ch. 279, 60 Stat. 229, 229 (granting North Dakota jurisdiction); Act of June 30, 1948, Pub. L. No. 80–846, ch. 759, 62 Stat. 1161, 1161 (granting Iowa jurisdiction).

58. See Duro v. Reina, 495 U.S. 676, 696 (1990); Brendale v. Confederated Tribes and Bands of the Yakima Indian Nation, 492 U.S. 408, 425 (1989); Merrion v. Jicarilla Apache Tribe, 455 U.S. 130, 141 (1982).

59. See Dussias, "Geographically-Based and Membership-Based Views of Indian Tribal Sovereignty" at 17 (citing language in Marshall's opinion in *Worcester*).

60. 358 U.S. 217 (1959).

61. Id. at 223 (citation omitted). Cohen is, however, unclear on this point: "It clearly appears, from the foregoing cases, that the powers of an Indian tribe are not limited to such powers as it may exercise in its capacity as a landowner. In its capacity as a sovereign, and in the exercise of local self-government, it may exercise powers similar to those exercised by any state or nation in regulating the use and disposition of private property, save insofar as it is restricted by specific statutes of Con-

gress." Cohen, *Handbook of Federal Indian Law,* 1942 ed., at 145. And in summarizing state power, Cohen concludes that states have jurisdiction in matters involving non-Indians "unless there is involved a subject matter of special federal concern." Id. at 121.

62. 455 U.S. 130 (1982).
63. Id. at 137.
64. 450 U.S. at 565.
65. Id. at 557.
66. Id. at 565–66. In this section I will primarily discuss the second category, but note should be taken of the Court's narrow reading of the first exception as well. See Atkinson Trading Co. v. Shirley, 121 S.Ct. 1825 (2001).
67. In one post-*Montana* case, a splintered Court reached a splintered decision on the power of a tribe to impose zoning regulations on nonmember fee land. See Brendale v. Confederated Tribes and Bands of the Yakima Indian Nation, 492 U.S. 408 (1989). Six Justices found tribal authority to zone fee land within an area of the reservation closed to the general public; a different majority of the Justices denied the tribe authority to zone fee land in an area which was open to the public and in which almost half the land was owned by nonmembers. The Justices offered differing interpretations of the rule secured by the *Montana* exception. See id. at 428–32 (White, Rehnquist, Scalia, and Kennedy), 449–50 (Blackmun, Brennan, Marshall); see also South Dakota v. Bourland, 508 U.S. 679 (1993) (considering whether a tribe had authority to regulate hunting and fishing by non-Indians in an area of the reservation acquired by the United States for a reservoir and dam; case remanded for application of the *Montana* exceptions).
68. 520 U.S. 438 (1997).
69. Strate v. A-1 Contractors, 520 U.S. 438, 458 (1997).
70. Id. at 459 (quoting *Williams,* 358 U.S. at 220).
71. Lower courts, both before and after *Strate,* have generally read the second *Montana* exception narrowly. See, e.g., County of Lewis v. Allen, 163 F.3d 509, 514–16 (9th Cir. 1998) (en banc); Lower Brule Sioux Tribe v. South Dakota, 104 F.3d 1017, 1023–24 (8th Cir.), cert. denied, 522 U.S. 816 (1997); Yellowstone County v. Pease, 96 F.3d 1169, 1176–77 (9th Cir. 1996), cert denied, 520 U.S. 1209 (1997). But cf. Montana v. EPA, 137 F.3d 1135, 1140–41 (9th Cir. 1998), cert. denied, 525 U.S. 921 (1998), (upholding the EPA's grant of power to tribe to enforce environmental regulations against nonconsenting non–tribal member under the federal Clean Water Act; EPA regulations recognized tribal health and welfare under the second *Montana* exception).

72. 121 S.Ct. 2304 (2001).
73. Id. at 2313.
74. In response to Justice O'Connor's statement that the Court's decision permitted state law enforcement officers to act with impunity on reservations (id. at 2332 (O'Connor, J., concurring in part and concurring in the judgment)), Justice Scalia left a window open a crack for suits against state officials off on a frolic: "We do not say state officers cannot be regulated; we say they cannot be regulated in the performance of their law-enforcement duties. Action unrelated to that is *potentially* subject to tribal control depending on the outcome of *Montana* analysis." Id. at 2317 (emphasis supplied). The Court further held that tribal courts could not entertain federal civil rights suits brought under 42 U.S.C. §1983. Id, at 2313–15. It noted, however, that tribal plaintiffs could sue in federal or state courts for civil rights violations. Id. at 2318.
75. Id at. 2310.
76. As Justice Souter's concurring opinion states, "The principle on which *Montana* and *Strate* were decided . . . looks first to human relationships, not land records . . . It is the membership status of the unconsenting party, not the status of the real property, that counts as the primary jurisdictional fact." Id at 2322.
77. Id. at 2312 (quoting Fort Leavenworth R. Co. v. Lowe, 114 U.S. 525, 533 (1885)).
78. Id. at 2323.
79. See United States v. McBratney, 104 U.S. 621, 624 (1881).
80. 435 U.S. 191 (1978).
81. Id. at 208.
82. Id. at 209–10.
83. 109 U.S. 556 (1883).
84. Id. at 571.
85. 435 U.S. at 211.
86. See, e.g., Philip P. Frickey, "Marshalling Past and Present: Colonialism, Constitutionalism, and Interpretation in Federal Indian Law," 107 *Harv. L. Rev.* 381, 420 n.162 (1993) ("Because of its facts, [that of the three thousand individuals living on the reservation, only fifty were actually members of the tribe], *Oliphant* was a horrible test case from the tribal perspective").
87. 495 U.S. 676 (1990).
88. Id. at 688.
89. Id. at 688.
90. Id.
91. Id. at 707 (Brennan, J., dissenting).

92. Id. at 694.
93. See Philip P. Frickey, "Adjudication and Its Discontents: Coherence and Conciliation in Federal Indian Law," 110 *Harv. L. Rev.* 1754, 1770 (1997).
94. 495 U.S. at 692 (quoting *Oliphant,* 435 U.S. at 211).
95. Id. at 693.
96. Duro v. Reina, 495 U.S. 676, 693 (1990).
97. Congress permanently overrode the Court's decision in *Duro,* granting the tribes criminal jurisdiction over non-tribal Indians who commit crimes on the reservation. See Act of Oct. 28, 1991, 105 Stat. 646. Compare Nell Jessup Newton, "Permanent Legislation to Correct *Duro v. Reina,*" 17 *Am. Indian L. Rev.* 109 (1992) (supporting the legislation), with L. Scott Gould, "The Congressional Response to *Duro v. Reina:* Compromising Sovereignty and the Constitution," 28 *U.C. Davis L. Rev.* 53 (1994) (arguing against the legislation). To my mind, Congress should have gone further, authorizing criminal jurisdiction over non-Indians as well. Newton suggests that extending jurisdiction over non-Indians was not politically possible because whites would never countenance it. See Newton, "Permanent Legislation to Correct *Duro v. Reina*" at 124.
98. See generally Jon D. Erickson et al., "Monitored Retrievable Storage of Spent Nuclear Fuel in Indian Country: Liability, Sovereignty, and Socioeconomics," 19 *Am. Indian L. Rev.* 73 (1994) (discussing temporary reservation storage of nuclear waste); William Claiborne, "Utah Resisting Tribe's Nuclear Dump," *Wash. Post,* March 2, 1999, at A3 (discussing same in regard to Goshute tribe in Utah).
99. See New York Ass'n of Convenience Stores v. Urbach, 699 N.E. 2d 904 (N.Y. 1998).
100. See, e.g., Cal. Penal Code §326.5. (West Supp. 1987). This provision of the California Penal Code was at issue in California v. Cabazon Band of Mission Indians, 480 U.S. 202 (1987). The Court in *Cabazon* prevented enforcement of the state provision, citing the compelling federal and tribal interests supporting tribal bingo. See id. at 221–22.
101. See Department of Taxation and Finance v. Milhelm Attea & Bros., 512 U.S. 61, 75–76 (1994) (upholding state law given legitimate state interest and minimal burden on tribe); see also *Williams,* 358 U.S. at 220 (reporting that the principle of *Worcester* had been modified "where essential tribal relations were not involved and where the rights of Indians would not be jeopardized").
102. See U.S. Constitution, Art. IV, §3 ("[N]o new state shall be formed or erected within the Jurisdiction of any other State; nor any State be

formed by the Junction of two or more States, or Parts of States, without the Consent of the Legislatures of the States concerned as well as of the Congress").

103. See U.S. Constitution, Art. IV, §2 (privileges and immunities clause); cf. City of Philadelphia v. New Jersey, 437 U.S. 617, 628–29 (1978) (holding states may not discriminate against out-of-state commerce).
104. See U.S. Constitution, Art. IV, §1 ("Full Faith and Credit shall be given in each State to the public Acts, Records, and judicial Proceedings of every other State. And the Congress may by general Laws prescribe the Manner in which such Acts, Records and Proceedings shall be proved, and the Effect thereof").
105. 411 U.S. 164 (1973).
106. Id. at 172.
107. Id.; see also White Mountain Apache Tribe v. Bracker, 448 U.S. 136, 143, 152 (1980) (holding that a state tax on non-Indian businesses on a reservation was preempted by federal policies and finding that "[t]he right of tribal self-government is ultimately dependent on and subject to the broad power of Congress"). The Court, of course, has backed away from the following statement in that case: "[We have] repeatedly emphasized that there is a significant geographical component which remains highly relevant to the preemption inquiry; though the reservation boundary is not absolute, it remains an important factor to weigh in determining whether state authority has exceeded the permissible limits." Id. at 151.
108. 480 U.S. 202 (1987). Note that this case preceded the enactment of the Indian Gaming Regulatory Act. See generally Act of Oct. 17, 1988, 102 Stat. 2467.
109. *Cabazon,* 480 U.S. at 215.
110. Id. at 216.
111. That this balance could tip in favor of the state became apparent in Department of Taxation and Finance of New York v. Milhelm Attea & Bros., 512 U.S. 61 (1994). At issue there was New York's regulation of cigarette wholesalers who made tax-exempt sales to Indians on reservations. New York believed that sales purportedly made to Indians on reservations (which would be tax-exempt) were actually made to non-Indians—a belief based on data showing that the volume of tax-exempt sales indicated per capita consumption rates far above average. In an attempt to ensure that tax would be collected on non-exempt sales, the state imposed quotas on the quantity of tax-exempt sales and record-keeping requirements. The Court noted that resolution of the case depended not on "'mechanical or absolute conceptions of state

or tribal sovereignty'" but rather on "'a particularized inquiry into the nature of the state, federal and tribal interests at stake.'" Id. at 73 (quoting White Mountain Apache Tribe v. Bracker, 448 U.S. 136, 142, 145 (1980)). The Court upheld the regulations, concluding that the state's interest in "ensuring compliance with lawful taxes" outweighed the tribes' "modest interest in offering a tax exemption to customers who would ordinarily shop elsewhere." 512 U.S. at 73.

112. See *Cabazon,* 480 U.S. at 215 n.17.
113. See id. at 222 (Stevens, J., dissenting); cf. Cotton Petroleum Corp. v. New Mexico, 490 U.S. 163, 175–76 (1989) (summarizing that, although a state may not tax the United States directly, it may do so indirectly absent a congressional action to the contrary).
114. 358 U.S. 217 (1959).
115. Id. at 223.
116. 520 U.S. at 457 (finding that the facts do not fit under the first exception of *Montana* and citing *Williams v. Lee* among a line of cases as an example of when the first exception does apply and as an example of a relation between a tribal member and a nonmember).
117. Id. at 442.
118. In a subsequent case, *El Paso Natural Gas Co. v. Neztsosie,* the Court narrowly read *Strate* when it upheld the general civil authority of tribal courts over non-Indians *on tribal land.* 526 U.S. 473, 483 n.4 (1999).
119. Id at (quoting White Mountain Apache Tribe v. Bracker, 448 U.S. 136, 141 (1980), quoting Worcester v. Georgia, 6 Pet. 515, 561 (1832)).
120. Id. at n. 4.
121. See Barry Friedman and Scott B. Smith, "The Sedimentary Constitution," 147 *U. Pa. L. Rev.* 1 (1998).
122. See Dussias, "Geographically-Based and Membership-Based Views of Indian Tribal Sovereignty" at 18–79.
123. See Gould, "The Consent Paradigm."
124. See Singer, "Sovereignty and Property," at 44 and n.221 (noting the inconsistency of the consent paradigm); see also Robert Laurence, "A Quintessential Essay on *Martinez v. Santa Clara Pueblo,*" 28 *Idaho L. Rev.* 307, 337 (1992).
125. See Dussias, "Geographically-Based and Membership-Based Views of Indian Tribal Sovereignty" at 92–94; Singer, "Sovereignty and Property" at 5–6.
126. Worcester, 31 U.S. at 559.
127. Id. at 559–60.
128. Id. at 557.

129. Milner S. Ball, "Constitution, Court, Indian Tribes," 1987 *Am. B. Found. Res. J.* 1, 32.
130. Department of Taxation & Fin. v. Milhelm Attea & Bros., 512 U.S. 61, 73 (1994) (quoting McClanahan v. State Tax Comm'n, 411 U.S. 164, 165 (1973)).
131. *Worcester,* 31 U.S. at 593 (McLean, J., concurring).
132. Id. at 556.
133. See, e.g., Russel L. Barsh and James Y. Henderson, *The Road: Indian Tribes and Political Liberty* (1980); Frickey, "Marshalling Past and Present"; McSloy, "Back to the Future."
134. See *The European Union: How Democratic Is It?* (Svein S. Andersen and Kjell A. Eliassen, eds., 1996).
135. See Philip P. Frickey, "A Common Law for Our Age of Colonialism." The 1990 census reported that Indians constituted just 54 percent of the total population living on reservations. Out of the 808,163 people living on reservations, only 437,431 were Indian. See Gould, "The Congressional Response to *Duro v. Reina*" at 125 (table 2).
136. 495 U.S. 676 (1990).
137. Id. at 688.
138. Id. at 693; see also Merrion v. Jicarilla Apache Tribe, 455 U.S. 130, 172–73, 183 (1982) (Stevens, J., dissenting) ("Since nonmembers are excluded from participation in tribal government, the powers that may be exercised over them are appropriately limited").
139. See *Duro,* 495 U.S. at 707 (1990) (Brennan, J., dissenting) (citation omitted): "[We have never] held that participation in the political process is a prerequisite to the exercise of criminal jurisdiction by a sovereign. If such were the case, a State could not prosecute nonresidents, and this country could not prosecute aliens who violate our laws. The commission of a crime on the reservation is all the consent that is necessary to allow the tribe to exercise criminal jurisdiction over the nonmember Indian." See also *Restatement (Third) of Foreign Relations Law of the United States* §421(2)(a) (1986) ("In general, a state's exercise of jurisdiction . . . is reasonable if . . . the person or thing is present in the territory of the state, other than transitorily").
140. See, e.g., Dussias, "Geographically-Based and Membership-Based Views of Indian Tribal Sovereignty" at 87.
141. See U.S. Constitution, Amend. XIV (persons born or naturalized in the United States are citizens "of the State wherein they reside"); see also Dunn v. Blumstein, 405 U.S. 330, 360 (1972) (striking down one-year state residency requirement coupled with three-month county residency requirement for voter registration in state).

142. Cf. United States v. Carolene Products Co., 304 U.S. 144, 152–53 n.4 (1938). It is noteworthy that this concern does not appear to carry over to the exclusion of residents of the territories and of the District of Columbia from representation in Congress.
143. See Mississippi Band of Choctaw Indians v. Holyfield, 490 U.S. 30 (1989); Ex parte Crow Dog, 109 U.S. 556 (1883).
144. This concern also seems to be at work in the Court's cases regarding reduction of reservation territory. For a discussion and critique of the so-called diminishment cases, see Frickey, "A Common Law for Our Age of Colonialism" at 17–27.
145. *Duro,* 495 U.S. at 693 ("The retained sovereignty of the tribe is but a recognition of certain additional authority the tribes maintain over Indians who consent to be tribal members").
146. According to 1980 data, Indians constitute a majority on just one of the ten most populous reservations. (Indians are a majority on all ten of the reservations with the largest Indian populations.) Gould, "Congressional Response to *Duro v. Reina*" at 134 (table 4), 137 (table 5).
147. See 435 U.S. at 192 n.1. Non–tribe members owned 63 percent of the land on the reservation. Gould notes thirty-three reservations with active tribal court systems in which Indians constitute a minority of the population (in five of which Indians constitute 10 percent or less). See Gould, "Congressional Response to *Duro v. Reina*" at 128–29 (table 3).
148. Brendale v. Confederated Tribes and Bands of Yakima Indian Nation, 492 U.S. 408, 445–46 and n.4 (1989); cf. South Dakota v. Yankton Sioux Tribe, 522 U.S. 329, 356–57 (1998).
149. On the role or blood quantum standards in tribal membership rules, see Margo S. Brownell, "Who Is an Indian? Searching for an Answer to the Question at the Core of Federal Indian Law," 34 *U. Mich. J. Rev.* 275, 279–81 (2000–2001); L. Scott Gould, "Mixing Bodies and Beliefs: The Predicament of Tribes," 101 *Colum. L. Rev.* 702, 718–26 (2001); Cohen, *Handbook of Federal Indian Law,* 1982 ed., at 23. Not all tribal membership rules are blood-based. More so in the past than today, tribes have permitted non-Indian spouses to become members and have endowed membership on non-Indians by adoption. See Nofire v. United States, 164 U.S. 657 (1897); United States v. Rogers, 45 U.S. (4 How.) 567, 572–73 (1846).
150. Nor can states discriminate against newcomers. See Saenz v. Roe, 526 U.S. 489, 502–4 (1999).
151. See *Ex parte Crow Dog,* 109 U.S. at 571 ("[To try Indians in federal court] tries them not by their peers, . . . but by superiors of a different race").

152. See, e.g., 25 U.S.C. §479 (1994) (providing rights under the Indian Reorganization Act for persons with one-half or more Indian blood); id. §601(d) (allowing membership for those children of one-fourth or more blood of the Yakima Tribes); id. §2007(a)(1)(A), (f) (determining allotment for BIA-funded schools by the number of Indian students with one-fourth or greater Indian blood). See generally Brownell, "Who Is An Indian"; Gould, "Mixing Bodies and Beliefs."
153. Morton v. Mancari, 417 U.S. 535, 553 n.24 (1974).
154. See, e.g., Rice v. Cayetano, 528 U.S. 495 (2000); Shaw v. Hunt, 517 U.S. 899 (1996); Shaw v. Reno, 509 U.S. 630 (1993).
155. See, e.g., Adarand Constructors, Inc. v. Pena, 515 U.S. 200 (1995); City of Richmond v. J. A. Croson Co., 488 U.S. 469 (1989).
156. *Strate,* 520 U.S. at 459.
157. *Oliphant,* 435 U.S. at 210–11 (quoting *Ex Parte Crow Dog,* 109 U.S. at 571). This was the reason why Indians should not be subject to trial in federal court, but Justice Rehnquist found the argument persuasive the other way around as well. See 435 U.S. at 211. Note, however, that by giving federal courts jurisdiction over major crimes committed by Indians on reservations, Congress ultimately subjected tribal members to procedures foreign to their "race [and] tradition." *Ex Parte Crow Dog,* 109 U.S. at 571.
158. *Duro,* 495 U.S. at 693 (citations omitted).
159. See, e.g., Printz v. United States, 521 U.S. 898 (1997); Seminole Tribe of Florida v. Florida, 517 U.S. 44 (1996); United States v. Lopez, 514 U.S. 549 (1995).
160. See Vicki Jackson, "Federalism and the Uses and Limits of Law: *Printz* and Principle?" 111 *Harv. L. Rev.* 2180, 2220–23 (1998).
161. See, e.g., Rice v. Cayetano, 528 U.S. 495 (2000); Shaw v. Hunt, 517 U.S. 899 (1996); Adarand Constructors, Inc. v. Pena, 515 U.S. 200 (1995); Shaw v. Reno, 509 U.S. 630 (1993).
162. 495 U.S. at 692.
163. Id. at 692–93.
164. Id. at 693.
165. Id. at 695.
166. See Graham v. Richardson, 403 U.S. 365, 371 (1971); Yick Wo v. Hopkins, 118 U.S. 356, 368–69 (1886).
167. See 495 U.S. at 708 (Brennan, J., dissenting). And Congress later did pass a statute granting tribal courts jurisdiction over nonmember Indians. See Act of Oct. 28, 1991, 105 Stat. 646.
168. Congress has taken up the "logic" of *Duro* in challenging tribal court jurisdiction over civil cases arising on reservations. In 1997 the Sen-

ate Appropriations Committee reported legislation that would have allowed non-Indians to bring civil actions against tribes in federal courts. (The provision was ultimately not enacted.) The committee justified the provision in the following terms:

> Citizens of the United States have the inherent right to have their disputes decided by a neutral court or arbiter. This right is significantly diminished for non-Indian citizens of the United States who live or work on or near Indian reservations and who find themselves in civil disputes with an Indian tribe. According to the 1990 census, there are over 300,000 non-Indians living on fee land within the exterior boundaries of the reservation. These 300,000 Americans currently lack the right to have their civil claims against an Indian tribe heard before a Federal court. This provision will guarantee that the due process rights of all American citizens and their right to be heard before a neutral legal entity is protected.

S. Rep. No. 105–56 at 63–64 (1997).

169. For a general discussion of these kinds of claims, see Peter J. Rubin, "Equal Rights, Special Rights, and the Nature of Antidiscrimination Law," 97 *Mich. L. Rev.* 564 (1998).
170. See Robert N. Clinton, "Isolated in Their Own Country: A Defense of Federal Protection of Indian Autonomy and Self-Government," 33 *Stan. L. Rev.* 979, 980–82 (1981) (describing calls for abolition of "special rights"); Francis Paul Prucha, *American Indian Treaties: The History of a Political Autonomy* 422–27 (1994).
171. William Claiborne, "Tribal Land Claim Meets Resistance in Illinois," *Wash. Post,* February 13, 2001, at A3.
172. American Indian Policy Review Commission, *Final Report* 579 (1977) (dissenting views of Cong. Lloyd Meeds, vice chairman of the commission).
173. National Gambling Impact Study Commission, *Final Report* 6–1 to 6–2 (1999).
174. See Practising Law Institute, *The Gaming Industry on American Indian Lands* 156 (1994); Naomi Mezey, "The Distribution of Wealth, Sovereignty, and Culture through Indian Gaming," 48 *Stan. L. Rev.* 711, 725 (1996). The identification of tribes with casino gambling is consistent with the Court's conception of tribes as voluntary associations. It permits the tribes to be portrayed as hugely profitable private corporations cloaked in governmental garb that guarantees them exemption from state taxation and immunity from suit. See, e.g., Mezey, "The

Distribution of Wealth, Sovereignty, and Culture through Indian Gaming" at 726 ("[T]he Pequots continue to reinvent their past and present identities with gaming profits"). Mezey discusses how the large profits of the Mashantucket Pequot Indians in southeastern Connecticut give the tribe the resources to hire anthropologists and archeologists to uncover their tribal past. To critics, this seems a far cry from the tribes' defense of sovereignty as a way to pursue traditional cultural values with an exemption from state taxation.

175. See Prucha, *American Indian Treaties* at 402–7.
176. See Indian Gaming Regulatory Act of 1988, §11(b)(1)(A), 102 Stat. 2467, 2472; Washington v. Washington State Commercial Fishing Vessel Association, 443 U.S. 658, 673 n.20 (1979).
177. Mezey makes the gaming-sovereignty connection explicit. Gaming, she says, has given the Pequots their first modern opportunity for self-governance: "As tribe member Joseph Carter puts it, 'You need money to practice sovereignty.'" Mezey, "The Distribution of Wealth, Sovereignty, and Culture through Indian Gaming" at 726–27. See also National Gambling Impact Study Commission, *Final Report* at 6–2 ("[G]ambling revenues have proven to be a very important source of funding for many tribal governments, providing much-needed improvements in the health, education, and welfare of Native Americans on reservations across the United States").
178. See Ronald Reagan, "Statement on Indian Policy," January 24, 1983, *Public Papers of the Presidents of the United States: Ronald Reagan, 1983,* 96; see also *Cabazon,* 480 U.S. at 217 n.21 (1987) (stating that gaming is consistent with Reagan's 1983 statement on Indian policy).
179. See Will Kymlicka, *Liberalism, Community, and Culture* ch. 8 (1991) (providing a liberal defense of cultural structures as a context for choice).
180. This is not to say that gaming has not engendered divisions within tribes. See Mezey, "The Distribution of Wealth, Sovereignty, and Culture through Indian Gaming" at 728–31 (stating that tribal "traditionalists" see the materialism of gaming as destructive of their Indian culture).

6. Indian Tribal Sovereignty beyond Plenary Power

1. See Act of Jan. 4, 1975, §3, 88 Stat. 2203, 2203–4; id. tit. 1, §104, 88 Stat. at 2207–8.
2. See Act of Oct. 25, 1994, Pub. L. No. 103–413, tit. 2, 108 Stat. 4250, 4270.

3. See, e.g., 7 U.S.C. §136u (1994); 33 U.S.C. §1377(e) (1994); 42 U.S.C. § 300j-11 (1994) (same, Clean Air Act); see also Mary Christina Wood, "Protecting the Attributes of Native Sovereignty: A New Trust Paradigm for Federal Actions Affecting Tribal Lands and Resources," 1995 *Utah L. Rev.* 109, 187, 188 and n.344, 189–92.
4. 59 Fed. Reg. 22,951 (May 4, 1994).
5. See Wood, "Protecting the Attributes" at 188 n.345.
6. See William Claiborne, "Bigger Role for Death Valley Tribe," *Washington Post,* April 6, 1999, at A21. For a skeptical view of some of the self-determination policies, see Robert B. Porter, "A Proposal to the *Hanodaganyas* to Decolonize Federal Indian Control Law," 31 *U. Mich. J. L. Rev.* 899, 963–69 (1998).
7. See L. Scott Gould, "The Congressional Response to *Duro v. Reina:* Compromising Sovereignty and the Constitution," 28 *U.C. Davis L. Rev.* 53, 124 (table 1).
8. Id.
9. See id. at 124 and n.312; L. Scott Gould, "Mixing Bodies and Beliefs: The Predicament of Tribes, 101 *Colum. L. Rev.* 702, 752 (2001).
10. U.S. Census Bureau, "Profile of General Demographic Characteristics, 2000 Census of Population and Housing," table DP-1 (May 2001), *http://www.census.gov/prod/cen2000/dp1/2kh00.pdf.* An additional 374,000 persons identified themselves as Native Hawaiian or Other Pacific Islander, either solely or in combination with other racial categories. Id.
11. See Robert H. White, *Tribal Assets: The Rebirth of Tribal America* (1990).
12. Nevertheless, general economic conditions on many reservations remain remarkably poor, and statistics regarding other indicia of well-being—employment rates, poverty levels, life expectancy—are deeply troubling. See Marlita A. Reddy, ed., *Statistical Record of Native North Americans* charts 441, 574, 655 (2d ed. 1995).
13. Vine Deloria, Jr., and Clifford M. Lytle, *The Nations Within: The Past and Future of American Indian Sovereignty* viii (1998).
14. See S. 1691, 105th Cong. (1998); Robert J. McCarthy, "Civil Rights in Tribal Courts: The Indian Bill of Rights at Thirty Years," 34 *Idaho L. Rev.* 465, 489 and nn.203–4 (citing bills and hearings). Under traditional doctrine, tribes—like states—cannot be sued without their consent. See Kiowa Tribe of Oklahoma v. Manufacturing Techs., Inc., 523 U.S. 751, 760 (1998); Three Affiliated Tribes of the Fort Berthold Reservation v. Wold Eng'g, 476 U.S. 877, 890–91 (1986).
15. H.R. 5523, 106th Cong., 2d Sess. (2000).
16. Cf. Kiowa Tribe of Oklahoma v. Manufacturing Techs., Inc., 523 U.S. 751, 758–60 (1998) (suggesting that continued sovereign immunity

for tribes may be hard to defend but that it was up to Congress to change the law).

17. U.S. Constitution, Art. I, §8.
18. U.S. Constitution, Art. I, §2.
19. See Francis Paul Prucha, *American Indian Treaties: The History of a Political Anomaly* chs. 1 and 2 (1994); Robert A. Williams, Jr., *Linking Arms Together: American Indian Treaty Visions of Law and Peace, 1600–1800* (1997).
20. U.S. Constitution, Art. VI (emphasis added).
21. U.S. Constitution, Art. I, §8; Art. IV, §3.
22. Worcester v. Georgia, 31 U.S. (6 Pet.) 515, 562 (1832).
23. See Elk v. Wilkins, 112 U.S. 94, 102–9 (1884).
24. See Oklahoma Tax Comm'n v. Citizen Band Potawatomi Indian Tribe of Oklahoma, 498 U.S. 505, 510 (1991).
25. Talton v. Mayes, 163 U.S. 376, 382–83 (1896).
26. See Steven P. McSloy, "Back to the Future: Native American Sovereignty in the 21st Century," 20 *N.Y.U. Rev. L. & Soc. Change* 217, 252–78 (1993).
27. Id. at 263.
28. See Rachel San Kronowitz et al., "Toward Consent and Cooperation: Reconsidering the Political Status of Indian Nations," 22 *Harv. C.R.–C.L. L. Rev.* 507, 620 (1987) ("The United States violates international law when it fails to respect Indian peoples' right to self-determination"). See generally S. James Anaya, *Indigenous Peoples in International Law* (1996).
29. See Nell Jessup Newton, "Federal Power over Indians: Its Sources, Scope, and Limitations," 132 *U. Pa. L. Rev.* 239 (1984).
30. See McClanahan v. State Tax Comm'n, 411 U.S. 164, 172 n.7 (1973).
31. See Art. 37, reprinted in Anaya, *Indigenous Peoples in International Law* at 215.
32. See Art. 20, reprinted id. at 212.
33. Newton, "Federal Power over Indians," 195, 249–61.
34. See Felix S. Cohen, *Handbook of Federal Indian Law* 221–225 (Rennard Strickland and Charles F. Wilkinson, eds., 1982) (citing cases) [hereinafter Cohen, *Handbook of Federal Indian Law,* 1982 ed.].
35. See Mary Christina Wood, "Indian Land and the Promise of Native Sovereignty: The Trust Doctrine Revisited," 1994 *Utah L. Rev.* 1471, 1508–13; see also United States v. Sioux Nation of Indians, 448 U.S. 371, 415–16 (1980); Lone Wolf v. Hitchcock, 187 U.S. 553, 565–66 (1903).
36. See Wood, "Indian Land and the Promise" at 1509–11; Wood, "Protecting the Attributes" at 117.

37. See *Sioux Nation of Indians,* 448 U.S. at 415.
38. Minnesota v. Mille Lacs Band of Chippewa Indians, 526 U.S. 172, 200 (1999).
39. See Menominee Tribe of Indians v. United States, 391 U.S. 404, 412 (1968). The Court, however, has said that there is no duty on Congress to so state on the face of the statute. See United States v. Dion, 476 U.S. 734, 738 (1986).
40. See Philip P. Frickey, "Marshalling Past and Present: Colonialism, Constitutionalism, and Interpretation in Federal Indian Law," 107 *Harv. L. Rev.* 381, 418–26 (1993). But see *Mille Lacs,* 526 U.S. at 218 (relying on canons in aid of tribe).
41. See Cohen, *Handbook of Federal Indian Law,* 1982 ed., at 220–28 (outlining the "trust responsibility").
42. See generally Wood, "Protecting the Attributes."
43. For instance, strategies that incorporate the constitutional protections of association and culture and family could limit the doctrine. See, e.g., Wisconsin v. Yoder, 406 U.S. 205 (1972) (First Amendment protection of religion); Pierce v. Society of Sisters, 268 U.S. 510 (1925) (substantive due process); Meyer v. Nebraska, 262 S. 390 (1923) (substantive due process); see also Newton, "Federal Power over Indians" at 264 ("The Court's willingness to protect . . . insular groups from forced homogenization demonstrates that values of cultural diversity may be protected by the Constitution in a proper case"). But see Employment Div., Dep't of Human Resources v. Smith, 494 U.S. 872, 890 (1990) (holding that the free exercise clause does not bar a state from criminalizing a tribe's religious use of peyote).
44. See note 34 and accompanying text.
45. Robert N. Clinton, "Redressing the Legacy of Conquest: A Vision Quest for a Decolonized Federal Indian Law," 46 *Ark. L. Rev.* 77 (1993).
46. See Anaya, *Indigenous Peoples in International Law* at 81–82.
47. The outcome would be different, however, vis-à-vis states themselves. The federal government must still identify a federal power that justifies the legislation, and we have learned that even the commerce power has its limits. See United States v. Morrison, 529 U.S. 598 (2000); United States v. Lopez, 514 U.S. 549 (1995). Regulation of the tribes remains plenary in the sense that Congress is deemed to possess full regulatory power without appeal to any particular delegated power.
48. See Indian Reorganization Act of 1934, Pub. L. No. 73–383, ch. 576, §16, 48 Stat. 984, 987.

49. 439 U.S. 463 (1979).
50. Id. at 501.
51. See 436 U.S. 49, 56 (1978). Similar language appears in the territories cases, as noted in Chapter 4.
52. 187 U.S. 553 (1903).
53. See id. at 564.
54. See id. at 554–55.
55. See id. at 557.
56. See id. at 559.
57. See id. at 566.
58. Id.
59. Id. at 568.
60. Id.
61. 430 U.S. 73, 84 (1977).
62. Russel L. Barsh and James Y. Henderson, *The Road: Indian Tribes and Political Liberty* 264–67 (1980).
63. See Newton, "Federal Power over Indians" at 261.
64. See Buckley v. Valeo, 424 U.S. 1 (1976); Boy Scouts of America v. Dale, 530 U.S. 640 (2000); Hurley v. Irish-American Gay, Lesbian and Bisexual Group, 515 U.S. 557 (1995).
65. See Wisconsin v. Yoder, 406 U.S. 205 (1972).
66. See Pierce v. Society of Sisters, 268 U.S. 510 (1925); Meyer v. Nebraska, 262 U.S. 390 (1923); Newton, "Federal Power over Indians" at 264.
67. *Meyer,* 262 U.S. at 402.
68. Cf. Roberts v. U.S. Jaycees, 468 U.S. 809 (1984).
69. See Newton, "Federal Power over Indians" at 236–88.
70. Id. at 266.
71. But see Employment Div., Dep't of Human Res. of Oregon v. Smith, 494 U.S. 872 (1990).
72. Compare Boy Scouts of America v. Dale, 530 U.S. 640 (2000) (invalidating on First Amendment grounds state law requiring Boy Scouts to admit gays as members).
73. See Judith Resnik, "Dependent Sovereigns: Indian Tribes, States, and the Federal Courts," 56 *U. Chi. L. Rev.* 671, 751 (1989), adopting term from Robert Cover, "The Supreme Court 1982 Term—Foreword: Nomos and Narrative," 97 *Harv. L. Rev.* 4 (1983).
74. Cf. Richmond v. J. A. Croson Co., 488 U.S. 469 (1989) (invalidating affirmative action program adopted by majority-black city council); Shaw v. Reno, 509 U.S. 630 (1993) (subjecting to "strict scrutiny" the use of race in drawing election districts).
75. See Richard W. Garnett, "Once More into the Maze: *United States v.*

Lopez, Tribal Self-Determination, and Federal Conspiracy Jurisdiction in Indian Country," 72 *N. Dak. L. Rev.* 433 (1996); Richard A. Monette, "A New Federalism for Indian Tribes: The Relationship between the United States and Tribes in Light of Our Federalism and Republican Democracy," 25 *U. Tol. L. Rev.* 617 (1994).

76. See Printz v. United States, 521 U.S. 898 (1997); United States v. Lopez, 514 U.S. 549 (1995); New York v. United States, 505 U.S. 144 (1992).
77. See *Printz,* 521 U.S. 898; *New York,* 505 U.S. 144.
78. This has been true from early days: Coyle v. Smith, 221 U.S. 559 (1911) (federal relocation of state capital prohibited). This limit, however, is not so entrenched in the context of voting; see, e.g., Baker v. Carr, 369 U.S. 186 (1962).
79. See, e.g., Kimel v. Florida Bd. of Regents, 528 U.S. 62 (2000); Florida Prepaid Postsecondary Education Expense Bd. v. College Savings Bank, 527 U.S. 627 (1999).
80. Patrick Macklem, "Distributing Sovereignty: Indian Nations and Equality of Peoples," 45 *Stan. L Rev.* 1311, 1333–35 (1993). "The legitimacy of Indian government is not based on the mere fact that indigenous people were prior occupants of the continent, but on the fact that they were prior sovereigns." Id. at 1333.
81. U.S. Constitution, Art. I, §8, cl. 3: Congress shall have power "[t]o regulate Commerce with foreign Nations, and among the several States, and with the Indian Tribes."
82. See Herbert Wechsler, "The Political Safeguards of Federalism: The Role of the States in the Composition and Selection of the National Government," 54 *Colum. L. Rev.* 542 (1954).
83. Which is not to say that they do not have power as interest groups lobbying the federal bureaucracy.
84. See Clinton, "Redressing the Legacy of Conquest" at 124–25.
85. 25 U.S.C. §476.
86. See Goldberg v. Kelly, 397 U.S. 254 (1970); Cleveland Bd. of Educ. v. Loudermill, 470 U.S. 532 (1985). See Charles A. Reich, "The New Property," 73 *Yale L. J.* 733 (1964).
87. Cf. Dandridge v. Williams, 397 U.S. 471 (1970).
88. See Julian N. Eule, "Temporal Limits on the Legislative Mandate: Entrenchment and Retroactivity," 1987 *Am. B. Found. Res. J.* 379.
89. Limitations on altering past agreements are reflected in constitutional norms disfavoring retroactive application of laws. See id. at 441–47.
90. See id. at 447–59.
91. See Stone v. Mississippi, 101 U.S. 814 (1879).

92. See Memorandum from Teresa Wynn Roseborough for the Special Representative for Guam Commonwealth, "Mutual Consent Provisions in the Guam Commonwealth Legislation," July 28, 1994 [hereinafter "Roseborough Memorandum"].

93. This can perhaps be traced to Dartmouth Coll. v. Woodward, 17 U.S. (4 Wheat.) 518 (1819); see also Eule, "Temporal Limits on the Legislative Mandate" at 419–24.

94. United States v. Sioux Nation of Indians, 448 U.S. 371 (1980). Technically, the Court held that if it could be shown that the measure appropriately advanced tribal interests—by exchanging the taken land for property of equivalent value—then the federal statute would not trigger the just compensation clause.

95. Cohen, *Handbook of Federal Indian Law,* 1982 ed., at 222–23; Menominee Tribe of Indians v. United States, 391 U.S. 404 (1968).

96. A contrary view is expressed in a 1963 memorandum of the Department of Justice's Office of Legal Counsel regarding a "mutual consent" provision in a proposed U.S.–Puerto Rico compact. The memorandum concludes that federal legislation could constitutionally create "vested rights of a political nature" that could not be taken back without mutual agreement of the United States and Puerto Rico. See Office of Legal Counsel, U.S. Department of Justice, "Power of the United States to Conclude with the Commonwealth of Puerto Rico a Compact Which Could Be Modified Only by Mutual Consent" (July 23, 1963).

97. I am adopting Bruce Ackerman's terms of "normal lawmaking" and "higher lawmaking/constitutional politics." See Bruce Ackerman, 1 *We the People: Foundations* 6–7 (1991).

98. Act of March 18, 1959, §7, 73 Stat. 4 (1959).

99. The process is described in detail in S. Rep. 80, 86th Cong., 1st Sess. (1959).

100. See Justice McLean's statement in his *Worcester v. Georgia* concurrence: "The exercise of the power of self-government by the Indians, within a state, is undoubtedly contemplated to be temporary." 31 U.S. (6 Pet.) 515, 593 (1832).

101. See Note, "Sovereignty, Referenda, and the Entrenchment of a United Kingdom Bill of Rights," 101 *Yale L. J.* 457 (1991).

102. Quoted in Jack N. Rakove, *Original Meanings: Politics and Ideas in the Making of the Constitution* 100 (1996).

103. Id. at 101. See Ackerman, *We the People* 169–75; *The Federalist No. 40* (James Madison).

104. See Rakove, *Original Meanings* at 105.

105. Id. at 130. See also McCulloch v. Maryland, 17 U.S. (4 Wheat.) 316, 377–78 (1819).
106. "Special Message to the Congress on Indian Affairs," July 8, 1970, in *Public Papers of the Presidents of the United States: Richard M. Nixon, 1970,* 564, 567.
107. Covenant to Establish a Commonwealth of the Northern Mariana Islands in Political Union with the United States of America, 90 Stat. 263, (1976) [§105]; Compact of Free Association Act of 1985, 99 Stat. 1770 (1986), published as note to 48 U.S.C. §1681 (1987).
108. See Office of Legal Counsel, "Power of the United States to Conclude with the Commonwealth of Puerto Rico a Compact Which Could Be Modified Only by Mutual Consent"; A. Mitchell McConnell, Jr., Acting Assistant Attorney General for Legislative Affairs, to Marlow W. Cook, co-chairman, Ad Hoc Advisory Group on Puerto Rico, May 12, 1975; sources cited in Roseborough Memorandum at 2 n.2.
109. Roseborough Memorandum at 2.
110. Id. at 4.
111. Id. at 6.
112. Anaya, *Indigenous Peoples in International Law* at 82. See Porter, "A Proposal to the *Hanodaganyas*" at 946–48.
113. Barsh and Henderson, *The Road* at 270–84; Clinton, "Redressing the Legacy of Conquest" at 124–25; Vine Deloria, Jr., and David E. Wilkins, *Tribes, Treatises, and Constitutional Tribulations* ch. 8 (1999); Kronowitz, "Toward Consent and Cooperation"; Steven Paul McSloy, "American Indians and the Constitution: An Argument for Nationhood," 14 *Am. Indian L. Rev.* 139, 181 (1989); McSloy, "Back to the Future"; Porter, "A Proposal to the *Hanodaganyas*" at 988–90; Alex Tallchief Skibine, "Reconciling Federal and State Power inside Indian Reservations with the Rights of Tribal Self-Government and the Process of Self-Determination," 1995 *Utah L. Rev.* 1105; Note, "Sovereignty by Sufferance: The Illusion of Indian Tribal Sovereignty," 79 *Cornell L. Rev.* 404 (1994).
114. Significantly, when adopting the Tribal Self-Governance Act of 1994, Congress indicated its intent that agreements negotiated between tribes and federal authorities "may not be altered unilaterally by the Department of the Interior." S. Rep. No. 205, 103d Cong. at 4 (1993). See Porter, "A Proposal to the *Hanodaganyas*" at 973.
115. Williams, *Linking Arms Together* at 122.
116. Even if my argument fails to persuade as a legal matter, a compact that requires mutual consent for its amendment might today be a powerful political document. That is, a Congress that sought unilaterally to change the terms of such a compact would pay a political price.

117. Barsh and Henderson, *The Road* at 270–84; Clinton, "Redressing the Legacy of Conquest" at 124–25; Deloria and Wilkins, *Tribes, Treatises and Constitutional Tribulations* ch. 8; Porter, "A Proposal to the *Hanodaganyas*" at 988–90; Note, "Sovereignty by Sufferance"; McSloy, "American Indians and the Constitution"; McSloy, "Back to the Future."
118. An example is provided by an agreement between the Department of the Interior and the Timbi-Sha Shoshone tribe, which gives the tribe a role in managing the 3.2 million acre Death Valley National Park. The tribe (which had been limited to just forty acres of land) now is granted one thousand acres for traditional harvesting of pine nuts and willow branches; its activities will become part of a cultural education program for visitors; and it is authorized to build fifty homes, a tribal government complex, a cultural center, and a visitors' inn. William Claiborne, "Bigger Role for Death Valley Tribe, *Wash. Post,* April 6, 1999, at A21.
119. Clinton, "Redressing the Legacy of Conquest" at 120.
120. These words are John Marshall's in Worcester v. State of Georgia, 31 U.S. (6 Pet.) 515, 556 (1832).
121. But see Sandi B. Zellmer, "Indian Lands as Critical Habitat for Indian Nations and Endangered Species: Tribal Survival and Sovereignty Come First," 43 *S.D. L. Rev.* 381 (1998) (supporting secretarial order of the Departments of Interior and Commerce for implementation of the Endangered Species Act that takes into account special circumstances of reservations and tribal sovereignty).
122. See Clinton, "Redressing the Legacy of Conquest" at 124–25.
123. It thus differs from Barsh and Henderson's proposal that virtually equates tribes with states, to be secured by a constitutional amendment. Barsh and Henderson, *The Road* at 279–82.
124. Cf. Saenz v. Roe, 526 U.S. 489 (1999) (privileges and immunities clause protects right of citizens to settle in state of their choice).
125. See David C. Williams, "The Borders of the Equal Protection Clause: Indians as Peoples," 38 *UCLA L. Rev.* 759 (1991): "If Indian law does rest on racial distinctions, and if many reservations are special racial preserves, their existence poses a challenge to the vision of an individualist, integrated American polity." Id. at 774.
126. For example, 25 U.S.C. §479 ("The term 'Indian' . . . shall further include all other persons of one-half or more Indian blood"); 5 C.F.R. 5.1 (2000) (Bureau of Indian Affairs hiring preference for persons of Indian descent who are "one-half or more Indian blood of tribes indigenous to the United States"); see generally Margo S. Brownell, "Who Is

an Indian? Searching for an Answer to the Question at the Core of Federal Indian Law," 34 *U. Mich. J. L. Ref.* 275, 279–81, 284–98 (2000–2001); L. Scott Gould, "Mixing Bodies and Beliefs" at 718–26.

127. 417 U.S. 535 (1974).
128. The regulation is quoted in the case upholding the constitutionality of the program, Morton v. Mancari, 417 U.S. 535, 553 n.24 (1974).
129. See Adarand Constructors, Inc. v. Pena, 515 U.S. 438 (1997).
130. Compare Williams, "Borders of the Equal Protection Clause," and Stuart Minor Benjamin, "Equal Protection and the Special Relationship: The Case of Native Hawaiians," 106 *Yale L. J.* 537 (1996).
131. See Williams, "Borders of the Equal Protection Clause" at 799, 803–4.
132. But see Barsh and Henderson, *The Road* at 244, noting that before the reservation period, "tribes freely naturalized nonmember Indians and non-Indians on the basis of their usefulness and willingness to respect tribal law."
133. Cherokee Intermarriage Case, 203 U.S. 76 (1906); Roff v. Burney, 168 U.S. 218 (1897). In United States v. Rogers, 45 U.S. (4 How.) 567 (1846), Chief Justice Taney held, as a matter of statutory construction, that a white U.S. citizen could not escape criminal prosecution under federal law by way of adoption into an Indian tribe.
134. Felix S. Cohen, *Handbook of Federal Indian Law* 136 (1942 ed.) [hereinafter Cohen, *Handbook of Federal Indian Law,* 1942 ed.].
135. Navajo Nation Code, tit. 1, §702(a) (1995): "A. No Navajo law or custom has ever existed or exists now, by which anyone can ever become a Navajo, either by adoption, or otherwise, except by birth. B. All those individuals who claim to be a member of the Navajo Nation by adoption are declared to be in no possible way an adopted or honorary member of the Navajo People."
136. See, e.g., Navajo Nation Code, tit. 1, §701(b)–(c) (1995); Confederated Tribes of Colville Reservation Law and Order Code §8–1–80; Confederated Salish and Kootenai Tribes Constitution, Art. II, §2. More than four-fifths of all federally recognized tribes include a blood requirement for tribal membership. Gould, "Mixing Bodies and Beliefs" at 721.
137. See Gould, "Mixing Bodies and Beliefs" at 720–21.
138. Gould reports that as of 1990 just over one-third of persons who identified themselves as Indian lived in Indian country in tribes acknowledged by the federal government. Id. at 762. The new categories of the 2000 census make the distinction between political and racial identification more dramatic. More that 4.1 million persons listed themselves as American Indian or Alaska Native, either solely or in combination with another racial category (see note 10)—a number

far exceeding estimates for tribal membership.

139. 417 U.S. at 553 n.24. See also Rice v. Cayetano, 528 U.S. 495, 517–23 (2000) (noting continued approval of *Mancari,* and distinguishing election of trustees of the Office of Hawaiian Affairs (deemed to be race discrimination when limited to Native Hawaiians) from tribal rules limiting the franchise to tribal members).

140. See Carole E. Goldberg-Ambrose, "Not 'Strictly' Racial: A Response to 'Indians as Peoples,'" 39 *UCLA L. Rev.* 169, 173 (1991) ("By denying that Indian-based classifications are racial, *Mancari* both defied logic and undermined federal policy supporting tribal self-determination"); Williams, "Borders of the Equal Protection Clause" at 810 ("Title 25 [of the United States Code] rests on racial blood quantum requirements. No amount of handwaving about Congress's broad article I powers over Indians or the political component of the category 'Indian' can make that reality go away").

141. Navajo Nation Code, tit. 1, §701(c) (1995).

142. See, e.g., id.; Confederated Tribes of Colville Reservation Law and Order Code, §8–1–80 (defining as members persons of at least one-fourth degree Colville blood and who were born to at least one parent who is a Colville member).

143. Immigration and Nationality Act of 1952, 66 Stat. 163, §301 (codified at 8 U.S.C. §1401 (1994)).

144. Irish Nationality and Citizenship Act of 2000, §7(1). Similarly, under the Israeli Law of Return, a Jew anywhere in the world can become a citizen of Israel irrespective of his or her parents' nationality. Law of Return, 1950, 4 L.S.I. 114.

145. See Gould, "Mixing Bodies and Beliefs" at 757–67; Brownell, "Who Is an Indian?" at 309.

146. There are exceptions, of course. Diplomats may have immunity from legal process, and their children born in the United States are not deemed to acquire U.S. citizenship at birth.

147. Treaties may carve out exceptions on behalf of nationals of state X who commit crimes in state Y. For example, under the NATO treaty, military authorities of one NATO state are authorized to exercise criminal jurisdiction over their soldiers stationed in other NATO states. "Agreement between the Parties to the North Atlantic Treaty Regarding the Status of Their Forces," June 19, 1951, 4 U.S.T. 1792, T.I.A.S. No. 2846 (effective August 23, 1953), Art. VII.

148. For example, Puerto Rico has full authority to prosecute crimes committed *by anyone* on the island.

149. Some scholars maintain that the Constitution should be read to deny Congress any authority to regulate tribal sovereignty. E.g., McSloy,

"American Indians and the Constitution"; McSloy, "Back to the Future." But, as discussed earlier, there is virtually no chance that the Court will reach this conclusion.

150. See Chapter 5.
151. Oliphant v. Suquamish Indian Tribe, 435 U.S. 191, 208 (1978); *Duro v. Reina,* 495 U.S. at 686.
152. See *Duro,* 495 U.S. at 698.
153. Charles F. Wilkinson, *American Indians, Time, and the Law* 111 (1987).
154. See Mathews v. Eldridge, 424 U.S. 319 (1976).
155. See, e.g., Saenz v. Roe, 526 U.S. 489 (1999); Dunn v. Blumstein, 405 U.S. 330 (1972); Shapiro v. Thompson, 394 U.S. 618 (1969).
156. Robert J. McCarthy, "Civil Rights in Indian Tribal Courts: The Indian Bill of Rights at Thirty Years," 34 *Idaho L. Rev.* 465, 486 (1998) (citing data regarding tribal courts). "[T]ribal courts appear to be no less protective—and much more accessible—than federal courts have been in protecting civil rights on Indian reservations." Id. at 490. "Effective implementation of the ICRA depends not so much on federal courts located far from poor reservation communities, more so on well-trained and financed tribal courts, but mostly on an Indian civil rights movement in which low income Native Americans have equal access to justice in tribal courts, in traditional peacemaking practices, and in the larger society." Id. at 515; see also Nell Jessup Newton, "Tribal Court Praxis: One Year in Tribal Courts," 22 *Am. Indian L. Rev.* 285 (1997).
157. Nell Jessup Newton, "Permanent Legislation to Correct *Duro v. Reina,*" 17 *Am. Indian L. Rev.* 125 (1994); see generally Gould, "The Congressional Response to *Duro v. Reina.*"
158. Wilkinson, *American Indians, Time, and the Law* at 117.
159. Id. at 115. See Santa Clara Pueblo v. Martinez, 436 U.S. 49 (1978).
160. This reasoning has been aided, inadvertently, by T. H. Marshall's famous conceptualization of citizenship rights as guaranteeing equality among citizens as political, civil, and social rights-holders. See Thomas H. Marshall, "Citizenship and Social Class," in Thomas H. Marshall and Tom Bottomore, *Citizenship and Social Class* (1992).
161. See Rainer Bauböck, *Transnational Citizenship: Membership and Rights in International Migration* (1994).
162. See Tomas Hammar, "State, Nation, and Dual Citizenship," in *Immigration and the Politics of Citizenship in Europe and North America* 81–95 (William Rogers Brubaker, ed., 1989); T. Alexander Aleinikoff, "Between Principle and Politics: U.S. Citizenship Policy," in *From Migrants to Citizens: Membership in a Changing World* 157–59 (T. Alexander Aleinikoff and Douglas Klusmeyer, eds., 2000).
163. Reported in Wilkinson, *American Indians, Time, and the Law* at 118–19.

Philip P. Frickey, "A Common Law for Our Age of Colonialism: The Judicial Divestiture of Indian Tribal Authority over Nonmembers," 109 *Yale L. J.* 1, 84 n. 377 (1999).

164. See Jamin B. Raskin, "Legal Aliens, Local Citizens: The Historical, Constitutional, and Theoretical Meanings of Alien Suffrage," 141 *U. Pa. L. Rev.* 1391, 1460–67 (1993) (identifying New York City and Chicago as allowing noncitizens the right to vote in elections and matters concerning local school boards and further identifying several smaller localities throughout the state of Maryland that extend the franchise to noncitizens for all local elections).
165. Barsh and Henderson, *The Road* at 280.
166. Jeffrey Wutzke, Comment, "Dependent Independence: Application of the Nunavut Model to Native Hawaiian Sovereignty and Self-determination Claims," 22 *Am. Indian L. Rev* 509, 539 (1998).
167. Id. at 534–40. The Nunavut Implementation Committee has stated that the government of the territory will "not [be] a form of ethnic self-government." Id. at 539.
168. Royal Comm'n on Aboriginal Peoples, 2 *Report of the Royal Commission on Aboriginal Peoples: Perspectives and Realities* 264 (1996), quoted in Charles J. Marecic, "Nunavut Territory: Aboriginal Governing in the Canadian Regime of Governance," 24 *Am. Indian L. Rev.* 275, 289 (2000).
169. See Newton, "Permanent Legislation to Correct *Duro v. Reina*" at 126 ("[T]o dictate to tribal governments who may partake in their political communities would be a breach of faith with Indian tribes unprecedented since the Dawes Act of the 1880s; a breach of treaty promises with many tribes; and a violation of developing standards of international law") (footnotes omitted).
170. E.g., Articles of Agreement and Confederation, September 17, 1778, U.S.–Delaware Nation, Art. VI, 7 Stat. 13, 14.
171. See Will Kymlicka, *Multicultural Citizenship: A Liberal Theory of Minority Rights* ch. 7 (1995) (canvassing forms of group representation, including New Zealand policies that establish separate electoral lists for Maori).
172. Northwest Ordinance of 1787, Art. III, ch. VIII, 1 Stat. 50, 52 (1789).
173. See Anaya, *Indigenous Peoples in International Law* at 43; see also U.N. Charter, ch. XI, Art. 73–74.
174. U.N. Doc. E/CN.4/1995/2, E/CN.4/Sub.2/1994/56 at 105, Art. 4.

7. Plenary Power, Immigration Regulation, and Decentered Citizenship

1. See Alexander M. Bickel, *The Morality of Consent* ch. 2 (1975).
2. Bridges v. Wixon, 326 U.S. 135, 161–62 (1945) (Murphy, J., concur-

ring). Cases seem to suggest that the First Amendment does not apply to immigration proceedings (that is, that aliens may be excluded from the country for speech protected by the First Amendment). Reno v. American-Arab Anti-Discrimination Committee, 525 U.S. 471 (1999) (alien cannot challenge removal proceeding based on claim that government selectively prosecuted owing to alien's political beliefs); Kleindienst v. Mandel, 408 U.S. 753 (1972) (alien seeking entry cannot assert First Amendment claim); see also Price v. U.S.I.N.S., 962 F.2d 836 (9th Cir 1992), cert. denied, 510 U.S. 1040 (1994) (naturalization proceeding). But another—and to my mind better—reading is also available. See American-Arab Anti-Discrimination Comm. v. Reno, 70 F.3d 1045 (9th Cir. 1995); T. Alexander Aleinikoff, "Federal Regulation of Aliens and the Constitution," 83 *Am. J. Int'l. L.* 862, 869 (1989).

3. To see how stark the difference is, consider that the Supreme Court has held that the exclusionary rule does not apply in immigration proceedings. I.N.S. v. Lopez-Mendoza, 468 U.S. 1032 (1984). And because removal proceedings are not deemed to impose "punishment" in the constitutional sense, none of the rights protecting criminal defendants apply in immigration proceedings. See T. Alexander Aleinikoff, David A. Martin, and Hiroshi Motomua, *Immigration and Citizenship: Process and Policy* 693–95 (4th ed. 1998).
4. Early on the Court held that aliens were "persons" entitled to the protections of the equal protection clause. Yick Wo v. Hopkins, 118 U.S. 356 (1886). Explicit discrimination on the basis of alienage was deemed subject to strict scrutiny in *Graham v. Richardson,* 403 U.S. 365 (1971).
5. Plyler v. Doe, 457 U.S. 202 (1982).
6. See Chapter 6.
7. Harisiades v. Shaughnessy, 342 U.S. 580, 597 (1952) (Frankfurter, J., concurring).
8. See Fiallo v. Bell, 430 U.S. 787 (1977).
9. See Kleindienst v. Mandel, 408 U.S. 753 (1972).
10. See Shaughnessy v. United States ex rel. Mezei, 345 U.S. 206 (1953); United States ex rel. Knauff v. Shaughnessy, 338 U.S. 537 (1950). But see Landon v. Plasencia, 459 U.S. 21 (1982) (due process applies at reentry of permanent resident alien).
11. See *Harisiades,* 342 U.S. at 580.
12. See Mathews v. Diaz, 426 U.S. 67 (1976).
13. Although exclusion of aliens from the federal civil service by the Civil Service Commission was invalidated in *Hampton v. Mow Sun Wong,* 426 U.S. 88 (1976), lower courts had no trouble sustaining the exclusion

once it was promulgated by the president. See, e.g., Vergara v. Hampton, 581 F.2d 1281 (7th Cir. 1978), cert. denied sub nom. Vergara v. Chairman, Merit Sys. Protection Bd., 441 U.S. 905 (1979).

14. See Haitian Refugee Ctr., Inc. v. Gracey, 600 F. Supp. 1396 (D.D.C. 1985), aff'd on other grounds, 809 F.2d 794 (D.C. Cir. 1987).
15. Chinese and Japanese aliens were not eligible to naturalize until the mid-1900s. For the first few decades of the century, a U.S. citizen woman who married an alien (even if the woman lived in the United States) lost her American citizenship. The Supreme Court had little difficulty upholding this provision. See MacKenzie v. Hare, 239 U.S. 299 (1915).
16. See Yamataya v. Fisher, 189 U.S. 86 (1903).
17. See, e.g., Galvan v. Press, 347 U.S. 522, 531 (1954); Fong Yue Ting v. United States, 149 U.S. 698, 730 (1893).
18. *Diaz,* 426 U.S. 67, 80 (1976). I argue later that this oft-quoted sentence is usually taken out of context and misunderstood.
19. *Fiallo,* 430 U.S. at 792 (quoting *Mezei,* 345 U.S. at 210).
20. Brief for Respondent at 22, Miller v. Albright, 523 U.S. 420 (1998) (No. 96–1060).
21. Id. See also Brief for Respondent at 26–31, Nguyen v. INS, 121 S.Ct. 2053 (200) (No. 99–2071), urging extreme judicial deference to congressional policies regarding birthright citizenship of persons born to U.S. citizens overseas. The brief cites the foundational plenary power cases, including the *Chinese Exclusion Case,* 130 U.S. 581 (1889).
22. Fong Yue Ting v. United States, 149 U.S. 698 (1893); *Chinese Exclusion Case,* 130 U.S. 581 (1889).
23. See Duncan Kennedy, "Toward an Historical Understanding of Legal Consciousness: The Case of Classical Legal Thought in America, 1850–1940," 3 *Research in Law and Sociology* 3, 8 (Rita J. Simon and Steven Spitzer, eds., 1980).
24. For example, in *Marbury v. Madison,* Chief Justice Marshall separated cases appropriate for judicial resolution from "[q]uestions in their nature political"—that is, cases in which executive officers "perform duties in which they have a discretion." 5 U.S. (1 Cranch) 137, 170 (1803).
25. 149 U.S. at 712 (emphasis added).
26. Id. at 731.
27. See Louis Henkin, "Is There a 'Political Question' Doctrine?" 85 *Yale L. J.* 597, 601, 610–12 (1976).
28. *Fiallo,* 430 U.S. at 793.
29. Id. at 796 (citing *Diaz,* 426 U.S. at 82).
30. Compare, e.g., United States v. Virginia, 518 U.S. 515 (1996) (gender classification requires "exceedingly persuasive justification") with

Fiallo, 430 U.S. 787 (1977) (reason for gender classification must be "facially legitimate and bona fide").

31. A mixture of constitutional and prudential considerations is well known in standing doctrine. See Valley Forge Christian College v. Americans United for Separation of Church and State, 454 U.S. 464, 471–76 (1982).
32. The analysis here owes much to Lawrence Sager's important article "Fair Measure: The Legal Status of Underenforced Constitutional Norms," 91 *Harv. L. Rev.* 1212, 1218–20 (1978).
33. See Cornelia T. L. Pillard and T. Alexander Aleinikoff, "Skeptical Scrutiny of Plenary Power: Judicial and Executive Branch Decision Making in *Miller v. Albright,*" 1998 *Sup. Ct. Rev.* 1, 53–58; Sager, "Fair Measure" at 1264.
34. *Mezei,* 345 U.S. at 212 (citation omitted); *Knauff,* 338 U.S. at 544 (citation omitted).
35. Landon v. Plasencia, 459 U.S. 21, 32 (1982).
36. 426 U.S. 67 (1976).
37. Id. at 79–80.
38. As it was, for example, in *Fiallo,* 430 U.S. at 792.
39. An exception is Justice Frankfurter's opinion for the Court in Galvan v. Press, 347 U.S. 522 (1954), which upheld the retroactive application of a statute mandating the deportation of any alien who at any time after entry had been a member of the Communist Party. Justice Frankfurter's statement that the formulation of immigration policies is "entrusted exclusively to Congress" (id. at 531) has been undercut by subsequent Supreme Court holdings that immigration regulations are subject to (albeit limited) judicial review. See *Fiallo,* 430 U.S. at 793 n.5, 795–96 n.6; *Diaz,* 426 U.S. at 81–82.
40. See Henry M. Hart, Jr., "The Power of Congress to Limit the Jurisdiction of Federal Courts: An Exercise in Dialectic," 66 *Harv. L. Rev.* 1362, 1389–96 (1953); Gerald L. Neuman, *Strangers to the Constitution* 118–38 (1996).
41. See Zadvydas v. Davis, 121 S. Ct. 2491, 2500–01 (2001) (holding that cases involving aliens stopped at the border are distinguishable from cases in which alien has entered the country; in latter situation, due process clause applies). See also Stephen H. Legomsky, "Immigration Law and the Principle of Plenary Congressional Power," 1984 *Sup. Ct. Rev.* 255, 276–77.
42. 426 U.S. at 81–82 (emphasis added and footnotes omitted), quoted with approval in *Fiallo,* 430 U.S. at 796.
43. United States Dep't of Commerce v. Montana, 503 U.S. 442, 458 (1992) (footnotes omitted).

44. See Baker v. Carr, 369 U.S. 186, 210–14 (1962). This connection is made even clearer in an earlier opinion, *Harisiades,* 342 U.S. 580 (1952). There the Court upheld a statute mandating the deportation of persons who had been members of the Communist Party. Justice Jackson, writing for the majority, stated that "any policy toward aliens is vitally and intricately interwoven with contemporaneous policies in regard to the conduct of foreign relations, the war power, and the maintenance of a republican form of government." Id. at 588–89. These references invoked subject areas that had been ruled political questions in the past. See, e.g., Commercial Trust Co. v. Miller, 262 U.S. 51, 57 (1923) ("[T]he power to declare [war's] cessation, and what the cessation requires . . . is legislative"); Oetjen v. Central Leather Co., 246 U.S. 297, 302 (1918) ("The conduct of the foreign relations of our government is committed by the Constitution to the executive and legislative—'the political'—departments of the government, and the propriety of what may be done in the exercise of this political power is not subject to judicial inquiry or decision") (citations omitted); Luther v. Borden, 48 U.S. (7 How.) 1, 42 (1849) ("Under [the guaranty clause] it rests with Congress to decide what government is the established one in a State . . . And its decision is binding on every other department of the government, and could not be questioned in a judicial tribunal . . . So, too, as relates to the clause in the above-mentioned article of the Constitution, providing for cases of domestic violence"). These cases thus offered support for Justice Jackson's conclusion that "[s]uch matters are so exclusively entrusted to the political branches of government as to be largely immune from judicial inquiry or interference." *Harisiades,* 342 U.S. at 589 (footnote omitted). Interestingly, despite this rhetoric, Justice Jackson examined the deportation ground under the prevailing First Amendment doctrine that the Court applied to domestic legislation. See id. at 591–92; Aleinikoff, "Federal Regulation of Aliens and the Constitution" at 868–69.
45. *Fiallo,* 430 U.S. 787.
46. Id. at 792–96.
47. *Diaz* can, with equal plausibility, be read as being consistent with the institutional deference position. The reason is that caution against judicial intervention in immigration regulations applies in cases of federal regulation, but because the immigration power is exclusively federal, no similar deference is warranted in cases involving state regulation of aliens.
48. 430 U.S. at 794.
49. Id. at 794–95.

50. Id. at 798.
51. A conclusion that the immigration cases embody the substantive norm position would put the burden on the government to provide a substantive theory as to why such regulations are subject to an exceedingly low standard of review. For a persuasive analysis and a rejection of such substantive theories, see Neuman, *Strangers to the Constitution* at 118–38, and Legomsky, "Plenary Congressional Power" at 260–78.
52. See Sager, "Fair Measure" at 1227.
53. See Pillard and Aleinikoff, "Skeptical Scrutiny of Plenary Power" at 53–63.
54. See notes 23–27 and accompanying text.
55. The arguments here are cursory because they have received a full and persuasive treatment in Neuman, *Strangers to the Constitution* at 118–38, and Legomsky, "Plenary Congressional Power" at 261–69.
56. 369 U.S. at 217.
57. Id.
58. See United States v. Lopez, 514 U.S. 549 (1995).
59. 369 U.S. at 211.
60. See Legomsky, "Plenary Congressional Power" at 268–69.
61. See Immigration and Nationality Act (INA) §212(f), 8 U.S.C. §1182(f) (1994 and Supp. IV 1998) (authorizing the president to suspend entry of classes of aliens whose admission "would be detrimental to the interests of the United States").
62. Brief for Respondent at 22, Miller v. Albright, 523 U.S. 420 (1998) (No. 96–1060) (citation and footnote omitted).
63. Brief for Respondent at 28, Nguyen v. INS, 121 S.Ct. 2053 (2001) (No. 99–2071).
64. Michael Walzer, *Spheres of Justice: A Defense of Pluralism and Equality* 62 (1983).
65. See Rogers M. Smith, *Civic Ideals: Conflicting Visions of Citizenship in U.S. History* (1997). There may be some deep psychological need that is served here. Do we help to maintain internal tolerance by having a forum (immigration regulation) for venting our intolerance?
66. See T. Alexander Aleinikoff, "Citizens, Aliens, Membership, and the Constitution," 7 *Const. Comment.* 9, 32–34 (1990).
67. See Yamataya v. Fisher, 189 U.S. 86 (1903).
68. 121 S. Ct. 2491 (2001).
69. Id at 2505.
70. Id at 2499.
71. Id. at 2510 (Kennedy, J., dissenting).
72. Brief for the Respondents at 22, Zadvydas v. INS, 121 S.Ct. 2491 (2001) (No. 99-7791).

73. 121 S.Ct. at 2506 (Scalia, J., dissenting).
74. 121 S.Ct. at 2501. The majority holds that the cases asserting plenary power at the border are distinguishable: "The distinction between an alien who has effected an entry into the United States and one who has never entered runs through immigration law." Id. at 2500.
75. See Yamataya v. Fisher, 189 U.S. 86 (1903).
76. Id at 2502.
77. *Nguyen v. INS,* 121 S.Ct. at 2053, 2078 (2001) (O'Connor, J., dissenting).
78. Additional evidence comes from two other cases decided in 2001. In INS v. St. Cyr, 121 S. Ct. 2271 (2001), the Court again adopted a (strained) reading of a provision of the immigration code in order to avoid a difficult constitutional issue. The question in the case was whether courts had habeas corpus jurisdiction to hear legal challenges to INS interpretations that gave retroactive effect to some provisions of the harsh 1996 immigration laws. A five-Justice majority of the Court held that the 1996 laws would not be read to cut off existing general habeas jurisdiction, based on the view that "a serious Suspension Clause issue would be presented if we were to accept the INS's submission that the 1996 statutes have withdrawn [the power of] federal judges [to adjudicate pure questions of law in habeas] and provided no adequate substitute for its exercise." Id. at 2282. In *Nguyen v. INS,* 121 S.Ct. 2053 (2001), the Court considered a provision in U.S. citizenship law that makes it easier for U.S. citizen women than U.S. citizen men to pass citizenship to children born out of wedlock overseas. Although the Court (by a 5-to-4 vote) sustained the law, it purported to apply the constitutional standards normally used for evaluating gender-based law, despite the government's invocation of the plenary power doctrine. For an argument that it may be difficult—and surely more difficult than the Court recognizes—to distinguish such *jus sanguinis* citizenship statutes from immigration statutes (thereby concluding that cases such as *Nguyen* ultimately undermine *Fiallo v. Bell*), see Pillard and Aleinikoff, "Skeptical Scrutiny of Plenary Power," 1998 *Sup. Ct. Rev.* 1.
79. Colegrove v. Green, 328 U.S. 549, 556 (1946).
80. See Peter Schuck, "The Thickest Thicket: Partisan Gerrymandering and Judicial Regulation of Politics," 87 *Colum. L. Rev.* 1325, 1379–81 (1987).
81. 342 U.S. at 597 (Frankfurter, J., concurring).
82. Id.
83. 347 U.S. 522 (1954).

84. Id. at 530–31.
85. Id. at 531.
86. T. Aleinikoff Aleinikoff, *The Basics: Immigration Reform* (2000).
87. See E. Clay Shaw, Jr., and Lamar Smith, "Immigrants, Welfare, and the GOP," *Wash. Post,* May 28, 1997, at A19.
88. 141 *Cong. Rec.* 8,514 (1995).
89. INA §237(a)(5), 8 U.S.C. §1227(a)(5) (Supp. IV 1998) (emphasis added).
90. Rodriguez ex rel. Rodriguez v. United States, 169 F.3d 1342 (11th Cir. 1999); Shalala v. City of Chicago, 189 F.3d 598, 608 (7th Cir. 1999), cert. denied, 529 U.S. 1036 (2000); Abreu v. Callahan, 971 F. Supp. 799 (S.D.N.Y. 1997); Kiev v. Glickman, 991 F. Supp. 1090 (D. Minn. 1998).
91. The Supreme Court chose not to review the Seventh Circuit's decision upholding the law. 529 U.S. 1036 (2000).
92. 426 U.S. 67 (1976).
93. See Bolling v. Sharpe, 347 U.S. 497 (1954), invalidating segregated schools in the District of Columbia. See also Frontiero v. Richardson, 411 U.S. 677 (1973) (gender discrimination in federal law).
94. Id at 85.
95. Id. at 82, 84.
96. *Shalala v. City of Chicago,* 189 F.3d at 608 (7th Cir. 1999), cert. denied, 529 U.S. 1036 (2000).
97. Id. at 607.
98. One exception is *Hampton v. Mow Sun Wong,* 426 U.S. 88 (1976), invalidating a rule of the U.S. Civil Service Commission excluding aliens from eligibility for jobs in the federal civil service. The Court reached its decision not on the basis of nondiscrimination norms, but rather on the view that the policy was beyond the authority of the commission. Following the Court's decision, the federal government repromulgated the policy—this time based on an executive order signed by President Ford. The lower courts upheld the order. See, e.g., Mow Sun Wong v. Campbell, 626 F.2d 739 (9th Cir. 1980), cert. denied, 450 U.S. 959 (1981).
99. 141 *Cong. Rec.* 8,553 (1995).
100. Note that citizenship-as-membership offers a set of premises that would provide support for the "substantive norms" reading of the Court's immigration cases as well as the "institutional deference" approach.
101. Minor v. Happersett, 88 U.S. (21 Wall.) 162, 166 (1874); id. at 165. The "nothing more" is used here by the Court to explain why exclud-

ing women—who clearly were citizens—from voting did not violate the clause of the Fourteenth Amendment that prohibits states from abridging the "privileges or immunities of citizens of the United States."

102. Afroyim v. Rusk, 387 U.S. 253, 268 (1967).
103. Citizenship carries other "rights," such as the ability to obtain a U.S. passport and protection against the acts of foreign states. Perhaps the most important implication of citizenship—and one that, surprisingly, is rarely thought about—is that citizens cannot be deported from the United States.
104. INA §337(a), 8 U.S.C. §1448(a) (1994).
105. *Minor,* 88 U.S. (21 Wall.) at 165–66.
106. See, e.g., Bruce A. Ackerman, *Social Justice in the Liberal State* 89–95 (1980); Peter Schuck, "The Transformation of Immigration Law," 84 *Colum. L. Rev.* 1 (1984). Schuck attempts to ground "classical immigration law" in nineteenth-century liberalism but seems to concede that "restrictive nationalism" may be a better description than "traditional liberalism."
107. 454 U.S. 432, 439–40 (1982) (emphasis added).
108. Oddly, however, in the early years of the republic, citizenship and political rights were not as closely linked as they are today. Aliens voted in many states, and many citizens (women, free blacks) did not.
109. But note that the first naturalization statutes limited naturalization to "white" immigrants, and that the naturalization of Asian immigrants was not permitted until the mid-twentieth century. See Ian F. Haney-López, *White by Law: The Legal Construction of Race* (1996).
110. As Robert Post has suggested to me, an alien who refuses to take advantage of opportunities to naturalize puts the nation in the position of a spurned lover.
111. 342 U.S. 580, 585 (1952). Jackson also noted the "advantages" enjoyed by a nonnaturalized alien residing in the United States: "The alien retains immunities from burdens which the citizen must shoulder. By withholding his allegiance from the United States, he leaves outstanding a foreign call on his loyalties which international law not only permits our Government to recognize but commands it to respect." Id. at 585–86. Today, though, we hear an opposite complaint. Immigrants are said to be naturalizing for the "wrong reasons," that is, in order to maintain welfare benefits or to further group interests through participation in the political system.
112. See Peter H. Schuck and Rogers M. Smith, *Citizenship without Consent: Illegal Aliens in the American Polity* (1985).

113. See Fong Yue Ting v. United States, 149 U.S. 698, 708 (1893) (citing Théodore Ortolan, 1 *Régles Internationales et Diplomatie de la Mer* 297 (1864)). A lower federal court, at an earlier stage in the same litigation, had invalidated the substantive deportability ground. See Reno v. American-Arab Anti-Discrimination Comm., 70 F.3d 1045, 1066 (9th Cir. 1995) ("We reject the government's contention that we apply gradations of First Amendment protection parallel to the rational distinctions that are permissible pursuant to the equal protection clause in determining which citizens and aliens may receive particular government benefits . . . [T]o deny citizens or aliens some measure of their admitted rights to First Amendment associational freedom would be to nullify the right in its entirety.") (citations omitted). Whether the Supreme Court agrees with that constitutional judgment remains to be seen. For further discussion and differing opinions on the ramifications of this case, see Gerald L. Neuman, "Terrorism, Selective Deportation, and the First Amendment after *Reno v. AADC*," 14 *Geo. Immigr. L. J.* 313 (2000); and David Cole, "Damage Control? A Comment on Professor Neuman's Reading of *Reno v. AADC*," 14 *Geo. Immigr. L. J.* 347 (2000).
114. See Aleinikoff, "Citizens, Aliens, Membership, and the Constitution" at 19; Linda Bosniak, "Membership, Equality, and the Difference That Alienage Makes," 69 *N.Y.U. L. Rev.* 1047, 1062 (1994).
115. Sugarman v. Dougall, 413 U.S. 634, 651 (1973) (Rehnquist, J., dissenting).
116. Id.; see Michael J. Perry, "Equal Protection, Judicial Activism, and the Intellectual Agenda of Constitutional Theory: Reflections On, and Beyond, *Plyler v. Doe*," 44 *U. Pitt. L. Rev.* 329, 334 (1983) (stating that the framers "seem to have" "embodied in the Constitution the judgment that citizens and aliens are morally different and therefore may be treated differently"). But see Alexander M. Bickel, *The Morality of Consent* 33 (1975) ("Remarkably enough . . . the concept of citizenship plays only the most minimal role in the American constitutional scheme").
117. See Frederick Schauer, "Community, Citizenship, and the Search for National Identity," 84 *Mich. L. Rev.* 1504, 1508–9 (1986).
118. See, e.g., United States v. Brignoni-Ponce, 422 U.S. 873 (1975). *Brignoni-Ponce,* however, may have been called into question by a later case, United States v. Verdugo-Urquidez, 494 U.S. 259 (1990). Four Justices in the *Verdugo-Urquidez* majority suggested in dicta that the First, Second, and Fourth Amendments' reference to "the people" encompasses only "a class of persons who are part of a national commu-

nity or who have otherwise developed sufficient connection with this country to be considered part of that community." Id. at 265 (citation omitted). The full majority later noted that statements in other cases are "not dispositive of how the Court would rule on a Fourth Amendment claim by illegal aliens in the United States if such a claim were squarely before us." Id. at 272.

119. The Fourteenth Amendment was adopted against a backdrop of decades of discrimination against Chinese aliens living on the West Coast, and the 1870 Civil Rights Act was clearly intended to protect the Chinese. See Charles J. McClain, Jr., "The Chinese Struggle for Civil Rights in Nineteenth-Century America: The First Phase, 1850–1870," 72 *Cal. L. Rev.* 529 (1984). A notable exception to the general point here is the privileges or immunities clause of the Fourteenth Amendment. John Ely's suggestion that the clause could be read to offer protection to aliens if one understands "privileges or immunities of citizens of the United States" as a bundle of rights held by all persons rather than as a designation of the beneficiaries is too clever by half. See John Hart Ely, *Democracy and Distrust: A Theory of Judicial Review* 24–25 (1980).

120. See Gerald M. Rosberg, "Aliens and Equal Protection: Why Not the Right to Vote?" 75 *Mich. L. Rev.* 1092, 1097–1100 (1977).

121. But see Schuck and Smith, *Citizenship without Consent.* Schuck and Smith argue that the Fourteenth Amendment need not be read to grant birthright citizenship to children of nonimmigrant or illegal immigrant parents, but rather only to the children of American and permanent resident alien parents. Id. at 94. Their reasoning is that "mutual consent is the irreducible condition of membership in the American polity." Id.

122. See Gerald M. Rosberg, "The Protection of Aliens from Discriminatory Treatment by the National Government," 1977 *Sup. Ct. Rev.* 275, 337 ("[T]he traditional premise of the country's immigration policy [is] that resident aliens are virtually full-fledged members of the American community, sharing the burdens of membership as well as the benefits").

123. 403 U.S. 365 (1971).

124. Id. at 380.

125. Id. at 372.

126. The phrase originated, of course, in the famous "Footnote Four" of United States v. Carolene Products Co, 304 U.S. 144, 152–53 n.4 (1938). In the third paragraph of the footnote, Justice Stone suggested that "more searching judicial inquiry" might be appropriate in

cases evidencing "prejudice . . . which tends seriously to curtail the operation of those political process ordinarily to be relied upon to protect minorities." Id. This justification, however, does not easily translate into protection for aliens, who—after all—may constitutionally be excluded from voting and officeholding. See Toll v. Moreno, 458 U.S. 1, 39–42 (1982) (Rehnquist, J., dissenting). To be sure, discrimination against aliens has a persistent and ugly history in this country, but such hatred has generally been based on racial or ethnic backgrounds, not the fact of "alienage." Aliens, as a class, are remarkably diverse and not particularly "insular." See *Diaz,* 426 U.S. 67, 78–79 (1976) ("[T]he class of aliens is . . . a heterogeneous multitude of persons with a wide-ranging variety of ties to this country") (footnote omitted). To a surprising degree, aliens participate in American life on equal terms with U.S. citizens. Moreover, they are often able to find allies in the political system who are eager to represent their interests. See, e.g., Nicaraguan Adjustment and Central American Relief Act, 111 Stat. 2160, 2193 (1997).

127. 403 U.S. at 376 (citations omitted).

128. Perhaps the most dramatic example of this expanding concept of membership is a case invalidating a Texas statute that authorized local school districts to exclude the children of undocumented aliens from public schools. In *Plyler v. Doe,* 457 U.S. 202 (1982), the Court specifically resisted (as it had before) labeling education a "fundamental right"; rather, its analysis was grounded in the recognition that undocumented children were likely to be permanent members of American society. In various passages the Court stated:

> This situation raises the specter of a permanent caste of undocumented resident aliens, encouraged by some to remain here as a source of cheap labor, but nevertheless denied the benefits that our society makes available to citizens and lawful residents.
>
> . . . By denying these children a basic education, we deny them the ability to live within the structure of our civic institutions, and foreclose any realistic possibility that they will contribute in even the smallest way to the progress of our Nation.
>
> . . . [T]he record is clear that many of the undocumented children disabled by this classification will remain in this country indefinitely, and that some will become lawful residents or citizens of the United States. It is difficult to understand precisely what the State hopes to achieve by promoting the creation and perpetuation of a subclass of illiterates within our boundaries,

surely adding to the problems and costs of unemployment, welfare, and crime. It is thus clear that whatever savings might be achieved by denying these children an education, they are wholly insubstantial in light of the costs involved to these children, the State, and the Nation.

Id. at 218–19, 223, 230 (citation omitted). Although other factors appear to have carried weight in the majority opinion (including the fundamental importance of education and the unfairness of injuring children because of their parents' violation of the immigration laws), Peter Schuck is clearly correct that *Plyler* "may mark a fundamental break with classical immigration law's concept of national community and of the scope of congressional power to decide who is entitled to the benefits of membership." Schuck, "The Transformation of Immigration Law" at 54.

129. For discussions of "denizenship" in the European context, see Rainer Bauböck, *Transnational Citizenship: Membership and Rights in International Migration* 173 (1994); Tomas Hammar, *Democracy and the Nation State: Aliens, Denizens, and Citizens in a World of International Migration* 13–18, 219 (1990).
130. Cf. *Knauff,* 338 U.S. 537.
131. Cf. *Mezei,* 345 U.S. 206.
132. Cf. Price v. U.S. INS, 962 F.2d 836 (9th Cir. 1992), cert. denied, 510 U.S. 1040 (1994) (finding no constitutional violation).
133. Cf. Mahler v. Eby, 264 U.S. 32 (1924).
134. Cf. *Reno v. American-Arab Anti-Discrimination Committee,* 525 U.S. 471.
135. See *Harisiades,* 342 U.S. at 585, quoted in text at note 111.
136. The fact that an alien almost always has a country to which to return may make us view the degree of harm inflicted by deportation as quite different from that imposed on a banished citizen (who may end up as a "person without a country"). This does not, however, provide an answer to the constitutional question.
137. See John Guendelsberger, "Implementing Family Unification Rights in American Immigration Law: Proposed Amendments," 25 *San Diego L. Rev.* 253 (1988).
138. Moreover, it is a fundamental constitutional interest that has protected the family in many contexts. See, e.g., Troxel v. Granville, 530 U.S. 57 (2000) (invalidating a state law allowing courts broadly to grant visitation rights to any person in the child's best interest); Moore v. City of East Cleveland, 431 U.S. 494 (1977) (invalidating a municipal zoning ordinance preventing extended family members from living

together); Pierce v. Society of Sisters, 268 U.S. 510 (1925) (invalidating a state law requiring parents to send their children to public school); Meyers v. Nebraska, 262 U.S. 390 (1923) (invalidating a state law forbidding the teaching of non-English languages to certain schoolchildren).

139. United States Dep't of Agric. v. Moreno, 413 U.S. 528, 534 (1973). See also Romer v. Evans, 517 U.S. 620, 634–35 (1996).

140. See *Moreno,* 413 U.S. at 533. Cf. Saenz v. Roe, 526 U.S. 489, 505 (1999) (applying the same standard to state legislatures).

141. This is not to say, though, that one could not otherwise construct a set of requirements more closely linked to the exercise of the immigration power. For example, under U.S. immigration law, an intending immigrant can overcome the "public charge" test by demonstrating either that he has a job in the United States (and is therefore self-supporting) or that he can submit an affidavit of support from a U.S. sponsor. While such affidavits of support were for years not legally binding, 1996 legislation changed that by requiring affidavits of support and rendering them legally binding. See Immigration Reform and Immigrant Responsibility Act of 1996, Pub. L. No. 104–208, §551, 110 Stat. 3009, 3009–675. This act provided that the income of the sponsor would be "deemed" to the federal or state government if the alien sought means-tested benefits. See §551(b)(1)(A), 110 Stat. at 3009–676. Unlike the full-scale cutoff, these provisions are more carefully tailored to the manner by which an alien seeks to overcome the public charge exclusion. They also avoid sending the binary message (citizens 1, legal immigrants 0) of the provisions terminating permanent resident alien eligibility.

142. Georgie Anne Geyer, *Americans No More: The Death of Citizenship* (1996).

143. Cabell v. Chavez-Salido, 454 U.S. 432, 439 (1982) (quoting Foley v. Connelie, 435 U.S. 291, 295 (1978)) (footnote omitted).

144. See *Evans,* 517 U.S. at 633 ("A law declaring that in general it shall be more difficult for one group of citizens than for all others to seek aid from the government is itself a denial of equal protection of the laws in the most literal sense"); *Moreno,* 413 U.S. at 534 ("For if the constitutional conception of 'equal protection of the laws' means anything, it must at the very least mean that a bare congressional desire to harm a politically unpopular group cannot constitute a legitimate governmental interest"). Cf. City of Cleburne v. Cleburne Living Ctr., 473 U.S. 432, 466 (1985) (Marshall, J., concurring in part and dissenting in part) ("Moral philosophers may debate whether certain inequalities are absolute wrongs, but history makes clear that constitutional principles of equality, like constitutional principles of liberty, property, and

due process, evolve over time; what once was a 'natural' and 'self-evident' ordering later comes to be seen as an artificial and invidious constraint on human potential and freedom") (citation omitted).

145. See David Martin, "Due Process and Membership in the National Community: Political Asylum and Beyond," 44 *U. Pitt. L. Rev.* 165, 208–34 (1983).
146. See T. H. Marshall, "Citizenship and Social Class," in T. H. Marshall and Tom Bottomore, *Citizenship and Social Class* 18 (1992) ("Citizenship is a status bestowed on those who are full members of a community. All who possess the status are equal with respect to the rights and duties with which the status is endowed").
147. Johnson v. Eisentrager, 339 U.S. 763, 771 (1950).
148. Rogers Brubaker, *Citizenship and Nationhood in France and Germany* 31 (1992).
149. See Stephen H. Legomsky, "Why Citizenship?" 35 *Va. J. Int'l L.* 279, 297–300 (1994).
150. See Kenneth L. Karst, *Belonging to America: Equal Citizenship and the Constitution* (1989).
151. John Rawls, *The Law of Peoples* 44 (1999).
152. Id. at 23 n.17, quoting John Stuart Mill, *Considerations on Representative Government* ch. XVI (1862). It is likely that members of some groups in society do not feel connected to the dominant version of American national history. Members of Indian tribes in particular may have quite different sentiments of "pride and humiliation, pleasure and regret" about incidents in the past. These differences may give additional credence to self-determination claims and notions of "differentiated citizenship." See Will Kymlicka, *Multicultural Citizenship: A Liberal Theory of Minority Rights* ch. 9. (1995). They do not, however, provide support for denying rights and opportunities to resident immigrants.
153. In his critique of Michael Walzer's discussion of the morality of immigration limits, Joseph Carens argues that "[a]ny approach like Walzer's that seeks its ground in the tradition and culture of *our* community must confront, as a methodological paradox, the fact that liberalism is a central part of our culture . . . For people in a different moral tradition, one that assumed fundamental moral differences between those inside the society and those outside, restrictions on immigration might be easy to justify. Those who are *other* might simply not count, or at least not count as much. But we cannot dismiss the aliens on the ground that they are other, because *we* are the products of a liberal culture." Joseph Carens, "Aliens and Citizens: The Case for Open Borders," 49 *Rev. of Politics* 251, 268–69 (1987).
154. See Marshall, "Citizenship and Social Class" at 8–17.

155. Legislation in 1870 put "all persons" on the same grounds as "citizens." See Act of May 31, 1870, ch. 114, §16, 16 Stat. 140, 144 (current version at 42 U.S.C. §1981(a) (1994)) ("[A]ll *persons* within the jurisdiction of the United States shall have the same right in every State and Territory in the United States to make and enforce contracts, to sue, be parties, give evidence, and to the full and equal benefit of all laws and proceedings for the security of person and property as is enjoyed by white *citizens*.") (emphasis added). See also McClain, "The Chinese Struggle for Civil Rights in Nineteenth-Century America" at 566–67.
156. See *Yick Wo v. Hopkins,* 118 U.S. 356.
157. See Jamin B. Raskin, "Legal Aliens, Local Citizens: The Historical, Constitutional, and Theoretical Meanings of Alien Suffrage," 141 *U. Pa. L. Rev.* 1391, 1460–67 (1993).
158. That is, it protects aliens in the sense of avoiding prison. Deportation, as mentioned earlier, is another matter and one that is still unanswered. See note 2. Consider, however, the remarks of Justice Murphy:

> Since resident aliens have constitutional rights, it follows that Congress may not ignore them in the exercise of its "plenary" power of deportation . . . [T]he First Amendment and other portions of the Bill of Rights make no exception in favor of deportation laws or laws enacted pursuant to a "plenary" power of the Government. Hence the very provisions of the Constitution negative the proposition that Congress, in the exercise of a "plenary" power, may override the rights of those who are numbered among the beneficiaries of the Bill of Rights.
>
> Any other conclusion would make our constitutional safeguards transitory and discriminatory in nature. Thus, the Government would be precluded from enjoining or imprisoning an alien for exercising his freedom of speech. But the Government at the same time would be free, from a constitutional standpoint, to deport him for exercising that very same freedom. The alien would be fully clothed with his constitutional rights when defending himself in a court of law, but he would be stripped of those rights when deportation officials encircle him. I cannot agree that the framers of the Constitution meant to make such an empty mockery of human freedom.

Bridges v. Wixon, 326 U.S. 135, 161–62 (1945) (Murphy, J., concurring).
159. Paul Johnston, "The Emergence of Transnational Citizenship among

Mexican Immigrants in California," in *Citizenship Today: Global Perspectives and Practices* 253–277 (T. Alexander Aleinikoff and Douglas Klusmeyer, eds., 2001); Jennifer Gordon, *Campaign for the Unpaid Wages Prohibition Act: Latino Immigrants Change New York Wage Law,* Carnegie Endowment for International Peace, Working Paper No. 4 (1999).

160. Cf. Neuman, *Strangers to the Constitution* at 99–100, 108–17 (proposing a "mutuality approach").
161. Madison's "Report on the Virginia Resolutions," reprinted in 4 *Elliot's Debates* 572, 583 (2d ed. 1836). See also Neuman, *Strangers to the Constitution* at 58–60 (1996) (quoting Madison's "Report" and also suggesting that protecting the rights of aliens made sense from a citizen's point of view).
162. See Yasemin Nuhoğlu Soysal, *Limits of Citizenship: Migrants and Postnational Membership in Europe* 136–62 (1994).
163. This is not to say that immigrants may not be concerned with this nation's future, particularly if their children are U.S. citizens, but there is nothing wrong with valuing a concept—such as citizenship—that makes that commitment central.
164. I have argued this at greater length in "Between National and Post-National: Membership in the United States," 4 *Mich. J. Race and Law* 241 (1999).
165. Henry James, *The American Scene* 61 (1907).
166. Id. at 60.
167. Id. at 61.
168. Id.
169. Id. at 62 (emphasis added).
170. See Nathan Glazer, *We Are All Multiculturalists Now* (1997).

8. Reconceptualizing Sovereignty

1. Matthew Frye Jacobson, *Whiteness of a Different Color* (1998).
2. See, e.g., Saavedra Bruno v. Albright, 197 F.3d 1153, 1159 (D.C. Cir. 1999) ("For more than a century, the Supreme Court has thus recognized the power to exclude aliens as 'inherent in sovereignty, necessary for maintaining normal international relations and defending the country against foreign encroachments and dangers—a power to be exercised exclusively by the political branches of government'") (quoting the *Chinese Exclusion Case*); United States v. Benitez-Villafuerte, 186 F.3d 651, 657 (5th Cir. 1999), cert. denied, 528 U.S. 1097 (2000) ("'The power to expel aliens is essentially a power of the political branches of government, which may be exercised entirely through

executive officers, with such opportunity for judicial review of their action as Congress may see fit to authorize or permit'") (quoting *Yamataya v. Fisher*). The offensive language, however, has not altogether disappeared. See Jean v. Nelson, 711 F.2d 1455, 1467 (11th Cir. 1983) ("'Whatever the procedure authorized by Congress is, it is due process as far as an alien denied entry is concerned'") (citing Shaughnessy v. United States ex rel. Mezei, 345 U.S. 206, 212 (1953)).

3. See *Mezei*, 345 U.S. at 212; United States ex rel. Knauff v. Shaughnessy, 338 U.S. 537, 543 (1950).
4. See Lone Wolf v. Hitchcock, 187 U.S. 553, 566 (1903).
5. See Yasemin Nuhoğlu Soysal, *Limits of Citizenship: Migrants and Postnational Membership in Europe* 136–62 (1994).
6. See T. Alexander Aleinikoff, "Between National and Post-national Membership in the United States," 4 *Mich. J. Race & L.* 241, 249–55 (1999).
7. Cf. City of Richmond v. Croson, 448 U.S. 469 (1989) (invalidating an affirmative action program adopted by a city council on which African Americans constituted a majority).
8. See Chapter 6.
9. See Chapter 4.
10. Rainer Bauböck, "Cultural Citizenship, Minority Rights, and Self-Government," in *Citizenship Today: Global Perspectives and Practices* 319–48 (T. Alexander Aleinikoff and Douglas Klusmeyer, eds., 2001). See Will Kymlicka, *Multicultural Citizenship: A Liberal Theory of Minority Rights* ch. 2 (1995) (distinguishing the claims of "national minorities" and immigrants).
11. Guam is a different story, since immigration over the past half-century has relegated the indigenous Chamorro population to minority status. Not surprisingly, the power to regulate immigration has been a central issue in the Guamanian status negotiations while it has not been in the Puerto Rican debates.
12. Rights and inclusion, then, offer "republican remed[ies] for the diseases most incident to republican government." *The Federalist No. 10* at 84 (James Madison) (Clinton Rossiter, ed., 1961).
13. See Kymlicka, *Multicultural Citizenship* at 77–79. Kymlicka notes a contrast between the experiences and desires of immigrant groups and those of indigenous minorities. Indigenous minorities have attempted to resist such "integration" and have indeed sought autonomous governance structures. See id. at 79.
14. See T. Alexander Aleinikoff and Rubén G. Rumbaut, "Terms of Belonging: Are Models of Membership Self-Fulfilling Prophecies?" 13 *Geo. Immigr. L. J.* 1, 18 table 4 (1998).

15. Arthur M. Schlesinger, Jr., *The Disuniting of America* (1992). Most of Schlesinger's attention is directed to "the cult of ethnicity" (his label) and Afrocentricity. The "new ethnic gospel," he asserts, "rejects the unifying vision of individuals from all nations melted into a new race. Its underlying philosophy is that America is not a nation of individuals at all but a nation of groups, that ethnicity is the defining experience for most Americans, that ethnic ties are permanent and indelible, and that the division into ethnic communities establishes the basic structure of American society and the basic meaning of American history." Id. at 16. Leaving aside Schlesinger's cartoonlike characterization of multiculturalism, his concerns are only tangentially relevant to issues of the legal and political aspects of sovereignty. Indian policy accepts the idea of "measured separatism," and no territorial government seeks to establish itself along ethnic lines. Thus, I am using Schlesinger's phrase ("the disuniting of America") without directly engaging his argument.
16. David Hollinger calls this characteristic "the diversification of diversity." See David A. Hollinger, *Postethnic America: Beyond Multiculturalism* 79–104 (1995). See also Kenneth L. Karst, "The Bonds of American Nationhood," 21 *Cardozo L. Rev.* 1141, 1163–70 (2000); T. Alexander Aleinikoff, "The Constitution in Context: The Continuing Significance of Racism,"63 *U. Colo. L. Rev.* 325, 371 (1992).
17. For an illustration of such disputes, see "Casino Boom Helps Tribes Reduce Poverty and Unemployment," *N.Y. Times,* September 3, 2000, at A18.
18. See Constitution of Puerto Rico, Art. II.
19. See Indian Civil Rights Act of 1968, tit. 2, §202, 82 Stat. 73, 77–78 (codified at 25 U.S.C. §1302 (1994)).
20. There would be the possibility of some accommodations, such as the Indian Civil Rights Act's decision not to apply the establishment clause to tribes. One interesting accommodation would be to lodge primary responsibility for interpreting constitutional norms in the courts of the territories and Indian tribes. Santa Clara Pueblo v. Martinez, 436 U.S. 49 (1978), has, in effect, produced this situation for tribes—with encouraging results.
21. See Rogers M. Smith, *Civic Ideals* 5–9 (1997). Smith's subtitle for the book makes the point: "Conflicting Visions of Citizenship in U.S. History."
22. Toni Morrison, "Unspeakable Things Unspoken: The Afro-American Presence in American Literature," 28 *Mich. Q. Rev.* 1, 11 (1989).
23. Again, the claim is not that the idea of citizenship necessarily must be invoked in this way.

24. 120 S. Ct. 1044 (2000).
25. Haw. Rev. Stat. §10–2 (1993).
26. *Rice,* 120 S. Ct. at 1063 (Stevens, J., dissenting).
27. Id. at 1072.
28. Id. at 1059.
29. Id. at 1060.
30. Id. It is also worth noting the concurring opinion's view that the statute was basically irrational because the class that it defined included "individuals who are less than one five-hundredth original Hawaiian (assuming nine generations between 1778 and the present)." Id. at 1061 (Breyer, J., concurring).
31. Id. at 1047, 1060.
32. Id. at 1051.
33. Id.
34. Id. at 1047.
35. 387 U.S. 253, 268 (1967).
36. 454 U.S. 432, 439–40 (1982).
37. Measuring the foreign-born population is not the same as measuring noncitizens, because some foreign-born persons are naturalized citizens.
38. See U.S. Census Bureau, *Current Population Reports, Profile of the Foreign-Born Population in the United States: 1997* at 14 (Series No. P23–195, August 1999) (available online at <http://www.census.gov/prod/99pubs/p23–195.pdf>).
39. See "The Gateway City," *N.Y. Times,* September 4, 2000, at A16.
40. See Alexander M. Bickel, *The Morality of Consent* ch. 2 (1975) (seeing traces of *Dred Scott* in such reasoning).
41. Frederick Schauer, "Community, Citizenship, and the Search for National Identity," 84 *Mich. L. Rev.* 1504, 1506 (1986).
42. See, e.g., U.S. Commission on Immigration Reform, *Becoming an American: Immigration and Immigrant Policy* 26–29 (1997).
43. E. J. Hobsbawm, "The Future of the State," 27 *Dev. & Change* 267, 267 (1996).
44. Id. at 276.
45. Id. at 277 (footnote omitted).
46. Cf. Charles Taylor, "Why Democracy Needs Patriotism," in *For Love of Country: Debating the Limits of Patriotism* 119 (Joshua Cohen, ed., 1996). Taylor describes democracies as fragile institutions and discusses both the need to adopt policies that prevent divisive inegalitarianism and the need for a common commitment in support of such policies. See id. at 119–21.

47. Benedict Anderson's oft-cited term is an "imagined community." See Benedict Anderson, *Imagined Communities: Reflections on the Origin and Spread of Nationalism* (1991).
48. Id.
49. Id. at 62.
50. See Randolph S. Bourne, "Trans-National America," in *War and the Intellectuals: Essays, 1915–1919* at 107 (1964).
51. Id. at 115–16.
52. See Philip Kasinitz, "A Third Way to America," <http://www.culturefont.org/culturefront/magazine/99/summer/article.3.html>. See generally Hollinger, *Postethnic America.*

Index